DEMOCRACY AND RULE OF LAW IN CHINA'S SHADOW

This book provides detailed insight into some of the most contentious events occurring in jurisdictions operating within China's vast shadow.

Epic clashes between law and politics have become a regular fixture throughout the world, and no region has seen more of these than Asia. In some cases these conflicts have involved newfound democratic aspirations or democratic deepening, while in others it has arisen because of pushback against authoritarian or semi-authoritarian governments. Indeed, many of these clashes centre on or involve the region's most powerful and controversial player: China. This book focuses on several of these critical struggles, examining how democracy and the rule of law play out in a number of jurisdictions highly influenced by China's presence.

The chapters provide insightful analysis on issues such as major threats to the rule of law and attempts to uphold the principle, oath-taking controversies, foreign judges and the disparagement of the judiciary, unconstitutional and undemocratic provisions, changing ideas of representation, a right to democracy in international law, same-sex marriage rights, and the legal responses to civil disobedience in Taiwan and Hong Kong, among others.

Ultimately, the book delivers a contemporary understanding of how democracy and the rule of law both complement and converge in this fascinating region.

Constitutionalism in Asia series

NUS National University of Singapore | Centre for Asian Legal Studies Faculty of Law

Democracy and Rule of Law in China's Shadow

Edited by
Brian Christopher Jones

•HART•
OXFORD • LONDON • NEW YORK • NEW DELHI • SYDNEY

HART PUBLISHING

Bloomsbury Publishing Plc

Kemp House, Chawley Park, Cumnor Hill, Oxford, OX2 9PH, UK

1385 Broadway, New York, NY 10018, USA

29 Earlsfort Terrace, Dublin 2, Ireland

HART PUBLISHING, the Hart/Stag logo, BLOOMSBURY and the Diana logo are trademarks of Bloomsbury Publishing Plc

First published in Great Britain 2021

A catalogue record for this book is available from the British Library.

Library of Congress Cataloging-in-Publication data

Names: Jones, Brian Christopher, editor.

Title: Democracy and rule of law in China's shadow / edited by Brian Christopher Jones.

Description: Oxford, UK ; New York, NY : Hart Publishing, an imprint of Bloomsbury Publishing, 2021. | Series: Constitutionalism in Asia series | Includes bibliographical references and index.

Identifiers: LCCN 2021008486 (print) | LCCN 2021008487 (ebook) | ISBN 9781509933969 (hardback) | ISBN 9781509949175 (paperback) | ISBN 9781509933983 (pdf) | ISBN 9781509933976 (Epub)

Subjects: LCSH: Rule of law—Taiwan. | Rule of law—China—Hong Kong. | Rule of law—Singapore. | Law—Taiwan—Chinese influences. | Law—China—Hong Kong—Chinese influences. | Law—Singapore—Chinese influences.

Classification: LCC KNC514 .D46 2021 (print) | LCC KNC514 (ebook) | DDC 340/.11—dc23

LC record available at https://lccn.loc.gov/2021008486

LC ebook record available at https://lccn.loc.gov/2021008487

ISBN:	HB:	978-1-50993-396-9
	ePDF:	978-1-50993-398-3
	ePub:	978-1-50993-397-6

Typeset by Compuscript Ltd, Shannon

Contents

PART III
CLEARING THE SHADOW

List of Contributors

Amy Barrow is Senior Lecturer at the Macquarie Law School, Macquarie University.

Anne SY Cheung is Professor of Law and Director of the Law and Technology Centre at the Faculty of Law, University of Hong Kong.

Lin Chien-Chih is Associate Research Professor at Institutum Iurisprudentiae, Academia Sinica, Taiwan.

Zhu Han is Research Assistant Professor at the Faculty of Law, University of Hong Kong.

Jimmy Chia-Shin Hsu is Associate Research Professor at Institutum Iurisprudentiae, Academia Sinica, Taiwan.

Fu Hualing is Warren Chan Professor of Human Rights and Responsibilities at the Faculty of Law, University of Hong Kong.

Michael Jackson is Associate Professor of Law at the Faculty of Law, University of Hong Kong.

Brian Christopher Jones is Lecturer in Law at the School of Law, University of Sheffield.

Hsiaowei Kuan is Associate Professor at the College of Law, National Taipei University, Taiwan.

Jack Tsen-Ta Lee holds an LLB (Hons) from the National University of Singapore, an LLM from University College London and a PhD from the University of Birmingham.

Jaclyn L Neo is Associate Professor at the Faculty of Law, National University of Singapore.

Glenn Patmore is Associate Professor at the Melbourne Law School, University of Melbourne.

Benny YT Tai is Former Associate Professor of Law at the Faculty of Law, University of Hong Kong.

Xiaobo Zhai is Associate Professor at the Faculty of Law, University of Macau.

Introduction

BRIAN CHRISTOPHER JONES*

> An imperfect democracy is a misfortune for its people, but an imperfect authoritarian regime is an abomination.[1]

IF UNBALANCED OR taken to their extremes, both democracy and the rule of law can lead to an undervaluing or diminishment of the other: rule of law may stifle the democratic spirit, while democracy may overrun rule of law ideals. Although both principles contain mutually reinforcing foundations, there remains a large space – even within healthy and well-functioning states – in which these ideals may conflict. The rule of law often appeals to fundamental notions of how law and government should operate, especially the essential characteristic that powerholders are not immune from the law and must operate within it. But it can also equate to a preference for law and order, with more emphasis on certainty and stability. Democracy, however, is often focused on fulfilling the general will, promoting equality, and realising the basic idea that citizens are the ultimate powerholders. Indeed, without citizen compliance, governments possess little, if any, authority. When it comes to balancing these principles, such concerns are especially relevant in Asia, where the degree of freedom among citizens, reliance on the rule of law, and the embracing of democracy within countries often varies considerably.

A focus on the rule of law has long dominated scholarship centred on Asia, and this is especially true when it comes to China. But this enduring principle no longer stands alone. Tensions between competing principles that have long been simmering are coming to a head. Now epic clashes between democracy and the rule of law increasingly arise in many Asian jurisdictions. In some cases this has involved democratic aspirations or democratic deepening, while in others it has arisen because of pushback against authoritarian or semi-authoritarian governments. Indeed, the rise of authoritarianism presents a global challenge for democracy, as its playbook often involves the use of law to suppress democratic ambition. In this new global reality, democracy and the rule of law not only complement one other and help to sustain governments and nations, but

* Lecturer in Law, School of Law, University of Sheffield.

[1] RA Dahl, *Democracy and Its Critics* (1989), p 78. Reproduced with the kind permission of Yale University Press.

also frequently converge, potentially jeopardising or even upending the delicate balance present in many jurisdictions.

Recent events in Asia have brought forward intriguing questions about the operation of – and balance between – democracy and the rule of law and demonstrate that the West is not alone in pushing the interaction between these contested concepts. Although previous texts have focused primarily on one of these principles within a particular jurisdiction,[2] from the perspective of economic development,[3] or from an authoritarian perspective,[4] little sustained attention has been provided to the unique ways that Asian jurisdictions grapple with both these principles, and how they may differ from interactions in other parts of the world. This collection provides a variety of perspectives on how these extremely important values play out both within China and in the shadow of its authoritarianism.

Some initial critiques of the way these two values converge were analysed in a previous collection on the 2014 social movements that occurred in Taiwan and Hong Kong.[5] There it was found that Hong Kong's devotion to rule of law proved instrumental in sustaining the Umbrella Movement,[6] but may have also contributed to its downfall, while Taiwan's embrace of the democratic force of the Sunflower Movement produced a lack of concrete outcomes, but ultimately led to some significant changes within the country. This collection furthers and expands on this focus, analysing the operation of democracy and rule of law both within and outside these jurisdictions. However before discussing the focus of this collection, I would like to explore some of the fascinating and alarming post-Movement developments in Hong Kong and Taiwan, as it is in these jurisdictions where the tension between democracy and rule of law is being pushed to its limit.

POST-MOVEMENT DEVELOPMENTS

Both Hong Kong and Taiwan have faced a number of significant challenges in recent years. Hong Kong's troubles stem from its lack of genuine democracy, and its story demonstrates an unfortunate lose–lose scenario, where the

[2] J Chan, CS Doh, and MS Williams, *East Asian Perspectives on Political Legitimacy* (2017); J Rajah, *Authoritarian Rule of Law: Legislation, Discourse and Legitimacy in Singapore* (2012); R Peerenboom, *China's Long March towards Rule of Law* (2002).

[3] Chen W (ed), *The Beijing Consensus: How China Has Changed Western Ideas of Law and Economic Development* (2017).

[4] M Gallagher, *Authoritarian Legality in China* (2017); Chen W and Fu H (eds), *Authoritarian Legality in Asia: Formation, Development and Transition* (2020).

[5] BC Jones (ed), *Law and Politics of the Taiwan Sunflower and Hong Kong Umbrella Movements* (2017).

[6] This is also known as the Occupy Central Movement (OCM), or its longer name: 'Occupy Central with Love and Peace.'

valiant pursuit to achieve genuine democracy has ultimately backfired, resulting in much less autonomy and a diminishing rule of law. Meanwhile, Taiwan's experience has generally been more positive, demonstrating that recognising the democratic force of something may be just as important, if not more so, than adhering to rule of law ideals. Indeed, such recognition does not have to lead to the trampling or overrunning of the rule of law, but can actually reinforce it. Additionally, having political space to allow for compromise – especially on highly controversial and polarising societal matters – is essential in democracies, as there are significant limits to what law and legal resolution can accomplish. Much of the variance between Hong Kong and Taiwan turns on the reaction to public sentiment by political and legal elites, and whether adequate space is available within the constitutional system to resolve complex societal issues.

It is no exaggeration to say that Hong Kong's political and legal autonomy has been under assault as the city struggles to maintain its freedoms under the Basic Law and the one country, two systems (OCTS) framework. Local booksellers have disappeared, prominent government critics have been arrested and imprisoned, democratically elected legislators have been removed from office, peaceful protestors have been silenced and sanctioned, and pro-democracy supporters have been banned from running for office and arrested on 'subversion' charges.[7] Some of these developments have come about because of a focus on upholding the rule of law, rather than recognising the democratic force of the issues involved. Beyond this, law has at times been weaponised in order to stamp out the democratic spirit. These instances have come in the form of dubious warnings to judges regarding jurisdiction, pre-emptive interpretations, and controversial new laws, some of which have circumvented normal constitutional processes.[8] At times, these worrying developments have pushed citizens to mobilise in larger numbers than ever before, and protests within the city have become increasingly confrontational. Ultimately, as Hong Kong's rights and freedoms under the Basic Law and OCTS framework have narrowed, the city has become increasingly contentious.

Given all these recent developments, it may appear that Hong Kong's political masters – both the HKSAR Government and the PRC – care little for public sentiment. If they did, conciliatory responses may have come more frequently over the past few years. After all, political mobilisation in the city often reached its peak in the post-Umbrella era. In June 2019 it was estimated that nearly 2 million people took to the streets after Chief Executive

[7] In fact, one of the authors in this collection, Benny Y.T. Tai, was arrested in a general sweep of pro-democracy advocates on 6 January 2021, and released on bail two days later. On 1 March 2021, Hong Kong police officially charged 47 pro-democracy supporters with 'conspiracy to commit subversion', and Benny was one of those arrested and charged. (See, 'Hong Kong charges 47 activists in largest use yet of new security law' BBC News (1 March 2021), https://www.bbc.co.uk/news/world-asia-china-56228363).

[8] See, eg, AHY Chen, 'Constitutional Controversies in the Aftermath of the Anti-Extradition Movement of 2019' (2020) 50 *Hong Kong Law Journal* 609.

Carrie Lam suspended – but did not scrap – the controversial Extradition Bill.[9] One million people were said to have marched a week earlier, and the city's annual 1 July march that same year was said to have reached its highest level ever: 550,000.[10] What started as widespread but peaceful opposition to the Bill grew into a more radicalised movement that openly used more confrontational tactics, including violence. At the 1 July march, perhaps the height of the Movement, protesters broke into the Hong Kong Legislative Council, defacing governmental symbols and damaging the building's interior. These protests were explicitly aligned with pro-democracy groups and those opposed to a loss of autonomy within the city. And yet, the increasingly radical tactics employed by protesters did little to rattle public sentiment. In the November 2019 local elections, pro-democracy parties made historically significant gains.[11] If there was any question as to whether the PRC or HKSAR Governments cared about public sentiment, these results certainly answered it.

It turns out that Hong Kong's political masters care deeply about public sentiment, and exercises in genuine democracy can frighten them to bits. Rattled by the ongoing protests and November 2019 election victories, Beijing decided to clamp down even harder. Even though Hong Kong's Basic Law explicitly states that national security measures should be enacted locally,[12] China's National People's Congress (NPC) decided to press ahead on its own terms. The Standing Committee of the NPC (NPCSC) essentially wrote and passed Hong Kong's new national security law, which gives China considerable power to intervene in Hong Kong's affairs, even in its cherished legal system. Symbolically, the new legislation came into force just hours before 1 July. Many people herald this development as a death-knell for Hong Kong's autonomy, and a decisive end for 'one country, two systems'.[13] Indeed, the recent arrests of high-profile governmental critics,[14] and the sweeping arrests of over pro-democracy campaigners and politicians for subversion charges,[15] demonstrate very few signs for optimism. It seems obvious from recent events that, as Benny Tai declared in early January 2021, Hong Kong has entered a harsh winter.

[9] 'Hong Kong protest: 'Nearly two million' join demonstration' BBC News (17 June 2019). Available at: www.bbc.co.uk/news/world-asia-china-48656471.

[10] 'Organisers say 550,000 attend annual 1 July democracy march as protesters occupy legislature' Hong Kong Free Press (1 July 2019). Available at: https://hongkongfp.com/2019/07/01/breaking-organisers-say-550000-attend-annual-july-1-democracy-march-amid-clashes-rear-legislature/.

[11] 'Hong Kong elections: Pro-democracy groups make big gains' BBC News (25 November 2019). Available at: www.bbc.co.uk/news/world-asia-china-50531408.

[12] Hong Kong Basic Law, art 23 ('The Hong Kong Special Administrative Region shall enact laws on its own to prohibit any act of treason, secession, sedition, subversion against the Central People's Government, or theft of state secrets, to prohibit foreign political organizations or bodies from conducting political activities in the Region, and to prohibit political organizations or bodies of the Region from establishing ties with foreign political organizations or bodies.')

[13] See, eg, J Perlez, 'One Country, Two Systems, No Future: The End of Hong Kong as We Know It' (2020) 99 *Foreign Affairs* 204.

[14] See, eg, 'Hong Kong pro-democracy tycoon Jimmy Lai charged under security law' BBC News (11 December 2020). Available at: www.bbc.co.uk/news/world-asia-china-55271020.

[15] 'National security law: Hong Kong rounds up 53 pro-democracy activists' BBC News (6 January 2021). Available at: www.bbc.co.uk/news/amp/world-asia-china-55555299. Under Hong Kong's national security law, those convicted of subversion can face life imprisonment.

Conversely, Taiwan's post-Movement developments have also led to challenges, but in a different fashion than Hong Kong's. Domestically, President Tsai Ing-Wen's Democratic Progressive Party (DPP) government took a more sympathetic view of Sunflower Movement participants. More protesters have been pardoned than convicted, candidates of parties stemming from the Movement have been elected to the legislature, and even the judiciary has, at times, provided legal justification for the protesters' actions. These outcomes – while certainly controversial – differ significantly from those in relation to Hong Kong, and in some respects demonstrate the impact that public sentiment and adequate space for political compromise can have within a democracy. Although rule of law concerns were still raised by many, the democratic element provided space for different results. Other developments show a healthy democracy in action. Taiwan loosened their referendum threshold, thus leading to a number of referendums over the last two election cycles, and the country has become the first in Asia to provide official recognition for same-sex marriage. This, however, does not mean to imply that the domestic situation has been calm. Taiwanese politics have been just as passionate and contentious as ever.

Taiwan has, however, faced significant challenges in the international arena. Without any formal power over Taiwan's political system, China has been increasingly willing to exert its international influence in the hopes of weakening Taiwan's international position, thus putting pressure on domestic politicians. After the election of President Tsai in 2016, whose government is more supportive of Taiwanese autonomy and independence, pressure came on multiple fronts. Some of Taiwan's longstanding allies dropped their recognition of the country after Chinese promises of money and future infrastructure investment, and international organisations have not been as amenable to Taiwan even sitting as an observer in high-profile meetings. Indeed, even as Taiwan has done so remarkably well with the COVID-19 pandemic, the World Health Organization (WHO) repeatedly refused to use Taiwan's expertise. Thus, for all its domestic achievements, the international arena has been difficult to navigate, as Taiwan remains in an extremely vulnerable position: unrecognised and largely unprotected by the international community.[16]

Overall, the divergence of Hong Kong and Taiwan over the past few years has been significant, and a good deal of it can be attributed to the interaction between democracy and the rule of law, which this collection tackles.

THE FOCUS OF THIS COLLECTION

A major focus of this collection is on Taiwan and Hong Kong, as both these jurisdictions have endured numerous high-profile examples of democracy and

[16] BC Jones, 'Taiwan: A derogation of international law?' *East Asian Forum* (12 August 2017). Available at: www.eastasiaforum.org/2017/08/12/taiwan-a-derogation-of-international-law/.

the rule of law converging in dramatic fashion. However, this book also takes China itself into consideration, and examines how the tensions between the rule of law and democracy are interacting domestically. Additionally, the book examines Singapore, a city-state that is often considered a mirror image of Hong Kong in many ways. Although Singapore does not possess any direct political influence from China, the PRC's shadow still looms large there. Singapore is often referred to as a 'Twin City' or 'Sister City' to Hong Kong, as its Chinese-majority, focus on commerce and industry, and devotion to the rule of law provide much in common with the Special Administrative Region. Given its similarities to Hong Kong and its restrictions on free speech, at times it is suggested that Singaporean citizens may be more amenable to Chinese-style rule. However, Singapore's parliamentary democracy is noticeably different from China's authoritarian regime. General elections employing genuine universal suffrage have been in place since 1959, and even though one party has long dominated the political process, a healthy opposition now operates and contests every election. Indeed, at the height of the Extradition Bill backlash in Hong Kong, three out of four Singaporean citizens supported the protests,[17] suggesting that its alignment with Hong Kong – rather than China – may be more apt. Outside Singapore, China's regional influence, and the prospects for improvement within China's vast shadow are also considered in this collection.

The book is divided into three sections. Part I ('Disobedience, Democracy and Law') focuses on the aftermath of the movements in Taiwan and Hong Kong. Fu Hualing and Michael Jackson begin by discussing how regime type can influence protest law, analysing how governments and courts within different regimes often treat political challengers. They conclude by noting that law can often be a double-edged sword: expanding citizens' rights but also limiting them. Ultimately, too much repression may lead to radicalism and even violence. Next, Jimmy Hsu and Anne Cheung examine the major legal cases in Taiwan and Hong Kong that have sprung from the two movements. Examining the theories and justifications put forward by both the Taiwan and Hong Kong courts, the authors find inconsistencies in the way the courts have dealt with civil disobedience. Far from being straightforward applications of the law, the courts have creatively and cautiously manoeuvred in both jurisdictions, with an underlying focus on institutional integrity. Finally, in this section, Zhu Han delves into the oath-taking controversies that erupted in Hong Kong and Taiwan under similar conditions: post-Umbrella Movement Hong Kong and during authoritarian Taiwan. She finds that conditions in Taiwan became less confrontational as democratic reform progressed, while in Hong Kong the situation became more stringent and focused on strict compliance. Han finds that weaponising law and treating those that challenge political

[17] D Sim, 'Singaporeans support Hong Kong protests against controversial extradition bill, survey shows' South China Morning Post (9 July 2019). Available at: www.scmp.com/week-asia/politics/article/3017908/singaporeans-support-hong-kong-protests-against-controversial.

and constitutional authority in an increasingly legal manner may backfire, and that dealing with these groups or individuals under the political process would be a more reasonable approach.

Part II of the book ('Democratic Struggles with Law') inspects clashes between democracy and the rule of law that have occurred in jurisdictions under China's shadow. I begin by looking at the tensions between democracy and judicial outcomes in both Hong Kong and Taiwan, and especially when judicial criticism may undermine the rule of law. Two major events in both Hong Kong and Taiwan that attracted significant judicial criticism are examined. Similar to Han's findings regarding oath-taking, I conclude that Taiwan's reliance on the democratic process aids, and even tempers, judicial criticism, while Hong Kong's lack of democracy inflames it. Kuan Hsiaowei addresses the situation regarding gay marriage in Taiwan after a major court ruling, which sparked further referendums on the issue. Her chapter is a detailed exposé into the post-judgment battle of how same-sex marriage in Taiwan would come to be recognised. While in the end Taiwan became the first state in Asia to allow same-sex marriage, Kuan notes many of the challenges that arose were potential populist threats to the rule of law, and may have long-term implications. Concluding this section, Jack Lee and Jaclyn Neo discuss how the mutually supportive view of democracy and the rule of law is changing the idea of representation in Singapore. The authors focus on recent decisions by the Singapore courts regarding legislative by-elections, and how the courts have responded to these, displaying that conceptions of 'rule of law' and 'representation' are highly contested even within the judiciary. Lee and Neo assert that even though the democratic process is still being perfected in Singapore, communitarianism may be here to stay.

Part III ('Clearing the Shadow') discusses the potential directions that democracy and the rule of law may be heading under China's shadow, and what solutions may be possible. First, Benny Tai examines the post-movement operation of the rule of law in HK, arguing that it has moved from semi-democratic to semi-authoritarian because of significant moves made by Beijing. Tai forensically examines the situation in Hong Kong over the past few years, detailing a number of controversial events and the impact that they may have on the jurisdiction's well-established rule of law and its future prospects for democracy. Ultimately, Tai believes that even though Beijing has clamped down on the city in recent years, feelings about democracy and self-government have been roused, and that resilience and creativity must be demonstrated in the face of authoritarian aggression. Lin Chien-Chih's chapter asserts that as long as Taiwan's 1947 Constitution retains its reference to the 'one-China' principle, constitutional law in the country will remain undemocratic. Hitting on something that has become a topical issue of late,[18] he argues that both formal amendment

[18] J Pan, 'Constitution "not valid": Experts' *Taipei Times* (15 September 2020). Available at: www.taipeitimes.com/News/taiwan/archives/2020/09/15/2003743448.

and informal constitutional change have been closed off in remedying this situation, and that innovation needs to come through other means. Lin finds hope in increasing political participation in Taiwan, especially the recent progress made on national referendums, which may be a vehicle to deepen Taiwan's constitutional democracy. Zhai Xiaobo confronts China itself, suggesting that its original rule of law aims were not far off other liberal standards. Nonetheless, over the past couple decades these aims have been watered down by successive governments, and now amount to 'rule by law'. If its original aims are ever going to be fulfilled, then the CCP's version of the rule of law requires democracy, including a robust space for public debate. Finally, Glenn Patmore considers the relationship between democracy, human rights, and the rule of law. He argues that most UN definitions of democracy are inadequate and have not helped to establish a right to democracy in international law, despite the fact that multiple definitions of the rule of law have been provided. In order to establish a right to democracy under international law, Patmore suggests that a grand 'Treaty of the Democracies' be fostered among nations.

Amy Barrow concludes the book by further exploring some of the tensions the authors touch on throughout the text. She warns that Hong Kong's new National Security Law contains not just local, but also regional implications. Additionally, the COVID-19 pandemic is another major challenge for those in China's shadow and will test the strength of the democratic commitment to wide civil liberties. Ultimately, these confrontations have the potential to tip the region's delicate balance between democracy and the rule of law.

Part I

Disobedience, Democracy and Law

1

Protest, Law and Regime Type

FU HUALING* AND MICHAEL JACKSON+

INTRODUCTION

ALTHOUGH POLITICAL UPROAR in Hong Kong has been evident in recent months, 2013 and 2014 witnessed one of the most volatile moments in the recent history of the Greater China region. Large, lengthy and well-organised political protests swept mainland China, Hong Kong and Taiwan. The protests were unprecedented; each challenged the core of the respective political system. All have had significant impact on the political development in the respective societies. In 2013, Xu Zhiyong led his New Citizens Movement (NCM) into street action in different cities in China. In a spirit of freedom, public interest and love, NCM protesters, organised around dinner tables and coordinated via social media, demonstrated on the streets in small groups with home-made banners and cards to demand equal opportunities in education, freedom of the press and disclosure of assets of Party and state leaders.[1]

While Xu was organising NCM activities, Benny Tai and his co-organisers in Hong Kong were designing one of the largest occupy movements that the world has seen, which he later referred to as: Occupying Central with Love and Peace. The three Occupy Central leaders announced their civil disobedience manifesto on 27 March 2013, while NCM protesters were rallying in different parts of China. Encouraged by the success of mass protests since 2003, Tai and his supporters were determined to use civil disobedience – through an indefinite and potentially unlawful occupation of Hong Kong's busiest business districts – if the central government refused to offer a pathway to "genuine democracy" in the 2017 election of Hong Kong's Chief Executive (CE).

* Warren Chan, Professor of Human Rights and Responsibilities, Faculty of Law, Hong Kong University. The authors would like to thank the generous funding from the Research Grants Council of the Hong Kong Special Administrative Region Government (Grant Number 17608917).

+ Associate Professor of Law, Faculty of Law, Hong Kong University.

[1] E Pils, 'From Independent Lawyer Groups to Civic Opposition: The Case of China's New Citizen Movement' (2018) 19 *Asian-Pacific Law & Policy Journal* 110–152.

The Decision of the Standing Committee of the National People's Congress (NPC) on 31 August singularly failed the test and, faithful to his promises and prompted by student activists taking to the streets of Hong Kong, Tai activated the Occupy Central Movement (OCM) on 28 September 2014. The protesters who flooded out in response occupied streets near the business district for the next 79 days.[2]

Six months earlier, another social movement similarly shocked Taiwan's political landscape. Protests arose against the alleged abuse of executive and legislative power and the corresponding lack of legislative oversight in attempting to pass a Cross-Strait Service Trade Agreement (CSSTA), as part of a series of economic cooperation agreements with Mainland China.[3] The Sunflower Movement, as it came to be known, lasted for 23 days, during which students and young activists initially occupied Taiwan's Parliament between 18 March and 10 April. Some members also attempted to occupy the Executive Office on 23 and 24 March.[4] Fearing economic dominance by the Mainland through trade and investment and potential political submission, the Sunflower Movement demanded democratic vigilance against any possible encroachment. Interestingly, Hong Kong served as a reference point for the Sunflower Movement in assessing the Mainland's potential impact, sending a powerful statement that Taiwan did not wish to become the next Hong Kong.

In many aspects, all three movements shared a common objective in questioning and challenging the Mainland's authoritarian political system and adopted similar strategies of using social protest to pursue legal and policy changes in their respective societies. Each movement, in its own way, reflected a primal fear unique to each society and targeted foundational political concerns: on the Mainland, the lack of political freedom and the deepening political corruption, allied with a determination to catalyse incremental reform through emancipation and street action; in Hong Kong, the slipping away of economic prosperity, the rule of law and Hong Kong's high degree of autonomy, along with a resolve to maintain and entrench its way of life through implementing genuine democracy; and in Taiwan, the young democracy facing a looming existential threat from the Mainland, coalescing around a collective effort to maintain Taiwan's democratic vibrancy and resilience.

[2] Fu H, 'Political Protest in High-income Societies: The Case of the Occupy Central Movement in Hong Kong' in BC Jones (ed) *Law and Politics of the Taiwan Sunflower and Hong Kong Umbrella Movements* (2017), 83–99; FLF Lee and JM Chan, *Media and Protest Logic in the Digital Era: The Umbrella Movement in Hong Kong* (2018); and N Ma and EW Cheung (eds), *The Umbrella Movement: Civil Resistance and Contentious Space in Hong Kong* (2020).

[3] I Rowen, 'Inside Taiwan's Sunflower Movement: Twenty-Four Days in a Student-Occupied Parliament and the Future of the Region' (2015) 74 *The Journal of Asian Studies* 5–21; JR Yeh, 'Marching Towards Civic Constitutionalism with Sunflowers' in Jones, n 2 above, 49–62; JT Martin, 'Policing an Occupied Legislature: Symbolic Struggle over the Police Image in Taiwan's Sunflower Movement' (2015) 45(1) *Hong Kong Law Journal* 229–248.

[4] WC Chang, 'The Right to Free Assembly and the Sunflower Movement' in Jones, n 2 above, 30–48.

In all three cases, a populist movement evolved because political institutions were seen to have failed to address these foundational political concerns and to meet public demand for reform or revitalisation. Additionally, in response to a pending crisis which, as the protesters perceived it, threatened to shake the foundations of the political community, each movement bypassed established political institutions and took the development and implementation of their respective constitutions into their own hands. For the protesters, this was an occasion when significant swathes of the public came together in an assertion of their sovereign powers, bound together by their entitlement as citizens to take charge at that historical moment of their political future. Protest, seen from this perspective, was a direct exercise of the people's sovereignty and evidence of popular or civic constitutionalism.

For their roles in organising civil disobedience campaigns, protest leaders in all three jurisdictions were subsequently prosecuted for various offences. Yet the prosecution outcomes contrasted sharply between the three jurisdictions, reflecting the differences in regime type: on the Mainland, protesters were harshly suppressed through national security laws or the criminal law; in Taiwan, many were found not guilty and protesters in general were celebrated as the guardians of the constitution and democracy; while in Hong Kong they were found guilty for their "unlawful" activities, but were sentenced with varying degrees of leniency. The focus of this chapter is on the different conceptualisation of protest under the different political systems and its impact in shaping protest laws and their implementation in the three jurisdictions. Our principal argument is that regime type is determinative of the laws and regulations surrounding protest and its subsequent punishment, the pre-protest regulations, the political meaning and significance of public protests manifested in assemblies, processions and demonstrations (referred to generically as protest in this article); and the subsequent punishment imposed on individuals. Different regimes assign drastically different political meanings and significance to public protest; empower or limit courts in offering different degrees of protection of the right to protest; and encourage or prohibit civil society organisations in their function of nurturing a society with the freedom to protest.

Regime, Law and the Perception of Protest

Different types of regime face distinct political challenges and develop their own unique measures to manage political crises.[5] Mainland China, Hong Kong and Taiwan, although linked by geography, history and similarly constituted

[5] H Johnston, *States and Social Movements* (2011); and (2012) 'State Violence and Oppositional Protest in High Capacity Authoritarian Regime' (2012) 6 *International Journal of Conflict and Violence* 55–74.

populations, have markedly different political systems, which have important implications for protest: China is a Party state that practises socialism with the leadership of the Communist Party at its core.[6] Taiwan is a young democracy which entrenches human rights protection and the separation of powers, but has struggled to achieve a constitutional foundation grounded in the rule of law, distinguished by such features as judicial independence and credibility.[7] Hong Kong has a hybrid constitutional system – quasi authoritarian politically, but with an entrenched rule of law, judicial independence and constitutional protection of rights and freedom, although this has been placed under a severe stress test.[8] In spite of a possible backsliding of the rule of law after the 2019 protests and the imposition of a National Security Law, Hong Kong could still maintain its stature as a free, tolerant and orderly society with strong aspirations for full democracy.

Authoritarian states generally regard protest as a political threat and prioritise its pre-emption and repression (if pre-emption fails). On the contrary, democracies commonly embrace protest as an integral part of the political process, with the state facilitating and supporting protest and citizens passionately participating. In between these views, a more legalistic approach to protest can be found, in which formal legal rules are rigidly applied and followed and where law and its institutions purport to maintain a high degree of autonomy independent of the political process. Below we articulate these in much more detail.

PROTEST AND AUTHORITARIANISM: CHINA

Protest abounds in China.[9] While the Chinese authoritarian system recognises and, to a lesser degree, offers protection to individual rights, it strictly restricts their exercise through collective and organised action. What defines authoritarian law is not the deprivation of rights but their anti-solidarity nature. It is authoritarian because the legal system recognises the legal rights of individual citizens on the condition that the claim-making and rights-asserting process is neither organised nor does it appear in a collective form.[10]

[6] H Fu and M Dowdle, 'The Concept of Authoritarian Legality: The Chinese Case' in W Chen and H Fu (eds) *Authoritarian Legality in Asia: Formation, Development and Transition* (2020) 63–89.

[7] JT Martin, 'Legitimate force in a Particularistic Democracy: Street Police and Outlaw Legislators in the Republic of China on Taiwan' (2013) 38(3) *Law & Social Inquiry* 615–642; See also his *Sentiment, Reason and Law: Policing in the Republic of China on Taiwan* (2019).

[8] EC Ip, *Hybrid Constitutionalism: The Politics of Constitutional Review in the Chinese Special Administrative Regions* (2019).

[9] KJ O'Brien (ed) *Popular Protest in China* (2008); T Wright (ed) *Handbook of Protest and Resistance in China* (2019).

[10] Fu and Dowdle, n 6 above.

Assemblies, processions and demonstrations are necessarily collective when they become the way to air grievances and articulate demands. On the authoritarian Mainland, public protest is pre-empted and restricted precisely because of its collective and organising manifestations. Indeed, the key external characteristic of assemblies and processions is that they involve a large enough number of people gathered to engage in collective action, although the threshold number triggering the law's attention varies considerably throughout different jurisdictions. In Taiwan, an illegal assembly can be constituted by as few as three persons in a procession; and in Hong Kong, where public space is even more limited, the equivalent number is 30 persons (although previous incarnations had set the legal threshold at three, which remains the threshold for the more serious offence of unlawful assembly).[11] On the Mainland, there is no specification for the number of participants constituting an illegal a protest.

What is more dangerous for authoritarian leaders is the internal dimension of a protest. To qualify as a public protest, participants in the protest must have a common objective and the degree of consensus necessitates a process of organisation, coordination and deliberation. Historically, this has commonly depended on coordination by an active social sector and protest leaders to claim representation; although the advent of social media has made it possible to organise and coordinate public protests without any overarching NGO structure. On the Mainland, any such process of collective claim-making independent of the Party state is treated as a political threat to the Party's monopoly on power, something that the Party is deeply concerned about and tries to pre-empt.[12]

In authoritarian regimes, protest is perceived as an indication of governance failure posing a clear danger to the regime's stability; order and stability are often a core key performance indicator in assessing the performance legitimacy of a local state. Protest, as a symbol of disorder and instability, undermines the performance of a local state and the legitimacy of the Party as a whole. The state therefore individualises disputes to pre-empt public protest in the name of social harmony, social stability or national security. What increasingly defines China's authoritarian system is not repression or violent crackdowns on protests, but pre-emptive action to disaggregate claims and prevent disputes from escalating into collective action.[13] According to Zhou

[11] Public Order Ordinance, s 13(2)(b), POO (cap 245): 'This section shall not apply to … (b) any *public procession* consisting of not more than 30 persons'; in relation to public meetings, the threshold for regulatory control is 50 persons, s 7(2)(a), POO. Participating in a procession or meeting exceeding these thresholds constitutes participation in an 'unauthorised assembly', an offence contrary to s 17A, POO. By contrast, three remains the threshold for an 'unlawful assembly', which gives rise to more serious offences, contrary to s 18, PPO.

[12] Fu H, 'Politicized Challenges, De-Politicized Responses: Political Monitoring in China's Transitions' in F Davis, N McGarrity and G Williams (eds) *Surveillance, Counter-Terrorism and Comparative Constitutionalism* (2014) 296–312

[13] Zhou K and Yan XJ, 'The Quest for Stability: Policing Popular Protest in the People's Republic of China' (2014) 61 *Problems of Post-Communism* 3–17.

and Yan, the effective pre-emptive strategy in China depends on three institutions: embedded police that can "deeply penetrate grassroots society" and closely monitor communities; effective online surveillance of protest-related information; and an intricate network of informants to identify and inform potential protest.[14] These all function together to send out a strong signal that public protest in any form or scale is politically offensive and therefore practically impermissible.

China's political system precludes grounds to protest for precisely the same political concern. Protest in China is still at a pre-rights stage in the sense that dense politicisation has effectively prevented protests from adopting a rights-based discourse on the Mainland. While the right to protest exists in law, there is not an independent court to safeguard the specific right to protest. This contrasts sharply, as discussed below, with Hong Kong's protest society and, for that matter, Taiwan's, which are both largely sustained by judicial protection. Indeed, Taiwan's Constitutional Court[15] and Hong Kong's Court of Final Appeal[16] have significantly enlarged the space for protesters against a backdrop of legislative restrictions on the right to protest.

Independent civil society organisations have historically been crucial for organising protests: another critical ingredient missing on the Mainland. In liberal societies, NGOs have commonly been the driving force behind protest. Labour unions, human rights organisations, women's groups, or consumer associations, acting as the representatives of sectoral interests independent of the government and credible at both state and societal levels, are well endowed with political, organisational and financial resources. However, the Chinese political system prohibits independent NGOs and places all organisations under tight political control. Cross-geographic and cross-professional alliances are prohibited and the government imposes severe restrictions to harshly crack down on independent civil society forces. These restrictive and repressive measures have effectively limited the development of independent social organisations and significantly diminished their capacity to effectively organise and mobilise. To be successful, protest must be organised and coordinated, something which is much more difficult to do without with a critical mass of resources experience and professional support.[17] The cases of Hong Kong and Taiwan demonstrate this reality. Alternatively, social media may provide a platform for communication and the organisation of a protest but it is strictly regulated and monitored on the Mainland, which limits its viability as a platform for protest purposes.

[14] Ibid.

[15] Chang, n 4 above.

[16] PJ Yap, 'Freedom of Assembly and Association' in J Chan and CL Lim (eds) *Law of the Hong Kong Constitution* (2015), Chapter 23.

[17] T Wright, *The Perils of Protest: State Repression and Student Activism in China and Taiwan* (2001).

It is in this political context that the constitutional rights to assembly, procession and demonstration[18] and, more generally, protest legislation, must be understood. The Mainland Chinese government enacted the Assembly, Procession and Demonstration Law (APDL) in the aftermath of the 1989 Tiananmen bloodshed to establish a regulatory framework for lawful assembly and protest.[19] This law ostensibly creates an approval system, according to which protest organisers can apply for permission from a public security organ. Reflecting the political significance of pre-emption, the Chinese APDL and the subsidiary legislation require the police, upon receipt of an application for assembly and procession, to pursue concrete goals, to assist the applicants to solve their underlining problems, thereby rendering the proposed protest unnecessary.[20]

In practice, however, the political imperative for stability and order has rendered the regulatory regime virtually irrelevant. While there may be hundreds of thousands of protest rallies, assemblies and demonstrations annually, most relating to environmental and labour rights, virtually none have received police approval, primarily for the reason that the protesters have not bothered to file an application. The protestors know perfectly well that not only will their application be denied, but also will also alert the police to a forthcoming mass gathering that may be perceived as disturbing social harmony. An application serves as an open invitation for police intervention that might not assist in resolving the issues that are the subject of the protest.

For organisers the proposed protest must be small, sudden and secretive, so that authorities are side-stepped in the planning stage and the police are caught by surprise. Organisation is limited to people who know and trust one other and the identity of organisers often remains hidden to avoid surveillance and punishment.[21] The overt use of social media is avoided due to censorship and surveillance. The operation aims to be quick sharp and symbolic with a protest typically completed and the protesters vanishing before the police can respond. It is only by using this complex process that public protests have become possible, protest leaders remain safe and the intended publicity impact is achieved. In authoritarian systems there is a deeply felt animosity and distrust between the state and its protesters, as protesters need to evade detection and the pre-emptive power of the state.[22]

[18] Constitution of the People's Republic of China, Art 35.

[19] The Law of People's Republic of China on Assembly, Procession and Demonstration Law http://en.pkulaw.cn/Display.aspx?lib=law&Cgid=4472&EncodingName=big5. For a detained analysis of the legislative history, see J Wang and N Truong, 'Law for What? Ideas and Social Control in China and Vietnam' (2020) *Problems of Post-Communism* DOI: 10.1080/10758216.2020.1783562.

[20] Implementation Rules for The Law of People's Republic of China on Assembly, Procession and Demonstration Law, Art 11, www.gov.cn/gongbao/content/2011/content_1860718.htm.

[21] Wright, n 17 above.

[22] Ibid.

There are other ways to bypass the regulatory and political prohibitions and these avoidance tactics are common to protest in most authoritarian states. So that they can protest without seeking police approval, organisers encourage residents to stroll collectively or take a walk together at a designated place and time. The subtlety of this indirect approach can effectively reduce the risk for the organisers and the level of fear among participants. Environmental protests can often appeal to the rising urban middle class. Such was the case with a well-known demonstration against the construction of PX plants in Xiamen and Chengdu, whereby organisers invited residents of the city to take a stroll at a specific place and time.[23]

Given the priority of stability and the pre-emptive measures in place to prevent protest, the principal objective of policing protest in authoritarian regimes is to end it swiftly after it starts. Protest, almost by definition, is unlawful and is therefore subject to multiple police regulatory powers and a range of punishments. Demonstrators will never receive police approval, so they have no legal right to proceed. The principal challenge for the police, is to figure out a more cost-effective way to make such occurrences infrequent or rare.[24]

PROTEST AND DEMOCRACY: TAIWAN

Taiwan's protest history is a textbook example of political transition, democratic resilience and historical legacy. In Taiwan and elsewhere assembly and procession is a constitutional right and has been regarded as an integral part of the freedom of expression. Although assembly and procession are the subject matter in Article 11 of the Republic of China Constitution, according to the Constitutional Court, it falls into the same category as the rights found in Article 14 of the Constitution. This forms part of a general right of expression including the freedom of expression, academic research, writing and publication, as provided for in Article 14 of the Constitution.[25] Often regarded as a negative or first-generation political right, freedom of expression fulfils an important instrumental and normative role. As such, assembly and procession serve an important supplementary role to the freedom of expression more generally. For people without access to mass media channels, who are therefore limited in terms of expression, the streets and other public spheres play an indispensable alternative role.

The constitutional rights of association and assembly were suspended in Taiwan until 1987 when the Martial Law Decree was lifted. While the social and

[23] HC Steinhardt, 'Environmental Public Interest Campaigns: A New Phenomenon in China's Contentious Politics' in Wright, n 9 above.

[24] S Biddulph, *The Stability Imperative: Human Rights and Law in China* (2015).

[25] Constitution of the Republic of China, https://law.moj.gov.tw/ENG/LawClass/LawAll.aspx?pcode=A0000001.

economic changes in Taiwan from the 1960s produced a surge of informal associations, assemblies and processions these were unlawful and were not legally protected. Taiwan's protest law was made towards the end of uninterrupted Guomindang authoritarian rule and has largely survived the democratic transition. Taiwan passed the first law on assembly and processions in 1988 when the government began to lift martial law. Somewhat ironically, the law that was purportedly passed to protect the right to assembly and procession was entitled the Law of Assembly and Processions during the Period of National Mobilization for the Suppression of Rebellion. That law laid a foundation for legal regulation of protest in Taiwan during the decades of democratic transition. In 1992, it was renamed the Assembly and Procession Act (APA) without substantive changes.[26]

Like the Mainland APDL, the Taiwanese APA requires a permit before protests can lawfully take place. Interestingly, despite its democratic transition, which has made protest an essential part of political participation, Taiwan previously possessed a high and difficult threshold for assembly and procession.[27] In spite of the regulatory restraints on protest in Taiwan, the court has stepped in to compensate for the democratic deficit. Through two Constitutional Interpretations of the APA by the Constitutional Court and in decisions on individual prosecution for violations of the APA, the Court has created a rich jurisprudence that has reshaped the contours of the APA and enlarged the scope of the freedom of protest, both substantively and procedurally.[28]

Substantively, the Constitutional Court of Taiwan has ruled that any content control and any pre-constraints on protest or free speech are unconstitutional. In Interpretation No 445,[29] the Constitutional Court, while upholding the constitutionality of a permit system on the ground of the necessity for the police to maintain order, limited the scope of discretion in the review and approval process first by invalidating an article in the APA which prohibited assemblies or processions that advocated communism or the secession of territory, ie the advocacy of the independence of Taiwan. For the court, no content control is permissible when a general freedom of expression is being exercised and the police are not allowed to conduct any merit-based review. Secondly and more significantly, in the same judgment, the court also struck down another section in the APA which commonly appears in protest laws elsewhere on the ground that it was too vague to form a clear legal basis for review. The invalidated section of the law allowed the police to deny an application if an assembly or process was likely to endanger national security, social order, or public welfare, among others. In doing so, the court significantly altered the APA and limited police control to purely

[26] The Assembly and Procession Act. Available at: https://law.moj.gov.tw/LawClass/LawAll.aspx?pcode=D0080058. For a historical review of the legislation, see Chang, n 4 above.

[27] Chang, n 4 above, 30–48.

[28] Ibid.

[29] Judicial Yuan Interpretation No 445 (1998). Available at: http://cons.judicial.gov.tw/jcc/zh-tw/jep03/show?expno=445.

time, place and form of a protest relying on subsequent punishment regarding seditious content or disorder.

The court also questioned the time needed for the police to approve an application. Under Articles 9 and 12 of the APA, organisers of assemblies or processions are required to apply for a permit six days before the event takes place; expedited review is possible in cases of natural disasters or other unforeseeable incidents, in which case the time limit for applications was shortened to 24 hours. The court considered that the expedited review period was too long to pass a constitutional test; it required the legislature to provide a proper revision to the law.

Interpretation No 718 was made on 21 March 2014 in the middle of the Sunflower Movement. This concerned the legality of an urgent protest without making an application: the Constitutional Court struck down the expedited review as unconstitutional as it imposed a disproportionate burden and allowed "urgent or spontaneous assemblies" without applying for a permit.[30] This decision shows that Taiwan is moving away from its rigid approval regime. The current ruling party, the DPP, has also made repeated undertakings that Taiwan will eventually opt for a record system.

In comparison with Hong Kong, the number of approval requests for assembly and processions in Taiwan is not large. This is counterintuitive given the vibrancy of Taiwanese politics and the large scope of anti-government demonstrations that defined Taiwan's path to democracy. The annual number of approved/unapproved assemblies and those without making application is uneven and fluctuates greatly. In the years between 1999 and 2016, the number varied from 1,265 in 1999, 1,448 in 2003, to 14,751 in 2014.[31] The size of assemblies and processions has generally been large. With the exception of 2017, when the number of participants declined to 608,540, the number had always been slightly over 1 million – indeed it reached nearly 12 million in 2004 – indicating the forceful mobilisation of the masses in direct political participation on the Island.[32]

What does protest embody and entail? In Taiwan's maturing democracy, assembly and processions are no longer merely regarded as serving an expressive function, a negative freedom to be exercised by individuals without undue government restrictions. In fact, assembly and process serve a constitutive function in building and solidifying democracy. Its political significance is best put by the Constitutional Court in Interpretation No 445:

> Based on the idea of people's sovereignty, only when people enjoy the right of free discussion and full expression of their opinions can they discover truth, achieve

[30] Judicial Yuan Interpretation No 718 (2014), para 2. Available at: http://cons.judicial.gov.tw/jcc/zh-tw/jep03/show?expno=718.

[31] Police Department, Interior Ministry. Available at: www.moi.gov.tw/stat/node.aspx?cate_sn=&belong_sn=6463&sn=6465.

[32] Ibid. It is worth noting that a large number of protests went ahead without seeking approval.

> consensus through democratic process and then make law and policies accordingly. Therefore, the freedom of expression is a significant basic right for the implementation of democratic politics.[33]

Freedom of expression is the cornerstone of a liberal society. The court has reiterated the rights and the corresponding duty of the government to protect and facilitate the exercise of constitutional rights so citizens can participate in protest 'without fear'. Beyond liberal individual rights, the court also takes notice of the collective nature of assemblies and processions and their function as incubators of the democratic will. Assemblies and processions offer a platform from which citizens deliberate on significant issues and engage in dialogue with the government and with each other. That interactive, deliberative process makes democratic societies vibrant and resilient.[34]

PROTEST AND THE RULE OF LAW: HONG KONG

Hong Kong possesses a mature and vibrant society whose citizens exploit limited public space to air grievances and express popular demands. Public meetings and processions have traditionally been an integral part of a broader process of public deliberation and interaction between society and the government. They are commonplace and a central feature of Hong Kong's freedom. Protest has become so regular that those who air their concerns in a public space are not regarded as extraordinary, radical, or deviant. In Hong Kong's political culture, protest has become a middle-class activity – involving journalists, religious leaders, university professors, doctors and lawyers. The participation of the middle class makes public protest mainstream and 'respectable'. Hong Kong, on average, experiences slightly over 1,000 processions per year: an increase from 1,007 in 2008 to 1,203 in 2017. The number of assemblies has increased sharply over the same period, from 4,287 in 2008 to 10,608 in 2017.[35] Even after recent episodes of violent confrontation between the police and demonstrators, protest remains highly credible and has received wide community support and understanding.[36]

Subject to the exercise of policing powers, Hong Kong has a well-structured protest law, despite its narrow streets and high population density. Freedom of demonstration is both accepted in Hong Kong's political culture and strongly

[33] Judicial Yuan Interpretation No 445, para 7.

[34] Ibid.

[35] Hong Kong Police Force, 'Public Order Event Statistics'. Available at: www.police.gov.hk/ppp_en/09_statistics/poes.html.

[36] 'Research Report on Public Opinion during the Anti-Extradition Bill (Fugitive Offenders Bill) Movement in Hong Kong' *Centre for Communication and Public Opinion Survey* (The Chinese University of Hong Kong), May 2020: 95); 'Anti-Extradition Bill Movement People's Public Sentiment Report' Hong Kong Public Opinion Research Institute, December 2019: 22.

protected under the law. Rule of law concerns matter in regulating public protests and Hong Kong's protest culture has been facilitated by the Public Order Ordinance (POO) which effectively governs assemblies and processions. The legal framework includes various offences relating to unlawful assemblies, but its central feature is a regulatory process that residents in Hong Kong understand and with which they comply. Until the anti-extradition bill protests in 2019, there was no perceived overt political censorship in the approval process and, historically, the police were relatively neutral in the city's public debates, committed more to managing than preventing protest. From the very beginning of colonial rule, legal rules have served to absorb complicated political disagreements.[37]

Hong Kong's regulatory framework imposes considerable restrictions on public assemblies and demonstrations, necessitated in part by its crowded and bustling nature, but also partly due to the experience of riots and disturbances in the 1960s during the Cultural Revolution. The current POO was enacted in the aftermath of those riots, although public order regulations date back to the nineteenth century.

The first of these was the Peace Preservation Ordinance 1884, passed to control the possession of firearms by the Chinese population with a sunset clause to limit its effect to the period through to 1885.[38] When the Ordinance was renewed in 1886, new sections were enacted to punish persons 'found … unlawfully, riotously or tumultuously assembled to the disturbance of the peace and to the terror of Her Majesty's subjects'.[39] Emergency regulations were passed to control large scale economic strife in the 1920s.[40] In the aftermath of the Second World War, Hong Kong enacted its first Public Order Ordinance. This aimed to provide a regulatory framework for maintaining law and order during peacetime. As an immediate post-war piece of legislation, intended to restore and maintain peace and order, the POO was short and broadly framed but also included draconian measures such as the power of the Governor to declare a curfew.

A permission system for public protests had been in place since 1932 in the Summary Offences (SO) Ordinance. Section 3(16) made it an offence for a person who 'in any public place organizes, equips or takes part in any procession without the permission of the Secretary for Chinese Affairs or a District Officer'.[41] When the POO was revised in 1967 in response to the rioting, a licensing system was created, according to which no public meetings or processions could take place without a licence issued by the Commissioner of Police,

[37] CAG Jones, *Lost in China: Law, Culture, Identity in Post-1997 Hong Kong* (2015).

[38] *Peace Preservation Ordinance* (No 22 of 1884).

[39] *Peace Preservation Ordinance* 1886 (No 15 of 1886), s 7.

[40] *Emergency Regulations Ordinance* 1922 (No 5 of 1922); and *Illegal Strikes and Lockouts Ordinance* 1927 (No 10 of 1927).

[41] *Summary Offences Ordinance* 1932 (No 40 of 1932).

subject to the condition that they are 'not likely to prejudice the maintenance of public order or be used for any lawful or immoral purpose'. An application would be rejected whenever any person or group directly, indirectly, or likely to be associated with the meeting or procession had at any time contravened Hong Kong law.[42]

This licensing system was subsequently liberalised, following a government undertaking to do so, when 'Hong Kong was sufficiently stable (and its population sufficiently responsible) to accommodate less sweeping control over public meetings'.[43] After a study by a working party, the POO was amended in 1980 and the licensing requirement for assemblies was replaced with an advance notification system. Under section 8 of the 1980s Amendment, individuals were required to provide the Police Commissioner with a written notice of a planned assembly seven days prior to the meeting. The Commissioner could prohibit the holding of a public meeting, among other reasons, if it was likely to prejudice the maintenance of public order. Public processions remained subject to licence until 1995, when the POO was uniformly liberalised.

Liberalisation was prompted by the enactment of the Bill of Rights Ordinance, which had a significant impact on Hong Kong law, including on law and public order. Under Section 13(1) of the 1995 amendment to the POO, the licensing system was replaced by a notice system for public processions, according to which the organisers of a procession had to notify the Police Commissioner of their intention to hold a public procession, with the Commissioner entitled to object on a number of grounds.

The Chinese government strongly objected to this amendment and, before the 1997 transition, the Provisional Legislature that was set up by China to oversee the transition invalidated the amendment for contravening the Basic Law. The notification system was abolished, but Hong Kong did not return to its former permit system. Instead, it adopted a non-objection system under which a public meeting or procession may take place if two essential conditions are satisfied: (a) the Commissioner of Police is notified of the intention to hold the meeting or procession; and (b) the Commissioner of Police indicates no objection to the meeting or procession taking place or is taken to have issued a notice of no objection.

In contrast to the authoritarian motherland, the policing of protest in Hong Kong has been characterised not by vigilantly looking for ways to preempt strikes but rather by negotiation with the applicants regarding time, place and form. To do that effectively, protest organizers are required to submit adequate information during the application process to facilitate the decision-making process. In this sense, although the differing systems of permit, notice or no objection may impose different liabilities on protest organisers who fail

[42] *Public Order Ordinance* (No 64 of 1967), s 7(2).
[43] Hong Kong *Hansard*, 23 July 1980, 1065.

to comply with the rules, historically, it had little impact on the capacity of the police. Organisers had to inform the police of their protest intentions and their plans in detail and the police retained the power to control the process and to disperse crowds regardless of the type of approval required.

A stable legal system like Hong Kong's offers a high degree of predictability: protesters apply in advance police duly issue a no-objection letter and the demonstration routinely takes place. Rules and conditions are clearly set understood and complied with; protesting is largely self-regulatory and well-disciplined; the police usually provide minimum oversight for most assemblies and processions. In general, there is a clear leadership structure: it is almost as if the police have shifted any liability to the protest organisers. As a microcosm of Hong Kong society, protest under this framework was normally well-organised, orderly and peaceful with a high degree of trust between protesters and the police. Occasionally, some organisers of protests that took place without permission or violated conditions that had been negotiated with the police were prosecuted.

The 2019–2020 protests, initially triggered by the introduction of an Extradition Bill, but which subsequently shifted to include a demand for universal suffrage, have changed the protest ecosystem in Hong Kong.[44] Hong Kong's streets were again besieged and ablaze with protest, the frequent confrontations between protestors and the police made Hong Kong even more of a protest society, with the government seemingly incapable of finding a political solution and direct armed intervention from the Mainland obliquely threatened on a number of occasions. Massive public demonstrations took place, with organisers claiming on several occasions that participation reached the millions. Ostensibly, the protests were broadly conducted within the legal framework outlined above and consisted of a wide cross-section of Hong Kong's society. But radicalised groups of protestors, left frustrated after OCM and confronted with a tone-deaf and unresponsive government, claiming to lack any other democratic means of pursuing their objectives, stepped forward, unleashing a tit-for-tat spiral of violence as confrontations between police and protestors escalated. On a weekly, if not nightly, basis, black-clad protestors sporting helmets, gas masks and umbrellas (the defining symbol of OCM), stepped out of the shadows of

[44] Ironically, these protests originated from the alleged murder of a Hong Kong woman by her Hong Kong boyfriend while in Taiwan. He had returned to Hong Kong before her body was discovered, making it legally difficult to return him to Taiwan due to the absence of an extradition or rendition arrangement. The Hong Kong Government seized the moment to introduce an extradition Bill enabling his extradition to Taiwan. But this proposed extradition Bill equally applied to the Mainland and public and business reaction was immediate, demanding withdrawal of the Bill. Echoing the concerns which sparked the Sunflower Movement in Taiwan, the Bill was portrayed as a major incursion into Hong Kong's autonomy and freedoms and as undermining the notion of 'one country two systems'. See, AHY Chen, 'A Prefect Storm: Hong Kong-Mainland Rendition of Fugitive Offenders' (2019) 49 *Hong Kong Law Journal* 419–430.

peaceful protest and, under the mantra 'be water', engaged in spontaneous, short-term activities intended to disrupt the city. Employing the tactics of 'urban guerrilla warfare', these protestors stormed the Legislative Council building, encircled police stations, flooded into shopping malls and other public venues, defiled national symbols and spontaneously and repeatedly blocked and closed down streets and transportation infrastructure, including Hong Kong's international airport. Bricks, laser pens and petrol bombs became the 'weapons' of confrontation. For their part, the police responded with an even more confrontational stance, with large numbers of officers deployed in riot gear, armed with tear gas and other crowd-control weapons, supported by water cannon vehicles. With public support for the protests seemingly staying strong, notwithstanding the escalating cycle of violence and police popularity plummeting, the Mainland authorities have taken on a more proactive role, speaking directly on several occasions about the protests and decrying the protestors' 'unlawfulness'. Ultimately, there appeared to be two movements taking place at the same time.[45] One followed Hong Kong's traditional regulatory framework and remained peaceful. The other was more radicalised, impassioned and willing to engage in violence.

Despite the escalating tensions, judicial independence in Hong Kong remained steadfast and was commonly perceived as a bulwark of Hong Kong's rule of law, ensuring that police powers in managing public order are subject to robust judicial oversight. However, least this was true prior to the enactment of the Law of the People's Republic of China on Safeguarding National Security in the Hong Kong Special Administrative Region on 30 June 2020 and then the Implementation Rules for Article 43 of the Law of the People's Republic of China on Safeguarding National Security in the Hong Kong Special Administrative Region (Implementation Rules) on 7 July 2020 now threatens to cast a shadow over this both judicial independence and this perception.[46]

The Hong Kong judiciary has always deferred to police determination on practical matters relating to time and venue restrictions on meeting and procession, but it has equally been cognisant of its role and responsibility as the last bastion of Hong Kong's rule of law, given the territory's anaemic legislature and its 'executive-led' system. To this end, the judiciary has stood ready to intervene when rights and freedoms are violated and has exercised a supervisory role in ensuring the legality of the application and approval process. When necessary, the courts have been rigorous in protecting the right of expression through protest against occasionally overzealous police. For example, Hong Kong's Court of Final Appeal (CFA) reduced the scope of police discretion by invalidating ordre

[45] K Kennedy, 'Can Hong Kong Turn Away from Violence and Learn the Lesson of Democratic Compromise?' *South China Morning Post* (28 Aug 2019).

[46] H Fu, 'National Security Law: Challenges and Prospects' in J Chan and CL Lim (eds), *Law of the Hong Kong Constitution*, 3rd edn, forthcoming 2021.

public as a legal ground for objecting to a protest, on the grounds of vagueness.[47] Even so, like the Constitutional Court in Taiwan, the CFA refused to invalidate the non-objection system itself for protest management. Further, the CFA confirmed the constitutionality of other statutory grounds for police objections, including national security and public order, unlike in Taiwan, where they were declared unconstitutional by Taiwan's highest court.[48]

Until recently Hong Kong's treatment of protesters was thus defined by a regard for rule of law and the effective protection of rights and freedoms predicated on conventions of police neutrality, apolitical prosecutions by the Department of Justice and independent judicial decisions. In dealing with OCM and its organisers and participants, the courts have maintained this perceived commitment to neutrality, professing to eschew consideration of motivation and instead focusing on the essential 'unlawfulness' of alleged criminal conduct. From the injunction order initially forcing the occupiers to exit the streets, to the initial prosecution of those initiating OCM, to the eventual prosecution of participants in a series of unlawful assembly cases and then the disqualification of pro-independence members of the Legislative Council, Hong Kong courts steadfastly reiterated their political neutrality. In practical terms, this perceived commitment to political neutrality is grounded in a clear separation between lawful and unlawful protests, with a sharp and decisive focus on the lawfulness of a protest. Lawfulness is claimed to be the only lens through which criminality is viewed. The following statement from the Court of Appeal captures the essence of the judicial attitude to unlawful assembly:

> ... this court is duty-bound to send a clear message to the public that when taking part in assemblies, processions, demonstrations or like activities, in the free exercise of their rights, participants must abide by the law and must not cause any damage to public order and public peace.[49]

Judicial consensus also maintains that an unlawful assembly involving any violence, including 'charging at or assaulting law-enforcement officers ... will be met by a substantial sentence, otherwise there will be no social accord or social progress and citizens' rights and freedom as safeguarded by law may altogether vanish'.[50]

'Lawfulness' thus serves as a starting point agreed upon by the courts at all levels and it is on the basis of this common understanding that judges have claimed to exercise their discretion in sentencing and also given expression to

[47] *Leung Kwok Hung v HKSAR* (2005) 8 HKCFAR 229.
[48] Judicial Yuan Interpretation No 445.
[49] Secretary for Justice and Wong Chi Fung, Law Kwun Chung and Chow Yong Kang Alex (17 August 2017) (Court of Appeal) (English Translation).
[50] Ibid, para 17.

the underlying values. One of Hon Yeung VPs' open statements, quoted below at length, is representative of a conservative law-and-order approach that disregards political motivations in sentencing:

> In recent years, an unhealthy wind has been blowing in Hong Kong. Some people, on the pretext of pursuing their ideals of freely exercising their rights conferred by law, have acted wantonly in an unlawful manner. Certain people, including individuals of learning, advocate 'achieving justice by violating the law' and, under the slogan, they encourage others to break the law. These people openly flout the law. Not only do they refuse to admit their lawbreaking activities are wrong, but they even go as far as regarding such activities as a source of honour and pride.[51]

To reverse the 'unhealthy wind', the Court of Appeal replaced community service orders, originally imposed by a magistrate on three student leaders for the offence of inciting others to enter a restricted place, with substantial custodial sentences. The Court of Final Appeal, in overturning this aspect of the Court of Appeal's decision, makes the same legal point, but with a more moderate tone:

> The fact of a conviction of the offence will necessarily mean that the offender has crossed the line separating the lawful exercise of his constitutional rights from unlawful activity subject to sanctions and constraints. In such a case, there is little merit in a plea for leniency on the basis that the offender was merely exercising constitutional rights since, by definition, he was not doing so at the time when the offence was committed.[52]

As the law stands in Hong Kong, motivation, however noble it is, is irrelevant in determining criminal liability and carries little weight in the sentencing process. While judges can consider political motivation when imposing a sentence, the consideration is based entirely on pragmatic and utilitarian grounds rather than any normative or principled considerations.[53] From a Hong Kong perspective, the mainland approach is politically repressive and legally unpersuasive. Conversely, Taiwan's democratic process has been so fast-moving, it has unleashed tremendous power and energy on both society and its institutions and requires consolidation to become rule-bound given that many protestors do not comply with the permit system, which is frequently not enforced by the police and in light of the Constitutional Court's ruling that the expedited approval process is too long to be constitutional, while leaving amendment and thus the fate of the permit system, as a matter for the Legislature to properly decide.

[51] Ibid, para. 6.
[52] Secretary for Justice and Wong Chi Fung (FACC No 9 of 2017) (Court of Final Appeal), para 70.
[53] Ibid, para 76, citing Lord Hoffmann in *Sepet v Home Secretary* [20003] 1 WLR 856, para 34.

THE POLITICS OF PROTEST

Protesters in all three jurisdictions commonly frame and legitimise their street activities in terms of civil disobedience. Many emphasise the peaceful, non-violent nature of their resistance. By and large, they practice what they preach and avoid confrontation with the authorities and counter-protesters. Yet, their protests took place in different political systems, challenged their respective systems to their core in different ways and ultimately received different treatments.

Civil disobedience has different meanings in different political systems. John Rawls famously pointed out the internal irony of civil disobedience, stating that its problem 'arise[s] only within a more or less just democratic state for those citizens who recognize and accept the legitimacy of the constitution'.[54] Civil disobedience lies between an act of defiance, violent resistance against and a radical break from a political community and submission to constituted authorities. It is thus a protest against the malfunctioning of a constitutional order, while also accepting the legitimacy of that order at a foundational level. It promotes evolutionary improvement of the existing order rather than a revolutionary change. It is thus 'an act of loyalty'.[55]

Defining civil disobedience in this way, at first sight, Taiwan's Sunflower Movement is a typical example of civil disobedience in the liberal sense in that it sought to undergird, not to undermine, Taiwan's democratic process. Upholding democracy, in Jones and Su's terms, was the endgame of the Sunflower Movement and it converges perfectly with Taiwan's constitutional design. For Yeh, the movement recognises the limit of 'formal institutions' in safeguarding democracy and offers a corrective mechanism to the democratic deficit within democratic institutions. The traditional oversight mechanisms, including constitutional review by the courts, periodic elections, or the related parliamentary process, often fail to safeguard young democracies from backsliding into stagnation. Representative democracy may also marginalise public participation in the day-to-day making of policy and effectively reduce the public to merely a passive audience – the trigger of the Sunflower Movement in Taiwan. Democratic institutions may actually work to damage the core values of democracy, with politicians and political parties hijacking the legislative process to advance their own interests. Periodic elections, as competitive as they may be, often fail to make the legislature democratically accountable. Legislatures may also be captured by special interests. For Yeh, the Sunflower Movement and the social forces it epitomised – referred to as 'civic constitutionalism' – may have saved Taiwan's democracy from degeneration and even collapse. Civic constitutionalism refers

[54] J Rawls, *A Theory of Justice* (1971), p 363.

[55] BR Roth, 'Democratic Political Obligation', p 196, in Jones, n 2 above. That explains the exception to the offence of seditious libel in common law. See, for example, s 9 of the *Crimes Ordinance*, Hong Kong.

to a process in which the 'people', centred around the civil society, replacing the legislature and the courts, understand, interpret and shape the meaning of the constitution to positively reinforce the judicial and legislative processes. Civic constitutionalism, therefore, does not challenge democracy as the endgame in Taiwan. On the contrary, it boosts democracy by requesting that people remain vigilant to democracy's vulnerability and be ready to mobilise to maintain and enhance the democratic value of the political process. In Jones and Su's formulation, the Sunflower Movement involves more than just 'disobeying'. It is a 'democratic contestation' that is 'democracy-compatible' and, indeed, democracy-promoting. It offers 'a duelling vision of democracy'.[56]

Some may argue that the Sunflower Movement is not based on civil disobedience in a liberal sense because the protesters did not plead guilty or accept responsibility and punishment, as they were expected to do according to the liberal theory of civil disobedience. On the contrary, the DPP, on winning the 2016 election, dropped charges against a large swathe of the protesters who attempted, in an aggressive if not violent manner, to break in and occupy Executive offices. Additionally, the courts then found 22 leaders of the Parliament occupation not guilty of any offences. The Sunflower protesters were either excused because of the circumstances of the cases or justified because of their democratic motivation and aspirations.

Protest on the Mainland, smaller in scope and secretive in its operation, but 'radical' in its impact, has a significantly different political meaning and repercussions. Protest takes place within a context that cannot tolerate it or integrate it as part of the official system. For the protesters in the NCM, the end game is not merely to hold the Party-state accountable to its own rhetoric and to improve governance under the existing political system. That is their mid-game, but their ultimate objective is to change the system from within. Their endgame is the replacement of the existing system with a new liberal constitutional democracy. These two systems, in the eyes of protesters, are mutually exclusive and irreconcilable at a foundational level. While protest on the Mainland contains similarities to those in Taiwan and Hong Kong, the challenge it poses to the Mainland's political system is a qualitatively different and is, in turn, perceived and treated as such. Directly or indirectly, protesters are subversive in terms of their ultimate goal.

The OCM in Hong Kong drew inspiration from both the NCM in the Mainland and the Sunflower Movement in Taiwan. Like the NCM, the OCM in Hong Kong challenged the Chinese political system in an open, direct and radical way: explicitly, that is 'give us democracy as we define it or we will paralyze Hong Kong'. This, of course, may have particular implications on the Mainland. The term occupying central in Chinese (佔中) can be read differently and can,

[56] BC Jones and YT Su, 'Confrontational Contestation and Democratic Compromise: The Sunflower Movement and its Aftermath,' in Jones, n 2 above, 15–29.

with some organising, evolve into occupying China （中）. After all, a major occupation occurred in Tiananmen Square in 1989.[57] In that sense, the OCM was a rebellious movement which squared up to the central government, with its organisers openly threatening to use serious unlawful activities to force the central government to change its policy towards Hong Kong. In the eyes of the central government, the OCM was part of the global colour revolution that used Hong Kong as a base to subvert the Chinese political system. It was, therefore, as dangerous as the NCM.

Hong Kong's 1997 reunification to China and the arrival of a new political master redefined the protest landscape. After all the celebrations and genuine efforts to finesse deeper fractures at a structural level, an adversarial relationship started to surface as Hong Kong came to the realisation that at the end of the day it is China's political system that makes democratic aspirations an impossibility. The incremental denial of Hong Kong's aspirations for democracy by the central government through various political and legal action has absorbed most of the city's political resources and has become the focal point of Hong Kong's political protest.[58]

From the 1989 protest in response to the Tiananmen bloodshed, the 2003 anti-national security bill, the 2008 anti-patriotic education, to the OCM, anti-central government rallies and demonstrations have redefined Hong Kong's political landscape.[59] Protest is both symbolic and expressive, intended to articulate political views, reconfirm political positions and provide a moral compass to a society that has lost its direction; it is also used as an instrument to push back against policy changes.[60]

Different from the NCM and similar to Sunflower Movement, the OCM aims to maintain and solidify the high degree of autonomy in Hong Kong that is entrenched in the Chinese Constitution and specified in the Basic Law. The OCM is thus internally contradictory in its objectives. Maintaining One Country Two Systems (OCTS) is the endgame for Hong Kong; but genuine democracy, as the protesters demanded, is unattainable under the OCTS framework. For them, the Party state has promised something that is not deliverable and Hong Kong has started to realise and come to terms with this eventuality. OCM leaders and participants decided to protest knowing they were in violation of the POO;

[57] Wright, n 17 above.

[58] J Chan, 'A Storm of Unprecedented Ferocity: Shrinking Space for Political Rights, Public Demonstrations and Judicial Independence in Hong Kong' (2018) 16(2) *International Journal of Comparative Constitutional Law* 373–388.

[59] W Cheng and WH Yuen, (eds) (2018) 社运年代：香港抗争政治的轨迹（The Age of Social Movement: The Trajectory of Hong Kong's Political Contention） (2018); Fu H, 'China's Imperatives for National Security Legislation,' in C Chan and F de Londras (eds), *China's National Security: Endangering Hong Kong's Rule of Law?* (2020).

[60] FLF Lee, 'Internet Alternative Media, Movement Experience and Radicalism: The Case of Post-Umbrella Movement Hong Kong' (2018) 27 *Social Movement Studies* 311.

they mostly pleaded guilty, as promised, and accepted punishment for their actions. The many frustrations associated with the OCTS formula eventually led to the radicalisation of political protest and it is the failure to achieve democracy that has ultimately planted the seeds for the advocacy of Hong Kong's independence,[61] leading to the epic protest of the 2019 with unprecedented levels of violence and the imposition of the National Security Law in 2020.[62] OCTS was initially designed, in part, to lure Taiwan back to the motherland; but the structural fault in the design is pushing Hong Kong toward Taiwan.

THE FUTURE OF PROTEST

The three systems generate three distinct perceptions of, and reactions to, protest. On the authoritarian Mainland, protest is a political provocation to be pre-empted and suppressed if pre-emption fails; in Hong Kong's liberal tradition it has been a legal right to be balanced against the rights and freedoms of others; and in Taiwan it is a democratic virtue and indeed a public duty of citizens to ensure democratic resilience. Protest, as exemplified in these three cases, attempts to challenge or reinforce the existing system and has received drastically different treatment. But after all the protests and prosecutions, what are the future prospects of public protest in these three jurisdictions? Could the NCM, OCM and Sunflower Movement happen again in their respective societies?

On the Mainland, political pre-emption and legal repression work to drive grievances underground. While the formal political and legal system allows assemblies, processions and demonstrations, the political reality is such that any sign of public protest and collective action would be regarded as a political risk and continues to be prohibited and suppressed. The case of Xu Zhiyong and his co-organisers and supporters illustrates both the determination and capacity of the Party state to prevent and prohibit any public protests that are deemed politically risky. But for civil society actors who have survived periodic crackdowns, the streets (in both the real and virtual worlds) remain the best platforms and battle grounds to create meaningful input into the decision-making process and to educate the general public. In authoritarian states, particularly where institutional participation through the legislative process, judicial process, or mass media is tightly controlled or entirely absent, public protest is the principal way to make claims and demands. Taking that avenue away without adequate institutional compensation, means society is left with no alternative mechanism to let off steam and air their grievances.

[61] B Tai, S Veitch, Fu H and R Cullen, 'Pursuing Democracy in an Authoritarian State: Protest and the Rule of Law in Hong Kong' (2019) 28(6) *Social & Legal Studies* 1–39.

[62] Chen, n 41 above; AHY Chen, 'Constitutional Controversies in the Aftermath of the Anti-Extradition Movement of 2019,' (2020) 50 (2) *Hong Kong Law Journal* 609–632.

Taiwan faces a different predicament; its democracy may be under stress due to other factors. In 2014, the Sunflower Movement galvanised political forces and eventually delivered a crushing defeat to the Kuomintang-led government, in a similar way to the Wild Lily Movement, another iconic movement which led to further liberalisation and democratisation, in 1990.[63] As a significant part of pan-DPP alliance, civil society actors, who led the civil society in Taiwan, were invited to join the government and leading lawyers, well-known academics and powerful NGO leaders felt duty-bound to join the government to further consolidate Taiwan's democracy. Previously opposition forces, these actors are now part of the ruling coalition. While protests about social and economic issues have continued and have even intensified in certain policy areas, civil society critique and supervision of the DPP government may no longer possess the vigour and challenge that it used to. Will Taiwan's democracy continue to create and nurture independent social forces to create further constitutional movements?

After the OCM and the subsequent crackdowns, Hong Kong police started to gear themselves up in preparation for future unrest. Prior to the anti-extradition protests, the foundation of the public's trust in the Hong Kong police was the latter's perceived political neutrality and its effectiveness and legitimacy depend on the survival of this trust.[64] But the OCM and subsequent protests have exposed social divisions and pushed the police into violent confrontation with citizens. Inevitably, taking this path poses a direct challenge to the police's ability to remain politically neutral but also effective. With the prospect of rising authoritarian legality on the horizon,[65] civil society actors who devoted themselves to the OCM have found themselves subject to a wide legal crackdown. Hundreds of activists were prosecuted, most were convicted and have received at least some form of punishment for their peaceful protest.

This demonstrates that law can be a double-edged sword. It can empower citizens to exercise their individual rights of protest; but it can also limit their advocacy to a narrowly defined legal space. The legalistic approach which criminalises any unlawful activity has had a powerful chilling impact, demonstrating that there is a stark price to be paid in Hong Kong for extra-legal mobilisation. But it remains uncertain whether legal repression in Hong Kong will, in the long run, tame the passionate youth or simply radicalise them. The resilient protests on Hong Kong's streets and their violent escalation tend to demonstrate that legal repression breeds radicalism and violence.

[63] Wright, n 17 above.

[64] Fu, n 2 above.

[65] See Benny Tai's chapter in this collection: 'Authoritarian Rule of Law in Hong Kong'.

2

The Ultimate Test of Fidelity: Judicial Responses to Civil Disobedience in Hong Kong and Taiwan

JIMMY CHIA-SHIN HSU* AND ANNE SY CHEUNG+

IN 2014 TWO large-scale social protests involving extraordinary acts of civil disobedience broke out in Taiwan and Hong Kong. The temporal proximity of Hong Kong's Occupy Central and Taiwan's Sunflower Movement was no coincidence, as both were aggravated social responses to the perceived threats from China.[1] The social responses soon spilled into the legal arena. In the case of Hong Kong, three student leaders of the Occupy Movement narrowly escaped a prison term before the Court of Final Appeal (CFA), but received a stern warning that future offenders in large-scale unlawful assemblies involving any degree of violence would be subject to stricter scrutiny.[2] In addition, nine pro-democracy activists, including the co-founders of Occupy Central, had been convicted by the District Court.[3] In contrast, in Taiwan's Sunflower Movement, legal responses varied and in general were less than severe. After the Democratic Progressive Party came into power in 2016, the government dropped charges against almost 200 individuals who had participated in the movement. For those cases that went through court trials, some defendants were acquitted while others were given lenient sentences.

The contrasting legal responses of the two jurisdictions provide profoundly rich cases for theoretical reflections on civil disobedience and

* Jimmy Chia-Shin Hsu, Associate Research Professor, Institutum Iurisprudentiae, Academia Sinica, Taiwan.

+ Anne SY Cheung, Professor, Faculty of Law, and Co-director of the Law and Technology Centre, the University of Hong Kong.

[1] BC Jones (ed), *Law and Politics of the Taiwan Sunflower and Hong Kong Umbrella Movements* (2017).

[2] *Secretary for Justice v Chow Yong Kang Alex and others* [2018] HKCFA 4.

[3] *HKSAR v Tai Yiu Ting and others* [2019] HKDC 450 [37]. At the time of writing, this case is pending on appeal before the Court of Appeal, to be heard in March 2021.

its relationship with law and democracy. When the protesters in the civil disobedience movements ended up as defendants in courts, court rooms in Hong Kong and Taiwan become high-tension arenas. In this chapter, we ask: How do we critically evaluate these judicial responses? What does the disparity in judicial responses of the two jurisdictions reveal about the courts' and protesters' understanding of what legitimates government coercion and what generates genuine political obligation for people to abide by the law and the political regime?

We draw on Philippe Nonet and Philip Selznick's models of law and society,[4] in particular their theories on repressive, autonomous and responsive law to identify relevant considerations suitable for Hong Kong and Taiwan societies. In repressive law, rules of law are subordinated to power politics, serving interests of the state; in autonomous law, law is independent of the state, acting as a restraint on political power, characterised by procedural justice; whereas in responsive law, law seeks not only to adjudicate but regulate society by responding to social needs and aspirations.[5] Their typology captures the intricate dynamics between law and political relations. We argue that when a state has to face a deeply divided issue as evident in massive scale of civil disobedience in society, different approaches to the rule of law are called for in different political regimes. For a democratic state, the court may waiver between autonomous law and responsive law, depending on how the court evaluates the merits of the issues and whether the court chooses to be a neutral arbiter or an advocate for change. For a semi-authoritarian state, responsive law may be better suited for a court that still upholds rule of law principles.

This chapter will first discuss proper theoretical frameworks for analysing the court decisions within the two jurisdictions. Most of the literature on civil disobedience centres on philosophical analysis of its definition and justification. Such theories are highly relevant, since they have provided moral and legal principles for the court to evaluate the legal relevance of civil disobedience. Yet we are still in need of a theoretical framework better suited for our inquiry, for the contrasted judicial decisions serve as focal points of complex legal–political phenomena that require explanation. For this purpose, the theoretical framework should illuminate relevant legal and political factors in a meaningful structure. Next, we examine the judicial reasoning in the cases concerned. The Hong Kong courts tried hard to reach 'a Solomonic solution'[6] that was agreeable to all sides by fending off political arguments and confining civil disobedience as a criminal act. In contrast, apart from those cases in which the government has withdrawn charges, Taiwan's courts have bent over backwards to accommodate

[4] P Nonet and P Selznick, *Law & Society in Transition: Toward Responsive Law* (2001), 33.

[5] Ibid, 16.

[6] P Yap, 'Twenty Years of the Basic Law: Continuity and Changes in the Geoffrey Ma Court' (2019) 49 *Hong Kong Law Journal* 209.

civil disobedience. Finally, we analyse the disparity in the judicial responses in the two jurisdictions and explore the profound implications of the contrast for the rule of law and democracy in each jurisdiction. Despite the fact that Hong Kong is arguably a semi-authoritarian state and Taiwan is a democracy, asking the courts to rule on civil disobedience will hardly yield satisfactory results. The courts' decisions will not have settled the validity of the legal or political doctrines embedded in the concept of civil disobedience. Rather, these complex disputes only reveal the limitations of the courts in handling political argumentation and their precariousness in guarding their role not to be a tool of publicity for the said cause. Throughout these events, law has had to constantly re-invent itself to live up to the ultimate requirement of fidelity to law, be it obedience to top-down black letter law, or adherence to the civility aspect of allowing the right to dissent. This is especially the case given that both societies are striving to advance the rule of law and democracy in the shadow of a dictatorial hegemon, China.

CIVIL DISOBEDIENCE AND THE JUDICIAL ROLE IN LAW AND SOCIAL CHANGE

Court cases tend to focus on individual defendants, but it cannot be overemphasised that the cases studied in this chapter arose out of large-scale protests. If, through public disobedience, protesters intend to appeal to the sense of justice of the majority, the scale of protests may be an important indicator of the extent to which their cause resonates with the majority's sense of justice. At the very least, large-scale protests signify a serious disintegration that the political system has failed to resolve. As Hannah Arendt remarked on the wave of disobedience present the West in the 1960s: 'If history teaches anything about the causes of revolution … it is that a disintegration of political systems precedes revolutions, that the telling symptom of disintegration is a progressive erosion of governmental authority, and that this erosion is caused by the government's inability to function properly, from which spring the citizen's doubts about its legitimacy.'[7]

Not all serious political dissatisfaction justifies civil disobedience. With regard to the appropriate object of civil disobedience, John Rawls, whose theory of civil disobedience is discussed in both Hong Kong and Taiwan's court decisions, clearly stated, 'there is a presumption in favour of restricting civil disobedience to serious infringements of the first principle of justice, the principle of equal liberty, and to blatant violations of the second part of the second principle, the principle of fair equality of opportunity'.[8]

[7] H Arendt, 'Civil Disobedience', in H Arendt, *Crisis of the Republic* (1972), 69.
[8] J Rawls, *A Theory of Justice* (1999), 326.

These presumptions are typically breached by vicious discrimination and serious violations of basic human rights. But it is doubtful whether the Umbrella Movement and the Sunflower Movement accord with this presumption in the goals they pursue. Yet both could be understood to fall under what Daniel Markovits calls 'democratic disobedience'.[9] Markovits argues that democratic disobedience is justifiable when it sets out to remedy systematic democratic deficits. It echoes Rawls's assumption that 'a state of near justice requires a democratic regime'.[10] As a matter of extra-legal legitimacy, it is not difficult to justify the Umbrella Movement, since its precise goal was to put pressure on a semi-authoritarian regime to honour its written promise of universal suffrage to the Hong Kong people for the election of the Chief Executive.[11] Taiwan's case is more complicated. By the time the Sunflower Movement broke out in 2014, Taiwan was widely acknowledged as a consolidated liberal democracy. The controversy concerned whether the ruling Kuomintang (KMT/The Nationalist Party) administration could sign the 'Cross-Strait Service and Trade Agreement' (CSSTA) with China that would open Taiwan to the Chinese service industry. The agreement would have allowed Chinese inflows not just of goods and investment, but also personnel. Ultimately, signing up to the agreement involved the development of new economic policies, without which, as argued by the KMT administration, Taiwan's economy would continue to stagnate and would become politically vulnerable to an economically powerful China. However, a significant segment of the public perceived the agreement to be a serious threat to the future of Taiwan's democracy. Ideally, these highly political controversies should have been resolved by the political branches. Unfortunately, Taiwan and Hong Kong's political systems failed. The Hong Kong political system's failure is obvious, precisely because it became unable to effectively respond to the people's demands for political reform with the straitjacket imposed on it by Beijing. In contrast, the flaw of Taiwan's system is convoluted. When the Sunflower Movement erupted, President Ma argued that he and his ruling party had already carried out extensive public hearings to accommodate public opinion.[12] What lies beneath Taiwan's situation is a fundamental divide regarding its national identity. This conflict has placed a serious strain on the political system. The CSSTA touched on the most sensitive nerve of the divide and the legal mechanism regulating normal democratic politics was strained to breaking point. The failure of both political systems raised serious challenges to the legal system as protesters considered that lawful means of persuasion had come to an end and decided to take extra-legal action.

[9] D Markovits, 'Democratic Disobedience' (2005) 114 *Yale Law Journal* 1897.
[10] Rawls, n 8 above, 319.
[11] Article 45 of the Basic Law of Hong Kong's Special Administrative Region.
[12] News release from the Presidential Office of Republic of China, on President Ma Ying-jeou's press conference on 29 March, 2014. Available at: www.president.gov.tw/NEWS/18494. (accessed 31 October 2020).

Before the cases entered the courtroom there was still a narrow window in which political considerations could play an explicit role: prosecutorial discretion. This issue has arisen before. Ronald Dworkin argued forcefully for not prosecuting those who disobeyed draft laws in protesting the Vietnam War.[13] His argument mainly rests on his view that the American legal system is open to political morality mediated through the US Constitution. If the protesters consider the constitutionality of the law doubtful, then, given that belief, they should not be prosecuted, let alone punished. In a later essay, he argued that utilitarianism should be a necessary condition for just punishment. He said, 'Nobody should ever be punished unless punishing him will do some good on the whole in the long run all things considered'.[14] This is partly why the Taiwanese Government dropped the charges against those defendants who broke into the Executive Yuan office building during the protest. The Premier stated that these cases involve political issues that are best resolved outside of a court.[15] However, it should be noted that the judgment on 'all things considered' can be political as well as partisan. In a polarised democracy such as Taiwan, there may not be one objective, neutral, perspective from which to have an 'all things considered' judgment. The political may not be clearly separable from the partisan. It is no wonder, then, that the charges were withdrawn only two years later by the new Democratic Progressive Party (DPP) Administration, after it defeated the KMT in both the presidential and legislative elections in the wake of the Sunflower Movement.

When civil disobedience cases reach the courts, the entanglement of the legal system with political controversy becomes inevitable. It tests the court's position on civil disobedience, the rule of law and its proper role within the political regime. First, let us focus on the core concept of civil disobedience. Rawls defines civil disobedience as 'a public, nonviolent, conscientious yet political act contrary to law usually done with the aim of bringing about a change in the law or policies of the government'.[16] Further, he sets justificatory conditions on civil disobedience. In addition to the object of disobedience, Rawls argues that civil disobedience should only occur when legal means of redress have proved to be of no avail.[17] Protesters should coordinate to avoid a breakdown in the respect for law and the constitution.[18] Rawls continues to

[13] R Dworkin, 'On Not Prosecuting Civil Disobedience' *The New York Review of Books* (6 June 1968).

[14] R Dworkin, 'Civil Disobedience and Nuclear Protest' in R Dworkin, *A Matter of Principle* (1985), 114.

[15] Lo TB (羅添斌), 'The Executive Yuan Declares Withdrawal of Charges Against the Sunflower Movement Protesters' [行政院宣布撤告太陽花學運人士], *The Liberty Times* [自由時報] (23 May 2016). Available at: https://news.ltn.com.tw/news/politics/breakingnews/1705434 (accessed 31 October 2020)

[16] Rawls, n 8 above, 320.

[17] Ibid, 327.

[18] Ibid, 328.

discuss the role of civil disobedience in a nearly just and democratic society. It is during this discussion that he offers some extraordinary insights into the conditions that make civil disobedience legitimate and practicable. He indicates that the basic point of disobedience is to appeal to the majority's sense of justice and ask them to reconsider the issue.[19] The assumption is that a sense of justice exists within the larger society. If this sense of justice is lacking, 'the majority may simply be aroused to more repressive measures if the calculation of advantages points in this direction'.[20] But this common sense of justice need not be based on strong consensus. Overlapping consensus will do. However, there may come 'a point beyond which the requisite agreement in judgment breaks down and society splits into more or less distinct parts that hold diverse opinions on fundamental political questions. In this case of strictly partitioned consensus, the basis for civil disobedience no longer obtains'.[21] Rawls' advice offers insight for us to assess the wisdom and the political repercussions of the two movements.

Another important aspect of civil disobedience is its strategy. Ronald Dworkin distinguishes persuasive strategy from non-persuasive or coercive strategy.[22] The former hopes to force the majority to listen to their arguments. The latter aims to increase the cost for the majority to pursue the protested subject matter, in the hope that the majority will drop the subject matter.[23] While the former has higher legitimacy, the latter can be justified in the following circumstances: if the wrong it seeks to address involves serious violations of equal liberty; if the political process offers no realistic hope; if there is no effective persuasive strategy available; nonviolent non-persuasive strategies hold out a reasonable prospect of success; and these techniques do not threaten to become counterproductive.[24] With some adjustments, all these insights may prove relevant in the assessment of the legitimacy and prudence of civil disobedience in Hong Kong and Taiwan.

Second, closely related to civil disobedience is the core, but contested, idea of the rule of law. Rawls requires those who engage in civil disobedience to do it in public, nonviolent manner and to accept the legal consequences of their actions, to show their 'fidelity to law'.[25] While Rawls' definition of civil disobedience has brought this act of defiance within the parameters of the law, it has also confronted the law with an acute dilemma – its own 'legal illegality'[26] – asking

[19] Ibid, 335.
[20] Ibid, 339.
[21] Ibid, 340.
[22] Dworkin, n 14 above, 109.
[23] Ibid.
[24] Ibid, 110.
[25] Rawls, n 8 above, 322.
[26] MR Hall, 'Guilty but Civilly Disobedient: Reconciling Civil Disobedience and the Rule of Law' (2006) 28 *Cardozo Law Review* 2083.

the law to make provision for its own violation. Yet, what exactly do we mean by law in the debate of civil disobedience? It is obvious that the theoretical debate between the thin and thick conceptions of the rule of law is implicated. Indeed, as Occupy Central leader Benny Tai argues, civil disobedience is justified by the rule of law.[27] Both share the common goal of pursuing justice. Tai maintains that the thin conception of the rule of law which focuses on formal legality, once understood to mean 'limitation from law', actually implicates thicker conceptions which focus on substantive justice through law.[28] The idea of the rule of law grows from thin to thick, toward a fuller and higher level of development.

Thirdly, we need a theory to capture the dynamics among the court, the political power and social change. Here, we find it useful to adopt Nonet and Selznick's three models of law and society, namely the repressive law, the autonomous law and the responsive law. First, under repressive law, law is identified with the state and subordinated to *raison d'état*; the conservation of authority is an overriding preoccupation to serve the interests of those in power; specialised agencies of control, such as the police and the security force, become independent centres of power that are weakly bound by legal constraints.[29] Second, under autonomous law, law is separated from politics and acts as a restraint on political power; the system proclaims the independence of the judiciary and draws a sharp line between legislative and judicial functions; the legal order espouses the 'model of rules' to enforce official accountability. Judges decide disputes solely by reference to formally promulgated legal rules or precedents 'Fidelity to law' is understood as strict obedience to the rules of positive law.[30] This model resembles closely with the fundamentals of the rule of law ideal. Third, under responsive law, the dynamics of legal development increase the authority of purpose in reasoning. Law seeks substantive justice and responds to calls for legal change. Judges interpret and re-formulate rules in light of actual consequences under broader principles of law, justice and public policy.[31]

Even though Nonet and Selznick consider responsive law to be more reflective of modern social dynamics, they admit that the responsive law model is a precarious ideal. Its desirability is historically contingent, for much depends on the delicate balance between the responsive pursuit of justice and over-responsiveness to particular ideologies and interests.[32] While any reader can discern that repressive law is by no means a desirable model, their theory leaves

[27] BYT Tai, 'Civil Disobedience and the Rule of Law' in MHK Ng, JD Wong (eds), *Civil Unrest and Governance in Hong Kong: Law and Order from Historical and Cultural Perspectives* (2017), 143.

[28] Ibid, 147, 153.

[29] Nonet and Selznick, n 4 above, 33.

[30] Ibid, 54.

[31] Ibid, 78.

[32] Ibid, xiii, 116.

a puzzle behind as to when autonomous law or responsive law is a desirable model under a particular historical circumstance. In critically applying Nonet and Selznick's theory to the dilemma that the Hong Kong and Taiwan courts are facing, we argue that they have underestimated the significance of autonomous law and have assumed that responsive law is the highest stage of legal development in a democratic state. They appreciated the merits of autonomous law for 'purchasing procedural autonomy at the price of substantive subordination' but have neglected the value of the autonomous law under different historical circumstances. As Jeremy Waldron's idea of 'circumstances of politics' illustrates, a society may come to a point where there is a 'felt need among the members of a certain group for a common framework or decision or course of action on some matter, even in the face of disagreement about what that framework or decision or course of action ... should be'.[33] The autonomous law model allows the court to play an arbitral role, not to identify with the political authority but to sustain a society riven by serious social–political conflict and to manage ongoing ideological wars. Once we address Nonet and Selznick's underestimation of the autonomous law, we have powerful conceptual tools to analyse the challenges faced by Taiwan's courts. Likewise, our later discussion will show – despite being caught in a stage of semi-authoritarianism – that it is crucial for Hong Kong judges to adopt the responsive law model to build upon its core principles of the rule of law, so as to achieve substantive justice in society.

CIVIL DISOBEDIENCE BEFORE HONG KONG AND TAIWAN COURTS

Hong Kong: From Occupy Central to the Umbrella Movement

Hong Kong – a former British colony – has been China's Special Administrative Region (SAR) since 1 July 1997. Under the Sino-British Joint Declaration of 1984, it should enjoy a 'high degree of autonomy' under the framework of one country, two systems (OCTS).[34] Yet, the precise content of this formulation has never been clearly stated. It is exactly this nebulous degree of autonomy that proves critical to its citizens. Will Hong Kong move from a state of semi-liberalism to semi-authoritarianism, enjoying semi-autonomy? Its mini constitution, the Basic Law, has promised the gradual and orderly development of political reform without precise details.[35] In particular, article 45 stipulates that the ultimate aim of the method for selecting the Chief Executive is 'by universal

[33] Jeremy Waldron, *Law and Disagreement* (1999), 102.

[34] Clause 3(2) of the Joint Declaration of the Government of the United Kingdom of Great Britain and Northern Ireland and the Government of the People's Republic of China on the Question of Hong Kong (1984).

[35] Article 45 and Annex I of the Basic Law states the method for selecting the Chief Executive, while article 68 and Annex II state the method for forming the Legislative Council.

suffrage upon nomination by a broadly representative nominating committee in accordance with democratic procedures'. In 2007, the National People's Congress Standing Committee (NPCSC) made a resolution in favour of orderly progression toward the implementation of the method of universal suffrage for the election of the Chief Executive in 2017.[36] Since then, struggle over the precise mode of political reform has become increasingly tense.[37] When CY Leung was selected as the Chief Executive in 2012, consultations for the 2017 election process turned out to be a bitterly contentious legal and political battle.[38]

In January 2013, Benny Tai Yiu-ting (a law professor) published an article in a local newspaper calling for acts of civil disobedience to be undertaken in Central – the heart of Hong Kong's financial district – to fight for a genuinely democratic method to elect the Chief Executive, ie one-person-one-vote.[39] Tai had a detailed plan for his Occupy Central movement.[40] However, in August 2014, the NPCSC issued a decision relating to the selection method of the Chief Executive starting from 2017.[41] Although it claimed that universal suffrage would be delivered, the Beijing Government allowed only two to three candidates to stand. Every candidate must first have received support from at least half of the members of the Beijing-controlled nominating committee. This caused a furore, with many condemning it as 'fake democracy'.[42]

Shortly after the announcement of the NPCSC's proposal, on 22 September 2014, more than 12,000 students, peacefully gathered outside the Legislative Council complex demanding political reform.[43] However, five days later, when

[36] 'Decision of the Standing Committee of the National People's Congress on Issues Relating to the Methods for Selecting the CE of the Hong Kong Special Administrative Region and for Forming the Legislative Council of the Hong Kong Special Administrative Region in the Year 2012 and on Issues Relating to Universal Suffrage', Instrument 21, Adopted at the Thirty First Session of the Standing Committee of the Tenth National People's Congress on 29 December 2007. Available at: www.basiclaw.gov.hk/en/basiclawtext/images/basiclawtext_doc21.pdf.

[37] S Hargreaves, 'From the Fragrant Harbour to Occupy Central: Hong Kong's Democratic Development & "Rule of Law" Discourse'. Available at: https://papers.ssrn.com/abstract=2714776.

[38] Ibid.

[39] YT Tai, 'Civil Disobedience as a Weapon of Mass Destruction' *Hong Kong Economic Journal* (16 January 2013), Available at: www1.hkej.com//dailynews/commentary/article/654855/%E5%85%AC%E6%B0%91%E6%8A%97%E5%91%BD%E7%9A%84%E6%9C%80%E5%A4%A7%E6%AE%BA%E5%82%B7%E5%8A%9B%E6%AD%A6%E5%99%A8.

[40] Benny YT Tai, 'Round Three of Hong Kong's Constitutional Game: From Semi-Democracy to Semi-Authoritarianism' (2019) 49 *Hong Kong Law Journal* 335, 344.

[41] 'Decision of the Standing Committee of the National People's Congress on Issues Relating to the Selection of the Chief Executive of the Hong Kong Special Administrative Region by Universal Suffrage and on the Method for Forming the Legislative Council of the Hong Kong Special Administrative Region in the Year 2016' (Adopted at the Tenth Session of the Standing Committee of the Twelfth National People's Congress on 31 August 2014), available at: www.2017.gov.hk/filemanager/template/en/doc/20140831b.pdf.

[42] ASM Ku, 'Performing Civil Disobedience in Hong Kong' in ASM Ku and others (eds), *The Civil Sphere in East Asia* (2019), 97.

[43] E Barber and C Campbell, 'Hong Kong Students Clash With Police' *Time* (27 September 2014). Available at: https://time.com/3434099/protest-arrested-hong-kong-democracy-students-occupy-central/.

the student leaders suddenly stormed the Civic Square (part of the government headquarters), the gathering quickly escalated into clashes between protesters and police and set in motion a series of unprecedented occupy movements in Hong Kong, known as the 'Umbrella Movement'.[44] It was only on 28 September 2014 that Tai and other organisers of the Occupy Central Movement declared the official launch of their campaign.[45] Throughout the Movement, Central was never occupied. Rather, different occupied zones popped up spontaneously in Admiralty, Mong Kok and Causeway Bay.[46] Besides, the event did not unfold as Tai had planned. Rather than ending after a few days, it lasted for 79.[47] Eventually, the student leaders and the organisers of the Occupy Central Movement were removed, prosecuted and convicted.

The Hong Kong Courts

The prosecution of social movement leaders has opened up a significant legal battle in Hong Kong's difficult fight for democracy. While the moral and political dimensions of civil disobedience readily appeal to many, its legal nature remains contentious. Social movements have forced Hong Kong courts to grasp and grapple with civil disobedience as a legal doctrine in theory and in practice, especially in *Secretary for Justice v Wong Chi Fung and others*[48] and *HKSAR v Tai Yiu Ting and others*.[49] What is distinctive about these two cases is that the arguments put forward by the defendants and the reasoning laid down by the judges are rife with contradictions. On the one hand, the student leaders pleaded not guilty but were willing to accept legal consequences.[50] The Occupy Central movement leaders turned themselves into police but refused to

[44] The name of the movement originated from protesters opening umbrellas to block tear gas and pepper spray fired by police. J Henley, 'How the Umbrella Became a Symbol of the Hong Kong Democracy Protests' *The Guardian* (29 September 2014). Available at: www.theguardian.com/world/2014/sep/29/umbrella-symbol-hong-kong-democracy-protests.

[45] T Branigan and J Kaiman, 'Tens of Thousands Join Pro-Democracy Protest in Hong Kong' *The Guardian* (28 September 2014). Available at: www.theguardian.com/world/2014/sep/28/hong-kong-occupy-central-teargas-police-electoral-limits.

[46] For a short period, Canton Road in Tsim Sha Tsui was also occupied. 'How Hong Kong Protests Evolved' *BBC News* (11 December 2014). Available at: www.bbc.com/news/world-asia-china-30390820.

[47] The Umbrella Movement was brought to an end by court injunctions applied for by different private parties, including the taxi drivers' association, a minibus operators' group and owners of commercial buildings. CH Ho, 'To Punish or Not to Punish: The Question of Civil Disobedience and the Umbrella Movement' in BC Jones (ed), *Law and Politics of the Taiwan Sunflower and Hong Kong Umbrella Movements* (2017), 126. For legal implications of the Umbrella Movement and Occupy Central, see AHY Chen, 'Social Movements and the Law: The Case of Hong Kong' in M Ng and J Wong (eds), *Civil Unrest and Governance in Hong Kong* (2017), 132–133.

[48] *Secretary for Justice v Wong Chi Fung and others*, n 2 above.

[49] *HKSAR v Tai Yiu Ting and others*, n 3 above.

[50] *Secretary for Justice v Wong Chi Fung and others*, n 2 above, paras 26, 34.

accept the more serious charge of public nuisance.[51] On the other hand, judges from the CFA recognised civil disobedience as an honourable act but confined it as criminal conduct. They paid tribute to the defining works of Rawls and Dworkin on civil disobedience but then adopted selective references from their writing, resulting in a distorted interpretation of their legal theories. Adhering to the CFA's ruling, the District Court judge condemned the defendants in the Occupy Central Movement for failing to comply with civil disobedience conventions but then refused to apply a similar standard on prosecutors and judges. What has to be carefully examined is civil disobedience as a legal doctrine and as interpreted by the court.

Secretary for Justice v Wong Chi Fung and others

The three young student leaders who stormed into Civic Square, the forecourt of the government headquarters and the Legislative Council Building, which triggered the Umbrella Movement, were subsequently convicted by the magistrates' court for taking part in an unlawful assembly[52] and for inciting others to take part in an unlawful assembly.[53] They were each sentenced to community service orders of various lengths.[54] The Secretary for Justice considered the sentences inadequate and far too lenient and applied for a review.[55] The Court of Appeal then substituted the original sentences with custodial sentences, ranging from six to eight months. Most importantly, the judgment laid down guidelines to future courts regarding sentences for unlawful assembly, with much stricter views on the involvement of disorder and any degree of violence, emphasising the deterrent aspect of sentencing.[56] In essence, the judgment allowed future courts to impose immediate imprisonment for the offence of unlawful assembly involving any degree of violence.[57] This stern approach gave rise to intense debate and the student leaders ultimately decided to appeal to the Court of Final Appeal (CFA).

The CFA ruled that while it was right for the Court of Appeal to provide sentencing guidance for unlawful assemblies involving violence and right for it to send a strong message that such acts would not be condoned, it

[51] *HKSAR v Tai Yiu Ting and others*, n 3 above, para 153. The leaders were Tai Yiu Ting Benny, Professor Chan Kin Man and the Reverend Chu Yiu Ming.

[52] This charge was against the first and third appellant: *Secretary for Justice v Wong Chi Fung and others*, n 2 above, para 4.

[53] This charge was against the second appellant, Ibid 1.

[54] Ibid, 33.

[55] Ibid, 36.

[56] Ibid, 40.

[57] The court would consider the seriousness of the case and actual factual circumstances including degree or scale of violence, the number of people involved and the consequences of the act. Ibid, paras 121–124.

was inappropriate for the Court to apply the new sentencing guideline retrospectively.[58] Although the CFA acknowledged civil disobedience as a recognisable concept in Hong Kong, it decided that the weight given to motive must vary depending on the circumstances.[59] In all, the CFA unanimously allowed the appeals, quashed the prison sentences imposed by the Court of Appeal and reinstated those imposed by the lower magistrates' court. However, the CFA stressed that those involved in large-scale unlawful assemblies involving violence would be subject to the new guidelines laid down by the Court of Appeal as from the date of that decision.[60]

Pertinent to our discussion is not only the judicial reasoning on the nature and role of civil disobedience in the criminal justice system, but also the positioning of the court. The two issues are so intertwined that the judges' understanding of their role inevitably influenced how they define and interpret civil disobedience. Insisting on being apolitical, the CFA has delivered a deceptively simplistic understanding of civil disobedience. At the outset, the CFA referred directly to Lord Hoffmann's famous dicta in the English authorities of *R v Jones (Margaret)* that 'civil disobedience on conscientious grounds has a long and honourable history'.[61] In fact, Lord Hoffmann was one of the presiding judges in *Wong Chi Fung*. The CFA further affirmed 'the concept of civil disobedience is one which is recognisable in any jurisdiction respecting individual rights, including Hong Kong'.[62] Additionally, the judges also endorsed the definition of civil disobedience by Rawls.[63] A preliminary gloss over the above may lead one to conclude that the Hong Kong courts are ready to embrace civil disobedience as a legal concept and may even absolve part, if not all, of the liabilities of the appellants. But behind this opaque reference to case authorities and legal theories lies a rigidly reserved judicial attitude of being apolitical, resulting in a highly selective interpretation of materials. This is especially true in regarding the form (direct or indirect) and nature (violent or non-violent) of civil disobedience and the need to administer punishment against those who engage in it.

First, in Rawls' seminal work, *A Theory of Justice*, he has provided not only a definition of civil disobedience but has also explicitly elaborated and recognised two forms of civil disobedience – direct and indirect – to be equally valid.[64] Direct civil disobedience refers to someone who breaches the same law that is being protested, while indirect civil disobedience covers situations where it is neither practical nor feasible to infringe the law or policy held to be unjust. For the latter form, Rawls uses the examples of protesting a vague and harsh statute

[58] Ibid, 124–126.
[59] *Secretary for Justice v Wong Chi Fung and others* (n 2) para 71.
[60] Ibid, 135.
[61] [2007] 1 AC 136 at [89], quoted ibid 70.
[62] Ibid 70.
[63] Ibid 72.
[64] Rawls, n 8 above, 320.

against treason, or an objectionable foreign policy. In both cases, Rawls points out, it will not be feasible to commit direct civil disobedience, as the consequence is either too drastic for one to bear, or it is simply impossible to directly violate the government policy. In *Wong Chi Fung*, the student leaders were convicted of the offences relating to unlawful assembly under section 18 of the Public Order Ordinance,[65] but they were protesting against government proposals for constitutional reform. It is simply not possible to breach a proposed policy on a system of election to demonstrate one's determination to fight for 'genuine democracy'. Although the CFA acknowledged the two forms of civil disobedience and ruled that a sentencing court may consider the motive of the protesters, it effectively recognised only the direct form, highlighting that there was no injustice in the application of the Public Order Ordinance[66] and there was nothing unjust in punishing the appellants. Relying on Lord Hoffmann's dictum in *Sepet v Home Secretary*, the CFA reasoned that:

> 'while the demonstrator or objector cannot be morally condemned … for following the dictates of his conscience, it is not necessarily unjust for the state to punish him in the same way as any other person who breaks the law. It will of course be different if the law itself is unjust. The injustice of the law will carry over into its enforcement. But if the law is not otherwise unjust … then it does not follow that because his objection is conscientious, the state is not entitled to punish him'.[67]

In the direct form of civil disobedience, if protesters are indeed breaking the 'unjust law' that they are objecting to, does this mean that there is a right to civil disobedience? How is the court going to 'carry over' the injustice of the law into its enforcement? In sending a strong message that a just law could not serve as a surrogate for targeted but unreachable justice,[68] the court has effectively denied indirect civil disobedience, without addressing the full force of direct civil disobedience.

Second, the CFA highlighted the peaceful and non-violent nature of the act of civil disobedience.[69] This becomes critical and determinative of the culpability of those participating in civil disobedience. The Umbrella Movement began with the student leaders' forced entry to the Civic Square. They pushed through the gate and jumped off a fence causing minor injuries to ten security guards on duty, including one who suffered a mild facture to his foot.[70] The magistrates' court did not regard this case as involving serious violence. The Court of Appeal disagreed; it considered the Umbrella Movement to be a case of unlawful assembly on a large scale, with risk of violent clashes.[71] Sharing

[65] Cap. 245, LHK.
[66] *Secretary for Justice v Wong Chi Fung and others*, n 2 above, para 73.
[67] Ibid at para 33.
[68] Hall, n 26 above, 2073.
[69] *Secretary for Justice v Wong Chi Fung and others* (n 2) para 72.
[70] Ibid, 22.
[71] Ibid, 40.

similar concerns with the Court of Appeal, the CFA stressed that civil disobedience must be peaceful and non-violent.[72] The difficulty, as pointed out by Johannes Chan, is that there is a full range of degrees of violence in major public demonstration and confrontation, ranging from extremely trivial to riotous in nature.[73] The Umbrella Movement was, by and large, peaceful, with the student leaders consistently reminding participants to be 'peaceful, rational, and non-violent'.[74] It is unrealistic to insist on a puritan standard of non-violence in large-scale social movements and unfair to use it as a ground to deprive one's claim to civil disobedience.

Third, what is being emphasised by the CFA is the acceptance of punishment by protesters and the role of the court in administering punishment. Other than being peaceful and non-violent, it is also an imperative requirement in Rawls' definition for those participating in civil disobedience to accept punishment to show their fidelity to law and to provide moral justification for their cause. It is, however, important to note that the willingness to accept punishment does not lead to a legal justification of the act.[75] Rather, the acceptance of punishment implies that the protesters know that their act was unlawful and there is no defence.[76] Before the law, regardless of how noble the cause is, civil disobedience is a crime and can only be considered as a mitigating factor in sentencing. Not only is there a need for those engaging in civil disobedience to accept punishment, but the law also has to be enforced and punishment must be administered. In confining civil disobedience as a criminal act, its political nature has been downplayed. Yet, as embedded in Rawls' theory, civil disobedience is innately a political act. However, the court refused to tread on this political terrain. The CFA stood firm and refused to 'enter into an evaluation of the worthiness of the cause espouses', as it was 'not the task of the courts to take sides on issues that are political or to prefer one set of social or other values over another'.[77]

What is in place is the overriding concern to punish protesters. This preoccupation to punish, has arguably led to the selective reference of authorities. For instance, the CFA referred to the famous dicta of Lord Hoffmann in *R v Jones (Margaret)*:

> 'But there are conventions which are generally accepted by the law-breakers on one side and the law-enforcers on the other. The protesters behave with a sense of proportion and do not cause excessive damage or inconvenience. And they vouch the sincerity of their beliefs by accepting the penalties imposed by the law.'[78]

[72] Ibid, 2, 74.

[73] JMM Chan, 'A Storm of Unprecedented Ferocity: Shrinking Space for Political Rights, Public Demonstrations and Judicial Independence in Hong Kong' (2018) 16(2) *International Journal of Constitutional Law* 373–388.

[74] *Secretary for Justice v Wong Chi Fung and others*, n 2 above, paras 20, 35.

[75] Ho, n 47 above, 127.

[76] Chan, n 73 above, 384.

[77] Ibid.

[78] [2007] 1 AC 136, para 89, quoted in *Secretary for Justice v Wong Chi Fung and others*, n 2 above, para 72.

What is missing, oddly, is the rest of the dicta on the required conventions on law enforcers and judges. The remaining part reads:

> 'The police and prosecutors, on the other hand, behave with restraint and the magistrates impose sentences which take the conscientious motives of the protesters into account. The conditional discharges ordered by the magistrates in the cases which came before them exemplifies their sensitivity to these conventions'.[79]

Since Lord Hoffmann was also one of the presiding judges in Wong Chi Fung, this omission was unlikely to be an oversight. In applying the dicta, one would have further asked: had the Secretary for Justice complied with conventions when he decided to seek a review for a harsher sentence against the appellants? Had the judges of the Court of Appeal adhered to conventions in sentencing? All these questions were left unanswered. Instead, the need to punish those involved in the disobedience became the centrepiece. Again, in concluding the discussion on civil disobedience, the CFA relied on another quote by Lord Hoffmann in *Sepet v Home Secretary*:

> 'In deciding whether or not to impose punishment, the most important consideration would be whether it would do more harm than good. This means that the objector has no right not to be punished. It is a matter for the state (including the judges) to decide on utilitarian grounds whether to do so or not. As Ronald Dworkin said in A Matter of Principle … "Utilitarianism may be a poor general theory of justice, but it states an excellent necessary condition for a just punishment".'

This final note raises two curious questions. First, application of the utilitarian formula inevitably involves political calculation in weighing the harm and benefit to the entire society when punishing protesters. Second, is not Dworkin a staunch supporter of civil disobedience? Mentioned earlier in Part I of our discussion, in his famous piece 'On not Prosecuting Civil Disobedience', Dworkin defended those draft offenders who were against the Vietnam War and condemned those who hold 'the mindless view that conscientious disobedience is the same as lawlessness'.[80] He further argued that there was a duty on prosecutors not to prosecute and for judges not to sentence when the validity of the law is doubtful in cases of civil disobedience.[81] In his later work, *A Matter of Principle*, Dworkin discussed civil disobedience in the context of nuclear protest in Germany.[82] He illustrated that civil disobedience not only causes minimum harm to society, but has also brought advancement and engaged the collective moral sense of the community.[83] The utilitarian benefits of civil disobedience considered by Dworkin in both pieces include fostering liberating and critical views in society, valuing reflective and committed members in the community,

[79] [2007] 1 AC 136, para 89.
[80] Dworkin, n 13 above.
[81] Ibid.
[82] Dworkin, n 14 above, 105.
[83] Ibid.

maximising the prospect that a democratic society will correct its own mistakes and intensely re-examining controversial societal decisions.[84] For serious readers, the CFA has added an unfair spin to Dworkin's work.

HKSAR v Tai Yiu Ting and others

Likewise, we see a similar judicial attitude in selective reliance on literature in *HKSAR v Tai Yiu Ting and others*. The case is largely concerned with the three Occupy Central leaders being charged with conspiracy to commit public nuisance, incitement to commit public nuisance and incitement to incite public nuisance.[85] Their defence was that they did not have the required intention to cause public nuisance,[86] they were exercising their constitutional rights of free speech, right of assembly and right of demonstration,[87] and that Occupy Central was a movement of civil disobedience.[88] They were convicted of the charges and were sentenced to 16 months' imprisonment by the District Court. At the time of writing, the case is pending on appeal.[89] While the District Court dealt largely with the factual argument as to whether there was public nuisance and whether the leaders' response was proportionate, we focus here on the court's civil disobedience analysis.

Judge Johnny Chan stressed that it was not for the court to find whether the situations were unjust,[90] nor to adjudicate the merits of the political cause behind civil disobedience.[91] Following the precedent set by the CFA, the District Court replicated the stance that civil disobedience does not constitute a defence to a criminal charge.[92] The issue under contention is whether the parties in a civil disobedience movement have followed the conventions set by Lord Hoffmann in *R v Jones (Margaret)* mentioned earlier in our discussion on *Wong Chi Fung*, 'there are conventions which are generally accepted by the law-breakers on one side and the law enforcers on the other'. So, had the protesters and law enforcers complied with the conventions?

The defendants argued that they had borne in mind the concept of proportionality throughout the civil disobedience movement, that their purpose was to cause a civic awakening and not to paralyse the city and that they had

[84] See also discussion in Hall, n 6 above, 2083.

[85] The three leaders in Occupy Central were Benny Tai, Professor Chan Kin-man and Reverend Chu Yiu-ming. Together with the trio, there were six other defendants. *HKSAR v Tai Yiu Ting and others*, n 3 above.

[86] Ibid, 32.

[87] Ibid, 31.

[88] Ibid, 36.

[89] *HKSAR v Tai Yiu Ting* [2019] HKCA 938.

[90] *HKSAR v Tai Yiu Ting and others*, n 3 above, para 157.

[91] Ibid, 261.

[92] Ibid, 261, 273.

urged all participants to abide by the principle of non-violence and to accept punishment.[93] Nevertheless, Judge Chan considered that the yardstick used by the leaders was totally wrong.[94] Rather than considering whether Central would be paralysed, the test, as interpreted by Judge Chan, should be whether the protesters had acted with restraint and behaved in a proportional manner in not causing excessive damage or inconvenience.[95] In imposing a standard of rigid proportionality, Judge Chan's ruling runs contradictory to the nature of a successful civil disobedience movement. The fact that an act of civil disobedience is, by its very nature, meant to engage the public is simply ignored. If civil disobedience is an honourable act, the more the public is involved, the better. Besides, the moral strength of civil disobedience is also directly dependent on its numerical strength, in terms of how many people it can reach.[96]

If the leaders had failed to comply with the conventions, what about the prosecutors? The leaders of the Occupy Central Movement were charged not with the substantive offence of public nuisance, but with its inchoate offence of conspiracy and incitement to incite. This was the first time that the offences of incitement to commit public nuisance and incitement to incite public nuisance had been used against defendants in Hong Kong regarding the exercise of a constitutional right to peaceful assembly.[97] The issue under contention was whether the prosecution should bring charges of other appropriate statutory offences that could be used against the defendants. In fact, in his closing submission before the court, Tai explained why he and others had decided to file a defence, rather than accept punishment; they believed the charges against them were excessive and unreasonable.[98] What was expected by Tai was that he and other participants would be charged with the lesser offence of unauthorised assembly,[99] governed under the Public Order Ordinance. This offence caried a maximum prison term of three years, usually punishable by a fine.[100] In contrast, breaching the inchoate offences relating to public nuisance carried a maximum prison term of seven years.[101]

Departing from his earlier position that there are conventions for all parties to follow, Judge Chan did not apply the same standard to the prosecutors. Instead, he ruled that the 'preferring of charges is the sole prerogative of the

[93] Ibid, 259, 262.

[94] Ibid, 269.

[95] Ibid.

[96] Arendt, n 5 above, 77.

[97] *HKSAR v Tai Yiu Ting and others*, n 3 above, para 294.

[98] Tai YT, Closing Submission DCCC480/2017, para 77, published in Holmes Chan, '"I Will Never Give up": Law Professor Benny Tai Takes the Stand in Trial of 2014 pro-Democracy Activists' *Hong Kong Free Press HKFP* (12 December 2018), Available at: https://hongkongfp.com/2018/12/12/i-will-never-give-law-professor-benny-tai-takes-stand-trial-2014-pro-democracy-activists/.

[99] Ibid, para 47.

[100] Public Order Ordinance, s 18, Cap 245 LHK.

[101] Public nuisance is a common law offence, the indictable offence is governed by the Criminal Procedure Ordinance, s 101I, Cap 221 LHK.

Prosecution'.[102] To him, whether the prosecutor can 'beat a convicted defendant with a bigger or extra stick' in the event of a conviction depends on the findings of the court on the convicted defendant's culpability.[103] In other words, Judge Chan brushed aside the conventions that required law enforcers to act with restraint, never mind examining whether these conventions were breached and what consequences should follow. Taking this judicial attitude further, little would one expect that a judge would ever scrutinise the conventions imposed on fellow judges, as originally required by the said conventions.

In tracing judicial reasoning and attitudes in the above two cases, we find that Hong Kong courts were ill-equipped to handle civil disobedience cases. They adhered to the strict interpretation of the criminal law and its demands. They tightly applied conventions on the protesters, but not on law enforcers nor their fellow judges. They filtered authorities and legal theories, in a piecemeal manner, to justify punishment against those who participated in civil disobedience. Despite the high-sounding affirmation that civil disobedience is an honourable act, the concept has never been given due recognition. Their insistence that they are an independent and apolitical institution suggests that the courts are anxious to avoid any crossfire between the authorities and the public. It is certainly difficult to explore the concept of civil disobedience beyond the ambit of the criminal law. The court may indeed be a powerful neutral authority for resolving private disputes, but this does not hold true when one of the disputants is the state.[104] After all, the court also belongs to the state.

TAIWAN COURTS IN RESPONSE TO THE SUNFLOWER MOVEMENT

The controversy that triggered the Sunflower Movement concerned the 'Cross-Strait Service and Trade Agreement' (CSSTA). This agreement was signed between Taiwan and China on 21 June 2013. It was based on a previous 'Cross-Straits Economic Cooperation Framework Agreement' (ECFA) (2010). The ECFA was the foundational agreement upon which the KMT government sought to construct a quasi-FTA with China. The KMT administration believed that a quasi-FTA with China was not only beneficial for Taiwan's economy, but was also a necessary step before Taiwan could seek to sign an FTA with other major trade partners.[105] As China is Taiwan's biggest export market, if the cross-strait trade barrier is further reduced, it makes Taiwan a more attractive trade partner

[102] *HKSAR v Tai Yiu Ting and others*, n 3 above, para 281.
[103] Ibid, 284.
[104] Hall, n 26 above, 2101.
[105] Press release of the Office of the President, President Ma Ying-jeou Press Conference (29 March 2014), Available at: www.president.gov.tw/NEWS/18494.

for other countries. Also, China may ease its opposition to Taiwan's FTA with other countries, if it first signs one with China.[106]

The status of executive agreement between Taiwan and China is peculiar in Taiwan's legal system and this is a source of controversy. A pivotal part of Taiwan's democratic transition, which began in 1987, was to dismantle the martial law regime that was legitimated by the prolonged state of civil war between the Chinese Communist Party (CCP) and KMT. In 1991, the Additional Articles to the ROC (Republic of China/Taiwan) Constitution were enacted by the National Assembly. The ROC Constitution regarded its territory as covering the whole of China, only temporarily divided and ruled by two governments. As a result, the Constitution required that cross-strait relations be treated differently from normal foreign relations. Article 11 of the Additional Articles mandated: 'Rights and obligations between the people of the Chinese mainland area and those of the free area, and the disposition of other related affairs may be specified by law.' This offered a constitutional basis for the 'Act Governing Relations between the People of the Taiwan Area and the Mainland Area' ('Cross-Strait Relations Act'), which was enacted the following year. Article 4-2 and 5 of this Act maintained that for any agreement reached between Taiwan and China, only that involving revision of law or enactment of a new law should be scrutinised by the Legislative Yuan. Since the CSSTA involved no legal revision or enactment, legally it needed only to be 'deposited' with the Legislative Yuan. Obviously, it is unthinkable that an agreement of such importance would circumvent legislative oversight. Therefore, after the CSSTA was signed in June 2013, the ruling KMT and the opposition negotiated a resolution in a legislative caucus meeting to scrutinise it item by item. However, the legal foundation of this resolution was dubious and eventually became the immediate cause of the movement. The caucus had to find the proper procedural basis to implement this resolution in the Legislative Yuan Function Act, which was made more difficult by the dubious legal status of CSSTA. As a result, the caucus meeting had to analogise it with other government actions. If the Legislative Yuan analogised it with a foreign treaty, the Legislative Yuan only had the power to accept or veto it *in toto*. The analogy on which they eventually settled was an executive order. This gave the Legislative Yuan the power to scrutinise the order. However, once the floor meeting commissioned the order to the committee, it had a maximum of six months to complete the process. If the committee did not meet the deadline, the executive order was regarded as taking effect.[107]

From August 2013 to early March 2014, the Legislative Yuan held 16 public hearings and the government was reported to have held dozens of 'explanatory

[106] Huang Hsinhua (黃心華), *Eight Main Reasons for ECFA from the Perspective of Sustainability of Taiwan's Industrial Department* [由產業存續的觀點，談為何要簽ECFA的八大理由], National Policy Foundation, 22 April 2010. Available at: www.npf.org.tw/3/7350.

[107] Article 61 of The Legislative Yuan Function Act.

workshops' for concerned trade unions or business associations. However, given the wide potential and deep impact on multiple service industries, these were severely criticised by concerned citizens as being too superficial and opposition was mounting. As the last legislative hearing was held in early March 2014, the six-month examination period neared its end and the legislative committee was thrown into serious conflict between the KMT and the opposition Democratic Progressive Party (DPP). As the ruling KMT perceived no intention of DPP legislators to conduct substantive discussion and anticipated endless filibustering, on 18 March 2014, at a chaotic committee meeting, the KMT committee chairman declared that the examination was complete within 30 seconds. That night, student protesters broke into the Legislative Yuan, to be followed and surrounded by an increasingly bigger crowd. The occupation of the legislative building lasted for 23 days and only ended when the President of the Legislative Yuan promised to enact a Cross-strait Agreement Oversight Act and re-examine the CSSTA.

The Taiwan Courts

Two waves of protests were prosecuted and tried in Taiwan courts; each generated a different judicial response. The primary protest was the occupation of the Legislative Yuan Building that began on the evening of 18 March 2014 and which lasted for 23 days. The other related protest was carried out by a breakaway group of protesters, who invaded the Executive Yuan complex on 23 March and were expelled overnight. For those involved in the primary protest, the courts made some radically accommodating interpretation of criminal defences and used civil disobedience to legitimate the creative interpretive approach. Protest leaders were found not guilty. The courts were less tolerant of those involved in the second protest and convicted the defendants. Nonetheless, all convictions resulted in short prison terms convertible to fines. Here, we can see how Taiwan's courts experimented with different approaches to accommodating and managing political conflicts under a highly strained rule of law.

Occupation of the Legislative Yuan: *The Prosecutor v KC Huang and others*

The first major court decision, *The Prosecutor v KC Huang and others*, was delivered by a three-judge panel in the Taipei District Court in March 2017.[108]

[108] *The Prosecutor v KC Huang*, Taiwan Taipei District Court Criminal Decision, 104 Zusuzi 1 (2017)(臺灣臺北地方法院刑事判決104年度矚訴字第1號). The pagination of Taiwan court decisions refers to the pages in the court decisions in pdf form retrievable from the open database on the Judicial Yuan website. Available at: https://law.judicial.gov.tw/FJUD/default.aspx.

The leaders of the Sunflower Movement were prosecuted for several offences. Since the defendants played different roles in the movement, not all of them were charged on the same counts. The first was the crime of inciting others to commit an offence (Article 153 of the Criminal Code). The offence incited was trespassing without just cause (Article 306 of the Criminal Code), because the defendants repeatedly called upon the crowd to break into the legislative building. The defendants were not charged with trespassing in the first place, because, in the Criminal Code, trespassing is an *Antragsdelikt*, a crime which cannot be tried without a private complaint. Since the Speaker of the Legislative Yuan, Wang Jingping, refused to press charges against the protesters, the prosecutor instead grounded the charges on incitement, an offence which can be tried without a private complaint. The second major criminal charge was obstruction of government officials in discharge of their duties (Article 135 of the Criminal Code), as some of the defendants jostled their way into the legislative building and, in the process, physically engaged with the police officers who were guarding the building.

On the count of incitement of trespassing, the three-judge panel examined three major elements, which included the act of incitement, the *mens rea* of incitement and, for the offence incited, whether the protesters had trespassed into the legislative building 'without just cause'. The court determined none of the criminal element was proved beyond reasonable doubt. First, the court adopted an unusually narrow definition of 'incitement'. It is taken to mean a communicative act to encourage others to commit a crime before the act is performed so the minds of others are effectively changed to commit the offence due to this encouragement.[109] The prosecutor presented facts regarding the leaders addressing the crowd who were already in the Legislative Yuan building. The address conveyed messages such as the following: 'the purpose of the action is to take the country back into the people's hands'; 'we intend to occupy the building to protest the KMT government's passage of the CSSTA'; 'those who support the cause are welcome to stay and those who want to leave can leave'. The court found that at the time of the address those people were already in the Legislative Yuan building, therefore it was not necessarily the case that those people had trespassed because of the defendants' incitement. The court found that many of the participating protesters had learned about the incident from their friends, through social media, or on the television news. They followed the defendants of their own free will. The defendants merely addressed them as cohorts or coordinators, not 'inciters'. Technically, therefore, the defendants' communicative act did not amount to 'incitement'.[110]

[109] Ibid, 24–29. Taiwan's court decisions are retrievable from the publicly available database on the Judicial Yuan website. The pagination here refers to that shown in the pdf file retrieved from the Judicial Yuan database.

[110] Ibid.

The same interpretive strategy applies to the element of *mens rea* for incitement. The court found that some of the defendants used megaphones outside the building to call on the crowd to join them. But the court interpreted the purpose of such calls as 'looking for cohorts and partners to join them', not as 'incitement', technically meaning, in this court's construal, that they changed people's minds. Perhaps the court realised that such an interpretation was quite tenuous, so it went on to add a paragraph elaborating on constitutional protections for freedom of speech. The court argued that political speech lies at the centre of free speech constitutional protections. Since the offence of incitement punishes a form of speech, the fundamental right should restrict the scope of punishable speech, especially when that act involves political speech. The offence incited, namely trespassing, can be regarded as one form of symbolic speech, which should be accorded a certain level of protection. The court did not reason further about the doctrinal content and limits of symbolic speech, concluding instead, that, in view of the defendants' understandable purpose of rectifying the serious procedural flaw of the KMT's passage of CSSTA, all the considerations added together rendered the *mens rea* of incitement absent.[111]

Thirdly, the court had to tackle whether the incited act constitutes trespassing without 'just cause'. This element is treated in judicial precedents not just as lacking the explicit or implicit consent of the landowner, but also as indicating a lack of 'justification'. In the absence of the explicit or implicit consent of the landowner, it refers to legally justifiable causes such as necessity, or justifiable convention, such as entering a yard without a fence simply to ask for help. In the present case, the court took advantage of the otherwise unmalleable 'conventional justifiability' and inserted into it a radical interpretation of the concept of 'substantive unlawfulness' (實質違法性) and 'social adequacy/soziale Adäquanz' (社會相當性). These concepts have been used in the past by Taiwan's courts to recognise extraordinary defences that do not fall into legally recognised justifications such as self-defence and necessity. Typical examples include extremely trivial harm (the theft of one piece of paper) and socially tolerated acts with deep historical roots, such as giving the postman an annual gift according to custom (not constituting bribery). The court added one more legal principle to make room for a radical interpretation of these concepts, that is, the principle of treating criminal punishment as a last resort. This principle is originally for guiding legislative policy in regard to criminalisation, rather than for individual case interpretation. Yet the court used it as a hydraulic distractor to pull apart an otherwise narrow crevice, thus allowing considerations of social utility and impact to flow through.[112]

[111] Ibid, 29–33.
[112] Ibid, 33–34.

What goes through is the court's discussion of civil disobedience. The court first marched through a series of civil disobedience theories, from Henry David Thoreau, John Rawls, the German jurist Ralf Dreier and the German criminal law scholar Claus Roxin. On the basis of these theories, it then devised a set of criteria for civil disobedience: (1) the object of protest must concern grave unlawfulness or injustice involving governmental or public affairs; (2) the offence must be committed out of concerns for the public welfare and common good; (3) the act of protest must have a discernible connection with the object of protest; (4) the act must be public and non-violent; (5) the measure of protest must be suitable for achieving the stated cause; (6) there is no other legal and valid alternative measures remaining; and (7) the harm must be outweighed by the good brought by the protest and must be limited to a minimal degree.[113]

Next, the court discussed whether the actions met these criteria. The court examined the events that led to the passage of CSSTA and agreed with the defendants that there were serious substantive and procedural flaws in this legislative act. One of the major points was the resolution of the legislative caucus meeting, which required item-by-item examination and it noted the eventual hasty passage violated the resolution. It should be noted that the court did not just recognise the reasonableness of protesters' view of the legislative flaws. It said, the legislative act 'objectively contains serious flaws'. Once the objectiveness of the serious flaw in the legislative act was established, it was not difficult for the court to reason in favour of the defendants. It is noteworthy that when the court analysed whether the protest was necessary, it considered the testimony of the KMT legislator Chang Chingchung (張慶忠) who, as the presiding chairman of the committee, declared the passage of CSSTA. The point of the court's usage of Mr Chang's testimony is to show that, according to legislative custom, once the committee declares the passage of an executive order, it automatically takes effect. Therefore, the protesters' actions could be deemed necessary, as the last resort to remedy the protested wrong had been lost. Interestingly, however, in his testimony, Chang Chingchung also explained the legal basis of his declaration and cited precedents of cross-strait agreements that had been passed using the same procedures. This raises the question of why the court did not discuss Mr Chang's testimony regarding the fundamental issue of whether there were serious flaws in the legislative act. In any case, after the court ruled that the protesters' action amounted to civil disobedience, it determined that the incited acts did not constitute trespass, because they possessed 'just cause'.

The prosecutor appealed the case to the Taiwan High Court and the High Court upheld the district court decision.

[113] Ibid, 36.

Invasion of the Executive Yuan: *The Prosecutor v Wei Yang and others*

In the evening of 23 March 2014, five days into the Sunflower Movement, a breakaway group of protesters, who had grown impatient with the KMT government's refusal to withdraw the CSSTA, began a new initiative to invade the main building of Taiwan's Executive Yuan. Later that night, the leaders of the movement in the Legislative Yuan Building denied that they had planned the invasion, claiming that it was a spontaneous action by protesters whose causes they shared and they hoped that no protesters or police got hurt. The breakaway protesters first used hydraulic shears to cut through the barbwire barricade, twisted and dismantled one of the building gates and broke into the building. Some used ladders to climb up to the second floor, smashed the windows of an office and broke into the building. Others damaged property in the office, using those items to blockade the police. In the process, the protesters had come into conflict with the police, who were generally restrained and maintained a stalemate. Around 2:00 am the next morning, the police lieutenant received a direct order from the Premier Jiang Yihuah to expel the protesters from the Executive Yuan. The police reinforcements stormed in and forcefully expelled the protesters. By 5:00 am, the Executive Yuan building was secured. In the process, violent conflict broke out and there were reports of excessive use of force by the police. Many of the protesters suffered injuries. In the wake of the incident, in addition to the prosecution of protesters, many pressed charges of attempted murder against President Ma Ying-jeou, Premier Jiang Yi-huah, the police lieutenant and individual police officers because of the police violence inflicted on them. In May 2016, after the DPP defeated the KMT in both the presidential election and the legislative election, DPP Premier, Lin Chuan, announced the withdrawal of charges against the protesters. This withdrawal rendered groundless the trial on the basis of trespass, as trespassing cannot be tried without a complaint. Instead, the trial at the Taipei District Court continued based on offences that could be tried without complaint, including obstruction of official duty, incitement and malicious mischief against government properties.

In April 2017, the Taipei District Court delivered its decision in *The Prosecutor v Wei Yang and others*.[114] In this decision, the three-judge panel convicted some defendants for malicious mischief against government property and obstruction of official duties. They were given sentences of three, four or five months in prison, all of which could be converted to fines at a rate of one day for 1,000 TW dollars (about 30 US dollars). In the decision, the court considered the defences of necessity, civil disobedience and right of resistance and denied their relevance. Notably, unlike *The Prosecutor v KC Huang and others*, this panel did not take a stance on the defendants' claims of

[114] *The Prosecutor v Wei Yang and others*, Taiwan Taipei District Court Criminal Decision, 104 Yuanzusuzi 1 (2017)[臺灣臺北地方法院刑事判決104年度原矚訴字第1號].

the 'unlawfulness' of CSSTA passage. It raised doubts about these claims and recognised the controversy surrounding these issues. Regarding those defendants charged on incitement, the court adopted a similar approach to that in *The Prosecutor v KC Huang*. The court expressed concerns about the less-than-clear definition of the elements of incitement and the tension it generates within freedom of speech. It opined that elements of incitement should be read narrowly and that it should consider the social context in which the speech was made. The court did not set out clear criteria and went on to find the defendants not guilty on the ground that statements such as the following do not constitute incitement: (1) Wei Yang addressed a crowd of protesters, 'as the on-site leader I take full responsibility for today's actions, … on my left-hand side is the Executive Yuan. There is a long row of police on guard of it. And there are one or two hundred students … Occupation of the Executive Yuan will relieve pressure from our friends in the Legislative Yuan'; (2) Chen Ting-Hau addressed the crowd with a megaphone near the Executive Yuan, 'now you people on site can continue to climb into the Executive Yuan, … Let's occupy the Executive Yuan and exercise our rights as citizens'; (3) Liu Jingwen and Ko Tingyu posted on their Facebook pages, 'please, let's gather at the Executive Yuan. We must take over the Executive Yuan … I strongly suggest we invade the Executive Yuan (personal suggestion)'.[115]

The prosecutor appealed the acquittal of incitement to the Taiwan High Court. In its April 2020 judgment, the three-judge panel at the Taiwan High Court reversed the decision of the District Court and convicted the defendants for incitement to trespass and obstruction of official duty.[116] The defendants were given prison sentences of two to four months, also convertible to fines at the rate of one day for 1,000 TW dollars. Most noteworthy in the decision is the court's rejection of the defences made by the defendants, which poses an interesting contrast with *The Prosecutor v KC Huang and others*.

First, the High Court rejected the defendants' claim that their actions were an exercise in freedom of speech. The Court's opinion implicitly rejected the more sophisticated view of the lower court, which expressed concern about the tension between incitement and free speech. The High Court pointed out that the protected legal interests of the offence of incitement is public order, personal life, body, liberty, property and privacy, to be reviewed by the court in concrete cases and the meaning of the elements was not overly vague. The statute already reflects the Legislature's balancing of free speech and these legal interests. Moreover, the offence of trespassing involves an act that could last for an extended duration of time. The incitement does not have to occur before the incited offence is performed. During the continued performance of trespassing,

[115] Ibid, 73–77.
[116] Taiwan High Court, 106 Zushangsu 3 (2020) [臺灣高等法院刑事判決106年度矚上訴字第3號].

instigation to continue nevertheless constitutes incitement. The court noted that while CSSTA had its supporters as well as opponents, the defendants should have aired their views peacefully and rationally. Their coercive measures to occupy the Executive Yuan went beyond the constitutional protection of free speech.[117]

Next, the Court discussed the right of resistance and civil disobedience. It first indicated that civil disobedience is not a legal concept, but it still recognised its relevance. The Court articulated a version of civil disobedience that is largely congruent with John Rawls': it refers to actions that seek to effect revision of law or change of government policy, through public, non-violent, conscientious, yet illegal measures. The justificatory conditions are: the protested object must represent a grave and clear injustice; actors must have exhausted legal remedies; and the actions must not jeopardise the people's respect for the law and the constitution. The Court then expressed doubts about whether the passage of the CSSTA is 'grave and clear injustice' and whether the legal remedies had already been exhausted.[118] At first glance, it may appear that the Court is taking sides against the defendants on political issues. But it went on to raise an interesting point that may indicate an alternative reading of its judgment. It indicated that the Court may be attempting to play the role of a neutral arbiter in the political dispute by stating that, based on constitutional protection of equality, no one should be privileged by their political viewpoint and, as a result, enjoy immunity from breaking the law. The Court opined that Taiwan is a representative democracy and operates on majority rule. If civil disobedience can be legalised, it may jeopardise Taiwan's representative government. The highly political nature of assessing civil disobedience almost ensures that it is difficult to predict, on the part of law enforcers and those engaging in disobedience, what type of governmental action constitutes grave injustice and what warrants resistance. To effectively legalise civil disobedience would threaten or eliminate the deterrent function of criminal law and could jeopardise the rule of law.[119]

The court ended the discussion with a reflection on the role of the judiciary. It stated that the judiciary is the enforcer of the law, not its creator. If otherwise, this would infringe the legislative power and the basic democratic principle of the separation of powers. Especially, the judiciary has no democratic legitimacy. To ensure democracy and the rule of law, the court should cautiously guard its limited role and abide closely to the law. The court should not cross the boundaries of separation of powers. Nor should it be biased out of personal preference or sympathy, otherwise fairness or justice would be jeopardised. Scholarly discussion can identify trends, but the court should exercise self-restraint and adhere to the role of being the guardian of the rule of law. Especially, it should

[117] Ibid, 41–42.
[118] Ibid, 42–43.
[119] Ibid, 43.

not sacrifice the consistency of law by supporting the political view of a segment of society.[120]

Assessing the Role of the Courts in Civil Disobedience Cases

It is impressive how civil disobedience as a political concept has made its way into the judicial discourse of both jurisdictions. Courts in Hong Kong and Taiwan have referred to the canonical civil disobedience theory of John Rawls and others. Nevertheless, the courts in both jurisdictions have been thrown into a position that is much more difficult and complex than the occasional extra-legal hurly-burly of a 'near just' liberal democracy.

The Hong Kong protesters' cause is clearly reasonable and just. All they ask for is genuine universal suffrage for the Chief Executive to be vertically accountable to the Hong Kong people. John Rawls thinks that only in a near just society does civil disobedience pose a genuine problem for the general obligation to obey the law and that a 'nearly just society' requires a liberal democratic regime. It means that for a people living under a semi-authoritarian regime, civil disobedience poses no real legitimacy problems and more aggressive resistance than civil disobedience could be politically justifiable. Ronald Dworkin distinguishes between persuasive strategy and coercive strategies: persuasive strategies are generally easier to justify than coercive strategies. Yet, as Dworkin explained, coercive strategies are justifiable when there are no effective persuasive strategies available. The Umbrella Movement aims both to persuade and to coerce a semi-authoritarian regime to democratise. Both the cause and strategy are reasonable and justifiable.

However, the challenge for Hong Kong protesters is not so much about fundamental legitimacy but about the prudence of their actions. As Rawls advises, if there is a lack of majority sense of justice to which the protest can appeal, then it risks arousing more repressive measures. Dworkin also mentions that one of the conditions for coercive strategy is that it does not lead to counter-productive results. The formidable challenges for the democratic movement in Hong Kong are two-fold. The first is, of course, that the political regime that is not fully accountable to the Hong Kong people. The second is that it must operate within a society that has been economically highly integrated with China, whose totalitarian and ultranationalist ideology is closely bound up with its economic prowess. As a result, coercive strategies, if not successful, risk polarising the society and may, in turn, undermine the democratic movement. Under these circumstances, Lord Hoffmann's convention of mutuality is very hard to obtain, because an unwritten convention can only be sustained in a society that in general retains a common sense of justice and shared history.

[120] Ibid, 43–44.

In contrast, Taiwan's challenge may not be as formidable, but it is also because of China that an otherwise reasonable dispute on economic policy has turned into an explosive political conflict. The KMT administration's strategy to revive the long-stagnated Taiwan economy was to promote further economic integration with China as well as with other trading partners. However, in doing this the Ma Ying-jeou Administration raised serious suspicion among the pro-Taiwan independence camp, not only about the soundness of the policy but about the suspected hidden agenda behind it. President Ma rose to political prominence in the final years of the 'old' KMT authoritarian regime and his late father was a deeply devoted Chinese nationalist, aspiring to eventual reunification with China. Just like it took a renowned anti-communist republican President Richard Nixon to initiate the normalisation of US–China relations in the Cold War, if there is any merit in the KMT's economic strategy, it may also take a green-camp administration to do it, to alleviate suspicion of motivation.

Moreover, the dubious legal framework of cross-strait relations has been a legacy of the KMT-domineered democratic transition. The failure of successive administrations to repair it reflects the mutual distrust and political polarisation between the blue and green camps, which are at odds over conflicting national identities and historical memory. The flawed legal framework governing the cross-strait agreement was destined to break when the KMT administration sought to wade deeper into the water with China, since any further economic integration with China makes it more difficult to fend off Chinese influence. Taiwan may have an overall democratic regime in place. However, the consolidation and stability of democracy requires a united *demos* that provides the political foundations for constitutional legitimacy and normative resources to face conflicts when the law does not govern disputes. Taiwan does not yet have this and a politically menacing and economically tempting China further depletes the shallow consensus on Taiwan's nationhood and future vision for its people.

It is impossible to do justice to the political issues involved in both Hong Kong and Taiwan. Yet the discussion so far is enough to demonstrate the complexity in the evaluation of the legitimacy and prudence of the two movements. The major question for this chapter is what role the courts should play in face of these movements. As mentioned before, the CFA of Hong Kong referred to Lord Hoffmann's famous dicta in *R v Jones* that 'civil disobedience on conscientious grounds has a long and honourable history'. However, this honourable history does not necessarily shine on a future path that is overshadowed by China, a technologically sophisticated, economically successful authoritarian regime. The convention of mutuality articulated by Lord Hoffmann that is supposed to govern the extra-legal space, namely that 'the protesters behave with a sense of proportion and do not cause excessive damage or inconvenience' and that 'the police and prosecutors behave with restraint and the magistrates impose sentences which take the conscientious motives of the protesters into account', prove to be legal commands only for the protesters, but could hardly restrain those in power. As to Dworkin's key idea on 'utilitarianism' and 'all things considered' approach to civil disobedience, what exactly should be considered and how? More fundamentally, how should the court conceive of its role in these politically charged cases? It is now pertinent to see the courts through the lens of Nonet and Selznick's three models.

Hong Kong courts have inherited a strong legacy of 'autonomous law' which emphasises separating law from the political. The spirit of autonomous law is for the court to reserve an autonomous territory from the political realm. By closely following a narrow concept of the rule of law, the court can, apparently, check political power on blatant wrongdoing, violation of rights, or bad governance, while giving ample room to political decision making. However, when facing the challenges posed by large-scale societal civil disobedience, the Hong Kong courts abdicated from their role of being truly autonomous and applied rules only against the protesters. Rather than paying lip service to the noble ideals of civil disobedience but pre-occupied with the preservation of institutional integrity and law and order, the court should have acted on its autonomy and responded to the social crisis. At a minimum, arguably it is enough for the courts to retain their autonomy by upholding the rule of law, but not imposing harsh punishments. Alternatively, from a societal perspective, another solution could be to have jury trials for cases with civil disobedience as a mitigating factor. In this way, the courts could have maintained their neutral arbitral position, in addition to focusing on legal analysis that could achieve just legal ends, but also channel the public desire for fundamental change within society. The tendency of some Hong Kong judges to hand down harsh sentences suggests that there may be a strong force moving the Hong Kong courts from 'autonomous law' to 'repressive law'.

Taiwan's courts exhibited two different understandings of the judicial function, which led to different approaches to civil disobedience. In *The Prosecutor v KC Huang and others*, the court adopted a radical, even distorted, interpretation of elements of the offences, to accommodate those who engaged in disobedience. Civil disobedience, in the court's opinion, impacted the elements such as *actus reus* and *mens rea* of incitement, as well as the 'just cause' of trespassing. The impact was made through mediation of legal concepts such as 'social adequacy', 'substantive unlawfulness' and constitutional protection of free speech and assembly. This approach shows features of responsive law, which include openness and flexibility of law, the prominent function of purposive legal interpretation and responsiveness to social advocacy and societal change. One crucial feature of responsive law is for the court not only to adjudicate but also to regulate, to effect social change, taking into account law, justice and public policy. The *KC Huang* court did just that in its evaluation of the defendants' claims regarding the perceived injustices of the CSSTA. In contrast, in *The Prosecutor v Wei Yang and others*, the High Court took an approach that is closer to autonomous law than to responsive law. It did not impose harsh sentences on the defendants. In fact, no defendant went to jail. However, the court emphasised its role as a neutral arbiter guarding the boundaries of a functioning liberal democracy. In the face of intense political controversy, the court should refrain from taking sides; no one should enjoy immunity for illegal acts because of his/her political viewpoints. Ultimately, the court gave autonomous law a new meaning that was not clearly grasped by Nonet and Selznick: autonomous law may be deemed conservative at times, when a society is clear on where it is heading. But when a society is torn apart by serious disagreement, autonomous law can help the court manage conflicts as a neutral unbiased arbiter. This is especially important in a democracy where the legislative branch remains generally accountable to the people.

CONCLUSION

In this chapter, we have compared and contrasted the judicial responses to civil disobedience in Hong Kong and Taiwan. The judicial reasoning in both jurisdictions is not a straightforward exposition of law in response to law's demands. Rather, the decisions reflect cautious manoeuvres in the troubled waters of politics and careful positioning of the judiciary when it is caught in the crossfire between law, morality and politics. After all, civil disobedience is a highly charged concept with political overtones. When the courts were confronted with concrete cases of civil disobedience, judges have guarded their autonomy by opportunistically setting new legal standards for what was envisioned to be a fair and just societal result. They strived to develop a legal system that could put society back in order by carving out a legal niche to accommodate civil disobedience, albeit a tiny corner of criminal law. We have thus landed on a curious and uncertain ground – civil disobedience is no longer dismissed outright by the court, but neither is it fully recognised.

What is reflected in the judgments is the judicial understanding of court autonomy and independence within the larger political and social context. When Hong Kong judges were determined to be apolitical in the autonomous law model, we found deeply established conventions being only selectively applied against the protesters. Behind their seemingly neutral stance, there is a repressive instrumentalism in which law is used to maintain institutional integrity. Across the Strait, the Taiwan courts wavered from adopting a responsive law model to a restrained autonomous law model in the application and interpretation of law. Contrary to the assumption that responsive law accords well with democratic states, adopting the autonomous law model may prove to be a more prudent move for Taiwan in the long run.

Furthermore, the autonomous and responsive law models are not necessarily evolutionary stages of legal development. Rather they point to the distinctive features of a legal system that warrant special attention at various points of societal development. The points of reference are inevitably other conditions in society and the well-being of other political institutions. On the vexing issue of civil disobedience, judges could only negotiate the meanings of illegality, justice and civility in the midst of increasing state–society tensions.

3

Democratic Legitimacy vs Rule of Law: A Comparative Study of Oath-taking Controversies in Hong Kong and Taiwan

ZHU HAN*

INTRODUCTION

AT THE INAUGURAL meeting of the 2016 Legislative Council (LegCo) of the Hong Kong Special Administrative Region (HKSAR), two pro-independence advocates, Leung Chung-hang and Yau Wai-ching, took their oaths in a manner of 'insulting Chinese' and abandoning the 'one country' principle, which triggered a judicial review that resulted in their disqualification. Their actions reflect the rising localism and pro-independence ethos in Hong Kong society since the failure of the 2014 Occupy Central (OC) Movement demanding universal suffrage. After the disqualification of the two pro-independence legislators-elect, four other pan-democratic LegCo members were also disqualified by the court for failing to take the oath validly.[1] Furthermore, many candidates were prohibited from running election campaigns due to their separatist or localist stances. The newly promulgated National Security Law for the HKSAR also required public office holders to swear allegiance to the HKSAR and pledge to the Hong Kong Basic Law.[2] The oath-taking dispute and its spill-over effects has sparked tremendous controversy and intense debate within Hong Kong.

* Research Assistant Professor, Faculty of Law, the University of Hong Kong.

[1] See generally J Chan, 'A Storm of Unprecedented Ferocity: The Shrinking Space of the Right to Political Participation, Peaceful Demonstration, and Judicial Independence in Hong Kong' (2018) 16 *International Journal of Constitutional Law* 373, 378–379.

[2] Art 6 of the Law of the People's Republic of China on Safeguarding National Security in the Hong Kong Special Administrative Region (2020).

While oath-taking remains a relatively new issue in Hong Kong, the topic has frequently arisen over the past two decades in Taiwan, where national identity and regime legitimacy have long been at the centre of politics. Since 1984, in order to stage their protest against the legitimacy of the Republic of China (ROC) and authoritarian rule, many central and local legislative members of the opposition have declined to take their oaths in the manner prescribed by the law. The oath-taking controversies in Hong Kong and Taiwan both revolve around the identity crisis associated with China and the political legitimacy of the existing constitutional framework. Oath-taking controversies have also occurred in other jurisdictions such as the United Kingdom (UK), where Sinn Féin members have used an abstentionism policy for more than a century as a gesture rejecting the legitimacy of Westminster.

The oath-taking controversies touch on the issue concerning the political legitimacy of an existing constitutional system, as they present tensions between the popular will (as represented by democratically elected lawmakers) and the law (as represented by legal norms and judicial decisions). Underlying the controversies is the question, closely related to the right to self-determination/secession, of whether and how a constitutional and legal system can accommodate activities and claims opposing the very foundation upon which the existing constitutional framework operates. Responses from the authorities aimed at tackling the issue may range from political negotiation to forceful suppression, which largely reveals the degree of authoritarian or democratic inclinations that characterise a regime.

This chapter first traces the series of events surrounding oath-taking disputes in Hong Kong and Taiwan. It then considers the differences in relevant laws and judicial decisions and analyses the factors contributing to the contrast. It aims to demonstrate that the way in which the oath-taking disputes have been handled in Hong Kong has exacerbated the inherent tension between democratic legitimacy and legality in this city under the shadow of authoritarianism. This chapter also refers to the abstentionism tactic used by Sinn Féin representatives in the United Kingdom, aiming to highlight the uniqueness of the conflict between democratic legitimacy and the law in a semi-democratic context such as Hong Kong's.

2016 LEGCO OATH-TAKING CONTROVERSIES IN HONG KONG[3]

In 2016, two young pro-independence activists, Leung Chung-hang and Yau Wai-ching, were elected to LegCo. On 12 October 2016, while they were taking

[3] The factual review of these two cases is mainly extracted from the author's article: H Zhu and AHY Chen, 'The Oath-Taking Case and the NPCSC Interpretation of 2016: Interface of Common Law and Chinese Law' (2019) 49 *Hong Kong Law Journal* 381. The author is grateful to the *HKLJ* for permission to cite relevant parts of the article. See also the judgments of the Court of First Instance in the *Leung and Yau* case (*Chief Executive of the HKSAR v President of the Legislative Council and Leung Chung Hang Sixtus*), HCAL 185/2016 and HCMP 2819/2016 (15 Nov 2016),

their oaths at the inaugural meeting, Leung and Yau flaunted a 'Hong Kong is not China' banner, used the term 'Hong Kong nation' in their oaths and slurred the 'People's Republic of China' into 'people's re-fucking of Chee-na'. Their oaths were declared invalid by the oath administrator.[4] On 18 October, the LegCo President permitted them to retake their oaths.[5] On the same day, the Chief Executive and Secretary for Justice filed an urgent judicial review application at the Court of the First Instance (CFI) of the High Court, which sought to disqualify Leung and Yau as legislators and quash the decision of the LegCo President to permit them to retake the oaths. At the LegCo meeting on 19 October, pro-establishment legislators staged a walkout to prevent Leung and Yau from retaking their oaths.[6]

On 3 November, the CFI heard the case but reserved judgment. On 7 November, the Standing Committee of the National People's Congress (NPCSC) issued an Interpretation on Article 104 of the Basic Law of the Hong Kong Special Administrative Region (the 2016 NPCSC Interpretation) which elucidated the requirements for a valid oath.[7] On 15 November, the CFI rendered its judgment and held that the two legislators-elect had been disqualified. The appeals of Leung and Yau were dismissed by the Court of Appeal (CA),[8] and their leave to appeal further to the Court of Final Appeal (CFA) was also denied.[9]

Following the decision of the CA on the *Leung and Yau* case, four other pan-democratic LegCo members, Nathan Law Kwung Chung, Leung Kwok Hung, Lau Siu Lai and Yiu Chung Yim, were also disqualified in subsequent legal proceedings initiated by the government on a similar basis. Unlike Leung and Yau, these four others had read out the prescribed LegCo oath completely without altering the substance, but had done so in a mocking manner, reading the oath at a slow pace, adding messages before and after the oath, or carrying out various flamboyant acts, such as holding an opened yellow umbrella (symbolising the OC Movement). Leung's and Law's oaths were deemed valid while Lau and Yiu were required to retake the oath. They subsequently did so and assumed office. When the government commenced judicial proceedings against the four

[2016] 6 HKC 417 and the subsequent case of four other LegCo members – *Nathan Law Kwun Chung and others*, HCAL 223-226/2016, HCMP 3378/2016 (14 July 2017), [2017] 4 HKLRD 115.

[4] See HCAL 185/2016 and HCMP 2819/2016, paras 5–6.

[5] See 'President's Ruling on the Validity of the Legislative Council Oath Taken by Six Members at the Council Meeting of 12 October 2016'. Available at: www.legco.gov.hk/yr16-17/english/pre_rul/pre20161018-ref-e.pdf.

[6] S Lau, 'Explained: Walkouts and Oath-Taking Controversy at Start of LegCo Term', *South China Morning Post (South China Morning Post)* (26 October 2016). Available at: www.scmp.com/news/hong-kong/politics/article/2040147/explained-walkouts-and-oath-taking-controversy-start-legco.

[7] NPCSC, 'Interpretation of Article 104 of the Basic Law of the Hong Kong Special Administrative Region of the People's Republic of China by the Standing Committee of the National People's Congress' (7 November 2016). Available at: www.basiclaw.gov.hk/en/basiclawtext/images/basiclawtext_doc25.pdf.

[8] CACV 224/2016 (30 Nov 2016), [2017] 1 HKLRD 460.

[9] FAMV 7/2017 (1 Sept 2017).

in December 2016, they had held office for nearly two months. In July 2017, the CFI held that they had been disqualified due to their failure to properly take their oaths.[10] Only Leung appealed to the CA, but his appeal was dismissed. His leave to appeal to the CFA was also denied in 2019.[11]

The disqualification rulings have had a substantial political impact, as the 'pro-democracy' bloc in LegCo lost its veto power over motions initiated by individual LegCo members which are subject to the separate counting mechanism (there is separate counting in two groups – legislators elected by universal suffrage and those elected by functional constituencies). As a result, the 'pro-establishment' legislators succeeded in amending the LegCo Rules of Procedure 2017 for the purpose of restraining filibusters, a tactic constantly used by the pan-democratic LegCo members.[12]

In addition to the oath-taking disputes, the 2016 NPCSC Interpretation has had a spill-over effect on Hong Kong elections, as the interpretation also stipulates that 'to uphold the Basic Law' and 'to bear allegiance to the HKSAR' are legal requirements and preconditions for candidates in elections to any public office specified in Art 104 of the Basic Law. Even before the promulgation of the Interpretation, the returning officers in the 2016 LegCo election had disqualified five localist[13] candidates from running for election on grounds of their political stance. One of these candidates, Chan Ho-tin, subsequently brought an election petition but the decision was upheld by the court, which relied on the 2016 NPCSC Interpretation.[14] In 2018, another five localist or pro-democratic candidates were disqualified in two by-elections and a village representative election. In some cases, the returning officers explicitly stated that they had taken the 2016 NPCSC Interpretation into account in their disqualification decisions. Two of the five disqualified candidates have separately brought an election petition.[15] How the court will adjudicate the cases and the full ramifications of the 2016 NPCSC Interpretation, remains to be seen.

[10] HCAL 223/2016 and HCMP 3378/2016, n 3 above.

[11] C Lau, 'Ousted pro-democracy legislator 'Long Hair' Leung Kwok-hung loses bid to take case to Hong Kong's Court of Final Appeal' *South China Morning Post* (13 June 2019). Available at: www.scmp.com/news/hong-kong/law-and-crime/article/3014375/ousted-pro-democracy-legislator-long-hair-leung-kwok.

[12] B Tai, 'Round Three of Hong Kong's Constitutional Game' (2019) 49 *Hong Kong Law Journal* 335, 348.

[13] Localism refers to a political movement that focuses on the preservation of Hong Kong's identity and autonomy. Localists include 'a multitude of groups with different goals, ranging from advocating greater autonomy to independence for Hong Kong'. See YH Kwong, 'The growth of 'Localism' in Hong Kong' 3 (2016) *China Perspectives* 63, 63.

[14] See *Chan Ho Tin v Lo Ying Ki Alan* [2018] 2 HKLRD 7.

[15] S Wong, 'Judge hears Chow vote fight' *The Standard* (18 June 2019). Available at: www.thestandard.com.hk/section-news.php?id=208727; A Lum and C Lau, 'Ousted Hong Kong lawmaker Lau Siu-lai to challenge decision to ban her from standing in Kowloon West by-election' *South China Morning Post* (18 January 2019). Available at: www.scmp.com/news/hong-kong/politics/article/2182693/ousted-hong-kong-lawmaker-lau-siu-lai-challenge-decision-ban.

HISTORICAL REVIEW: OATH-TAKING DISPUTES IN TAIWAN

Oath-taking controversies have also occurred in Taiwan, both before and after the 1987 transition to democracy. Like the localist and pan-democratic LegCo members in Hong Kong, delegates of the *Tangwai* (outside the party) and the opposition party have either declined to take the oath or have taken it in a distorted form to express their political opinion against the legitimacy of the regime.

The first oath-taking incident occurred in the swearing-in ceremony for the 1984 Legislative Yuan. At the beginning of the ceremony, two *Tangwai* elected members, Yu Chen Yueh-ying and Cheng Yu-cheng, questioned the exact meaning of the term 'not pursuing personal profits' in the oath and requested further clarification. After their demand was rejected by the President of the Legislative Yuan, they simply stood up with other oath-takers during the swearing-in proceeding, without raising their hands and read out the oath. Cheng submitted his written oath afterwards, while Yu did not but retook her oath the next day.[16] This was the first time that opposition deputies had refused to take the oath, which set a precedent for using oath-taking to stage protests against the legitimacy of Kuomintang (KMT) rule and the existing constitutional system.

Following this incident, the period from 1986 to 1991 witnessed the most contentious oath-taking conflicts, which happened in conjunction with the democratic transformation. The following section documents a series of high-profile oath-taking conflicts in the National Assembly (a constitutional convention and electoral college to elect the President and Vice President) and Legislative Yuan) which reached their apex in 1990.

In September 1986, 132 *Tangwai* members created Taiwan's first opposition party, the Democratic Progressive Party (DPP) which was closely associated with advocacy for Taiwanese identity. The DPP was broadly tolerated by the ruling KMT and, during the next year, martial law was officially lifted, as were other bans on political parties and speeches. Consequently, opposition parties enjoyed more freedom and legality to openly advocate for Taiwanese identity and protest against the legitimacy of the KMT government. On 23 February 1987, at the 1987 inauguration ceremony of the Legislative Yuan, DPP legislators disrupted the administration of oaths and the oath-taking procedures were completed amid chaos and protests. The 12 DPP legislative members who had refused to be sworn in retook their oaths in March of the same year.[17]

At the 1990 swearing-in ceremony, to protest the legitimacy of the delegates who represented overseas nationals and were appointed by the authorities, the DDP legislators obstructed the ceremony by preventing the oath administrator

[16] '立委要求解釋誓詞' (Legislators require clarification of the oath) *China Times* (24 February 1984), 2; '余陳月瑛完成宣誓' (Yu Chen Yueh-ying takes oath) *China Times* (24 February 1984), 2.

[17] Shih HE, '宣誓與監督法令之研究' (Research on regulations regarding oath-taking and supervision) (1992) 148 *Faxue congkan* (*China Law Journal*) 1, 4–5.

from entering the chamber and covering his head with protest banners. The swearing-in ceremony came to an unceremonious end due to the ensuing chaos.[18] The DDP legislators who had refused to take the oath retook their oaths three days later. After some negotiation, the DPP and KMT legislators agreed that the DPP legislators could take their oaths without singing the national anthem or saluting the national flag, since such procedures were not prescribed by the ROC Oath Act.[19]

In Taiwan contention around oath-taking reached their apex in the eighth session of the first National Assembly, inaugurated on 19 February 1990. At the beginning of the swearing-in ceremony, the DPP representatives protested the 'ten-thousand-year Congress delegates' ('tenured' delegates chosen in 1947 from mainland China) and obstructed the administration of the oath. Most of the representatives, except for 11 DPP members, took their oaths despite the chaos.[20] When retaking their oaths on 24 February, the 11 DPP members stood away from the national flag and the picture of Sun Yat-sen, the founding father of the ROC and swore themselves in when the oath administrator was absent. They did not raise their right hand as required by Art 4 of the Organic Act of the National Assembly and read out a revised written oath in Taiwanese. Their oaths were ruled invalid by the administrator.[21] On 5 May, they retook their oaths in a similarly disputed manner and submitted their revised written oaths, in which the term 'representing people of the ROC' and 'seventy-ninth year of the Republic' were deleted and changed to 'representing Taiwanese people' and '1990'. Their oaths were once again deemed invalid by the oath administrator.[22]

Consequently, the Presidium of the National Assembly, controlled by the KMT, declared that a delegate who had failed to be sworn in was not entitled to attend the meeting. Thousands of police were mobilised to lock the entrance to the conference venue to prevent DPP delegates from entering, leading to a confrontation between the police and DPP delegates and their supporters. The latter demonstrated outside the venue but their efforts failed and they were excluded from the session at which the ROC President was elected.[23]

At the same time, the National Assembly applied to the Judicial Yuan for an interpretation on whether a National Assembly delegate who has sworn an oath contrary to the legal requirements is still eligible to perform his/her duty. The Judicial Yuan quickly issued Interpretation No 199 on 16 March, ruling that '[a] delegate of the National Assembly who has failed to swear an oath or

[18] Ibid.

[19] Ho HC, '省略國歌及向國旗行禮：民進黨立委補宣誓(Omitting singing national anthem and saluting national flag: DPP legislators retake oath) *United Daily News* (14 February 1990), 2.

[20] Shih, n 17 above, 5.

[21] Hsu LP, '民進黨國代未依法定程序進行 "宣誓"' (DPP delegates fail to take oath in accordance with legal procedure) *United Daily News* (25 February 1990), 3.

[22] Hsu LP, '民进党国代补宣誓改词' (DPP delegates retake and revise oaths) *United Daily News* (6 March 1990), 2.

[23] Lin CC, '民进党国代受阻起冲突' (DPP delegates obstructed, clash with police) *China Times* (14 March 1990), 1.

intentionally sworn an oath contrary to the manner or the wording stipulated under the Act is not eligible to perform his/her duty'.[24] It also ruled, however, that 'the issue of whether a delegate who has failed to swear an oath is entitled to attend the meetings of the National Assembly shall be decided by the National Assembly according to its self-governing rules'.[25]

Without the participation of DPP and non-party delegates (who resigned in protest), the National Assembly was dominated by KMT members, who attempted to further consolidate their power. These circumstances triggered the Wild Lily Student Movement, which started on 16 March, calling for popular elections for the President and all National Assembly delegates.[26] Although the conflict caused by the oath-taking dispute was largely eclipsed by the Wild Lily Movement, it ultimately yielded a positive impact and mutual compromise for resolving future oath-taking disputes. While DPP members subsequently continued to use distorted oath-taking manners to express their dissidence, none were ever barred from assuming office. The severe conflict and the fact that it resulted in the disadvantage of DDP delegates also made the DPP adjust its strategy, so that its members no longer revised the written oaths. Compromises on both sides led to milder oath-taking confrontations during the stage which followed.

For instance, during the swearing-in ceremony for the second provisional session of the first National Assembly on 8 April 1991, eight DPP delegates read a revised oath that adopted the term 'Republic of Taiwan' and the year '1991'. The oaths were declared invalid and they retook them on 13 April but with the barest adherence to the legal requirements, which were described as follows: 'One wore a headband emblazoned with a statement of protest, one held the DPP flag as he pledged an oath to the ROC, several drew maps of Taiwan on their pledge statement, and some mumbled inaudibly or read the oath in Taiwanese rather than Mandarin.'[27]

This time, however, drawing on the experience of the 1990 National Assembly, the DPP delegates did not delete any words of the written oath but simply added 'I love Taiwan' or drew a map of Taiwan beside the term 'ROC'. Their oaths were ultimately declared valid by Herbert Ma, then a grand justice, who claimed that his decision was 'made out of his consciousness and consideration of the country's future and the interests of constitutional development' and, for those reasons, 'the procedural defects would not be taken into account'.[28] Henceforth written, rather than oral oaths, have become more important in measuring oath validity.

[24] Judicial Yuan Interpretation No 254 (1990). Available at: http://cons.judicial.gov.tw/jcc/en-us/jep03/show?expno=254.

[25] Ibid.

[26] G Katsiaficas, *Asia's Unknow Uprisings Volume 2: People Power in the Philippines, Burma, Tibet, China, Taiwan, Bangladesh, Nepal, Thailand, and Indonesia* (2013), 198.

[27] AM Wachman, *Taiwan: National Identity and Democratization: National Identity and Democratization* (1994), 188–9.

[28] Shih, n 17 above, 6.

After further consolidation of democratisation in Taiwan, the oath-taking disputes continued but became much less dramatic. In 1992, all the seats of the National Assembly were popularly elected for the first time. For the National Assembly swearing-in ceremony, the DPP delegates chose to take the oath at another venue and read the revised oath in Taiwanese. In subscribing the printed written oaths, they added 'Taiwan' besides the term 'ROC' and used '1992' instead of the 'eighty-first year of the Republic'. Their written oaths were ruled valid on the ground that they did not substantively alter the oath, despite adding extra words.[29]

In 1992 Taiwan also held the first full election of the second Legislative Yuan. In the swearing-in ceremony on 1 February 1993, DPP legislators did not stand up to take the oath but walked out of the venue after the ceremony and swore themselves to the 'Taiwanese people'. But on the written oaths they only added '1992'so their oaths were ruled valid.[30] In 2000, then-President Chen Shui-bian also adopted a similar strategy, as he walked outside to swear a different version of the oath to the Taiwanese people after taking the official oath inside the presidential office.[31]

During the swearing-in ceremony of the third Legislative Yuan in 1996, DPP members did not walk outside to take the oath, but instead turned their back on the national flag and read out revised oaths. According to the Oath Act, written oath documents shall be submitted to the Judicial Yuan to be recorded. DPP members submitted revised written oaths, printed by themselves, with the name of an oath administrator of their choosing instead of the officially appointed one, ie then a Grand Justice, as prescribed by the law. The Judicial Yuan found the oaths contrary to legal requirements and returned them to the Legislative Yuan for re-submission. The requirement was ignored by the legislature. In the same year, DPP legislators requested two constitutional review, which were rejected by the Judicial Yuan on the ground that the applicants had not assumed office as they had failed to effectively take their oath.[32] DPP representatives had to compromise and re-submitted their written oaths in accordance with the law.[33]

After the successful transfer of power from the KMT to the DPP in 2000, oath-taking conflicts further receded despite some individual occurrences. For example, at the 2005 Legislative Yuan swearing-in ceremony, Li Ao, a non-partisan representative and a prominent figure of dissent, swore allegiance

[29] Ibid, 8.

[30] Yang SM, '司法院否認 處理有雙重標準(Judicial Yuan denies double standards in handling oath-taking disputes) *China Times* (12 April 1996), 9.

[31] Lo HH, '戶外就職大典 與人民同在' (Outdoor swearing-in ceremony with the public) *China Times* (21 May 2000), 2.

[32] See '第1050次大法官會議不受理案件' (Cases rejected by the 1050th Meeting of the Grand Justices of the Judicial Yuan) (7 June 1985). Available at: https://law.judicial.gov.tw/FINT/default.aspx.

[33] Kang TT, '55位民進黨立委識時務 同意補正' (55 DPP legislators agree to resubmit new oaths) *China Times* (11 June 1996), 7.

to his own picture instead of that of Sun Yat-sen, but he signed the written oath and was able to assume office.[34] While oath-taking disputes have also occurred in Taiwan's local legislatures since the authoritarian period, most of the oath-takers involved were allowed to assume office after submitting their written oaths[35] or re-taking the oath.[36]

Hong Kong vs Taiwan: Comparative Observations

The oath-taking disputes in both Hong Kong and Taiwan under KMT rule occurred in a semi-democratic context amid crises of national identity. The defiant oath takers were all democratically elected and the agenda expressed through their irregular swearing-in enjoyed a certain degree of popular support. Compared to the oath-taking disputes in Taiwan, oath-taking controversies in Hong Kong present some similarities, but also salient differences.

First, in both Hong Kong and Taiwan, refusing to take an oath or taking an oath in a disputable way is a method used by opposition politicians to protest against authoritarianism or the existing constitution order. Yet, the two regions have experienced different developmental trajectories of oath-taking contention. In Taiwan, the atmosphere has turned much less confrontational as democratic reform has progressed over the past decades. With the achievement of full democratisation, the political agenda and dissidence expressed through oath-taking have been mediated through constitutional and political processes. The pro-independence claim and identity issues have gradually become legitimised and even mainstream in the course of democratisation.

By contrast, in Hong Kong, the authorities' attitude towards oath-taking has transitioned from being more tolerant to more stringent. This change is best illustrated by the case of four LegCo members, which invalidated the irregular oath-taking manners that had been accepted in previous LegCo terms. In response to the 2016 oath-taking incident staged by the two pro-independence LegCo members and, with fears of rising pro-independence activism, the central and local authorities have imposed stricter compliance with the law in respect to oath taking.

Second, judiciaries in both Hong Kong and Taiwan have denied the validity of oaths taken in a manner inconsistent with the law, but the legal consequences of invalid oath-taking in Taiwan, even during the authoritarian period, have

[34] '李敖對自己宣誓' (Li Ao swears in to himself) *United Evening News* (1 February 2005), 1.

[35] Wang PJ, "'宣誓'僅具形式並無實質意義" (Oath taking only has a formal, unsubstantive, meaning), *China Times* (14 March 1990), 4; '北高市議會混亂中成立' (Taipei and Kaohsiung City councils inaugurated amid chaos), *China Times* (26 December 1989), 1.

[36] See, eg, '三峽五鎮代擇期補宣誓' (Five representatives of Sanxia Town Council will retake oath), *China Times* (6 August 1986), 5; Cheng HJ, '穎艾達利阿美族語宣誓就任議員' (Ingay Tali takes oath in Amis) *China Daily News* (9 January 2019), C02N.

been more lenient than those in Hong Kong. There are two major reasons for this different approach, one practical and one legal.

The practical reason is that the two regions have different forms of oath-taking. In Hong Kong, LegCo members must take the oath one by one, while deputies in Taiwan are sworn in collectively. Given the large number of deputies, it is, in practice, difficult for the oath administrator in Taiwan to determine whether one individual legislator among more than 100, has taken the oath strictly in accordance with the law. This has also provided more leeway for an oath administrator to circumvent the issue by simply claiming not to have seen how a legislator has taken the oath.[37] As to the written oath, Taiwan oath-taking laws require deputies to subscribe written oaths to the Judicial Yuan for recording. As previously mentioned, since 1991, written oaths have been crucial in measuring oath validity. In contrast, the signing of written oaths is not compulsory under Hong Kong law. The Oaths and Declarations Ordinance (ODO) in Hong Kong prescribes only oral oath-taking and the internal rules of the LegCo leaves the matter to the legislators' own choice.[38] The dual-track approach of oath-taking in Taiwan provides more space for stakeholders to achieve compromise. In practice, opposition deputies have been tolerated in using the oral oath to express their dissidence publicly, catering to their constituencies, while non-publicly, they must still submit complete written oaths to fulfil their legal obligations.

The legal reason for difference between the two jurisdictions is that the oath-taking laws in the two regions have different legal consequences for failing to validly take the oath. The current oath-taking law in Hong Kong can be traced back to the ODO enacted in 1972 in colonial Hong Kong. After the 1997 handover, the ODO was revised in accordance with the new constitutional order, but the basic structure and main features of the law have largely remained the same. Section 21 of the ODO stipulates the legal consequences of declining or neglecting to take the oath as follows:

> Any person who declines or neglects to take an oath duly tendered which he is required to take by this Part, shall —
>
> (a) if he has already entered on his office, vacate it, and
> (b) if he has not entered on his office, be disqualified from entering on it.

Applying section 21 of the ODO to the two oath-taking cases, Hong Kong courts further held that such consequences were automatic and immediate.[39] This interpretation has been reinforced by para 2(3) of the 2016 NPCSC

[37] See, eg, Yang SM, '負責監誓大法官：宣誓過程很順利' (Grand Justice in charge of oath administration: oath-taking proceedings went smoothly) *China Times* (2 February 1993), 4.

[38] Para 3.33, 'A Companion to the History, Rules and Practices of the Legislative Council of the Hong Kong Special Administrative Region'. Available at: www.legco.gov.hk/general/english/procedur/companion/main_toc.html.

[39] *Leung and Yau case* (HCAL 185/2016), n 3 above, para 94.

Interpretation, which stipulates that '[a]n oath taker is disqualified forthwith from assuming the public office … if he or she declines to take the oath'.

The Oath Act in Taiwan was promulgated in 1930 and has since been amended numerous times. The latest version was adopted in 2006. In 1979, Article 6 of the Oath Act stipulated the legal consequences of invalid oath-taking for the first time. This was revised by Article 8 of the 1983 Oath Act, which was, in turn, incorporated into the 2006 Oath Act. According to Article 8 of the 2006 Oath Act, public office holders who have not validly taken the oath shall be deemed as not to having assumed office; public office holders who are unable to take the oath on the designated date shall do so on an alternative date and, if they have not validly taken the oath, they shall be deemed absent; if public office holders who have, for particular reasons, assumed office before taking the oath fail to take it within three months of taking office, they shall be deemed to have resigned. Judicial Yuan Interpretation No 199 further ruled that if delegates have not validly taken the oath, they shall not be eligible to perform their duties, but this does not necessarily mean that they will be disqualified. According to the Oath Act and judicial decisions, invalid oath-taking in Taiwan will not immediately and automatically lead to disqualification of a deputy and retaking of the oath is allowed.

Compared to the Oath Act in Taiwan, the ODO in Hong Kong prescribed disqualification as a more stringent legal consequence. The NPCSC and Hong Kong's judiciary, moreover, elucidated the already stringent legal consequence in a narrower way. The legal consequence of immediate and automatic disqualification has ultimately stripped LegCo of its power to determine the validity of its members' oaths and to permit retaking the oath.

Third, the courts in both Hong Kong and Taiwan have asserted their authority to have the final say over the validity of the oath and have denied the effect of an oath taken in a distorted manner. The administrative authorities and judges in Taiwan, however, have shown more respect towards the self-governing rules of the National Assembly and Legislative Yuan over oath-taking disputes than the Beijing and Hong Kong authorities have towards those of the LegCo. In the case of oath-taking disputes in Hong Kong, both the central government and the HKSAR administration appeared quite hands-on and assertive. It was the HKSAR administration that initiated the judicial review against the LegCo members, while in Taiwan it was delegates who applied for constitutional review in the oath-taking disputes. In practice, retaking of the oath was allowed in Taiwan as a result of negotiation and compromise among different political forces; the National Assembly and Legislative Yuan have the power to allow the retaking of oaths. However, according to the Hong Kong court's interpretation of section 21 of the ODO, the LegCo President has no power to permit LegCo members to retake the oath, but the retaking of the oath is not even applicable because any disqualification resulting from an invalid swearing in is immediate and automatic. This process in Hong Kong appears unduly harsh and overly dramatic.

It is worth noting that judges serve as oath administrators in Taiwan, but they have generally, despite frustration in many circumstances, adopted a tolerant attitude towards delegates who took their oaths in a disputable way and have been inclined to validate them. As the historical review above demonstrates, even during the authoritarian period, DPP delegates were seldom banned from assuming their office for invalid oaths, nor were they disqualified.

It must be admitted that the China factor played a more critical role in the resolution of oath-taking controversies in Hong Kong than in Taiwan, as China's central government has a strong influence over the three branches of the Hong Kong government, as well as the city's legal and political dynamics. The Chinese government served as the supreme authority in the backing up and legalisation of the disqualification of those oath-takers who dared to cross the 'red line' of undermining sovereignty and central authority. In contrast, during the transitional period in Taiwan, there was no supreme authority who could use coercive power and have a final say over the oath-taking disputes and the popular will had far more leverage. Hence, different governmental branches and political powers in Taiwan were able to work out a more flexible and balanced way to resolve the oath-taking disputes through political and legal mechanisms.

THE UNITED KINGDOM: ABSTENTIONISM AND SEPARATISM

The contrast between Hong Kong and Taiwan echoes differences between the oath-taking laws and practices in the United Kingdom and Hong Kong. For a long while Hong Kong's oath-taking law largely imitated that of the United Kingdom. Section 21 of the ODO, which stipulates the legal consequences of invalid oath-taking, literally borrows section 7 of the 1868 Promissory Oaths Act (the 1868 Act) in the United Kingdom.

The UK oath laws differentiate between Parliamentary oaths and oaths taken by other public office holders. However, Hong Kong's oath-taking law does not differentiate popularly elected legislators from other public office holders. Therefore, the legal consequences for legislators who fail to take an oath are also different. In Hong Kong, any public office holder, including LegCo members, who invalidly takes an oath, will be disqualified. The UK's 1868 Act stipulates the same legal consequences, but this only applies to senior public officers, rather than elected legislators.[40]

For members of the United Kingdom Parliament, the 1866 Parliamentary Oaths Act (the 1866 Act) stipulates more lenient legal consequences. If a member of parliament (MP) does not validly swear the oath, they will not be disqualified but they cannot sit in any debate and they cannot formally vote. Any MP who has violated these rules will be subject to a fine and their seat will then be

[40] Promissory Oaths Act 1868, Schedule.

vacated. In addition, MPs who have not taken their seats may still enjoy access to Parliamentary facilities and allowances to a limited extent.[41]

Vacation of MPs' seats following failure to swear the oath has seldom occurred in the United Kingdom.[42] In recent decades, however, pro-separatism Sinn Féin members have adopted an abstentionist policy: they have refused to take the Parliamentary oath because they do not recognise the British Crown's sovereignty over Ireland. Consequently, they have not been able to participate in the proceedings of the House of Commons. In contrast to the situation in Hong Kong, however, Sinn Féin members are able to maintain their titles as MPs.[43] In 1997, one such member, Martin McGuinness, challenged the decision of the House of Commons to deny MPs access to facilities of the House because they had not taken their seats. He also sought to challenge the oath-taking requirement stipulated by the 1866 Act as a violation of freedoms of expression and religion. The challenge failed in the UK courts and at the European Court of Human Rights (ECtHR).[44] The UK court refused the application for judicial review on the ground that the decision by the House of Commons speaker lay within the realm of the internal arrangements of the House and the court did not have the jurisdiction to review primary legislation, ie the 1866 Act.[45] The ECtHR further held that an oath of allegiance to the reigning monarch can be viewed as an affirmation of loyalty to the constitutional principle which supports the workings of representative democracy in the United Kingdom.[46] Referring to the *McGuinness* case, it is legally and politically difficult to argue in favour of the two pro-independence elected LegCo members on the basis of ICCPR and international human rights law.[47]

In the United Kingdom, the legal regime for oath taking has further evolved in recent decades. As separatism has become more of an issue, the legislation on oath-taking by members of devolved legislatures provides an interesting comparison with Hong Kong. According to the law, members of the Scottish Parliament and the National Assembly for Wales (Welsh Assembly) have to be

[41] Section 5 of the 1866 Act.

[42] The year 1924 was the last time an MP's seat was declared vacant on the ground of violation of s 5 of the 1866 Act. See M Everett and D Nash, 'The Parliamentary Oath (House of Commons Library Briefing Paper, 2016)' 10. Available at: https://researchbriefings.parliament.uk/ResearchBriefing/Summary/CBP-7515#fullreport.

[43] Ibid, 12.

[44] See *Martin McGuinness v United Kingdom* (39511/98) 8 June 1999. Available at: http://hudoc.echr. coe.int/eng?i=001-4860.

[45] Ibid.

[46] Ibid, para 1.

[47] In 2003, the High Court of Justice in Northern Ireland rejected the application for judicial review brought by another Sinn Féin MP, Michelle Gildernew, who challenged a policy development grant awarded to political parties with two or more MPs who have taken the oath. Sinn Féin was excluded from the grant funding because of its abstentionism policy. The court refused the application on the ground that (i) the policy did not restrain Sinn Féin members' freedom of speech; and (ii) since Sinn Féin members did not take their seats, Sinn Féin was not equally restricted by the daily demands of parliamentary life which impair the capability of political parties to develop long-term party policies. See *Sinn Féin, Re Application for Judicial Review* [2003] NIQB 27 (11 April 2003).

sworn in or affirm within two months of being elected; otherwise they will be disqualified.[48] These provisions seem to imply that a member of the Scottish Parliament or the Welsh Assembly may attempt to take the requisite oath more than once within the two-month period; they would only be disqualified if, after the two months have elapsed, they still have not validly taken or re-taken the oath. Such provisions are similar to the oath-taking practice in Taiwan. By contrast, members of the Northern Ireland Assembly are not required to take an oath, but only need to sign the Assembly's Roll of Membership[49] and an undertaking on anti-paramilitarism.[50]

It may, therefore, be seen that the legal consequences for members of the Scottish Parliament and Welsh Assembly who refuse to take their oaths are more severe than those for MPs at the Westminster Parliament who fail to take the oath. Some pro-nationalist members of the Scottish Parliament have been opposed to the content of the oath, which requires swearing allegiance to the monarch. To demonstrate their political opposition, they prefaced their oath with a declaration that pledged loyalty to the Scottish people. In practice, this manner of oath-taking has been accepted as valid,[51] in sharp contrast with the case of the four LegCo members in Hong Kong. One of the four members, Nathan Law Kwun Chung, adopted a similar approach to the devolved legislators, but was ultimately disqualified.[52]

DILEMMA: INHERENT TENSION BETWEEN RULE OF LAW AND POLITICAL LEGITIMACY

The oath-taking issue, a seemingly insignificant procedural requirement, highlights the tension between democratic legitimacy (as represented by popularly elected lawmakers) and the law; this is particularly true in a semi-democratic context. Underlying the controversies is the question of whether and how a constitutional and legal system can accommodate activities and claims opposing the very foundation upon which the existing constitutional framework operates. In the post-cold war era, democracies often opt to absorb the extremists into the democratic equation rather than silencing them or pushing them underground.[53]

[48] Section 84 of the Scotland Act 1998; s 23 of the Government of Wales Act 2006. The two-month period may be extended under certain circumstances.

[49] Order 3(7)(8), Standing Orders of the Northern Ireland Assembly (2016).

[50] Section 8 of the Northern Ireland (Stormont Agreement and Implementation Plan) Act 2016.

[51] Everett and Nash, n 42 above, 32–33.

[52] In this case, Nathan Law Kwun Chung, one of the four LegCo members concerned, was disqualified for inserting additional phrases before and after he read out the words of the affirmation. He also adopted a distinct high-rising tone (as if he was asking a question) whenever he spoke the word 'Guo'(nation): see *Nathan Law Kwun Chung and others*, n 3 above, paras 79–83.

[53] Y Mersel, 'The Dissolution of Political Parties: The Problem of Internal Democracy' (2006) 4 *International Journal of Constitutional Law* 84, 87.

Such an approach is evidenced by the models of the United Kingdom and Taiwan regarding the handling of oath-taking disputes, where the authorities have tried to strike a delicate balance between recognising democratic legitimacy and respecting the law. By contrast, the Hong Kong case exacerbates the inherent tension between the political legitimacy and legality in its semi-democratic context under the unique 'one country, two systems' (OCTS) arrangement. This tension can be demonstrated in several ways.

Firstly, the Hong Kong oath-taking law itself, inherited from the colonial period, has foreshadowed the potential friction between the law and political legitimacy. Unlike the United Kingdom's law, the oath-taking law in colonial Hong Kong did not distinguish legislators from other public officer holders. This is probably because all branches of the Hong Kong government lacked any democratic input at the time. LegCo members were all appointed by the Governor during the colonial period. This non-discriminatory approach continued after 1997, although the 70-member LegCo is now completely elected (35 seats from geographical constituencies and 35 seats from functional constituencies). Thus, the Hong Kong oath law imposes more stringent legal consequences, ie disqualification, for popularly elected legislators, while the British and Taiwanese oath-taking laws and practices have taken the political legitimacy enjoyed by deputies into consideration. Given the change to a completely elected LegCo, perhaps it is time that Hong Kong revisit their law.

Secondly, judicial overreach in the Hong Kong oath-taking cases further situates the judiciary in an intractable counter-majoritarian position. By interpreting the already stringent legal consequences in a narrower sense, ie the disqualification should be 'automatic and immediate', the courts engaged in an obvious case of judicial activism when they excluded from the scope of the 'non-intervention principle' the LegCo President's decisions to re-administer the oath and held that the past practice of LegCo in adopting a lenient standard for the determination of the validity of oaths of office was irrelevant. In other jurisdictions, such as Taiwan and the UK, such a politicalised issue was largely left to the self-governance of the representative institution. The Hong Kong oath-taking cases point to a significant counter-majoritarian dilemma that courts could face within a democracy (or semi-democracy in the case of Hong Kong): When should the court exercise the judicial power to unseat a popularly elected legislator and to what extent may the judiciary be used to negate voter choice?

Thirdly, lack of political and democratic restraint on the legislature impairs the legitimacy of the law and judicial decisions. In the course of the first oath-taking case, the NPCSC issued an interpretation which incorporated and further reinforced the strict requirement in existing Hong Kong law regarding oath-taking.[54] The Hong Kong judiciary has exhibited a highly deferential attitude towards the NPCSC interpretation in all the oath-taking cases, as it

[54] NPCSC, n 7 above.

has done in other politically sensitive cases.[55] Such deference could be conveniently justified under the OCTS framework, as while the NPC and its standing committee are the highest organs of state power, only the NPC is vested with the power to revise or revoke improper decisions made by the NPCSC.[56] It is, therefore, hardly applicable, either normatively or practically, for Hong Kong courts, as sub-national courts, to exert legal control over acts of the supreme organs of the state.

The lack of legal and political control over the NPC and NPCSC is an issue of great concern, particularly when the NPCSC interpretations touch on basic civil rights and the autonomy of Hong Kong. The NPCSC has tended to interpret the Basic Law to the advantage of the central government's interests, ie maintaining the priority of the 'one country' principle and constraining political movement.[57] Underlying such concern is the absence of any democratic input in the NPC and the NPCSC, which are, de facto, controlled by the ruling party. As Chan pointed out, despite the doctrine of parliamentary supremacy in the United Kingdom (as there is no constitutional or judicial constraint on the exercise of Parliament's legislative power), free elections there serve as the main source of political control.[58] However, in the absence of any legal and political check on the supreme power, the indiscriminate application of the NPCSC's interpretation by the courts and the emphasis on complying with the existing constitutional order will inevitably give rise to legitimacy concerns, even in a well-developed legal system such as Hong Kong's.

Furthermore, the way the Beijing and Hong Kong authorities handled the oath-taking disputes has given rise to a worrying trend of rising authoritarian legalism in Hong Kong. The threshold for restricting the expression of pro-separatism is lower while the scope of contexts in which undesired speech is banned is wider in Hong Kong than in other democratic jurisdictions. For instance, the ECHR ruled in *McGuinness* that the oath-taking requirement did not violate the applicant's freedom of speech, on the ground that there is nothing to prevent the applicant from expressing his views in other contexts.[59] Though unable to take their seats in Parliament, Sinn Féin members still fully enjoy the rights of association and political participation. By contrast, constraints on pro-independence speech in Hong Kong have expanded from oaths of office to expressions in many other contexts. Pro-independence

[55] See PY Lo, 'Two Kinds of Unconstitutional Constitutional Interpretations in China's Hong Kong' *Blog of the International Journal of Constitutional Law* (23 December 2020). Available at: www.iconnectblog.com/2016/12/ two-kinds-of-unconstitutional-constitutional-interpretations/.

[56] PRC Const., art 62.

[57] H Zhu, 'Beijing's "Rule of Law" Strategy for Governing Hong Kong: Legalization without Democratization' (2009) 1 *China Perspectives* 23, 28.

[58] C Chan, 'The Legal Limits on Beijing's Powers to Interpret Hong Kong's Basic Law' *HKU Legal Scholarship Blog* (3 Nov 2016). Available at: http://researchblog.law.hku.hk/2016/11/cora-chan-on-legal-limits-of-beijings.html.

[59] *McGuinness v UK*, n 44 above.

activists' right to political participation has been curtailed simply because of their political stance, regardless of whether they resort to violence. As previously mentioned, many pro-independence localists running in the LegCo, or even village representative elections, have been stopped at the starting line for their political opinions. The pro-independence Hong Kong National Party was outlawed by the government on national security grounds under the Societies Ordinance, marking the first time the anti-triad legislation had been invoked against a political group.[60] Facing the central government's zero tolerance policy for separatism, the Hong Kong government has utilised various legal technicalities, which had been rarely used in the past, to crack down on pro-independence activism. Such use, or what some may characterise as 'abuse', of the law bears some similarity to the widespread use of legalism in many authoritarian regimes where governments have sought to use the law to 'suppress dissent in almost all forms while maintaining legal and political credibility'.[61] Ironically, an advanced rule-of-law system in a semi-democratic context such as Hong Kong (and in similarly situated jurisdictions, such as Singapore) seems to be a more efficient and justified instrument than an undeveloped legal system for containing and suppressing political dissent.[62]

CONCLUSION

Overall, the comparisons above show that, in settling oath-taking disputes, the law has become the dominant tool employed by both the Beijing and Hong Kong authorities to stifle those who challenge the existing constitutional configuration. This places Hong Kong in sharp contrast with Taiwan during its transitional period, where similar disputes were mainly mediated through the political process and gradually faded away as democratisation came about. In Hong Kong, the law has been employed to legalise a highly politicised issue, without leaving any room for achieving political comprise. Compared to Taiwan and many other democratic jurisdictions, the Hong Kong authorities have exploited the law to set up a lower threshold for constraining the freedom of speech and the right to political participation for pan-democratic and localist groups. The weaponisation of the law to suppress radical dissenting voices and political claims, which are supported by a certain portion of the populace but run against the current constitutional system, highlights the tension between legality and democratic legitimacy in Hong Kong.

[60] J Lam and T Cheung, 'Hong Kong separatist political party given 21-day ultimatum to contest unprecedented ban', *South China Morning Post* (17 July 2018). Available at: www.scmp.com/news/hong-kong/politics/article/2155566/hong-kong-separatist-political-party-faces-landmark.

[61] D Gurnham, 'Book Review: Authoritarian Rule of Law: Legislation, Discourse and Legitimacy in Singapore.' (2012) 22 *Law and Politics Book Review*, 525–527. Available at: www.lpbr.net/2012/11/authoritarian-rule-of-law-legislation.html.

[62] Zhu, n 57 above, 26.

The pro-independence/localist claims point directly to the legitimacy of the ultimate source of law in Hong Kong – which lacks democratic input – as well as to the legitimacy of the state sovereignty that denies the city full democracy. The tension between democratic legitimacy and legality burgeoned in the OC Movement, developed further in the oath-taking controversies and culminated in the 2019 anti-extradition bill crisis; there is little doubt it will continue to grow under the OCTS framework. While employment of the law appeared to have settled the OC Movement and the oath-taking disputes peacefully, although controversially, it has apparently failed in fixing the anti-extradition bill crisis. In the OC movement, protesters remained willing to act within the constitutional and legal framework in pursuing their democratic agenda, while in the oath-taking cases and anti-extradition bill crisis, the basic underlying constitutional structure and legal order have been directly challenged and even openly defied. The oath-taking cases have, therefore, gone beyond the seemingly trivial legal procedure issue, raising the important question of whether it is possible for the legal system in Hong Kong, within the current framework, to accommodate anti-OCTS voices and activities. How the authorities deal with these claims provide a benchmark to test whether Hong Kong is experiencing what Tai called the transition from semi-democracy to semi-authoritarianism.[63] Unfortunately, the recent promulgation of the highly controversial National Security Law for the HKSAR paints a bleak outlook for the implementation of the OCTS framework. Facing rising disobedience, the PRC and HKSAR authorities hope that this law will be a type of endgame for Hong Kong. However, such a legal strategy completely ignores Hong Kong society's demand for democracy, thus the law's long-term efficacy remains questionable.

Beijing authorities would be wise to take into account a 500-year-old oath of the subjects of the Spanish Kingdom of Aragon. It goes:

> We who are as good as you swear to you who are no better than we, to accept you as our king and sovereign lord, provided you observe all our liberties and laws; but if not, not.[64]

[63] Tai, n 12 above, 335–356.

[64] M Konnert, *Early Modern Europe: The Age of Religious War, 1559–1715* (2006), 38.

Part II

Democratic Struggles with Law

4

Court Criticism and the Rule of Law: From 'Foreign' to 'Dinosaur' Judges

BRIAN CHRISTOPHER JONES*

LAW AND LEGAL institutions have long endured harsh criticism from a variety of prominent individuals. In *Henry IV*, Shakespeare calls law 'the rusty curb of old father antick' and in *Henry VI*, he feeds Dick the butcher the harsh line: 'The first thing we do, let's kill all the lawyers.' In *Oliver Twist*, Dickens wrote that 'the law is an ass – an idiot'. And Dickens was not the only person to call the law an 'ass'; George Chapman did so almost two centuries before him, in *Revenge for Honour* ('I am ashamed the law is such an ass'). John Arbuthnot once referred to the law as a 'bottomless pit'; while Jonathan Swift likened the law to 'cobwebs', which 'may catch small flies, but let wasps and hornets breakthrough'. So, too, have those in the legal profession been accustomed to biting condemnation. Mark Twain once wrote that, 'to succeed in other trades, capacity must be shown; in the law, concealment of it will do',[1] and John Mortimer said: 'No brilliance is needed in the law. Nothing but common sense, and relatively clean fingernails.'[2]

Although it is difficult to find a historical period where law has not been openly and harshly disparaged, a stronger affinity (or perhaps more awareness) for upholding the rule of law in recent years has brought forward allegations that some types of criticism were crossing the line. When major societal clashes erupt judiciaries can sometimes get stuck in the middle, having to adjudicate the legal issues involved. These decisions may be perceived as taking sides and can often lead to harsh criticism of particular judges or decisions from the groups involved – especially those on the losing side. Both Hong Kong and Taiwan have seen a number of these over the past few years and judicial criticism in both

* Lecturer in Law, School of Law, University of Sheffield. This chapter builds on a blog post by the author: Brian Christopher Jones, 'Court Criticism and the Rule of Law: A Three-Part Test' (5 September 2018) *International Journal of Constitutional Law Blog*.

[1] M Twain, *Following the Equator* (1897).

[2] J Mortimer, *A Voyage Round My Father* (1971).

jurisdictions has become a prominent issue at times. In an age of burgeoning rule of law, the types of criticism that have come forward in both jurisdictions can help us understand the dynamics, value, and potential downsides of court criticism.

Although much court criticism is essential to the operation of democracy, determining when such criticism violates the rule of law is a valuable endeavour. One of the major problems in relation to court criticism is that we do not have an agreed-upon standard to determine what is democratically acceptable and what threatens the rule of law. Scholars and journalists often use a common sense 'smell test' to decide whether certain statements traverse the rule of law, ie 'you know it when you see it', but this is imprecise and does not produce much consensus. This chapter hopes to add more sophistication to the discussion and debate surrounding court criticism and the rule of law. It begins by considering the tensions present between democracy and law and how these – especially in an age of significant judicial power – may come into conflict. It then recommends a three-part test for determining whether criticism crosses the bounds of acceptability, which attempts to discern credible threats to the rule of law from merely harsh criticism. The chapter goes on to examine both Hong Kong and Taiwan, investigating court criticism from two separate incidents in each jurisdiction.

Both Hong Kong and Taiwan provide differing perspectives, given their respective semi-democracy and full-democracy statuses.[3] The Hong Kong judiciary, long known for its dedication to judicial independence and the rule of law, has recently encountered some harsh and, at times unfiltered and abusive, disparagement. Although this treatment is new for the Hong Kong judiciary, it may be indicative of wider tensions within Hong Kong's constitutional framework, especially the one country, two systems (OCTS) relationship with China. Recent controversial events in Taiwan, such as determining the innocence or guilt of Sunflower Movement leaders and whether same-sex couples should receive the same marital rights as heterosexual couples, have also prompted judicial criticism. Indeed, while no judiciary is exempt from criticism, lately it has been at fever pitch not only in Hong Kong in Taiwan but worldwide.

Before continuing, a few disclaimers should be noted: here I use a relatively thin conception of the rule of law. Borrowing words from Article 10(2) of the European Convention on Human Rights (ECHR), I primarily look at criticism that may challenge 'the authority and impartiality of the judiciary'.[4] The test laid out below is designed to allow as much criticism as possible, provided that

[3] Of course, some people may take issue with me characterising Hong Kong as a semi-democracy. I use the term here, but acknowledge that Hong Kong's democracy is quickly withering into the 'semi-authoritarian' realm. It should also be noted that Hong Kong is a common law system, while Taiwan relies on a civil law system.

[4] ECHR Art 10(2).

this criticism does not traverse the rule of law. Additionally, I am only concerned with high-level public criticism, eg criticism from the media, government ministers or elected lawmakers and not necessarily low-level criticism, eg tweets from members of the general public or comments on a webpage. Finally, this chapter does not advocate legally restricting speech based on concerns for the rule of law, but merely being able to discern between legitimate threats to the rule of law and harsh criticism.

THE TENSIONS BETWEEN DEMOCRACY, PUBLIC CRITICISM, AND THE RULE OF LAW

A bedrock principle of democracy is that governments and political leaders can and should be criticised. Indeed, intensely criticising elected politicians is a legally sanctioned, time-honoured tradition in jurisdictions throughout the world. For example, in the United Kingdom case of *Derbyshire County Council* it was said: 'It is of the highest public importance that a democratically elected governmental body, or indeed any governmental body, should be open to uninhibited public criticism'.[5] Similar expressions can be found in other courts, such as the European Court of Human Rights (ECtHR). In *Castells*, they noted:

> The limits of permissible criticism are wider with regard to the Government than in relation to a private citizen, or even a politician. In a democratic system the actions or omissions of the Government must be subject to the close scrutiny not only of the legislature and judicial authorities but also of the press and public opinion.[6]

For all intents and purposes, the elected branches are supposed to be able to withstand strong attacks from the public. Any type of fettering of such criticism that went beyond normal libel and slander standards would go against the basic right of freedom of speech. This principle has been enacted in a host of significant constitutions and international bills of rights throughout the years.

And yet, the same type of resilience is not expected in relation to the judiciary. For example, the European Convention on Human Rights has a special carve-out for the judiciary in relation to speech. Article 10(2) notes that if speech threatens the judiciary's authority of impartiality, then that provides a justification for it to be curtailed. Similar protections can often be noted at the state level. In the UK, a charge of 'scandalising the court' could be brought under the common law until 2013,[7] although its use was minimal. No doubt the widespread use of contempt of court proceedings in many jurisdictions fall within the ECHR provision and are legally permissible in any states with an established

[5] *Derbyshire CC v Times Newspapers* Ltd [1993] UKHL 18, 6.
[6] *Castells v Spain*, 14 EHRR 445 (1992).
[7] Law Commission, 'Contempt of Court: Scandalising the Court' (2012)(Paper No 207).

rule of law. These protections regarding the judiciary, although often situated around preserving judicial independence, portray the branch as inherently weaker and more susceptible to criticism than the elected branches. Whether this is still the case is debateable, but there is no question that when it comes to the operation of the legal system, perception matters. As Lord Heward said close to a century ago, 'Justice should not only be done, but should manifestly and undoubtedly be seen to be done'.[8] If not – as many judges have found over the years – court criticism may come in abundance.

The tensions between democracy and law have only been heightened over the past few decades, as more written constitutions and bills of rights have come into place,[9] more apex constitutional courts and regional human rights courts have been established and judiciaries around the world have become increasingly powerful.[10] In many jurisdictions, judiciaries have been provided the final word on constitutional matters, as apex courts are allowed to strike down whole statutes and also intervene in the legislative process if they so wish.[11] These developments have placed democratic accountability and the mechanisms of criticism in an awkward position, as laws that have been passed by elected and accountable officials now frequently come under increased scrutiny from unelected and much less accountable judiciaries. Even if citizens decide to play their trump card and amend the written constitution, some courts are even empowered to strike down constitutional amendments.[12] These significant changes in judicial power vis-à-vis the elected branches have heightened the tension between law and democracy, given that law can sometimes be said to overrule or trump democratic outputs.

Much of the 'us v them' rhetorical scaffolding has largely been supplied by the judiciary, in the name of the rule of law and other values. Indeed, a significant part of the anti-majoritarian perception of the courts has been built up either by the courts themselves or from scholars and those who advocate that the courts uphold the rule of law and fundamental rights, protect citizens from 'overzealous' executives and 'overreaching' legislatures, or defend ideas of justice and fairness. For example, in his classic text on the rule of law, Bingham noted that a 'truly independent judiciary is one of the strongest safeguards against

[8] *R v Sussex Justices, Ex Parte McCarthy*, [1924] 1 KB 256.

[9] Comparative Constitutions Project, 'Data Visualizations: New Constitutions', Available at: https://comparativeconstitutionsproject.org/ccp-visualizations/.

[10] R Hirschl, *Towards Juristocracy: The Origins and Consequences of the New Constitutionalism* (2007).

[11] Sometimes, through *a priori* review, laws and legal rules can be struck down before they finish their legislative stages. A number of jurisdictions allow apex courts to determine whether legislation travelling through the legislative process is constitutional (M de Visser, *Constitutional Review in Europe: A Comparative Analysis* (2015), 99–111).

[12] Y Roznai, *Unconstitutional Constitutional Amendments: The Limits of Amendment Powers* (2017); Albert R, *Constitutional Amendments: Making, Breaking, and Changing Constitutions* (2019).

executive lawlessness'.[13] Others have noted that courts protect against rule of law and fundamental rights violations by the legislature.[14] Beyond this and in an era of adjudicated constitutionalism it is clear that many '[p]olitical losers and political minorities turn to the independent, that is, unelected and unaccountable, judiciary in the hopes of persuading judges of claims that fail to command a majority in the legislature'.[15] Through these overtures, judiciaries can and often do respond by overturning statutes, intervening in political affairs and essentially playing a policy-making function.

Despite the suggestion that we need to curtail criticism of judges, some writers have acknowledged that judges and public criticism go hand in hand. Shetreet and Turenne state that '[a] robust and informed public debate about judicial affairs promotes judicial accountability'.[16] Indeed, this view aligns with that of Keith Ewing, who stresses that: 'Those who would presume to sit in judgment of democracy and indeed determine its content and values must themselves be exposed to some form of democratic scrutiny'.[17] Effective scrutiny of the courts, just like that of the other branches, is essential for a well-functioning state and has been labelled the 'most important of all checks on the judiciary'.[18] In fact, public criticism may be more essential for the courts compared to the other branches, given that oftentimes the judiciary is not the most transparent of branches and also because there are a lack of accountability structures in place to hold judges to account.

Given the widespread tension present between law and democracy, I have devised a test as to when court criticism violates the rule of law.

THE RULE OF LAW TEST

Below is a three-stage test that could be used to determine whether comment or criticism from a journalist, minister, lawmaker or other individual traverses the rule of law. In order for criticism to challenge rule of law principles, all three criteria must be met: targeted, element of abuse of belligerence, and a focus on the validity or legitimacy of the decision maker. The test is a way to further understand how criticism may cross the line and could be useful for scholars, journalists, and other public figures when discussing how judicial criticism could be understood.

[13] T Bingham, *The Rule of Law* (2011), 25.

[14] M De Visser, *Constitutional Review in Europe: A Comparative Analysis* (2015), 61.

[15] A Hollis-Brusky, 'An Activists Court' in Z Courser, E Helland and KP Miller, *Parchment Barriers: Political Polarization and the Limits of Constitutional Order* (2018).

[16] S Shetreet and S Turenne, *Judges on Trial: The Independence and Accountability of the English Judiciary* (2013), 382.

[17] K Ewing, 'The Unbalanced Constitution' in T Campbell, KD Ewing and A Tomkins, *Sceptical Essays on Human Rights* (2001), 117.

[18] Shetreet and Turenne, n 16 above, 382.

Step 1: Targeted

The first consideration when assessing judicial criticism is whether a specific judge or group of judges has been targeted. One thing that the jurisprudence of the ECtHR highlights as unacceptable is personal attacks on judges. Such attacks present problems for both authority and impartiality. In analysing this type of criticism, whether the attack was professional or personal is often taken into consideration, as the former tends to be more accepted than the latter. But distinguishing between these is difficult and there is no bright line. The Court has also differentiated between criticisms made inside the courtroom compared to criticism made outside of it, highlighting that the former is more acceptable than the latter.[19] This criterion connects to the ECtHR case law but does not necessarily distinguish between personal and professional attacks. The reason that I do not differentiate is because personal attacks can often employ professional elements (such as affiliations) and distinguishing between them sometimes becomes arbitrary.

One recent example highlights how this condition can be fulfilled. After the England and Wales High Court's Brexit decision in 2016,[20] the three judges who made the decision were specifically targeted. Much of the criticism focused on the individual judges, rather than on the judgment as a whole. The *Daily Mail* labelled the trio of judges 'Enemies of the People' whilst displaying their pictures underneath,[21] and then proceeded to individually (and personally) attack the judges, labelling the most senior judge a 'committed Europhile' and noting that another judge was 'openly gay'. I come back to this example below but suffice it to say that this criticism was especially targeted. Such targeted criticism need not be so vicious, however: it is often seen in family law situations, or in other situations where judges may be questioned about their sentencing practices. These examples can be separated from more general (or collective) criticism of the judiciary or of the administration of justice. Criticism that judges are 'too political' or that the justice system is 'unfair' or 'biased' is not targeted criticism – even if accurate and meaningful – and will not pass the first step.

Step 2: Element of Abuse or Belligerence

If criticism is targeted, the second leg of the test is whether the criticism exhibits an element of abuse or belligerence. This is not a factor that has been used

[19] *Morice v France*, 23 April 2015 [GC].

[20] *R (on the Application of Miller) v Secretary of State for Exiting the European Union* [2016] EWHC 2768 (Admin).

[21] J Slack, 'Enemies of the people: Fury over "out of touch" judges who have "declared war on democracy" by defying 17.4m Brexit voters and who could trigger constitutional crisis' (3 Nov 2016) Daily Mail. Available at: www.dailymail.co.uk/news/article-3903436/Enemies-people-Fury-touch-judges-defied-17-4m-Brexit-voters-trigger-constitutional-crisis.html.

in jurisprudence, such as the ECtHR's, but I think it is an essential component when assessing whether it traverses the rule of law. Here there must be a decidedly strong reaction or condemnation of a judge or a particular decision. Targeted criticism that is not abusive or belligerent can and often does happen. For example, a judge may say something especially biased or provocative,[22] and will then be reprimanded in the media and elsewhere because of it. Or perhaps a specific court has been systematically favouring one party over another,[23] and this has recently been condemned by a government official. The situation in both these cases would be that a specific judge or court was targeted, but that the criticism lacked the element of abuse or belligerence needed to send it over the line.

The elements of abuse or belligerence that I am most concerned with usually focus on an inherent personal characteristic of judges, eg age, ethnicity, mental capacity, etc. For example, older and younger judges are often susceptible to attack. As noted below, in Taiwan the label 'dinosaur judges' (*kong long fa guan*) is widely used,[24] and is often placed on older judges considered 'out of touch' (but this can also be applied to young, 'naïve' judges). The most common event to trigger such a label tends to be a judge's sentencing discretion. Oftentimes sentences are deemed too lenient, and here we may often see criticism[25] that is targeted[26] and includes an element of abuse. Such criticism may get extensive coverage in the press or on social media and there may even be an element of abuse – especially for older or younger judges, who are particularly vulnerable to such attacks. Criticism displaying elements of belligerence could also fall into this category. Such criticism may be highly provocative, such as an unfiltered ministerial reaction to a court judgment that is widely quoted in the press. Or, perhaps some type of unreasonable and sustained campaign against a particular judge or specific judgment would qualify.

However, even though these two elements are present, this does not mean that the criticism violates the rule of law (even if the criticism comes from ministers or elected lawmakers). In order for it to do so, the third hurdle must also be passed.

Step 3: Focus on the Validity or Legitimacy of the Decision-Maker

The final part of the test is that there must be a focus on undermining the validity or legitimacy of the decision maker. Here, the concern is questioning the

[22] A Liptak, 'Ruth Bader Ginsburg, No fan of Donald Trump, critiques latest term' (10 July 2016) *New York Times*. Available at: https://nyti.ms/29I7mE4.

[23] PS Green and J Mazor, 'Corrupt justice: what happens when judges' bias taints a case?' (18 October 2015), The Guardian. Available at: www.theguardian.com/us-news/2015/oct/18/judge-bias-corrupts-court-cases.

[24] J Pan, 'Judicial reform, jury system promoted' (5 June 2017) *Taipei Times*. Available at: www.taipeitimes.com/News/taiwan/archives/2017/06/05/2003671944.

[25] 'Editorial: Public fed up with "dinosaur judges"' (6 December 2017) *Taipei Times*. Available at: www.taipeitimes.com/News/editorials/archives/2017/12/06/2003683498.

[26] J Pan, 'Court hands murderer a "lenient" 18-year sentence' (30 November 2017) *Taipei Times*. Available at: www.taipeitimes.com/News/taiwan/archives/2017/11/30/2003683188.

judge's *very right* to make the decision. Although the first two elements of the test could be met and the criticism levied could be harsh, if it does not cross the boundary of questioning the judge's right to make that decision, it may not threaten the rule of law. Let me give you a couple examples that do traverse the rule of law.

An example of ethnic criticism that traversed the rule of law came in 2016 from then-US presidential candidate Donald Trump. After a decision against Trump University, Mr Trump criticised Judge Curiel on numerous occasions on Twitter[27] and in interviews,[28] displaying evidence of targeted and abusive comments. Notably, he attempted to delegitimise Mr Curiel's very right to make the decision by noting the judge's 'Mexican' ethnicity, even though he was born in Indiana and is an American citizen. This criticism crossed the line.

Going back to the earlier example regarding Brexit and the *Daily Mail*, to label the trio of judges 'enemies' was an attempt to invalidate or undermine the decision makers, as it implies not only that they were actively working against the British citizenry, but that they also had a predetermined view on this issue and were therefore unfit to make such a decision.

JUDICIAL CRITICISM IN A WITHERING SEMI-DEMOCRACY: HONG KONG

Ever since the 2014 Umbrella Movement, judicial criticism in Hong Kong has become an increasingly prominent and problematic issue. Throughout the 79-day occupation, there were numerous points when people advocated judicial intervention. Eventually a judicial order did ultimately bring an end to the Movement, but the heights of judicial criticism came later. Court decisions regarding Umbrella Movement leaders, the actions of the police during the protests, the disqualification of elected members of the Legislative Council and other contentious decisions, have led to continuously harsh criticism from many sides. Opening the legal year in January 2020, Hong Kong Chief Justice Geoffrey Ma addressed the seemingly unrelenting issue of court criticism head-on. In his speech, he noted:

> [W]hen attacks are made against the integrity and impartiality of the courts, or against the soundness of the legal system, or personal and highly offensive attacks are made against judges based solely on the outcome of cases, something needs to be said to inform the community about the operation of the law.[29]

[27] Donald J Trump (30 May 2016) *Twitter*, https://twitter.com/realdonaldtrump/status/737399475509985280?lang=en. (Donald Trump has now been banned from Twitter.)

[28] ZB Wolf, 'Trump's attacks on Judge Curiel are still jarring to read' (28 February 2018) CNN, https://edition.cnn.com/2018/02/27/politics/judge-curiel-trump-border-wall/index.html.

[29] 'Chief justice opens legal year with pledge to uphold Hong Kong's judicial independence' (13 January 2020) *South China Morning Post* – YouTube. Available at: https://youtu.be/S369YwbClzI.

Ma's noteworthy comments on court criticism, made during the last time he would open the legal year as head of the Hong Kong judiciary, were significant for another reason: prior to 2014, criticism of the courts in Hong Kong had been relatively mild. As a semi-democracy with an enduring focus on the rule of law, widespread criticism had certainly not been the norm in Hong Kong; nor had it ever been present at such high levels. However, given its history as a British colony, the rule of law encapsulates a thicker conception than it does within mainland China,[30] as it connects to rights and freedoms in the city that are more aligned with international standards. Since the handover in 1997, the balance between democracy and the rule of law has been tipped largely in favour of the latter. Although a good amount of Hong Kong's Legislative Council (LegCo) is popularly elected, the primary power holder – the Hong Kong Chief Executive (CE) – is not. The lack of a direct method of election for the CE is primarily what sparked the 2014 Umbrella Movement. However, elections do take place at the local level. Hong Kong is divided into 18 local districts, comprising 479 seats that are elected by citizens every four years. The November 2019 elections gave a prominent indication that citizens supported the ongoing city-wide protests and were potentially fed up with China's incursions into Hong Kong law.[31]

Tension between Hong Kong's colonial past under British rule and its current status as a Chinese special administrative region (SAR) often boils up, and the legal system is not immune from such strain. In 2014, judicial independence became a hot button issue in Hong Kong, as a Beijing white paper on 'one country two systems' (OCTS) suggested that judges should be 'patriotic'.[32] Although the Hong Kong judiciary challenged this view,[33] the tensions brought about by the Umbrella Movement and its aftermath certainly tested the judiciary's independence. Given Hong Kong's deficiency of formal democratic mechanisms,[34] the rule of law is Hong Kong's most authoritative constitutional principle. Thus, to violate the rule of law may mean more here than in other jurisdictions, where it may not be valued as highly or may be propped up by other underlying constitutional principles. Nevertheless, court criticism in Hong Kong has experienced the same problem as it has in other jurisdictions: where is the line drawn and

[30] Although, see Zhai Xiaobo's chapter in this collection, which argues that China's original rule of law plans were relatively thick and similar to other liberal democracies.

[31] 'Hong Kong elections: Pro-democracy groups makes big gains' BBC News (25 November 2019). Available at: www.bbc.co.uk/news/world-asia-china-50531408.

[32] S Lau, A Chiu and B Yap, 'Hong Kong lawyers march to defend judiciary in wake of Beijing's white paper' (27 June 2014) *South China Morning Post*. Available at: www.scmp.com/news/hong-kong/article/1541814/hong-kong-lawyers-stage-silent-march-oppose-beijings-white-paper.

[33] P So, 'Judges don't need to be patriots, says former top judge Andrew Li' *South China Morning Post* (15 August 2014). Available at: www.scmp.com/news/hong-kong/article/1573867/judges-dont-need-be-patriots-andrew-li.

[34] It should be acknowledged that although parts of the Hong Kong LegCo are elected by universal suffrage, not all members are. Additionally, further restrictions on Hong Kong's electoral system have recently come into place, which are designed to curb democratic representation.

what traverses the rule of law? Some have suggested that particular rhetoric against the judiciary has crossed the line.[35]

But there has been one unique feature of criticism within the Hong Kong context: the nationality of judges has come into question. Given Hong Kong's historical reliance on UK common law, some members of the judiciary are indeed 'foreign'. The Basic Law stipulates that judges from other common law jurisdictions may be invited to sit on the Court of Final Appeal and on other Hong Kong courts.[36] For example, Lord Neuberger and Baroness Hale, both former presidents of the UK Supreme Court, serve as guest judges on the Court of Final Appeal (CFA). According to the Basic Law, only two judges must be 'Hong Kong Chinese': the chief justice of the CFA and the chief judge of the High Court.[37] But, more broadly, this examination of the 'foreign' versus 'local' judges debate has turned into a dispute about democracy versus rule of law.

For this section I have decided to focus on two incidents where judicial criticism was present: the trials of the Occupy Central Movement student leaders;[38] and the later conviction of police officers for assault occurring during the Movement. These two incidents brought about different types of judicial criticism. Here, I primarily used articles from the *South China Morning Post*, Hong Kong's leading English-language newspaper, to determine what type of criticism was being levied on judges.

Occupy Central Movement Student Leaders

In 2016, three prominent student activists who had participated in the Umbrella Movement – Joshua Wong Chi-fung (黃之鋒), Nathan Law Kwun-chung (羅冠聰) and Alex Chow Yong-kang (周永康) – were given community service orders and suspended prison sentences for their participation in the 2014 activities. However, almost a year after these sentences were given, Justice Minister Rimsky Yuen decided to apply to the Court of Appeal for a sentencing review to bring about harsher sentences. The review eventually recommended just that and the trio were given much stiffer sentences, which included six to eight months' prison time. The increased penalties came with a good deal of scrutiny. Some critics accused the appellate court of acting 'politically', 'excessively', and outside their traditional role,[39] given that the student leaders

[35] J Lam, '"Ungrounded" attacks on Hong Kong's judiciary are a threat to the city's rule of law, say legal experts' *South China Morning Post* (26 August 2017). Available at: www.scmp.com/news/hong-kong/politics/article/2108408/ungrounded-attacks-hong-kongs-judiciary-are-threat-citys.

[36] HK Basic Law, arts 82 and 92.

[37] HK Basic Law, art 90.

[38] For more information on this case, see the chapter by Jimmy Hsu and Anne Cheung in this collection.

[39] J Hollingsworth and C Lau, 'Judiciary in the dock: jailing of student activists opens door to debate' *South China Morning Post* (25 August 2017). Available at: www.scmp.com/news/hong-kong/politics/article/2108186/judiciary-dock-jailing-student-activists-opens-door-debate.

had already completed their initial penalties and because appeal courts do not usually meddle in the factual findings of lower courts.

While some wider condemnation of the decision arose, the vast majority of those in the legal community attempted to protect the courts, aiming any criticism at the person who initiated the review, Justice Minister Yuen. Some reports suggested that Mr Yuen had neglected the advice of his top prosecutor to drop the review. In some ways this focus on the Justice Minister insulated the courts against increased criticism, even though it was a unanimous decision by the Court of Appeal – not the Justice Minister – which ultimately recommended the tougher sentence.

But good reasons may have existed to accuse the courts of acting politically and for not upholding the strict judicial independence that Hong Kong is widely known for. In the judgment, the Vice President of the Court of Appeal wrote some inflammatory material, which perhaps should have received more criticism than it did. In the sixth paragraph, Justice Wally Yeung Chun-kuen noted that:

> In recent years, an unhealthy wind has been blowing in Hong Kong. Some people, on the pretext of pursuing their ideals or freely exercising their rights conferred by law, have acted wantonly in an unlawful manner. Certain people, including individuals of learning, advocate "achieving justice by violating the law" and, under this slogan, they encourage others to break the law. These people openly flout the law. Not only do they refuse to admit their lawbreaking activities are wrong, but they even go as far as regarding such activities as a source of honour and pride. It is unfortunate that such arrogant and conceited ways of thinking have influenced some young people and have caused them to engage as they please in activities that are damaging the public order and disruptive of the peace at assemblies, processions or demonstrations.[40]

Whatever Justice Yueng was attempting to articulate through this passage, it is difficult to say that it upholds the principles of judicial independence. After all, it displays bias against the three defendants in this case and potential bias against any future defendants likely to come before the court in civil disobedience scenarios. And given that this judgment came from the Court of Appeal, it makes an especially strong statement to the lower courts. Additionally, Justice Poon wrote that, although the defendants themselves did not commit any violent acts, they should have foreseen violence erupting between the police and protesters. But even with passages like this present in the judgment, many in the legal community still set out to protect the courts, acting as if the court's hands were tied on whether to enhance the sentences, which they certainly were not; the Court of Appeal did this through their own volition.

Although there was criticism of the courts during this incident, much of it was based around legitimate criticism of how the judiciary and the criminal justice process was operating and whether the judges should have allowed the appeal. A good deal of it merely questioned whether the legal system was

[40] *Secretary for Justice v Wong Chi Fung and Others* [2017] HKCA 320, para 6 (Yueng).

operating correctly. And that, of course, is always a legitimate question to ask. Thus, if the three-stage test is taken into consideration, the criticism did not violate the rule of law. There were some accusations that the courts were acting politically or unreasonably, but there may have been good reasons for that. In fact, this is a case where the judiciary was lucky that the legal community mostly sprung to their defence. In the midst of a highly questionable increase in the youngsters' penalties and some suspicious statements from the bench, many legal scholars and others protected the judiciary, attempting to pile criticism on the Justice Minister. Of course, the Minister's actions are what sparked the review, but it was the review itself, not Mr Yuen, that increased the penalties of the three youths.

The Conviction of Police Officers for Assault During Occupy Central

During the Occupy Central Movement, a video emerged of a man being beaten by a number of police officers. The officers involved were eventually charged and, in February 2017, the Hong Kong District Court sentenced seven local policemen to prison terms of two years (the original charge against the officers was grievous bodily harm, which is a more serious offence, but this was reduced to assault).[41] The judge in the case, David Dufton, also lowered the original sentence by six months because of the police officers' service to the community and the intensity of the conditions that they were policing in. But when the judgment was given, a tidal wave of criticism followed. The judge was labelled a 'yellow heart'[42] – implying that he was sympathetic to the Umbrella Movement – and also a 'dog'.[43] Further, his validity as a decision maker was questioned, as he was deemed to be a 'foreign' judge who may hold 'allegiance to other sovereigns'.[44] Of course, the Basic Law allows for foreign judges to partake in adjudication throughout Hong Kong courts, as noted above.[45] Nevertheless, the suggestion that Mr Dufton's ethnicity should not have allowed him to decide this case, given that he was not of Chinese or Hong Kong descent, raises interesting questions about court criticism and the operation of law more generally.

[41] J Siu and E Lee, 'Outrage at two-year prison terms for Hong Kong policemen who beat up political activist' (17 February 2017) *South China Morning Post*. Available at: www.scmp.com/news/hong-kong/law-crime/article/2071703/two-years-jail-seven-policemen-who-beat-occupy-activist-ken.

[42] C Leung and T Cheung, 'Hong Kong lawmaker brands British judge a "yellow heart" after seven policemen are jailed' (17 February 2017) *South China Morning Post*. Available at: www.scmp.com/news/hong-kong/law-crime/article/2071853/hong-kong-lawmaker-brands-british-judge-yellow-heart-after.

[43] E Tong, 'HKFP Person of the Month, February 2017: Judge David Dufton of the Ken Tsang assault case' (1 March 2017) *Hong Kong Foreign Press*. Available at: www.hongkongfp.com/2017/03/01/hkfp-person-month-february-2017-judge-david-dufton-ken-tsang-assault-case/.

[44] C Lau and N Kang-chung, 'Criticism over judges' nationality unhelpful and disappointing, expatriate judge in Hong Kong says' (30 May 2017) *South China Morning Post*. Available at: www.scmp.com/news/hong-kong/law-crime/article/2096143/criticism-over-judges-nationality-unhelpful-and.

[45] HK Basic Law, arts 82 and 92

The backlash against the ruling displayed strong evidence that it crossed the bounds of acceptability under the rule of law test. The first criterion targeted, was definitely met. Dufton was the only judge sitting on the case and he was clearly targeted. Regarding the second criterion, the labelling of the judge as a 'yellow heart' by a Hong Kong lawmaker crossed the line, as there was nothing written in the judgment (nor in Mr Dufton's extra-legal activities) to suggest that he was sympathetic to the Umbrella Movement. In terms of the third criterion, it seems clear that the criticism of Judge Dufton as 'foreign' was a genuine attempt to undermine his legitimacy as a decision maker. It implies that a Hong Kong or Chinese judge would have come to a different result and that 'foreign' judges should not be allowed to sit on Hong Kong courts. But if concern over 'foreign judges' was to be levied, then it should have been levied at the Basic Law itself, which explicitly allows foreign judges to adjudicate Hong Kong cases, not at Mr Dufton. By raising Mr Dufton's ethnicity into such a prominent issue, his validity as a decision-making authority was challenged. Thus, all three elements of the test were fulfilled and the criticism went beyond the bounds of the rule of law.

Digesting Hong Kong's Court Criticism

Hong Kong's court criticism is interesting and relevant because it highlights the relationship between the cultural aspects of law and legal study and the more practical aspects of how the law operates. To those criticising the use of 'foreign' judges within Hong Kong, the idea that inclusion in a wider society or culture impacts upon judicial philosophy is inherently intertwined. Such cultural values become absorbed by those judging, who then pass on those values in their judgments and application of the law. Conversely, those who see the use of 'foreign' judges as acceptable – not just because their use is written into the Basic Law – may subscribe to a more principled operation of judicial independence: whether or not judges are 'foreign' is unlikely to change the result of any application of law.

There is little doubt that Hong Kong is currently going through a period of transition, as the 1997 handover is now over two decades old and the PRC has begun to assert its authority through interpretations of the Basic Law and in other ways. Thus, the use of 'foreign' judges contains multiple meanings and functions. For some it portrays judicial independence at one of the deepest levels possible, as even foreign judges are able to adjudicate issues in the territory and help uphold rule of law. It also connects to Hong Kong's history as a British colony, which has significantly influenced its legal system. One only has to watch the opening of the legal year in Hong Kong to see the bagpipes being played and the use of wigs for judges to ascertain its origins and connections to the UK. But many argue that, given the handover to PRC rule, this connection to the UK should no longer be maintained. Of course, Hong Kong is supposed to be operating on a 'one country, two systems' framework, but whether and how the use of foreign judges fits into that framework is debateable. And it seems increasingly clear that the protections provided by the Basic Law are limited.

Given the controversial cases the Hong Kong courts have heard over the past few years, the increase in judicial criticism remains unsurprising. Concerns regarding the integrity and impartiality of the system are bound to be aired by those who think that the courts simply got it wrong. The real threat for Hong Kong is that the rule of law is so dominant and the role of democracy is relatively weak. Any criticism traversing the bounds of acceptability is a much larger threat than normal: the system simply cannot cope with both democracy and the rule of law in disarray. As Geoffrey Ma said in his January 2020 comments:

> The rule of law is rightly cherished by the community, and is the foundation of a cohesive society. We must all do our best to preserve it, and to treasure it. Because once damaged, this is not something from which our community can easily recover.[46]

JUDICIAL CRITICISM IN A STABLE DEMOCRACY: TAIWAN

Taiwan is a relatively young but stable democracy that underwent a transition to democratisation in the 1980s and 1990s. The president and legislature are fully elected by the general public. The country has a commitment to liberal constitutional principles, eg, freedom of speech, rule of law, etc. and it has a similar judicial structure and commitment to judicial independence as other constitutional democracies. Taiwan's Constitutional Court has been issuing interpretations since 1949. Its institutional stature and influence has grown throughout the years, both from the sometimes-bullish insistence within its own jurisprudence[47] and also from the respect with which its judgments have been received both inside and outside Taiwan. Given Taiwan's commitment to democracy and the rule of law, the country has a young but stable foundation. That being said, judicial reform, the quality of justice and the performance of the legal system more generally are all hot-button and highly contested issues that are frequently debated.[48]

In Taiwan, a common expression among those criticising the judiciary is the phrase: *kong long fa guan*, or 'dinosaur judge'.[49] This label is often given to one specific judge but can also be applied more generally to the judiciary as a whole. Originally used to refer to a judge that was 'out of touch', the label has

[46] SCMP YouTube Channel, n 29 above.

[47] See, eg, BC Jones, 'Assessing the Constitutionality of Legislation: Constitutional Review in Taiwan's Legislative Yuan' 23(2) *Asia Pacific Law Review* 37, 48–51.

[48] N Chisholm, *Judicial Reform in Taiwan: Democratization and the Diffusion of Law* (2019).

[49] People in Taiwan also use 'baby judge' (娃娃法官) and 'pacifier, comforter judge' (奶嘴法官), which are referring to the same thing.

expanded into a catch-all for various complaints, often focusing on judges being: rash, biased, corrupt, incompetent and even brutal to court participants.[50] One recent Control Yuan official even cited three different types of 'dinosaur judge' that he was going to focus on in terms of judicial reform: 'those who bend the law to punish pan-green camp politicians, [those who] shield pan-blue camp members, and [those who] protect the Chinese Nationalist Party's (KMT) illegally acquired assets'.[51] Describing efforts to update the Taiwanese judicial system, one scholar recently noted that Taiwan was 'moving from dinosaur to dynamism'.[52] Thus, as much as the phrase is entrenched in the cultural lexicon, these examples also demonstrate that its use is still evolving.

I analysed two separate incidents to investigate court criticism in Taiwan: the legal case regarding the leaders of the Sunflower Movement and the period just before and after the Constitutional Court decision on same-sex marriage. These were both high-profile events and intensive periods of court-focused activity. Regarding the first, the Sunflowers had many supporters in Taiwan, but also had some bitter enemies.[53] The latter believed their dramatic actions deserved punishment. Also around this time, the Constitutional Court agreed to hear a case regarding same-sex marriage, which heightened the tension of an already court-focused public.

The Sunflower Movement Leaders

The Taiwan Sunflower Movement began on 18 March and lasted 23 days. Protestors occupied the main legislative chamber of Taiwan's Legislative Yuan, effectively halting all work by the legislature.[54] Given the prominence and scale of the protests, after the occupation 22 Sunflower Movement participants, including prominent leaders Lin Fei-fan (林飛帆), Chen Wei-ting (陳為廷), Huang Kuo-chang (黃國昌) and Wei Yang (魏揚), were charged with various crimes such as: incitement to commit an offence, obstruction of police officers, etc. On 31 March 2017, the Taipei District Court acquitted all 22 participants. The court studied and cited various theories and intricacies around civil disobedience so that they were better able to discern the arguments for and against the

[50] CF Wu and S Hsiao, 'Biased judges with bad attitudes are dinosaurs, head of reform group says' (7 May 2019) *Taipei Times*. Available at: www.taipeitimes.com/News/taiwan/archives/2019/05/07/2003714706.

[51] 'INTERVIEW: Chen eyes fair fight against "dinosaur judges"' (30 January 2018) *Taipei Times*. Available at: www.taipeitimes.com/News/taiwan/archives/2018/01/30/2003686686/1.

[52] MK Lewis, 'Forging Taiwan's Legal Identity' (2019) 44 *Brooklyn Journal of International Law* 489, 492.

[53] HHM Hsiao and PS Wan, 'The student-led movements of 2014 and public opinion: A comparison of Taiwan and Hong Kong' (2018) 3(1) *Asian Journal of Comparative Politics* 61.

[54] For more information on the protests, see BC Jones, *Law and Politics of the Taiwan Sunflower and Hong Kong Umbrella Movements* (2017).

leaders' actions. Ultimately, all those involved were acquitted. This decision was also upheld by the High Court on 13 March 2018.[55]

Close to three years after the controversial Movement took place, it may come as no surprise that many high-level politicians and other officials reacted mildly to the District and High Court judgments. But there were some unfavourable comments. KMT Vice Chairman Hau Lung-bin said that the decision ran counter to public approval and rhetorically asked, 'How many legal boundaries can a person be allowed to cross in the name of [upholding their] political beliefs?', further suggesting that this decision would probably lead to the occupation of other government buildings.[56] Another KMT Legislator, Lin Wei-chou, expressed that the judiciary must have the same standard for all types of civil disobedience and that faith in the judiciary needed to be restored.[57] The Tsai administration's Minister of Justice, Chiu Tai-San, also expressed disapproval with the court's decision and the Taipei Police force said that they were worried about its impact on the rule of law.[58] One journalist even noted: 'Obviously, the judiciary is and should be in theory independent of political pressures, but judicial rulings are very clearly influenced by political sentiment in Taiwan'.[59]

Three years after the Movement took place, perhaps we would not expect to see passionate reactions to the acquittal of the Sunflower leaders. That being said, although the criticism here was less harsh than during the same-sex marriage decision, it also followed some of the same patterns. None of it seemed focused on one or two individual judges; much of it concerned the wider implications of the decision for its impact on things such as the rule of law and the perceived independence of the courts. According to the three-stage test, these criticisms do not traverse the rule of law; in fact, it is arguable that they even seek to uphold it.

Taiwan's Same-Sex Marriage Case[60]

In 2017 Taiwan's Constitutional Court issued a landmark ruling on same-sex marriage,[61] paving the way for Taiwan to become the first country in Asia to

[55] 'High court upholds acquittal of Sunflower Movement leaders' (13 March 2018) *Focus Taiwan*. Available at: https://focustaiwan.tw/politics/201803130016.

[56] J Pan, 'Sunflower leaders, lawyer hail court ruling' (1 April 2017) *Taipei Times*. Available at: www.taipeitimes.com/News/front/archives/2017/04/01/2003667851.

[57] Ibid.

[58] B Hoie, 'Not guilty verdict upheld for sunflower movement protesters after appeal by prosecutors' (14 March 2018) *New Bloom*. Available at: https://newbloommag.net/2018/03/14/second-ruling-sunflower/.

[59] Ibid.

[60] For an excellent summary and analysis of this case, see Kuan Hsiaowei's chapter in this collection: 'Taiwan's Civil Code v Special Law Debate'.

[61] Taiwan Constitutional Court, Interpretation No 748.

allow such a practice.[62] However, the case was extremely controversial and Taiwan's Constitutional Court received a heavy amount of criticism both before and after the decision was issued. Effectively, the judgment said that same-sex marriage was an equality issue and that the legislature must pass an effective form of union for same-sex couples to remedy the situation within two years. If it failed to do this, then the Court would intervene. Although accusations of 'legislating from the bench' were thrown at the justices, the attacks that I found from opponents did not get much more personal and tended to concentrate on appropriate uses of judicial power. In one account, a member of an NGO stated: 'Judicial power should always be passive and reactive. It should wait for the Legislative Yuan to introduce a bill and be approved to become law. After that, the Council of Grand Justices makes a legal interpretation. This is the proper and legal way to go about it'.[63] This was indicative of the type of criticism the justices faced.

There was some stronger condemnation of the Court both before and after the decision. Legal experts noted that the group of justices making the decision was 'the most liberal group ever', given President Tsai's seven appointments to the Council. After the decision, which sparked fury in some quarters, chants of 'shame on the judiciary', 'the judicial process is unfair' and 'Justice is dead and buried' could be heard in the streets.[64] One personal attack noted was the chanting of 'down with the Judicial Yuan president', which was followed by 'down with Tsai Ing-Wen'.[65] There were even suggestions that the Justices had 'rigged the process' and pleas from some that a probe into the proceedings should be launched.[66] A few interest groups were especially harsh in their responses to the ruling, suggesting that 'ghost money' be thrown at the Judicial Yuan, that the justices had let 'politics override the law', and that the Court's members should be investigated for dereliction of duty.[67] However the response from Taiwan's politicians were not as divisive; all sides seemed to react positively or neutrally to the judgment.[68] Nonetheless, scholars have noted that Taiwan's Constitutional Court has been especially receptive to social movements and that they have come to respond favourably to them.[69] On that note, another critic of the decision noted: 'The grand justices should not become spokespeople for movements that

[62] MS Ho, 'Taiwan's Road to Marriage Equality: Politics of Legalizing Same-sex Marriage' (2019) 238 *The China Quarterly* 482.

[63] J Pan, 'Groups oppose legalizing same-sex marriage' (10 May 2017) *Taipei Times*. Available at: www.taipeitimes.com/News/taiwan/archives/2017/05/10/2003670298.

[64] J Pan, 'Same-sex marriage: Same-sex marriage decision sparks fury' (25 May 2017) *Taipei Times*. Available at: www.taipeitimes.com/News/taiwan/archives/2017/05/25/2003671254.

[65] Ibid.

[66] Ibid.

[67] 'Group calls for ghost money to be thrown at judiciary' (26 May 2017) *Taipei Times*. Available at: www.taipeitimes.com/News/taiwan/archives/2017/05/26/2003671315.

[68] WH Chen, 'Same-sex Marriage: Politicians praise ruling, undecided on next step' (25 May 2017) *Taipei Times*. Available at: www.taipeitimes.com/News/front/archives/2017/05/25/2003671246/1.

[69] Ho, n 62 above.

advocate social causes. The ruling shows our justice system is biased toward certain groups'.[70]

Analysing the court criticism on the whole, the same-sex marriage judgment produced some heavy condemnation and even some ominous suggestions that the Justices should be investigated. However, there was no sustained campaign or personal attacks on specific members of the Court, or any attempt to undermine or de-legitimise a specific justice or justices. The criticisms voiced often considered the role of law and of the courts and whether judges should be intervening in something that many viewed as a legislative, rather than a judicial, issue. These concerns are not unreasonable; they are similar to those in other jurisdictions regarding the issue. The consensus response from Taiwanese legislators and other prominent officials were also relatively mild. Ultimately, the criticism did not violate the three-stage test and was within the bounds of the rule of law.

Digesting Taiwan's Court Criticism

Just as Hong Kong's criticism of 'foreign judges' connects to culture and the impact that it may have on judicial philosophy, so too does Taiwan's criticism of 'dinosaur judges'. Labelling a judge in this way suggests some type of disconnect from the culture in which the judge is doing the adjudicating, as if the judges are living in their own bubble or are somehow disconnected from the wider society and the values that it holds. Thus, both criticisms connect to significant and age-old questions regarding law and judging: How much does the law stand independent of culture? Is being engaged in the culture a necessity for judges in their application of the law?

But Taiwan's court criticism is important for a couple of other reasons. First, it often coalesced around the proper roles and functions of constitutional actors and in some sense, touches on separation of powers issues. To some this may seem unsettling, as a written constitution is supposed to delineate these spheres of activity. In actuality, wide scope exists in democracies for difficult and increasingly sophisticated problems to be resolved through both judicial and extra-judicial means. Determining which branch or what mechanisms may resolve these issues is part of a healthy democratic debate. This type of deliberative debate, eg whether certain judgments uphold or hinder the rule of law and whether the legislature or the courts should provide rights to citizens, is what Taiwan displayed in the two examples above. Additionally, it is also significant that – even though Taiwan's issues were extremely controversial – the criticism did not fall foul of the rule of law.

[70] Pan, n 64 above.

CONCLUSION

There is little doubt that some judicial criticism threatens the rule of law, but journalists, scholars and others need to be cautious in waving this banner. Too much clamour about this type of speech could desensitise citizens as to its importance and also provides the impression that any court criticism – even tough but legitimate criticism – violates the rule of law. This chapter has attempted to add some sophistication to such an assessment. After all, if we are going to take judicial criticism seriously, then we must establish a more precise method of determining acceptability.

The examples of court criticism presented in this chapter reveal some important types of criticism, where judiciaries have been put under significant pressure following major political and cultural incidents. Two jurisdictions in East Asia were used to help understand what types of criticism may arise and how some speech may be helpful and other speech harmful. The types of criticism that took place in Taiwan reveal a democracy attempting to harmonise difficult cultural and political issues while debating how best to resolve difficult issues. Taiwan's cultural understanding of the 'dinosaur judge' has changed throughout the years, but its continued use demonstrates that, even in healthy democracies, the nuanced world of law often struggles to explain its decisions to citizens. Additionally, as some scholars have pointed out, Taiwan's highest court has been especially receptive to social movements, thus perhaps avoiding the 'dinosaur judge' label. Overall, the criticism that came forward in Taiwan was often focused around legitimate concerns regarding the function and operation of the judiciary within the constitutional state, a debate which is certainly acceptable.

Hong Kong's court criticism was different and, at times, represented a frustrated 'lashing out' towards the judiciary. This was certainly the case in relation to 'foreign judges', which the Basic Law explicitly allows. Other times, an anxious legal community already concerned about the damage being done to the rule of law refused to condemn judges for highly questionable statements being made from the bench. Just as some court criticism may cross the line of acceptability, a lack of holding judges to account for their decisions also threatens the rule of law.

Far from being unwelcome speech, this chapter has also highlighted that appropriate judicial criticism is one way of holding the judiciary accountable. As Shetreet and Turenne note: 'Judicial accountability is no longer simply construed as accountability to other judges as a group sharing an ethos, particular values and skills, and through decision making, by way of appeal and review'.[71] Court criticism has the potential to highlight injustice, ensure judicial

[71] Shetreet and Turenne, n 16 above, 429.

independence, and allow for increased societal debate on prominent issues. Such statements may even enhance the rule of law, as it brings into a sharper focus the delicate issues surrounding the operation of law and democracy. However, as this chapter set out to discern, there is a line between harsh criticism and criticism that violates the rule of law. The latter does not help democracy, and there remains little doubt that it also damages the rule of law.

5

Taiwan's 'Civil Code v Special Law' Debate in the Same-Sex Marriage Controversy: A Populist Threat to the Rule of Law?

HSIAOWEI KUAN*

INTRODUCTION

ON 30 NOVEMBER 2019, 75 per cent of the voters in Taiwan voted 'yes' on initiatives to restrict the definition of marriage in the Civil Code to a union between one man and one woman. This represented a political backlash against a decision made by the Constitutional Court in the form of Judicial Yuan Interpretation No 748 (JYI No 748). That decision decreed that Taiwan's Civil Code was unconstitutional because denying same-sex couples the right to get legally married constituted a violation of both the right to equality and the right to marry. The religious right in Taiwan launched a series of campaigns attempting to overrule JYI No 748 in order to try to prevent the Parliament from legalising same-sex marriage (SSM). These campaigns were similar to those seen in other democratic societies and were led by conservative activists who sought to hinder the progress that had been made in advancing the rights of homosexual persons. Theories of public policy, as well as empirical research, have suggested that the rights of minority groups are exceptionally vulnerable to the processes of referendum or initiative.[1] However, a campaign calling for legislative initiatives that would enclose a legislative principle at the statutory level, aimed at overruling a constitutional decision rendered at a higher

* Associate Professor, College of Law, National Taipei University, Taiwan.

[1] B Gamble, 'Putting Civil Rights to a Popular Vote' (1997) 41 *American Journal of Political Science* 245, 249. See also K Redfield-Ortiz, 'Government by the People for the People-Representative Democracy, Direct Democracy and the Unfinished Struggle for Gay Rights' (2011) 43 *Arizona State Law Journal* 1367.

level, was something previously unheard of in comparative practices.[2] Evidence shows that religious activists clearly knew that even if the initiatives they were proposing passed the threshold, they would not supersede the constitutional decision; yet they still devoted considerable resources to the campaign anyway. In the ensuing campaign, which lasted almost a year, religious activists first manipulated the pre-existing controversy over 'the Civil Code vs Special Law' in Taiwan's SSM debate. They purposely designed propositions with ambiguous wording and misled voters to support their stand. Most importantly, they stirred up popular hostility toward the judiciary by sewing the idea of adversity between 'the people' and 'the judicial elite' in the public consciousness, thereby posing a threat to constitutionalism and the rule of law. The tactics adopted in the religious Right's campaign were based on an ideology of populism.[3]

Matthijs Rooduijn argues that populists in different times and places have had four common characteristics: (1) they emphasise the central position of the people; (2) they criticise the elite; (3) they perceive the people as a homogeneous entity; and (4) they claim a serious crisis exists.[4] These characteristics can all be readily identified in the religious right's campaign. By carefully examining the way in which the campaign unfolded, this chapter explores and answers the following questions: How did the campaigners against SSM set their agenda? How did they use the oft-romanticised political mechanism of popular voting to advance their goals? How did they capitalise on the ambiguity of JYI No 748 to convince the authorities to allow them to begin their campaign? How did they design the initiative propositions with wording that appeared to mean one thing, but had another hidden meaning underneath? After the initiatives passed the legal threshold, what did the government and the Parliament do to strike a balance between the demands of the people and the Constitutional Court's decision? Did this process jeopardise the rule of law in Taiwan? What lessons can be learned from this campaign? To answer these questions, we first need to understand why popular voting has played a unique role in Taiwan's democracy.

[2] A former Justice, Yung-chin Su, who was a vocal scholar opposing the enactment of the Popular Voting Act, said in the press interview that a campaign for legislative initiatives at the level of a statute in order to overrule a constitutional decision at higher level was something unheard of in comparative practices. See Wei-chi Lo, 'Can the Anti-Same-sex marriage Initiatives Overrule the Interpretation made by the Constitutional Court? Yung-chin Su said the Justices Have the Final Say' (25 December 2017) *Storm Media*, www.storm.mg/article/376727.

[3] Cas Mudde defined popularism as an ideology or political movement that 'consider society to be ultimately separated into two homogeneous and antagonistic groups, the pure people versus the corrupt elite, and which argues that politics should be an expression of the general will of the people'. See Cas Mudde, 'The Populist Zeitgeist' (2004) 39 *Government and Opposition* 541, 543.

[4] M Rooduijnatthijs, 'The Nucleus of Populism: In Search of the Lowest Common Denominator' (2014) 49(4) *Government and Opposition* 572.

THE CONTROVERSY OVER POPULAR VOTING UNDER THE SHADOW OF CHINA

Direct Democracy in the ROC Constitution

The original design of the ROC Constitution (hereinafter, the Constitution) took a cautious and restrictive attitude towards whether citizens could take legislative or public decision-making power into their own hands. Article 17 of the Constitution explicitly guarantees the right to vote on both referendums and legislative initiatives. However, it should be noted that the Constitutional framers did not give the right to vote on national policy directly to the people. Instead, only the National Assembly could exercise the 'right' of referendum and initiative at the national level. In the framers' minds, although the members of the National Assembly were not ordinary citizens, they did form part of the mechanism designed to exercise direct democracy. In addition, the National Assembly cannot exercise the right to cast popular votes until a threshold is met whereby one-half of the counties in the nation have held referendums or initiatives, the exercise of which, according to Article 136 of the Constitution, shall be prescribed by law. In keeping with the oppression of political freedom during the Martial Law era, the ruling Kuomintang (KMT) had no intention of enacting any law that would grant citizens the right to cast ballots on referendums and legislative initiatives.

The Partisan Debate on the Legalisation of Popular Voting

In Western countries, it can be argued that the driving force behind the call for popular suffrage came from populist and progressive movements that arose from a distrust of government and a desire to restore the function of agenda-setting to the people.[5] In Taiwan, however, the debate regarding popular voting has been strongly associated with the political debate about the issue of unification and independence (*tong du*, 統獨). Under the shadow of Communist China, the KMT reckoned that the constructed status quo, ie one sovereign state (the Republic of China) with two areas (Mainland China and Taiwan), best served the party's interests while ruling the island. While the eventual lifting of Martial Law saw the rise of oppositional movements and opened the door to the first direct national election in 1992, the authoritarian government still considered the concept of popular voting taboo. For the KMT elites and its supporters, granting the right to popular voting was equivalent to the realisation of Taiwan's independence as a separate state.[6] As a result, throughout the

[5] KP Miller, 'Constraining Populism: The Real Challenge of Initiative Reform' (2001) 41 *Santa Clara Law Review* 1037, 1039–1045.

[6] CY Tseng, 'Referendum in Taiwan: System and Vision' (2012) 10 *The Journal of Chinese Public Administration* 243, 250; H Chi, 'Stop Advocating Taiwan Independence through Referendum' (2008) 208 *Straits Review Monthly* 34, 36.

intervening decades, the controversy over the legalisation of popular voting in Taiwan has been closely tied to the debate about Taiwan's independence from or unification with China. This linkage has made the former controversy even more partisan and adversarial than it might have been otherwise. On the one hand, after 1990, the most zealous advocates of taking back people's right to vote on referendums and initiatives were groups promoting Taiwan's independence.[7] They viewed popular voting as the most direct way for people who actually resided on the island to exercise popular sovereignty and criticised the constitutional framework that was established after constitutional amendment for recognising what they saw as fictitious sovereignty over the territory of mainland China. On the other hand, the opposition Democratic Progressive Party (DPP) also envisaged popular voting as an effective way to garner popular support for its causes, such as 'Going Back to the UN',[8] 'Taiwan for WHO',[9] 'Taiwan's New Constitution',[10] and 'Anti-Nuclear Plant No 4'.[11] Some KMT supporters thus called popular voting 'DPP's memorial shrine' (*shen chu pai*, 神主牌).[12]

Constitutional Petition Against the Popular Vote Act

Political promotion of these causes allowed the DPP to claim the moral high ground and, in turn, helped to gain public support for the enactment of the 'Popular Vote Act' (PVA). Recognising that public demand for the new law was unstoppable, the KMT and the People First Party (PFP) took the initiative to propose counter bills, which included procedures that were comparatively more restrictive than the proposed legislation. Collaboration between the KMT and PFP ensured that a more restrictive version of the PVA was passed by a majority vote in Taiwan's parliament on 31 December 2003. This caused indignation among advocates of popular voting and the DPP. The party's legislators subsequently filed a petition with the Constitutional Court in January 2004, requesting that the Justices strike down the newly enacted PVA. The argument underpinning the constitutional petition was twofold. First, the petitioners argued that the PVA's granting of power to propose referendums to parliament was repugnant to the constitutional design of representative democracy and constituted an encroachment on administrative power. Second, the petitioners zeroed in on the PVA's creation of a review agency – the National Referendum

[7] PC Chen, TR Chai, CL Lin, YM Hsu, IC Chen, CY Tseng, IC Lai, YL Huang, KJ Chen and CL Li, 'Democracy All the Way: Referendum Movement in Taiwan' (2007) 7 *Chung Hua Journal of Humanities and Social Sciences* 210, 211.

[8] Tseng, n 6 above, 138.

[9] Ibid, 142.

[10] Ibid, 143–144.

[11] Ibid, 141.

[12] LC Chang, YC Su, LP Nan, CC Yang and LW Cheng, 'Referendum? Populism? Please Follow the Conscience and Make Correct Decision' (2003) 152 *Straits Review Monthly* 56, 60.

Review Committee (NRRC) – and its bestowal of the legal authority to conduct substantive scrutiny of proposed referendums and initiatives. According to the PVA, the NRRC members were to be recommended by all parties in proportion to the number of seats held by each party caucus in the parliament and were appointed by the President upon nomination. The Premier had no say in the nomination of these candidates for NRRC posts and was obliged to accept the nominations. The petitioners argued that the aforementioned procedure for nominations and appointments undermined the administrative power of personnel appointments, which was the exclusive purview of the government's Administrative branch.

The case was before the Constitutional Court for four years before the Justices finally rendered their decision on 11 July 2008, in the form of Judicial Yuan Interpretation No 645 (JYI No 645). The Justices found the first argument unconvincing, holding that parliament's enactment of the PVA was squarely within its legislative power and did not run contrary to the fundamental premise that Taiwan's constitutional system is based on representative democracy. In the Justices' reasoning, as long as the law provides 'the people with a channel to express directly their opinions on important policies' and can assist 'the people in exercising their rights of initiative and referendum, it is certainly not contrary to the Constitution'. As to the second argument, the constitutional challenge to the composition of the NRRC and the appointment of its members, the Justices found that the relevant provisions were indeed unconstitutional. They opined that the NRRC was part and parcel of the government's executive power, therefore the power to make decisions concerning the actual personnel structure thereof, including staff officers and political appointees, was properly conferred by law on the Administrative Yuan. They noted that the authority to appoint personnel is an indispensable prerequisite for the satisfactory performance of the functions of the executive power in a country that values the rule of law. Since the NRRC was an internal organisation of the Administrative branch, it was beyond dispute that the Administrative Yuan should have the power to make decisions on the appointment of NRRC members.

Breaking the Birdcage

For over a decade, the PVA led to popular voting in Taiwan being mockingly referred to as 'Popular Voting in The Birdcage'. From the enactment of the PVA in 2003 to its first revision in January 2018, all six of the propositions put to referendums at the national level failed.[13] The existence of a high double threshold requiring a minimum 50 per cent voter turnout threshold, in addition to

[13] The list of the six propositions during this era can be found on the website of the Central Election Committee (see Referendums Profile, the Central Election Commission, Taiwan www.cec.gov.tw/english/cms/rProfile.

50 per cent support to carry a referendum, made the passage of any such referendum or initiative extremely difficult, if not impossible. In fact, many propositions never even made it to the voting stage because they were not approved by the NRRC. Indeed, public distrust of parliament's handling of a trade agreement with China initially triggered the Sunflower Movement in 2014.[14] In the post-Sunflower era, the overarching idea of comprehensive political reform by putting the power back in the people's hands (還權於民) was in tune with the demand for an overall reform of the PVA from both major political parties and also from vocal elements of civil society.[15]

In March 2016, the newly founded New Power Party (NPP), committed to reforming Taiwan's problematic representative democracy, proposed a Bill to revise 'the 'birdcage' Popular Voting Act'. However, it took almost two more years for legislators from different parties to reach an agreement on the specific issues in the Bill. The result was a compromise which lowered the threshold for the number of signatures required for a referendum to take place and also lowered the threshold for passage. The NPP bill not only lowered the passage threshold to a simple majority of voters;[16] the new threshold for the outcome of the vote to be legally binding was set at just 25 per cent of eligible voters, as opposed to the previous 50 per cent.[17] The impact of lowering the thresholds was twofold. First, as the signature requirement threshold was set at 0.01 per cent of all eligible voters in the first stage (as opposed to 0.2 per cent originally) and 1.5 per cent of eligible voters in the second stage (as opposed to the original 5 per cent), proposals in the form of a ballot question became more accessible

[14] About the history of Taiwan's Sunflower Movement and its aftermath, see BC Jones and YT Su, 'Confrontational Contestation and Democratic Compromise' in BC Jones (ed), *Law and Politics of the Taiwan Sunflower and Hong Kong Umbrella Movements* (2017).

[15] For a similar opinion, see JR Yeh 'Marching Towards Civic Constitutionalism with Sunflowers' in BC Jones (ed), *Law and Politics of the Taiwan Sunflower and Hong Kong Umbrella Movements* (2017).

[16] The revised Article 29 of the PVA provides: 'with regard to the result of voting for a proposal of referendum, if valid ballots of assent are more than ballots of dissent and reach 1/4 of eligible voters, the proposal is adopted. If valid ballots of assent are less than ballots of dissent or do not reach the quantity prescribed in the preceding Paragraph, the proposal is vetoed'.

[17] According to Article 30 of the PVA, if a proposal passes the threshold, the relevant government authorities are legally bound in the following fashion:

1. For the proposal of referendum of a statute or municipal ordinance, the original statute or ordinance will be repealed from the third day counted from the day of the Central Election Commission announces the result.
2. For a proposal of initiative of the legislative principles for a statute or municipal ordinance, the Executive Yuan or the municipal or county (city) government shall propose a statute or municipal ordinance based on the legislative principle within three months and send it to the Legislative Yuan or the municipal or county (city) council for deliberation. The Legislative Yuan or the municipal or county (city) council shall complete the procedure of deliberation before the adjournment of the next session.
3. For a proposal of referendum on a policy of paramount importance, the President or the authority shall take the necessary measures to implement the policy.
4. For a Constitutional referendum, the Legislative Yuan shall advise the President to grant assent to the amended constitutional provision.

for the people. What is more, after the PVA was successfully revised in 2018, the ballot questions became more diversified and less party orientated. Among the 16 propositions that have been put to public vote (as of October 2020), before the revision, four propositions (Propositions No 1, 2, 5 and 6) related to Taiwan's relationship with China or were about Taiwan's international status; but only one proposition (Proposition No 13) was related to Taiwan's status or the relationship with China after the revision. Secondly, the lower threshold for passage meant the initiative to give policy-making power to the people was no longer just an empty promise. This is evidenced by the fact that seven out of the 16 propositions which met the threshold after 2018 were passed.

SAME-SEX MARRIAGE ON THE BALLOT

Perhaps it never occurred to reformists and advocates of popular voting that the very thing they were vociferously calling for – ballot voting – would one day be used as a tool in a campaign against the civil rights of a minority group in Taiwan. However, just three weeks after the revised PVA's promulgation, the Coalition for the Happiness of our Next Generation (下一代幸福聯盟, CHNG), a group opposed to same-sex marriage and composed of conservative parents with evangelical leanings,[18] successfully collected enough signatures on a petition to meet the first threshold. The group's proposals were duly submitted to the Central Election Committee (CEC), which had become the competent authority in charge of national ballot voting after the NRRC was abolished in 2018. When the first round of ballot casting based on the revised PVA was held in November 2018, two out of the ten propositions (Propositions 12 and 14) involved the law on same-sex marriage, while two others dealt with inclusion of LGBT-related materials in school educational curricula (Propositions 11 and 15).

POPULAR VOTING AS A STRATEGY FOR THE CAMPAIGN TO OPPOSE SAME-SEX MARRIAGE

The vote in 2018 was not the first time a group opposed to same-sex marriage had promoted its cause through a ballot campaign. In 2013, the Taiwan Alliance to Promote Civil Partnership Rights (TAPCPR) had publicised a 'Bill for Diverse Forms of Families' (多元成家法案), which sought to legalise same-sex marriage, grant legal recognition to civil partnerships among both heterosexuals and homosexuals and expand the legal rights of members of multiple families. The proposal of this bill sparked a backlash, led by the religious Right, against the social and legal reform of the traditional family. The three marriage/family

[18] YC Kao, 'Organizing Transnational Moral Conservatism: How US Christian and Taiwanese "Pro-Family" Movements Converge, Diverge, and Collide' (DPhil thesis, Rutgers University 2018) 90.

reform components not only put the bill squarely in the sights of conservative religious groups, but also fuelled their distrust of the political elite. In September 2015, the first Christian political party in Taiwan, the Faith and Hope League (信望盟, FHL), was formed to fill the gap left by the breakdown of trust and collaboration between political parties and Christian conservatives.[19] Although the draft 'Bill for Diverse Forms of Families' had not reached the substantive review stage in parliament, its growing distrust of the political class prompted religious organisations to launch a pre-emptive strike at the Bill.

In November 2015, the FHL announced it was collecting signatures for a petition. Two months later, the group submitted the signed documents to the NRRC for approval. The draft proposition to be included on the ballot ticket asked: 'Do you agree that any change of the provisions regarding husband and wife, consanguineal relationships, and relationship-defined principles set forth in the Chapters of Marriage, Parents and Children, Guardianship, and Family, of the Family Part of the Civil Code, shall not be made without being approved by a referendum?' The wording of the proposition was confusing, in the sense that it essentially purported to block a road that had not yet been built. The law targeted by the proposition was only a draft at that stage, so could not be repealed. Instead, implementing a formidable procedural hurdle in the form of a referendum was seen as the only way to prevent the legislature from reviewing the Bill.

The NRRC rejected the aforementioned proposal in February of 2016 on the grounds that its wording was too obscure and it did not contain any specific legislative principle – the latter being required by the PVA for a proposed legislative initiative to be approved. Although the first round of the popular ballot campaign had failed, the fact that enough signatures had been collected to allow the petition to pass the threshold showcased the ability of religious organisations to flex their political muscle.

Believing that the 'silent majority' would stand firmly on its side, religious organisations began to be obsessed with the idea of pushing their anti-same-sex marriage agenda through by ballot. By November 2016, when religious groups organised a demonstration to oppose new draft bills to legalise same-sex marriage proposed by cross-partisan legislators,[20] the main framework for the anti-same-sex marriage movement –'Let Marriage and Family Matters be decided by the People' ('婚姻家庭 人民決定') – had been established.[21] In December 2016, legislators reached a consensus at the committee level for the first time and drafted a cross-party Bill for further partisan consultation. Worried that the elites of the ruling party would push the Bill through, the

[19] Ibid 95–96.

[20] HW Kuan, 'The Development of LGBT Rights in Democratic Taiwan: An Analysis from the Perspective of Law and Social Movements' (2019) Special Issue *Academia Sinica Law Journal* 551, 599.

[21] Coalition for the Happiness of our Next Generation, 'Let the Matters on Marriage and Family be Decided by the People' Urgent Mobilization Order' (10 November 2016).

religious Right again decided to rely on ballot voting in response to this new parliamentary challenge.

The populist discourse of the anti-same-sex marriage camp attempted to situate it on the side of the 'people', as opposed to the political elite. This carefully crafted ethos has since permeated the anti-same-sex marriage movement. When the revision of the PVA was discussed in Taiwan's parliament, religious Right groups welcomed the proposal to lower the thresholds. They stressed that popular sovereignty is the foundation of the Constitution and a well-designed popular voting system is the best way to allow the people to exercise their sovereignty, in addition to being a tool to constrain the power of the parliament. In addition, they asserted that important and controversial social issues should be decided by the people instead of by proxy, or, in other words, by the political elite,[22]

Opposition to the Judicial Elite's Role in Legalising Same-sex Marriage

Populist hostility toward the political elite from the religious right not only paints politicians as the enemy, but also espouses negative attitudes toward the judiciary. On 10 February 2017, the Judicial Yuan announced that the Constitutional Court would hold a public hearing on same-sex marriage on 24 March 2017. The CHNG subsequently expressed its strong opposition on multiple occasions, through a press conference and sit-ins outside the Judicial Yuan. The CHNG insisted that the Constitutional Court should undertake a fact-finding mission to decide whether homosexuality is a result of biological or environmental factors and to consider whether it might be a psychological illness.[23] In the press conference, self-proclaimed 'post-gay' protesters asserted that homosexuality can be 'cured' through proper therapy.[24] The CHNG contended not only that the definition of marriage should not be a matter for Constitutional review,[25] but also that it should not be decided by the Justices because the judiciary itself lacked democratic legitimacy.[26] The protesters reiterated that it should be left to the people to decide the core definition of marriage. They demanded that the Constitutional Court Justices refrain from interfering with their initiative calling for a popular vote on the definition of marriage. This initiative, which

[22] Coalition for the Happiness of our Next Generation, 'Let the Matters on Marriage and Family be Decided by the People' Coalition for the Happiness of our Next Generation Urges All Parties to Amend the "Popular Votes Act"' (11 May 2017).

[23] Coalition for the Happiness of our Next Generation, 'Children Should Not Become Guinea Pigs. Justices Should Undergo Facts Investigation to find Evidence with Regard to whether Homosexuality is Natural or Not' (10 February 2017).

[24] Coalition for the Happiness of our Next Generation, 'The Procedure of Constitutional Court was Seriously Prejudiced. The Definition of Marriage Shall be Decided by the People' (17 May 2017).

[25] CHNG, n 19 above.

[26] CHNG, n 20 above.

had already been launched, sought to restrict marriage to a union between one man and one woman. They admonished the Justices, 'not to side with the dominant minority by bullying the oppressed majority'. They further called for the Justices to respect the consensus of society and the people's right to democratic participation.[27] The religious Right's relentless mantra of leaving the matter of definition of marriage to a popular vote served to create the impression of a dichotomy between the judicial elite and the ordinary people.

The Constitutional Court rendered its decision on 24 May 2017. The Justices found that denying the right of two persons of the same sex to marry violated both their right to equality and their constitutional right to marry. The Justices gave the Parliament two years to amend the current law or to enact a new law to allow same-sex couples to marry. Otherwise, it was held that same-sex couples would automatically be allowed to register their marriages under the current framework. This ruling incensed the religious groups. Their immediate response to JYI No 748 was a noisy protest in front of the Judicial Yuan on the day the decision was announced, with demonstrators shouting slogans such as: 'The judicial elite shall not bully the mass majority!'[28] Group leaders claimed the public majority would never accept the alteration of the definition of marriage because of the decision of a few Justices. They openly questioned the neutrality and independence of the Constitutional Court, suggesting the whole process of Constitutional review had been a political farce staged by President Tsai Ing-wen, who had already made her stance in support of same-sex marriage legalisation clear. They also contended that the judiciary was biased in favour of the same-sex marriage camp and even accused the Justices of being spokespersons for same-sex marriage advocacy. The CHNG then wasted no time before announcing it was launching an initiative campaign to overrule the ruling of the Constitutional Court and take back the people's power to define marriage as a union between a man and a woman. The initiative campaign began on 25 May 2017, the day after JYI No 748 was issued.[29] The CHNG insisted that the majority's opinion was not sufficiently reflected in the process of Constitutional review. They argued that the people should have the right to participate in the policy-making process with regard to important issues. They further opined that if Taiwan was truly proud of its democratic success, the government should let the people fully participate in decisions about crucial issues that impinge on social and cultural development, such as same-sex marriage. Some of the arguments made by the CHNG were legitimate and could be rationally

[27] CHNG, n 20 above and Coalition for the Happiness of our Next Generation, 'CHNG: Justices Only Heard LGBT's Side of Testimony' (24 March 2017).

[28] Coalition for the Happiness of our Next Generation, 'Announcement in the Press Conference Regarding the Decision of the Case on Same-sex Marriage' (24 May 2017).

[29] Coalition for the Happiness of our Next Generation, 'CHNG Held Press Conference: Same-sex Marriage Shall be Decided by Popular Voting' (25 May 2017).

debated, but the rhetoric and tone in the distributed pamphlets and messages in the conservative community were more militant. This fiery rhetoric aimed to widen the dichotomy between the judicial elite and the majority of ordinary Taiwanese and stoke the level of confrontation and hostility to a fever pitch.

Linking the Proposition Against LGBT-Inclusive Education to the Proposition Against Same-sex Marriage

It is noteworthy that the strategy of the campaign against same-sex marriage in Taiwan has a unique defining feature. Namely, it is inseparable from the anti-LGBT inclusive education movement, in which the major driving force behind is conservative parents. One of the earliest causes of the anti-LGBT rights movement was the fight against LGBT-inclusive curricula. The first conservative mobilisation against LGBT civil rights at the national level occurred in 2011, when the True Love Alliance (TLA) was formed.[30] The Alliance aimed to put an end to the promotion of gender diversity and sexual diversity on school campuses. Although these efforts were not met with official success, the pitched ideological battle waged between progressive and conservative camps exposed the fact that the inclusive education activism was weak in grassroots mobilisation. The controversy also highlighted the extent to which Taiwanese parents were susceptible to manipulation tactics. Parents in contemporary Taiwan are extremely anxious about childrearing and education because of rapid transition in social values and economic restructure.[31] Therefore, when it comes to issues regarding children's education, these are more likely to raise concerns from parents. Thus, when the CHNG was established, the group's leadership craftily amalgamated two anti-LGBT-rights causes – anti-LGBT education and anti-same-sex marriage – into a single main priority. Under the guise of protecting the best interests of children, the CHNG stressed that legalisation of same-sex marriage would spell the ruin of Taiwan's youngest generation. Furthermore, they played on parents' insecurities, intimating that society occupied a precarious position at the edge of a slippery slope; if same-sex marriage were legalised, the curriculum would need to be adjusted accordingly, with children being 'turned into gays' as a result. The CHNG thus capitalised on parents' fears of increased homosexual behaviour, using it as a powerful motivational tool to mobilise its followers. A parallel, two-pronged framework was thus employed to attack LGBT education and same-sex marriage simultaneously. The natural analogy to 'Let Marriage and Family Matters be decided by the People ('婚姻家庭 人民決定')'

[30] Kao (n 18) 76.

[31] See generally PC Lan, *Struggling to Raise Children: Globalization, Parental Anxieties and Unequal Childhoods* (2019).

turned into: 'Let Matters of Education for Children be decided by the Parents ('子女教育 父母決定').' The emergence of the latter showed that a network of national and local parents' organisations had proven its ability to provide robust grassroots support for anti-same-sex marriage mobilisation.

Set against this background, it becomes clear why the movement to initiate a ballot proposition against same-sex marriage would be twinned with a similar one in opposition to LGBT and gender equity education and the promotion of sexual diversity on campuses, in the wake of JYI No 748. The announcement of the launch of a ballot initiative campaign to oppose changing the definition of marriage came in lockstep with a call for a referendum on abolishing LGBT inclusive education in Taiwan's middle and elementary schools. The CHNG claimed that the results following from JYI No 748 would have a significant negative impact on children's education and social morality. They insisted that parents could not accept a change in the definition of marriage in course materials taught at schools and argued that whether children should be taught about new concepts of marriage should be parents' decisions, rather than the purview of non-elected Justices or the government. As it was, the two aforementioned proposals later evolved into three separate propositions. Two of these propositions advanced by the religious organisations were about the definition of marriage, while the remaining one was about gender equity education. The propositions were worded as follows:

> *Proposition 10 (Definition of Marriage)*
>
> 'Do you agree that marriage defined in the Civil Code should be restricted to the union between a man and a woman?'
>
> *Proposition 11(Alteration of Current Gender Equity Education)*
>
> 'Do you agree that the Ministry of Education and schools (elementary and junior high schools) should not implement the gender equity education defined by the Enforcement Rules for Gender Equity Education Act to students undergoing primary and junior high school education?'
>
> *Proposition 12 (Protection of Same-sex Couples by other forms)*
>
> 'Do you agree with implementing the protection of same-sex couples' rights of permanent cohabitation by forms other than amending the definition of marriage in the Civil Code?'

On 24 January 2018, CHNG announced that the number of signatures in support of putting the propositions to a popular vote had reached the legal threshold and this was submitted to the CEC on 9 February.[32]

[32] The Central Election Commission, Taiwan, 'TSENG,HSIEN-YING submitted the proposition on "Do you agree to protect same-sex couples' rights of permanent cohabitation by forms other than amending the marriage definition in the Civil Code?" for National Initiative'. Available at: www.cec.gov.tw/english/cms/proposal/27236.

THE 'CIVIL CODE VS SPECIAL LAW' DEBATE IN THE SAME-SEX MARRIAGE CONTROVERSY IN TAIWAN

In many countries, the core issue in SSM legalisation is whether the intimate relationship between same-sex couples should be protected under the existing institution of marriage, or under an alternative form, that resembles a marriage-like relationship, at least to some extent. In practice, individuals in these alternative forms of relationship including domestic partnership, registered partnership and civil union, typically enjoy different levels of legal protection. Once same-sex relationships are institutionalised by law, whether in the form of marriage or in one of the alternative forms, the legalisation thereof may be accomplished either through the amendment of an existing law or the enactment of a new law. Theoretically speaking, it is the 'form of relationship' that matters, because welcoming same-sex couples to enter into the institution of marriage not only manifests the equality rights of gays and lesbians, but also implies social acceptance of same-sex relationships. It can be reasonably inferred that inasmuch as same-sex couples are granted equality right to marriage, the 'form of legislation' becomes an almost insignificant issue. However, such was not the case in Taiwan, where debate over the form of the relevant SSM legislation became a significant point of controversy.

The 'Civil Code vs Special Law' Debate

Activists in the SSM camp never wavered in their insistence that the legal institution of marriage should be extended to include same-sex couples; the acceptance of any compromise that might provide comparatively less protection to persons in alternative forms of relationship was never an option. When several bills were proposed after the tragic death of Professor Jacques Picoux, who committed suicide after he knew he had no right of inheritance to the assets of his deceased partner and would soon to be evicted from the apartment where he and his partner had lived for decades, the political climate in Taiwan was dominated by voices supporting SSM. During heated legislative debate on 24 November 2016, the anti-SSM camp for the first time raised the idea of enacting a 'special law' to protect the rights of same-sex couples.[33] This represented a softening of the religious right's firm stand of total opposition to extending legal protection to same-sex couples and signified an acceptance of the notion that same-sex couples should be protected by law, as long as the definition of marriage in the Civil Code was kept intact. This led to a proposal centred on the idea that 'Same-sex Couples Shall be Protected by Enacting a Special Law ('另立專法保障同志')'.

[33] Gazette of the Legislative Yuan in Taiwan (2017) 197–253.

Outwardly, 'enacting a special law' looked like a compromise – and perhaps the best way – to settle the confrontation between two feuding camps. However, the anti-SSM camp never clearly articulated what should be contained in the 'special law'. Key questions were left unanswered; for instance, to what extent would the special law protect same-sex relationships? Would same-sex couples enjoy the same level of protection as heterosexual married couples? Would the relationships or unions protected by the special law be referred to as marriages, unions, or partnerships? Could same-sex couples have their own families? Would they be allowed to adopt children? Unless a promise of substantial and definite protection was given for same-sex families who lacked any legal protection, the proposal to enact a special law offered, at best, hollow hope. Some feared it was akin to a Trojan horse – a surreptitious bid to deny same-sex families full participation in society – particularly, the right to marry – under the guise of helping them.

In response to the imprecise proposals put forward by the anti-SSM camp, the pro-SSM camp chose to reiterate the necessity of ensuring equal right to marriage by amending the Civil Code and rejecting the proposal of a parallel system provided by a special law. Those opposed to amending the Civil Code steadfastly refused to give ground and the SSM controversy became one based on 'Civil Code vs Special Law'. The nature of the debate thus shifted from the 'form of the relationship', ie marriage vs alternative forms, to the 'form of the legislation', ie Civil Code vs Special Law. Logically, when both factors are considered, there are four possible positions with regard to the SSM debate (see Figure 5.1). Enacting a special law can, in theory, give same-sex couples the same level of protection as the Civil Code affords traditional families (Position C). Conversely, amending the Civil Code does not necessarily give same-sex couples an equal right to marry (Position B). Stakeholders in the rival camps well knew that the 'Civil Code camp' supported full protection of marriage equality (ie Position A) and when the 'special law camp' spoke about a special law, they sought to only give the recognition accorded to alternative forms to same-sex couples (ie Position D). Moreover, the latter camp's strategy of focusing on the legislation's form, while leaving the content ambiguous, was a deliberate effort to garner support from people holding opinions somewhere in the middle (ie Position B or C), or others who were largely indifferent about the controversy and just wanted to put the issue to rest as soon as possible.

Since no legislator had proposed a bill to enact a special law by the end of the 2016 legislative debate, the legislators on the Judiciary and Organic Laws and Statutes Committee of the Legislative Yuan were not interested in taking either Position C or Position D. The cross-partisan proposal that was eventually sent for consultation was a Bill to revise the current Civil Code. Although the special law camp failed to win this battle, the 'Civil Code vs Special Law' dichotomy had become deeply rooted in the minds of Taiwanese people.

Figure 5.1 Four Positions in the SSM Debate

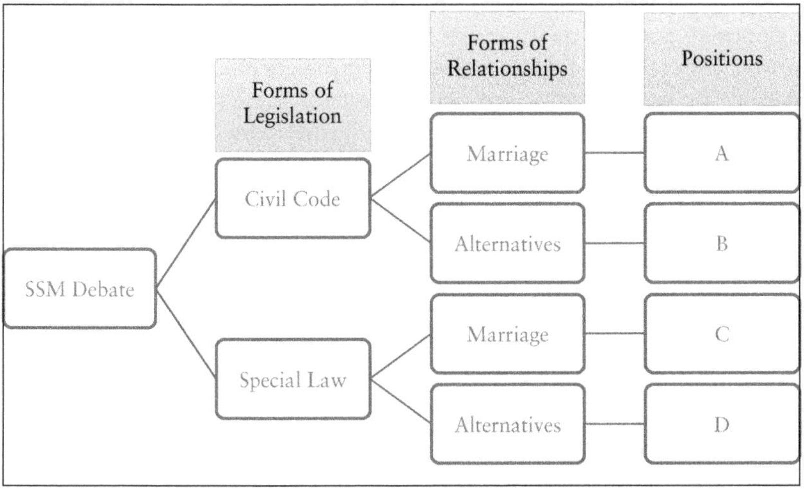

The Lingering Impact of the 'Civil Code vs Special Law' Dichotomy

This idea of a dichotomy between legislative forms later made it all the way to the Constitutional Court. Influenced by the 'Civil Code vs Special Law' debate, the Constitutional Court made an announcement before it convened the public hearing that one of the issues it would be considering, among others, was the following:

> If the Parliament enacts a law to create an institution of relationship other than marriage, for instance, same-sex partnership, would it be in accordance with the right to equality protected under Article 7 and the freedom of marriage protected under Article 22?

The issue the Justices raised was whether a law that conformed to Position D would be a violation of the Constitution and it is noteworthy that they not only mentioned the specific legislative form (an enactment of law) but also the form of relationship (institution of relationships other than marriage).

The petitioners in the case rejected this position outright, for two reasons. First, one of the petitioners claimed the issue was a hypothetical question, insofar as there was no existing law that created alternative protection for same-sex couples. A hypothetical law, so the argument went, could not constitute a subject for the case since it did not meet the prerequisite of 'ripeness' for judicial review. Secondly, the petitioner also argued that the alternative form of protection, even if it was 'separate but equal' to the institution of marriage, would, by its very nature, constitute discrimination based on sexual orientation and would therefore be repugnant to the notion of equal protection. In other words, the petitioners insisted that only Position A was constitutional. In contrast, as the opposing party in the case, the Ministry of Justice (MoJ) contended that enacting a special law did not necessarily constitute discrimination. Moreover, a special law would better serve the interests of same-sex families because it would be carefully tailored to their needs. Furthermore, the MoJ asserted that it was within the power of legislative discretion to decide, in law, what form of relationships and in what form of legislation the rights of same-sex couples would be protected. In sum, the MoJ considered it to be within the power of the Parliament to choose among Positions A to D.

The Constitutional Court did not respond directly to this issue in its holding contained in JYI No 748. Yet in paragraph 17 of its reasoning, the Court stated:

> Given the complexity and controversy surrounding this case, longer deliberation time for further legislation might be needed. On the other hand, overdue legislation will indefinitely prolong the unconstitutionality of such underinclusiveness, which should be prevented. This Court thus orders that the authorities concerned shall amend or enact the law as appropriate in accordance with the ruling of this Interpretation within two years after the date of announcement of this Interpretation. It is within the discretion of the authorities concerned to determine the form (for example, amendment of the Marriage Chapter, enactment of a special Chapter in Part IV on Family of the Civil Code, enactment of a special law, or other forms) for achieving the equal protection of the freedom of marriage for two persons of the same sex to create a permanent union of intimate and exclusive nature for the purpose of living a common life.

To paraphrase, the Justices did not rule the Civil Code immediately void, but gave the authorities concerned, ie the Administrative Yuan and the Parliament, two years to 'amend or enact the laws' as appropriate in accordance with the decision. Furthermore, the Justices left it to the authorities concerned to decide 'the form' for achieving the equal protection of the freedom of marriage between two persons of the same sex as mandated by the Constitution. Although the Justices did not explicitly use the words 'form of legislation' in this paragraph, it can be readily inferred from the inclusion of examples in the quoted section of the reasoning that 'form' should be taken to mean the 'form of legislation'. In the above quotation, the Justices gave examples of legislative forms to clarify that the word 'form' should mean one of the following: amendment to the chapter which stipulates the definition of marriage in the Civil Code; enactment of a particular chapter to address SSM in the Family Part of the Civil Code; or enactment of a special law other than the Civil Code. The first two examples would have entailed a revision of the Civil Code, while the third would have required the enactment of a special law. Clearly, the Justices were concerned with the need to achieve 'the equal protection of the freedom of marriage' inherent in the Constitution, regardless of the form of legislation used to achieve it. In other words, the Constitutional Court had taken a position closer to Positions A and C in Figure 5.1. It would be difficult to conceive how legal professionals or scholars would interpret the paragraph in any other way.

The Voters' Confusion by Design

Unfortunately, religious groups misinterpreted this paragraph and distorted its meaning in an attempt to overrule JYI No 748 by a popular vote. As previously mentioned, the CHNG began collecting signatures for the proposition on the definition of marriage immediately after the decision of the Constitutional Court in May 2017. Simultaneously, the CHNG began collecting signatures for another proposition relevant to SSM, which would demand that Parliament pass a special law to protect the rights of same-sex couples. The original wording of these two propositions were as follows:

> *Proposition 10 (Definition of Marriage)*
>
> Do you agree that marriage should be restricted to the union between a man and a woman?
>
> *Proposition 12 (Protection of Same-sex Couples by Special Law)*
>
> Do you agree with protecting same-sex couples' rights of permanent cohabitation by enacting a special law on the premise that the definition of marriage is not altered?

These two propositions followed the rationale of a 'Civil Code vs Special Law' dichotomy that was prevalent before the issuance of JYI No 748. They had the clear goal of (1) keeping the Civil Code unchanged, which would mean that the sacrosanct status of heterosexual marriage would remain intact; and (2) locating same-sex relationships in the confines of a special law, thereby implying the deviation of homosexuals from sexual normativity and reiterating the existence of a difference between homosexual and heterosexual couples.[34] However, JYI No 748 had already ruled that such a dichotomy of 'us vs others' or 'marriage vs alternative forms of relationship' could no longer be allowed under the Constitution and affirmed that same-sex couples should enjoy 'equal protection of the freedom of marriage'. Therefore, when these two propositions were brought to the CEC, the expert witnesses who took the stand raised red flags about their wording. They reminded the proponents that referendums and initiatives regulated by the PVA were bound by the Constitution, so a proposition *per se* could not be worded in a way that would violate the Constitution. They

[34] In the public hearing held in the Legislative Yuan in November 2016, the scholars and opinion leaders from the anti-SSM camp constantly referred to the Act on Life Registered Partnership in Germany, enacted in 2001, which did not give same-sex couples the same protection as married heterosexual couples. Some argued that same-sex couples should be viewed as cohabiting non-consanguineous family members who only deserved limited protection from the law. See *Bulletin of the Legislative Yuan* 105:95 197–253 (2016). Some other opinion leaders considered homosexuality as deviant social behaviour and a form of sexual liberation. See *Bulletin of the Legislative Yuan* 105:93, 154–155 (2016).

went on to say that since the Justices had already made it clear in JYI No 748 that the Civil Code's denial of same-sex couples' right to marry was a violation of their equal rights to marry, a proposition for a referendum or an initiative could not once again mandate the Parliament to legislate to confine the definition of marriage in the Civil Code to a union between a man and a woman and thereby exclude same-sex couples from marriage. In the same vein, since Proposition 12 was also premised on a limitation of the definition of marriage, it would likewise be abhorrent to JYI No 748. The CEC therefore requested that the proponents either alter or supplement the original proposition so that it would not be repugnant to JYI No 748.

Left with narrow room to manoeuvre for a popular vote, the CHNG altered the propositions to home in on what the Justices left for legislative discretion under JYI No 748. Specifically, since the Court's Interpretation left the government with only two options regarding the form of legislation, that is, Positions A and C, the newly drafted propositions aimed to steer people toward voting for Position C, which the CHNG saw as the sole possible outcome that would not be repugnant to JYI No 748. The wording of Proposition 10 was thus changed to read as follows:

> Do you agree that marriage as defined in the Civil Code should be restricted to the union between a man and a woman? (the underlined words amended the original referendum question)

This new proposition would mandate the legislators not to take Position A, for this position (Civil Code-marriage) should be left to heterosexual couples.

Proposition 12 was also altered to read as follows:

> Do you agree with protecting same-sex couples' rights of permanent cohabitation by forms other than amending the definition of marriage in the Civil Code?' (the underlined words amended the original question)

The new proposition was supposed to restrict the legislators' choice to Position C (special law-marriage), which would be the only position in conformity with JYI No 748. However, by circumventing the use of the word 'marriage' to describe the relationships of same-sex couples and instead portraying them as 'permanent cohabitation' instead of 'marriage', this question implied that relationships of permanent cohabitation were different from marriage.

What made Proposition 12 confusing was the use of the word 'forms'. If 'forms' meant 'forms of legislation', the proposition was valid because it would be in line with Position C. But if the 'forms' meant 'forms of relationship', which would mean it fell under Position D, it would be deemed inconsistent to JYI No 748 and would therefore be rejected by the CEC. The CEC explicitly reminded the CHNG that the 'other form' in JYI No 748 meant the form of legislation, not the form of relationship. If the CHNG insisted on proposing the initiative with the intention to address the question on the form of relationship, the CEC had no choice but to reject the proposal. After a back-and-forth confirmation process between the CEC and CHNG, the CHNG acknowledged that the proposition must be premised on achieving equal protection for the freedom to marry. These propositions were both later approved by the CEC in April 2018, after alteration of their phrasing.

In the months that followed, the anti-SSM initiative campaign was a textbook case of introducing voter confusion into the process of popular voting, a phenomenon commonly seen in many initiative or referendum practices.[35] Proponents of the initiative continued to lead the public to believe they stood for Position D, despite the fact that the official phrasing of the propositions indicated something else. If voters believed they were going to vote for Position D and the propositions to support it were passed, the intent behind the initiatives apparently purported to overrule JYI No 748, in contradiction to the promise made to the CEC by the CHNG. Judging from the pamphlets and digital advertisements used in the campaign leading up to the ballot initiative, the CHNG's intent contradicted the phrasing of the propositions that would be presented to voters. Fearing that voters would be confused when they read the questions on the ballot tickets, the CHNG sent thousands of volunteers to distribute aide-mémoire cards outside polling stations to help voters memorise the numbers of the propositions and the corresponding answers they should choose. As a result, Proposition 10 received 7.65 million votes, which accounted for 72 per cent of the votes, while Proposition 12 received 6.4 million votes, which accounted for 61 per cent.[36] The two propositions regarding SSM were both passed at the end of November 2018.

A Populist Threat to the Rule of Law?

It became a formidable challenge for both the Administrative Yuan and the Parliament to balance adherence to the stipulations of JYI No 748 with the outcome of the popular vote. As a constitutional state committed to basing its democracy on constitutionalism after democratisation, Taiwan is committed to the rule of law. It has maintained the supremacy of the Constitution through repeated constitutional practices and this has been maintained in decisions made by the Constitutional Court. The Prime Minister and the DPP, the ruling party, vowed to strike a balance between the Constitutional Court decision and the referendum results. In February 2019, the Administrative Yuan proposed a Bill named 'the Act for Implementation of J.Y. Interpretation No. 748' (hereinafter,

[35] J Verhulst and A Nijeboer, *Direct Democracy: Facts, Arguments and Experiences on the Introduction of Initiative and Referendum* (Democracy International, 2007) 78–79; JN Eule, 'Judicial Review of Direct Democracy' (1990) 99 *Yale Law Journal* 1508–1509; E Chemerinsky, 'Challenging Direct Democracy', 2007 *Michigan State Law Review* 297–299.

[36] 7.65 million was 39 per cent of all eligible voters; 6.4 million was 32 per cent of all eligible voters.

the Act for 748).[37] The bill purported to protect what it called the 'same-sex married relationship (同性婚姻關係)'. In this draft version, Article 2 defined a same-sex married relationship as 'a permanent union of intimate and exclusive nature for the purpose of living a common life', phrasing which was identical to that of JYI No 748. In other parts of the Bill, a same-sex married relationship was referred to as a 'relationship defined in Article 2', instead of using the Civil Code terms 'spouse' or 'marriage' to refer to married couples. Yet even so, it still gave same-sex couples almost equal rights to those enjoyed by heterosexual married couples.[38] As the Administrative Yuan explained, the Act for 748 had accomplished what JYI No 748 required. It provided equal protection of the freedom to marry, while at the same time fulfilling the legislative principles established by the initiatives, namely, giving protection to same-sex couples' permanent cohabitation by the enactment of a special law, without altering the definition of marriage in the Civil Code.

Religious groups, however, were furious about the bill, accusing the government of intentionally ignoring the will of the people. They insisted that popular sovereignty should be the highest power in the state and it followed that that the ruling of the Constitutional Court should be vacated because it was contradictory to the peoples' will. Therefore, they insisted the government should follow the will of 7.56 million voters to give same-sex couples legal protection in a form such as 'same-sex cohabitation' or 'same-sex partnership' because that was what Proposition 12 had already demanded.[39] By this time, the CHNG had revealed its true intent to mandate the legislators to take Position D, despite their self-proclaimed support for Position C. On its website, the CHNG fiercely asserted that JYI No 748, which should only impinge on the effect of the 'old' Civil Code, had no binding power over the 'new' principle of legislation after the outcome the initiative had produced. They therefore asked, 'Who has greater power: fifteen Justices or the People who cast the 7.56 million votes?' and 'Who are the masters of the country: 15 Justices or the People?'[40]

The rationale behind the opposition was based on a populist ideology of the existence of a dichotomy between the people and the judicial elite. As previously discussed, the early advocacy of popular voting in Taiwan was anchored in the belief that Taiwanese people should have the right of self-determination, particularly with regard to Taiwan's future with respect to China. Advocates of the popular vote did not likely foresee that the direct democracy they were so passionate about could one day be used to limit or deprive a minority of their

[37] The Act for Implementation of JY Interpretation No 748 was passed on 17 May 2019 and enforced on 24 May 2019.

[38] As to the protection of same-sex headed families, however, Article 20 of the Act for 748 only allows one of the couple to establish parentage by adopting the children who have the biological connection with his or her spouse.

[39] Coalition for the Happiness of our Next Generation, 'Should the Decision of 15 Justices Supercede the People's Will?' (16 May 2019).

[40] Ibid.

fundamental rights. Likewise, they could not possibly have envisaged that popular voting could ever endanger constitutionalism and the very rule of law itself. Indeed, popular voting had long been romanticised and was closely associated with the dream of Taiwanese independence. It was members of the pro-unification camp who often decried popular voting as 'populism' in the debate on legalisation of the PVA.[41]

The literature on direct democracy reveals a heated debate over whether ballot voting could become a political mechanism which endangers minority rights both in theory and in practice and perpetrates a 'tyranny of majority'.[42] Many scholars contend that the referendum and initiative processes can be tyrannical measures of majority power over minorities,[43] especially those who belong to the most vulnerable groups in society.[44] Yet in Taiwan, the tension between direct democracy and the principles of constitutionalism, which include, inter alia, rule of law and equal protection of minority rights, was never an issue in the enactment process and amendment of the PVA. In fact, the possibility of popular voting results being repugnant to the Constitution or to decisions of the Constitutional Court, or even endangering people's rights, was seldom discussed.[45] The SSM controversy marked the first time in Taiwan's constitutional history that a debate over the legal effects and impact of citizen-initiated measures had become the focus of serious controversy. Activists from the religious right asserted that the result of the popular votes were a clear manifestation of popular sovereignty and should trump the Constitution itself.[46] However, the Judicial Yuan clarified the matter immediately after the passage of the propositions: while the Parliament should follow the legislative principles mandated by the result of popular votes when enacting laws, such legislation should still be

[41] Chang et al, n 12 above.

[42] JN Eule, 'Judicial Review of Direct Democracy' (1990) 99 *Yale Law Journal* 1503; DC Lewis, *Direct Democracy And Minority Rights: A Critical Assessment of the Tyranny of the Majority in the American States* (2013); SL Vargas, 'Judicial Review of Initiatives and Referendums in which Majorities Vote on Minorities' Democratic Citizenship' (1990) 60 *Ohio State Law Journal* 399; KR Johnson, 'An Essay on Immigration Politics, Popular Democracy, and California's Proposition 187: The Political Relevance and Legal Irrelevance of Race' (1995) 70 *Washington Law Review* 629; SJ Clark, 'A Populist Critique of Direct Democracy' (1998) 112 *Harvard Law Review* 434; J Schacter, 'The Pursuit of Popular Intent: Interpretive Dilemmas in Direct Democracy' (1995) 105 *Yale Law Journal* 107; ML Stearns, (2012) 'Direct (Anti-) Democracy' (2012) 80 *Washington Law Review* 311.

[43] Gamble, n 1 above; DC Lewis, *Direct Democracy and Minority Rights: A Critical Assessment of the Tyranny of the Majority in the American States* (2013).

[44] AL Stone, 'Rethinking the Tyranny of the Majority: The Extralegal Consequences of Anti-gay Ballot Measure' (2015) 19 *Chapman Law Rev* 219, 219–239; DC Lewis, 'Direct Democracy and Minority Rights: Same-sex Marriage Bans in the US States' (2011) 92 *Social Science Quarterly* 364, 364.

[45] A few exceptions in academia include TL Hsu, 'Constitution and Referendum: The Constitutional Analysis of Referendum and the Establishment of Referendum Act' (1998) 2 *New Century Forum* 35; YH Liao, 'Oppression or Emancipation? Preliminary Recommendations for Crafting a Challenging and Subversive Plebiscite System' (2005) 30 *The Constitutional Review* 445.

[46] HI Yu, 'Popular Voting is the Highest Manifestation of Popular Sovereignty; It Should be Higher Than the Constitution' (26 November 2018). Available at: www.facebook.com/You.HsinYi/posts/966847410105603.

situated at level of law and cannot contradict JYI No 748, the binding effect of which is at a level equivalent to that of the Constitution.[47]

Under extreme public pressure, Taiwan's Parliament passed the Act for 748, with mild modification. The term 'same-sex marriage' in Article 2 was removed. The only place where the term 'marriage' appeared was in Article 4, in which the process of registration was stipulated. The fact that the other provisions were not altered or extensively discussed evidenced that it was the *name* given to the relationship in the enactment of the special law that mattered most to the opposition camp, since the definition of marriage in the Civil Code was left intact. The legislators who supported the Bill laboured to explain to their constituents why the questions on the ballot tickets proposed by the CHNG actually meant Position C, so the Act for 748 was not in contradiction to the outcome of Propositions 10 and 12, while, at the same time, was in conformity with JYI No 748. The majority of the members in the Parliament voted 'yes' and passed the Act for 748 on 17 May 2019.

CONCLUSION

Religious organisations in Taiwan pursued an anti-SSM agenda through an initiative campaign they aligned in tandem with a parallel anti-LGBT-inclusive education platform. Religious right groups also craftily drafted the phrasing of the related propositions to make them misleading and ambiguous, to conceal their real intent from the CEC. The groups further stimulated public discontent against the Constitutional Court Justices by promulgating the populist ideology of an unbridgeable rift between common people and the judicial elite. The populist manipulation of ballot measures in the anti-SSM initiatives in 2019 was aimed at striking down a decision of the Constitutional Court. The recognition that the Constitution is the supreme law of the land was manifested in a scene that transpired in the last sitting of the Legislature before the third reading of the Act for 748 on 17 May 2019. The party whip of the DPP, Chien-Ming Ko, stood before his colleagues and spoke these words: 'As you all know, I always stood up against SSM, but even a person like me must face the authority of the Constitution.' He further explained: 'The Justices interpreted the Constitution and demanded that we enact a law to allow same-sex couples to marry. Do we

[47] YH Chang, "Does the Legal Effect of Popular Votes Rank Higher Than the Constitution? Judicial Yuan Spoke' (30 November 2018) CTS. Available at: https//news.cts.com.tw/cts/politics/201811/201811301944569.html. The interpretation of the Constitution made by the Justices has the binding effect on either the government and administration, the legislature, the lower courts, or the people. In 1984, Judicial Yuan Interpretation No 185 clarified the disputed issue by stating that 'the interpretations of the Judicial Yuan shall be binding upon every institution and person in the country and each institution shall abide by the meaning of these interpretations in handling relevant matters'. See Judicial Yuan Interpretation No 185.

legislators have any room to negotiate and compromise otherwise? We need to bow to the Constitution. No one can stand opposed to the Constitution.'[48]

The extent to which voters were confused by the religious right's manipulation of the wording of the propositions is a matter for debate. These are questions that should be left for research by legal scholars or political scientists.[49] In any case, a poll conducted one year after the passage of the Act for 748 showed that 53 per cent of people supported the legalisation of SSM and, moreover, the rate of such support was still rising.[50] Even so, the experience of the anti-SSM campaign has raised eyebrows among human rights workers and a few key questions remain unanswered. Most importantly, how can Taiwan maintain a robust referendum mechanism while also continuing to protect minority rights? In the end, the Parliament and the Administrative Yuan decided to defy significant political pressure and uphold their constitutional duty to abide by the decision of the Constitutional Court. Nevertheless, these circumstances could change in the future and constitutionalism and the rule of law may again be under threat. The challenge for Taiwan's democracy going forward is how to balance its dynamic democratic impulse with the rule of law, ultimately ensuring that important minority rights remain protected and valued by the citizenry.

[48] 'Chien-Ming Ko: 'I always stood up against SSM, but still have to face the authority of the Constitution' (17 May 2019). Next Magazine. Available at: https:/tw.nextmgz.com/realtimenews/news/469786.

[49] See, eg JS Schacter, 'The Pursuit of Popular Intent: Interpretive Dilemmas in Direct Democracy' (1995) 105 *Yale Law Journal* 107, 1995.

[50] YY Zhou, 'Poll After One Year of Same-sex Marriage Legalization, the Acceptance Rate Increased 15.1%' (8 May 2020) *Apple Daily*. Available at: https:/tw.appledaily.com/politics/20200508/R3Y3UKPCHN4T66YPJCKJQMOZG4/. Another poll by the Taiwan Equality Campaign showed that 92.8 per cent of people think the legalisation of SSM does not affect their everyday life. See Taiwan Equality Campaign, 'Does LGBT Widely Accepted One Year After Same-Sex Marriage was Legalized?' (15 May 2020). Available at: https://equallove.tw/news/65.

6

Communitarian Rule of Law and the Judicial Articulation of the Right to be Represented in Singapore

JACK TSEN-TA LEE* AND JACLYN L NEO+

INTRODUCTION

IN JULY 2020, Singapore went to the polls to elect a new Parliament and government, in the midst of the COVID-19 outbreak. It was the Republic's fourteenth general election since its independence in 1965, but only the second time in recent history that all parliamentary seats were contested.[1] A total of 11 political parties contested this election,[2] with several newly formed parties adding to those which were more established.[3] At the centre of the electoral contest was the People's Action Party (PAP), which has formed every government in Singapore since independence. In fact, after the opposition party Barisan Sosialis quit Parliament in protest in 1965,[4] the PAP enjoyed a monopoly of seats in Parliament until 1981, when an opposition leader won a seat in a by-election. That, however, did not lead to any radical change in the composition of Parliament, even though the opposition presence has

*LLB (Hons) (National University of Singapore), LLM (University College London); PhD (Birmingham).

+Associate Professor, Director of the Centre for Asian Legal Studies, National University of Singapore Faculty of Law.

[1] R Sim, 'Singapore GE2020: All 93 Seats to be Contested at July 10 Election; 192 Candidates from 11 Parties File Papers on Nomination Day', *The Straits Times* (30 June 2020). Available at: www.straitstimes.com/politics/singapore-ge2020-all-93-seats-to-be-contested-at-july-10-polls-192-candidates-from-11.

[2] Ibid.

[3] F Koh, 'Singapore GE2020: With New Leaders and New Parties, a Much-changed Opposition Gets Ready for Battle', *The Straits Times* (23 June 2020). Available at: www.straitstimes.com/politics/singapore-ge2020-with-new-leaders-and-new-parties-a-much-changed-opposition-gets-ready-for.

[4] Ho AL, 'Opposition MPs Boycott S'pore's First House session', *The Straits Times* (6 December 2015) www.straitstimes.com/singapore/opposition-mps-boycott-spores-first-house-session.

increased over the decades, partly because opposition parties won more seats and partly due to deliberate institutional design on the part of the government to introduce more opposition voices while maintaining the political status quo. In the 2015 general election, the PAP retained its supermajority with 83 out of 89 seats in Parliament and increased its vote share to 69.9 per cent.[5] The key question at each general election has never been *who* is going to form the government, but what the victory margin will be for the PAP.

The state of elections in Singapore poses a fascinating puzzle. While critics may point to the PAP's dominance and laws purporting to restrict freedom of speech, among other things, as indicative of a 'fundamentally undemocratic'[6] regime, others have conceded that Singapore is at least 'semi-democratic'[7] or, grudgingly, 'competitively authoritarian'.[8] Indeed, even though elections have been held regularly since Singapore's independence in 1965, it consistently scores and ranks poorly in various democracy indices. On the Economist Intelligence Unit's Democracy Index, Singapore is consistently classified as a flawed democracy, with concerns raised every year about its legal restrictions on freedom of speech.[9] At the same time, Singapore ranks very highly on rule of law indices. It has ranked first out of 140 countries in terms of the '[e]fficiency of [its] legal framework in settling disputes' by the World Economic Forum.[10] Singapore was also ranked among the top countries worldwide in respect of its fidelity to the rule of law by the World Bank[11] and the World Justice Project.[12] In 2020, the World Justice Project ranked Singapore above the United Kingdom on its Rule of Law Index.[13] In 2016, the International Monetary Fund Chief praised Singapore as an example to be emulated for its eradication of corruption and its

[5] S Tan, 'GE2015: PAP Vote Share Increases to 69.9%, Party Wins 83 of 89 Seats including WP-held Punggol East' *The Straits Times* (12 September 2015). Available at: www.straitstimes.com/politics/ge2015-pap-vote-share-increases-to-699-party-wins-83-of-89-seats-including-wp-held-punggol.

[6] S Reyes, 'Singapore's Stubborn Authoritarianism' *Harvard Political Review* (29 September 2015) Available at: https://harvardpolitics.com/world/singapores-stubborn-authoritarianism/.

[7] W Case, 'Singapore a Stable Semi-democracy' in *Politics in Southeast Asia: Democracy or Less* (2002), 81.

[8] S Ortmann, 'Singapore: Authoritarian but Newly Competitive' (2012) 22(4) *Journal of Democracy* 153.

[9] 'Asia Remains Stagnant in the Democracy Index 2019', *The Economist* (27 January 2020), https://country.eiu.com/article.aspx?articleid=538983237&Country=Singapore&topic=Politics&subtopic=Forecast&subsubtopic=Democracy+index.

[10] K Schwab (ed), *The Global Competitiveness Report 2015–2016* (Geneva: World Economic Forum, 2015), 321. Available at: www3.weforum.org/docs/gcr/2015-2016/Global_Competitiveness_Report_2015-2016.pdf.

[11] 'Worldwide Governance Indicators: Country Data Report for Singapore, 1996–2014', *World Bank* (15 September 2015). Available at: http://documents1.worldbank.org/curated/en/666041467993465894/pdf/105564-WP-PUBLIC-Singapore.pdf.

[12] 'WJP Rule of Law Index: Singapore', World Justice Project (2020). Available at: https://worldjusticeproject.org/rule-of-law-index/country/2020/Singapore/.

[13] World Justice Project Rule of Law Index 2020,World Justice Project, 2020, 7. Available at: https://worldjusticeproject.org/sites/default/files/documents/WJP-ROLI-2020-Online_0.pdf.

establishment of honest and competent public institutions.[14] Others, however, argue that what Singapore has is not the rule of law, but rule by law.[15]

The discrepancy between how Singapore ranks in terms of the rule of law vis-à-vis democracy raises a fascinating puzzle. How does a country rank so highly on rule of law indexes but score so poorly on democracy indexes? More importantly, what does this say about the relationship between the rule of law and democracy? The first puzzle is probably easier to address and the clue lies in the factors used in how the rule of law indexes were compiled and scored. Singapore scores very highly on rule of law indexes that take into account a wide range of indicators that go beyond those used in democratic indexes. On the World Justice Project's Rule of Law Index, for instance, it comes at or near the top of the table on order and security, non-corruption, civil justice, criminal justice, as well as regulatory enforcement, but not so high on other aspects such as constraints on government powers, openness of government and fundamental liberties. On one level, therefore, the discrepancies could be said to reflect an old debate about the meaning and content of the rule of law. Indeed, scholarship parsing through these is plentiful and has become a small cottage industry unto itself. Martin Krygier highlights how the concept has evolved from a 'controversial legal ideal' to an 'opposed international cliché/slogan'.[16] Melissa Curley, Björn Dressel and Stephen McCarthy point to the deeply contested and politicized nature of the discussion on the rule of law.[17] Jeremy Waldron famously called the rule of law an essentially contested concept.[18]

Distinctions are commonly drawn between formal and substantive concepts of the rule of law,[19] or alternatively, between thin and thick senses of the rule of law.[20] Within this discourse, the question of whether individual rights protection should be considered part of the rule of law has become a critical flashpoint. Indeed, critics argue that restrictions on freedom, especially freedom of speech, association and assembly, are often an indicator of an insufficiently democratic system. Jothie Rajah characterise Singapore as a country that employs an authoritarian form of the rule of law.[21] She presents an analysis of authoritarian

[14] 'IMF Chief Cites Lee Kuan Yew's "Zero-tolerance" Stance towards Corruption as Example for Rest of World', *Today* (12 May 2016). Available at: www.todayonline.com/world/imf-chief-cites-lee-kuan-yews-zero-tolerance-policy-towards-corruption-example-rest-world.

[15] For a discussion situated within the rule of law v. rule by law debate, see G Silverstein, 'Singapore: The Exception that Proves Rules Matter', in T Ginsburg and T Moustafa (eds) *The Politics of Courts in Authoritarian Regimes* (2008), 73–101.

[16] M Krygier, 'The Rule of Law: Pasts, Presents, and Two Possible Futures' (2016) 12 *Annual Review Law & Social Science* 199.

[17] See, for example, M Curley, B Dressel and S McCarthy, 'Competing Visions of the Rule of Law in Southeast Asia: Power, Rhetoric and Governance' (2018) *Asian Studies Review* 1.

[18] J Waldron, 'Is the Rule of Law an Essentially Contested Concept (in Florida)?' (2002) 21 *Law & Philosophy* 137.

[19] See, for example, B Tamanaha, *On the Rule of Law: History, Politics, Theory* (2004).

[20] See, for example, Thio LA, 'Lex Rex or Rex Lex? Competing Conceptions of the Rule of Law in Singapore' (2002) 20(1) *Pacific Basin Law Journal* 1–76.

[21] J Rajah, *Authoritarian Rule of Law: Legislation, Discourse, and Legitimacy in Singapore* (2012).

legalism, showing how prosperity, public discourse and a rigorous observance of legal procedure have enabled a reconfigured rule of law such that liberal form encases illiberal content. This disagreement is not merely a dispute among academics or theorists. The 'rule of law' has become a useful and desirable label for governments seeking international approval. Thus, Brian Tamanaha has cautioned that 'rampant uncertainty' raises the risk that the rule of law 'might devolve to an empty phrase' that could be instrumentalised and 'proclaimed with impunity by malevolent governments'.[22]

Common among rule of law indicators is the quality of the judiciary. Without a doubt, the judiciary in Singapore is extremely well regarded for the quality of its doctrinal analysis, its efficiency and uncorrupted reputation. At the same time, critics have argued against what they perceive as a pro-establishment stance in public law cases.[23] This, however, presents an insufficiently nuanced view of the judiciary. The Singapore judiciary has, in recent times, contributed to a thicker conception of the rule of law, alongside an emphasis on Westminster constitutionalism, separation of powers and its co-equality with the political branches of government. In addition, the court has started to articulate a theory of representative democracy that seeks to balance the right to be represented with competing interests rooted in a communitarian conception of democracy. This judicial articulation is significant, as it demonstrates a shift in judicial philosophy towards greater engagement with constitutional issues, instead of employing notions of justiciability in order to not decide such issues. There has been a move towards a constitutional rule of law, albeit a nascent one that is constrained by a communitarian approach to politics. Communitarianism is a multi-faceted theory which, at its core, posits that there are 'common formulations of the good' and the good is not left to be determined by individuals by and for themselves.[24] Beyond this, there is significant disagreement, not least with 'liberal communitarians' seeking to distinguish themselves from what they consider to be more 'authoritarian' strains of communitarianism, which arises when states employ the common good to suppress individual rights.[25] For our purposes, we employ the term communitarian democracy to refer to a political philosophy that sees democracy as serving the common good and emphasizes a more consensual form of politics that prioritizes social solidarity.[26]

This chapter will examine three cases concerning the right to be represented in Singapore, employing them as useful devices to consider some of the more thorny

[22] Tamanaha, n 19 above, 114.

[23] For example, R Worthington, 'Between Hermes and Themis: An Empirical Study of the Contemporary Judiciary in Singapore' (2002) 28(4) *Journal of Law & Society* 490.

[24] A Etzioni, 'Communitarianism revisited' (2014) 19(3) *Journal of Political Ideologies*, 241, 242.

[25] Ibid, 244–245.

[26] For more on communitarianism in Asia, see Daniel Bell, 'Communitarianism' Stanford Encyclopedia of Philosophy (4 October 2001, rev. 21 March 2016). Available at https://plato.stanford.edu/entries/communitarianism/.

issues concerning the relationship between the rule of law and democracy in a communitarian dominant party state like Singapore.

CONTESTED CONCEPTS OF THE RULE OF LAW IN SINGAPORE

A Communitarian Rule of Law

The idea that Singapore practises a communitarian rule of law has been articulated by the Government as well as by judges in extra-judicial speeches. In a 2016 speech delivered by Chief Justice Sundaresh Menon at the American Law Institute's 93rd Annual Meeting, he observed that Singapore's 'fidelity to the rule of law' coexists with 'an emphasis on communitarian over individualist values'.[27] This emphasis includes a preference for 'dialogue, tolerance, compromise and placing [of] the community above self'. As he further observed, '[t]hese values have modulated the court's approach in ensuring that the rule of law rules'.[28] This focus on communitarianism adds another layer of complexity to the idea of the rule of law in Singapore, which had for some time focused on formal or procedural aspects. For instance, in 1999, in response to a parliamentary motion by an opposition member, a Government Minister sketched out a procedural idea of the rule of law, rejecting the opposition member's more substantive claims. The Minister stated that the rule of law:

> [...] refers to the supremacy of law, as opposed to the arbitrary exercise of power. The other key tenet is that everyone is equal before the law. The concept also includes the notions of the transparency, openness and prospective application of our laws, observation of the principles of natural justice, independence of the Judiciary and judicial review of administrative action.[29]

Lee observes that in subsequent years the government's attitude towards the rule of law shifted from a more procedural idea of the rule of law to one that is not quite focused on human rights, but is nonetheless richer.[30] For example, in its response to a 2008 report on the state of human rights, democracy and the rule of law in Singapore by the International Bar Association Human Rights Institute,[31] the government drew a link between the rule of law and certain

[27] S Menon, 'The Rule of Law: The Path to Exceptionalism' (2016) 28 *Singapore Academy Law Journal* 413.

[28] Ibid, para 24.

[29] Ho PK (Minister of State for Law), 'Rule of Law', *Singapore Parliamentary Debates, Official Report* (24 November 1999), vol. 71, col. 592. See, generally, JTT Lee, 'Shall the Twain Never Meet? Competing Narratives and Discourses of the Rule of Law in Singapore' [2012] *Singapore Journal of Legal Studies* 298, 319–320.

[30] Lee, ibid, 326.

[31] *Prosperity versus Individual Rights? Human Rights, Democracy and the Rule of Law in Singapore* (London: International Bar Association, 2008). Available at: www.ibanet.org/Document/Default.aspx?DocumentUid=93326691-C4DA-473B-943A-DD0FC76325E8.

substantive values. It stated that the fundamentals for Singapore's success include '[f]ree and fair elections held regularly' and '[a] free society where individual human dignity is protected'.[32] At the same time, the government argued that '[t]he reality is that there are often situations where the pursuit of one norm conflicts with another and decisions have to be taken on the appropriate balance to be struck between them'.[33]

This conception of the rule of law in Singapore 'favours communitarian values over individual rights'.[34] It is no longer a thin or formal view that merely requires observance of the law and a system of judicial oversight, but one that recognises the need to embrace representative democracy and 'human dignity' within the doctrine (though the implications of the latter remain uncertain). Yet the protection of fundamental liberties or human rights is not a lexically prioritized aspect of the rule of law. Instead, it is implied that when public interests such as economic growth and public order clash with individual rights, the latter will be outweighed by the former.[35] The Law Minister has said that the rule of law should be applied 'with hard-nosed practicality',[36] so as 'to achieve good governance and to promote the general welfare'.[37]

It seems evident that the judiciary also aligns with this view. Extra-judicially, Chief Justice Menon explained that within the 'communitarian rule of law', the judiciary is independent but 'plays a supporting role to good governance by articulating clear rules and principles by which the Government should abide, and serving as the last line of defence if and when those principles are breached'.[38] He further explained that 'a court which is respected by the other branches of government can effectively shape the debate and ensure the legality of government actions by setting out its concerns openly and potentially obviating a binary clash between the Judiciary and the Executive'.[39]

[32] 'Singapore's Response to the International Bar Association's Report on Singapore', annexed to a letter (reference no LAW/06/021/026) dated 14 November 2008 from Mark Jayaratnam, Deputy Director, Legal Policy Division, Ministry of Law, to the Chairman of the Human Rights Institute Council of the International Bar Association. Available at: http://app2.mlaw.gov.sg/LinkClick.aspx?fileticket=gDkKt5ebvTY%3d&tabid=204, paras 22 and 32.

[33] Ibid.

[34] Lee, n 29 above, 326.

[35] Thio LA, 'Rule of Law within a Non-liberal "Communitarian" Democracy: The Singapore Experience' in R Peerenboom (ed), *Asian Discourses of Rule of Law: Theories and Implementation of Rule of Law in Twelve Asian Countries, France and the US* (2004), 183, 208 (regarding the Government's approach as a "competing 'thick' version [of the rule of law] fashioned after an illiberal model which prioritises statist goals like economic growth and social control by a relatively incorrupt government").

[36] K Shanmugam, 'The Rule of Law in Singapore' [2012] *Singapore Journal of Legal Studies* 357, 358.

[37] Ibid, 357.

[38] Menon, n 27, para 25, citing Chan SK, 'Judicial Review – From Angst to Empathy: A Lecture to Singapore Management University Second Year Law Students' (2010) 22 *Singapore Academy of Law Journal* 469, para 29.

[39] Menon, n 27, above, para 29.

This echoes the opinion of former Chief Justice Chan Sek Keong that the Singapore judiciary takes a 'green-light' view of judicial review where the courts are not 'the first line of defence against administrative abuses of power: instead, control can and should come internally from Parliament and the Executive itself in upholding high standards of public administration and policy'.[40] This is preferred to a 'red-light' view, where the courts are 'locked in an adversarial or combative relationship with the Executive and functioning as a check on administrative power'.[41]

THE RULE OF LAW'S RELATIONSHIP TO DEMOCRACY WITHIN SINGAPORE

The relationship between the rule of law and democracy is not always clear. It is possible to differentiate between the two, though they may at times be conflated. Furthermore, some may see it as complementary and mutually reinforcing, while others point out that they can frequently be in conflict with one other. Waldron suggests that the rule of law is part of a 'constellation' of mutually reinforcing ideals, which include democracy, human rights, economic freedoms, good governance and development.[42] In Tamanaha's view, the formal version of the rule of law adds democracy to formal legality, that is, as part of the understanding of the rule of law. In this regard, the two have an intrinsically co-legitimating function. As he puts it:

> Without formal legality democracy can be circumvented (because government officials can undercut the law); without democracy formal legality loses its legitimacy (because the content of the law has not been determined by legitimate means).[43]

The exact relationship is complex; the rule of law could serve to reinforce majority rule, while also supporting limits on it.[44] Others have claimed a causal relationship in what Gordon Silverstein calls the 'economic engagement-rule of law process', which sees the rule of law in the form of judicialisation as translating economic incentives into political and social liberalisation. Silverstein, however, cautions against this assumption, pointing to Singapore (among other

[40] Chan, n 38 above, para 29.

[41] Ibid. Chan, who was Chief Justice of Singapore between 2006 and 2012, adopted the red-light/green-light terminology from: C Harlow and R Rawlings, *Law and Administration* (3rd edn) (2009). Chan's preference for the green-light view was cited with approval by the Court of Appeal in *Jeyaretnam Kenneth Andrew v Attorney-General* [2014] 1 SLR 345 at paras 48–50 and *Wong Souk Yee v Attorney-General* [2019] 1 SLR 1223 at para 93 (CA); and by the High Court in *Nagaenthran a/l K Dharmalingam v Attorney-General* [2018] SGHC 112 at para 123.

[42] J Waldron, 'The Rule of Law and the Importance of Procedure' in JE Fleming (ed), *Getting to the Rule of Law* (2011), 3, 8.

[43] Tamanaha, n 19 above, 99.

[44] I Salevao, *Rule of Law, Legitimate Governance & Development in the Pacific* (2005), 3.

jurisdictions) as an example where this assumed trajectory had not taken place.[45] Instead, there is an increasingly confident articulation of a democracy that is less defined by liberal rights, but by a more communitarian outlook that values political stability and social cohesion.[46] There is a coalescing of communitarian democracy with the rule of law, Singapore style.

JUDICIAL ARTICULATION OF THE RIGHT TO BE REPRESENTED

The Case of Vellama: Articulating the Right to be Represented

The occasion for judicial engagement with the idea of representation and democracy in Singapore came in the wake of a casual vacancy that arose in a Single Member Constituency (SMC), one of the two types of electoral divisions in Singapore. The elected members of Singapore's unicameral Parliament are chosen by the electorate in a 'first-past-the-post' system either through SMCs in which each voter casts a ballot for an individual candidate, or through Group Representation Constituencies (GRCs) in which a ballot is cast for a group of candidates contesting as a team.

The parliamentary seat in question had fallen vacant after its Member of Parliament (MP) was expelled from his political party. According to Article 46(2)(b) of the Constitution,[47] which is an anti-hopping provision, when a Member of Parliament is expelled from the party under the banner of which he/she stood for election, the seat becomes vacant.[48] The Prime Minister, who was asked in Parliament when he was going to call a by-election to fill the seat, answered that while he intended to do so, he had not decided on the date and that, in any case, the 'timing of the by-election is at the discretion of the Prime Minister'.[49] He further asserted that:

> The Prime Minister is not obliged to call a by-election within any fixed time frame. This absence of any stipulated time frame is the result of a deliberate decision by Parliament to confer on the Prime Minister the discretion to decide when to fill a Parliament vacancy.[50]

According to the PM, his decision would depend on 'all relevant factors including the well-being of [the constituency's] residents, issues on the national agenda, as

[45] See G Silverstein, 'Globalisation and the Rule of Law: "A Machine that Runs of Itself?"' (2003) 1(3) *International Journal of Constitutional Law* 427.

[46] See, generally, Thio, n 35 above.

[47] Constitution of the Republic of Singapore (1985 Rev Ed, 1999 Rep).

[48] Article 46(2)(b) states: 'The seat of a Member of Parliament shall become vacant – [...] if he ceases to be a member of, or is expelled or resigns from, the political party for which he stood in the election'.

[49] Lee HL (Prime Minister), 'By-election in Hougang' *Singapore Parliamentary Debates, Official Report* (9 March 2012), vol 88, 2426.

[50] Ibid.

well as the international backdrop which affects our prosperity and security'.[51] This argument was particularly controversial because the constituency seat was one of a handful that were in opposition hands.

A voter in the constituency filed an application for judicial review, seeking the court's assistance to declare that the Prime Minister had to call a by-election to fill the vacancy. In *Vellama d/o Marie Muthu v Attorney-General*,[52] the High Court held in the government's favour but was overruled by the Court of Appeal. The judgments diverged not only in interpretive approaches, but also in their conceptions of democracy. In its judgment, the High Court took a formalistic approach, which affirmed the Prime Minister's position that there was no constitutional requirement for him to call a by-election to fill a casual vacancy.[53] The issue turned on the interpretation of Article 49(1) of the Constitution which stated that a vacancy 'shall be filled by election'. The High Court held that this referred to 'the process of how this vacancy is to be filled and not the event of an election'.[54] Part of the reasoning hinged on the fact that there are three types of MPs: elected MPs, Non-constituency Members of Parliament (NCMPs) and Nominated Members of Parliament (NMPs). NCMPs are opposition members who did not win seats during the general election, but are nonetheless offered seats in Parliament because they attained the highest percentage of the votes in the constituencies they contested. Their number is currently capped at 12. NMPs are nominated members who are non-partisan and who are selected based on achievements in their fields and are meant to contribute to the diversity of voices in Parliament. Both the NCMP and NMP schemes were introduced by the PAP Government to introduce political plurality in the parliamentary chamber, but without affecting the political status quo. In particular, the government acknowledges that the NCMP scheme serves to give the electorate the assurance that they can safely vote for the PAP because there will always be opposition voices in Parliament under the scheme.[55]

Thus, the High Court held that the constitutional requirement that a vacant seat 'shall be filled by election' only means that the particular seat is not to be filled by any other means, for example, by nomination. The Court was reinforced in this view by the contrast between the phraseology in Article 49(1) and Article 66, which deals with when general elections are to be called. Article 66

[51] Ibid.

[52] *Vellama d/o Marie Muthu v AG* [2012] 4 SLR 698 (*Vellama* (HC)).

[53] Ibid, para 115.

[54] Ibid, para 80.

[55] Remarks to this effect were made during the campaigning period of the 2020 general election: see, for example, D Cheong, 'Singapore GE2020: PAP Will Not have "Blank Cheque" because of NCMP Scheme, say Chan Chun Sing and Indranee Rajah', *The Straits Times* (2 July 2020). Available at: www.straitstimes.com/politics/singapore-ge2020-pap-will-not-have-blank-cheque-because-of-ncmp-scheme-say-chun-sing-and; L Lai, 'Singapore GE2020: Workers' Party Using Fear of Opposition Wipeout to Sway Voters, says Heng Swee Keat', *The Straits Times* (5 July 2020). Available at: www.straitstimes.com/politics/singapore-ge2020-workers-party-using-fear-of-opposi tion-wipeout-to-sway-voters-says-heng.

states: 'There *shall be a general election* at such time, within 3 months after every dissolution of Parliament, as the President shall, by Proclamation in the *Gazette*, appoint.' The reference in Article 49 to *election* rather than *an election*, the Court reasoned, compared to *a general election* in Article 66, suggested that Article 49(1) referred to the process by which a casual vacancy was to be filled rather than the event of holding an election.[56]

The judgment notably did not examine the rationales for democratic representation. Observing that '[j]udicial review is founded on the rule of law',[57] the Court made reference to passages affirming that the principle of the rule of law entails that 'all legal power has limits and is subject to judicial review to enforce those limits'.[58] Despite these references, the High Court nonetheless endorsed the Prime Minister's view that he is not subject to any constitutional limits or obligations when it comes to deciding when to call by-elections.

In contrast, the Court of Appeal held that the Prime Minister is, in fact, under a constitutional obligation to call by-elections though he retains broad, good-faith discretion to do so within a reasonable time. It disagreed with the High Court's interpretation of Article 49(1):

> Even reading the word 'election' in the context as prescribing only a process, we fail to see how that necessarily leads to the conclusion that the Prime Minister has thereby an unfettered discretion as to whether he will tender advice to the President to issue a writ of election.[59]

The Court of Appeal further argued that the High Court had not considered the possibility that the phrase *shall be filled by election* could be read in a 'double-barrelled sense', such that it was both mandatory for the Prime Minister to fill a casual vacancy that had arisen in Parliament and to do so by way of election.[60] In other words, the Court of Appeal recognised that a purely literal interpretation of the provision did not lead to any particular conclusion as to the issue at hand.[61]

[56] *Vellama* (HC), n 52 above, paras 57–61.

[57] Ibid, para 2.

[58] Thio LA, *A Treatise on Singapore Constitutional Law* (2012) at para 03.026, cited in *Vellama* (HC).

[59] *Vellama d/o Marie Muthu v Attorney-General* [2013] 4 SLR 1 at para 75 (CA) ('*Vellama* (CA)'). The Court of Appeal said: 'Whether we construe the word "election" as a process or an event, the [question as to whether the Prime Minister has the discretion not to call for a by-election] still remains. It seems to us that the omission of the word "an" in the phrase "shall be filled by election" ('the phrase') is neither here nor there.' Ibid.

[60] Ibid, para 76.

[61] This is a remarkable departure from formalism and strict interpretivism, which had characterized many of the earlier decisions by the Singapore courts in constitutional cases. For a critique on formalistic approaches in Singapore, see Yap PJ, 'Uncovering Originalism and Textualism in Singapore' in JL Neo (ed), *Constitutional Interpretation in Singapore: Theory and Practice* (2017), 117–136.

The Court of Appeal's holding was hailed as a robust affirmation of the right of representation in Singapore. The Court articulated a link between representation and Westminster-style constitutionalism. The most important passage in the judgment is this:

> Having regard to the role of an MP in the Westminster form of government and on a plain reading of Art 49, it seems clear to us that the Constitution places a duty upon the Prime Minister to call a by-election (unless he intends to dissolve Parliament in the near future) to fill casual vacancies of elected MPs which may arise from time to time.[62]

This reference to the Westminster form of government points to the British model of parliamentary democracy, which Singapore inherited from its British colonials. It envisages a form of government which emphasizes the important role of each MP. As the Court explained, an MP 'represents the people of the constituency who voted him into Parliament', therefore voters of each constituency are 'entitled to have a Member representing and speaking for them in Parliament'.[63] The constitutional duty to call a by-election is imperative because '[i]f a vacancy is left unfilled for an unnecessarily prolonged period that would raise a serious risk of disenfranchising the residents of that constituency'.[64]

Comparing the two judgments, the idea of the rule of law has been invoked in such divergent ways that it is hard to determine what actual normative force it serves. The High Court's conception of the rule of law is vindicated through formal adherence to the constitutional text and even through an emphasis on ensuring the 'right' process is followed. Like the High Court, the Court of Appeal also emphasised the role of the rule of law, stating that it is 'a basic proposition of the rule of law that all discretionary power is subject to legal limits'.[65] However, it took the normativity of the rule of law differently, holding that this therefore means the Prime Minister's discretion as to when a by-election should be held is subject to judicial review. Furthermore, while Article 49(1) does not set out any time limit within which a by-election must be conducted, the rule of law eschews absolute discretion and therefore a reasonable time requirement would be imposed, having regard to all the circumstances.[66]

Another aspect of disagreement lies in the divergent conceptions of representation. While the High Court appeared to see representation as primarily a way to elect the government, the Court of Appeal saw elections as protecting the representative link and the right of voters in the constituency to be represented in Parliament. Thus, one might see the Court of Appeal's approach as tending

[62] *Vellama* (CA), n 59 above, para 82.
[63] Ibid, para 79.
[64] Ibid, para 85.
[65] Ibid, citing *Chng Suan Tze v Minister for Home Affairs* [1988] 2 SLR(R) 525 at para 86 (CA).
[66] *Vellama* (CA), n 59 above, para 84, citing the Interpretation Act (Cap 1, 2002 Rev Ed), s 52: 'Where no time is prescribed or allowed within which anything shall be done, that thing shall be done with all convenient speed and as often as the prescribed occasion arises.'

towards a more robust and protective idea of representative democracy, which is nonetheless balanced against communitarian considerations. One can see this, for instance, in the Court of Appeal's caveat:

> As the timing for the holding of an election to fill a vacancy is a polycentric matter which would involve considerations which go well beyond mere practicality and the Prime Minister could justifiably take into account matters relating to policy, including the physical well-being of the country, it is impossible to lay down the specific considerations or factors which would have a bearing on the question as to whether the Prime Minister has acted unreasonably for not, to date, calling a by-election to fill a vacancy.[67]

Accordingly, the Court would only be prepared to intervene in 'exceptional cases',[68] as it appears to balance the right to be represented against the need to maintain social and political stability.

Communitarian Democracy and the Group Representation Constituency: The Case of Wong Souk Yee

One might also understand the Court of Appeal's decision in a subsequent case through this communitarian lens. The case of *Wong Souk Yee v Attorney-General*,[69] an appeal from the High Court,[70] arose when one MP resigned her parliamentary seat to contest the 2017 presidential election. She was part of a GRC, which serves to ensure minority representation by requiring that at least one of the parliamentarians in the team is from the Malay, Indian, or some other minority community in Singapore.[71] While the GRC scheme was instituted through a constitutional amendment, the procedure for filling a vacancy in a GRC is provided for by statute. The Parliamentary Elections Act (PEA)[72] states that no by-election needs to be held 'unless all the Members for

[67] Ibid, para 85. The Court mentioned transboundary haze and, presciently given the current COVID-19 pandemic, a public health concern such as severe acute respiratory syndrome (SARS) as factors that would possibly warrant the Prime Minister postponing a by-election: para 84.

[68] Ibid, para 85.

[69] *Wong Souk Yee*, n 41 above.

[70] *Wong Souk Yee v Attorney-General* [2018] SGHC 80 (HC).

[71] Singapore Constitution, n 43 above, art 39A(1) (which declares the GRC scheme to be 'in order to ensure the representation in Parliament of Members from the Malay, Indian and other minority communities') and arts 39A(2)(a)–(b); Parliamentary Elections Act (Cap 218, 2011 Rev Ed) ('PEA'), ss 27A(4)–(8). The President, acting on the Cabinet's advice, declares before an election which GRCs must have at least one MP from the Malay community and which must have at least one from the Indian or other minority communities: PEA, ibid, s 8A(1)(b). Three-fifths (or, if that is not a whole number, the next higher whole number) of all GRCs must have at least one Malay MP: PEA, ibid, s 8A(3). For general commentary on the GRC scheme, see Thio LA, 'The Right to Political Participation in Singapore: Tailor-making a Westminster-modelled Constitution to Fit the Imperatives of "Asian" Democracy' (2002) 6 *Singapore Journal of International & Comparative Law* 181; and TT Hang, 'Singapore's Electoral System: Government by the People?' (2008) 28(4) *Legal Studies* 610.

[72] PEA, ibid.

that constituency have vacated their seats'[73] in the midst of a parliamentary term. This raises difficult questions about the proper interpretive relationship between a supreme constitution, which contains more general texts and an ordinary statute, which contains more specific provisions governing a particular situation. The Constitution, as we saw earlier, provides at Article 49(1) that vacancies 'shall be filled by elections'. But the statute says that this is only if all the seats in the GRC have become vacant.

This was the issue that the Singapore courts had to grapple with in this case. The appellant, a resident of the constituency who had stood for election at the 2015 general election, argued the statutory provision was unconstitutional and sought to constitutionally oblige the Prime Minister to call for a by-election to fill the vacant seat or, alternatively, to fill all the seats in the GRC. The High Court decided against the applicant. This time the Court of Appeal agreed with the High Court's ruling but disagreed on the reasoning. While conceding there is a discrepancy between the texts, the Court of Appeal noted that when Article 49(1) was enacted in 1965, the concept of GRCs did not exist, therefore how the article applied to GRCs was unclear. Indeed, both sides agreed that there must have been a legislative oversight when drafting the constitutional amendments which implemented the GRC scheme. The parliamentary debates concerning the GRC scheme indicated that it had never been the government's intention for a by-election to be called unless all the seats in a GRC had been vacated. However, the debates were unclear as to how Parliament had intended to implement its intention.[74]

The appellant argued that the article should be interpreted as requiring a by-election for all the seats in a GRC whenever any vacancy arises. The Court was very uneasy with this suggestion as there was no mechanism by which it could force the resignation of the remaining MPs in the team. In the end, it adopted the government's interpretation that Article 49(1) had no application to GRC seats as the words *seat of a Member* in that provision refer only to the seat of an MP of an SMC.[75] This was also in line with Parliament's intention when it established the GRC scheme, whereas the appellant's interpretation would have led to the precise result that legislators had sought to avoid.[76]

As regards the appellant's point that the minority representation rationale underlying the GRC scheme would be undermined if, as had happened in this particular constituency, it is the minority MP's seat which is vacated and not filled through a by-election,[77] the Court noted that this had been considered by Parliament and it had decided that a diminution in the proportion of minority representation in Parliament was 'an acceptable trade-off' to prevent one MP

[73] Ibid, s. 24(2A).
[74] *Wong Souk Yee*, n 41 above, paras 49–56.
[75] Ibid, para 58.
[76] Ibid, paras 70–73.
[77] Ibid, para 74.

in a GRC from being able to hold the other MPs to ransom, for example, by threatening to resign his or her seat, thus forcing a by-election. If the appellant's preferred interpretation of Article 49(1) was adopted, the Court would be reversing Parliament's policy choice. This 'strikes at the heart of the concern behind judicial legislation, and would result in our overstepping our constitutional role'.[78]

In the reasoning set out thus far, the Court of Appeal focused on construing the constitutional text in the light of Parliament's intention in enacting the GRC scheme in 1988 and did not expressly have regard to any rationale for democratic representation. However, it did allude to the latter point when responding to one of the appellant's arguments. The appellant had relied on the Court's statement in *Vellama* that '[t]he voters of a constituency are entitled to have a Member representing and speaking for them in Parliament',[79] and the fact that in the later case of *Yong Vui Kong v Public Prosecutor*[80] the Court had said this articulation of the Westminster model of government provided the 'philosophical underpinnings of the right to vote'[81] which might possibly be 'part of the basic structure of the Constitution'.[82] On this basis, the appellant submitted that the Constitution's basic structure also embodies the right of voters to be represented in Parliament and that this right includes the right to be represented by the full complement of elected MPs returned at each general election. Thus, if a vacancy in a GRC remained unfilled, an aspect of the Constitution's basic structure had been violated.[83]

It is significant that the Court did not dismiss outright the possibility that such a right of representation might be implied into the Constitution. It noted that the Court had not yet conclusively held whether the basic structure doctrine as articulated in *Kesavananda Bharati v State of Kerala*[84] applies in Singapore – that is, in a way that obliges the courts to invalidate purported constitutional amendments inconsistent to the Constitution's basic structure. Assuming, though, the right to representation is part of the basic structure, this did not mean there is a particular form of representation that is 'fundamental and essential' to the Westminster model of government and which cannot be modified. There was nothing in principle preventing Parliament from allowing a GRC to be represented by fewer than its full complement of MPs if some of them had vacated their seats.[85]

Nonetheless, the Court expressed the opinion that if *all* the seats in a GRC fell vacant, it did not necessarily mean that the Prime Minister was not

[78] Ibid, para 75.
[79] *Vellama* (CA), n 59 above, para 79.
[80] [2015] 2 SLR 1129 (CA).
[81] Ibid, para 70.
[82] Ibid, para 69.
[83] *Vellama* (CA), n 59 above, para 76.
[84] AIR 1973 SC 1461 (SC, India).
[85] *Vellama* (CA), n 59 above, para 78.

constitutionally (rather than statutorily) obliged to call a by-election. In this scenario, it was 'at least arguable that an implied right to representation might be invoked to fill this lacuna in the Constitution', though obviously it would be more desirable if Parliament amended the Constitution to deal with the situation instead.[86]

Interestingly, in the later case of *Daniel De Costa Augustin v Attorney-General*,[87] an unsuccessful attempt to challenge the holding of the 2020 general election in the midst of the COVID-19 pandemic, the Court confirmed that the right to vote is 'plainly a constitutional right'[88] which is 'best understood as a right that is found in the Constitution either as a matter of construing it in its entirety or as a matter of necessary implication' from certain constitutional provisions.[89] The Court also accepted 'as a statement of principle elections must be free and fair',[90] but held the appellant had not presented an arguable case as to what this requires, how the aspects of the principle attract constitutional status and how a breach was threatened on the facts of the case.[91]

Right to be Represented, but How?

Arguably, the holding in *Wong Souk Yee* that the right of representation tolerates a sub-optimal level of democratic representation in GRCs detracts from a substantive conception of the rule of law, which would require individual rights to be guaranteed. This assumes, though, that one emphasises the substantive conception, which has never been accepted in Singapore. Instead, the judiciary has affirmed that the right to be represented is constitutionally protected, but not necessarily in specific ways that could be contrary to social and political stability. The Court of Appeal's acceptance of the government's argument that by-elections should not be required unless all the seats in a GRC are vacated lest one or some of the MPs use the threat of resignation to hold the others to ransom serves the aim of not disrupting the political status quo.

Accordingly, there is a right to be represented, but the mechanics of representation are not certain. We know from *De Costa* that the right to vote, which is implied in the Constitution, requires a free and fair election, but what the latter means has yet to be worked out. As such, the precise form of democracy is still in flux in Singapore, though communitarianism is clearly part of the equation.

[86] Ibid, para 72.
[87] [2020] SGCA 60 (CA).
[88] Ibid, para 10.
[89] The Court identified art 66 which requires a general election to be held within three months of a dissolution of Parliament and art 39(1)(a) which states that Parliament consists of, among others, 'such number of elected Members as is required to be returned at a general election': see *De Costa*, ibid para 9.
[90] *De Costa*, ibid, para 13.
[91] Ibid, para 14.

What we might see is a periodic renegotiation of the balance between the right to be represented against the communitarian interests of political and social stability, framed through the lenses of the rule of law and democracy.

Even while the cases have not embraced a substantive version of the rule of law, the courts have definitely advanced a thicker procedural idea of the rule of law. In *Wong Souk Yee*, the Court of Appeal made two procedural rulings that underscore the rule of law's role in upholding representative democracy. The High Court had dismissed the appellant's application for leave to bring judicial review proceedings on the ground that it failed to disclose an arguable or *prima facie* case of reasonable suspicion in favour of granting the remedies sought. Disagreeing, the Court of Appeal noted that the threshold for granting leave is low since the requirement for leave is only intended to 'filter out groundless or hopeless cases at an early stage'.[92] The appellant had met the threshold.[93]

The Court of Appeal also set aside the High Court's order that the appellant should pay costs to the respondent. It held that where a serious question of constitutional law is raised, courts have discretion to depart from the usual rule that costs follow the event. By emphasising that the threshold for granting leave for applications for prerogative orders is low and holding that in cases where serious constitutional law questions are raised an unsuccessful applicant may not be required to bear the government's legal costs, the Court thus signalled that appropriate challenges seeking to uphold democratic representation will not be turned away.

CONCLUSION

We have seen that the Singapore courts have relied on the concept of the rule of law in a way supportive of the right to be represented. However, they have developed this right within the specific contexts in Singapore, particularly framed by the idea of a 'communitarian rule of law'. This has meant that the approach sits on the tightrope of ensuring the availability of judicial review as an aspect of the rule of law, while stating that this power will only be strongly exercised in exceptional situations, thus according the executive and legislature much leeway. Hence, while Singapore has witnessed an expansion in political space for debate and opposition in recent years,[94] there have been contrary developments in more recent times.

[92] *AXY v Comptroller of Income Tax* [2018] 1 SLR 1069, para 34 (CA).

[93] *Vellama* (CA), n 59 above, para 85.

[94] See Thio LA, 'Singapore: Regulating Political Speech and the Commitment "to Build a Democratic Society"' (2003) 1(3) *International Journal of Constitutional Law* 516 but compare Derek Da Cunha's critique that this opening up of space may be more apparent than real: D da Cunha, *Singapore in the New Millennium: Challenges Facing the City-State* (2002), 271–274.

While the current Prime Minister Lee Hsien Loong has been associated with a more inclusive and open political style,[95] recent legal changes such as the Protection from Online Falsehoods and Manipulation Act 2019 (POFMA)[96] have raised concerns among critics about a reversion to a more constricted democratic space. At the same time, Singapore now has a highly educated population who use the Internet to inform themselves, connect with one another, as well as share ideas and opinions. While the population may generally agree with an approach to governance that is more communitarian, rather than strictly orientated towards individual rights, they have shown less willingness to accept a top-down, authoritarian approach. The further inroad that the Workers' Party made in the 2020 general election by capturing ten parliamentary seats, the best showing by an opposition party since the nation's independence,[97] is probably as much a testament to its ability to connect with the electorate as it is a vote against what some saw as the heavy-handed use of the law to control public discourse.[98] As Singapore sees a further maturing of its democracy, it is likely that a greater conceptual distinction will need to be made between authoritarian and communitarian conceptions of the rule of law.

[95] For instance, in his 2006 National Day message, Prime Minister Lee Hsien Loong explicitly stated that the government would build a more open society and encourage freer debate: see Lee Hsien Loong, 'Prime Minister Lee Hsien Loong's National Day Message 2006' (8 August 2006) at para 13, Archives Online, National Archives of Singapore. Available at: www.nas.gov.sg/archivesonline/data/pdfdoc/2006080801.htm.

[96] No 18 of 2019.

[97] C Yong and J Iau, 'Singapore GE2020: Signs of Young Voters' Crucial Role in Election Outcome' *The Straits Times* (16 July 2020). Available at: www.straitstimes.com/singapore/signs-of-young-voters-crucial-role-in-ge2020-outcome.

[98] G Ho and Y Sin, 'Singapore GE2020: A watershed election and new normal?' *The Straits Times* (12 July 2020). Available at: www.straitstimes.com/politics/a-watershed-election-and-new-normal.

Part III

Clearing the Shadow

7

Authoritarian Rule of Law in Hong Kong

BENNY Y T TAI*

FOR MANY YEARS, Hong Kong's rule of law (ROL) has been recognised as well established.[1] According to the World Justice Project's Rule of Law Index, Hong Kong's global ranking in 2019 was 16 among 126 countries and jurisdictions.[2] Although throughout the years Hong Kong has not possessed a fully democratic political system, much confidence has been displayed in its commitment to the ROL.

In 2013–2014, the Umbrella Movement hit Hong Kong. At that time, it was the largest social movement in the territory's history, which used a form of civil disobedience to strive for the introduction of universal suffrage.[3] Since then, Hong Kong has gradually slid into a new era. Not only has there been no real advancement in the democratic direction; there are signs that the nature of the governing system is deteriorating from semi-democratic to semi-authoritarian. Hong Kong's sovereign, the Chinese Communist Party (CCP), has readjusted its policy towards Hong Kong. In the years after the Umbrella Movement, the CCP and its local agent, the Government of the Hong Kong Special Administrative Region Government (HKSAR), have been more prepared to stretch their authoritarian muscles in the territory.

In this very different political environment, Hong Kong's well-established ROL is now facing its most severe challenge. Many people, including senior members in the legal profession and the judiciary, did not see these coming. Before Hong Kong's citizens had sufficient space to recover their breath and adjust to

* Former Associate Professor, Faculty of Law, University of Hong Kong, Hong Kong.

[1] A Chen and A Cheung, 'Debating Rule of Law in the Hong Kong Special Administrative Region, 1997–2002' in R Peerenboom (ed) *Asian Discourses of Rule of Law* (2004).

[2] World Justice Project, *Rule of Law Index 2019*, Available at: https://worldjusticeproject.org/sites/default/files/documents/ROLI-2019-Reduced.pdf.

[3] Chan KM, 'Occupying Hong Kong: How deliberation, referendum and civil disobedience played out in the Umbrella Movement' (2005) 21 *International Journal on Human Rights* 129; BYT Tai, 'Stages of Hong Kong's Democratic Movement' (2019) 4(4) *Asian Journal of Comparative Politics* 352.

the new environment, the city was unexpectedly struck again by another wave of large-scale street protests, less than five years after the Umbrella Movement. The latest movement, larger in scale, longer in duration and rougher in style, was triggered by the launching of a bill (the Extradition Bill), to amend the Fugitive Offenders Ordinance, by the Chief Executive (CE) of the HKSAR: Carrie Lam. The bill proposed to expedite and extend the arrangement of the extradition of suspected offenders of certain criminal offences to mainland China and Taiwan. If the aftermath of the Umbrella Movement has dragged Hong Kong into a semi-authoritarian era, then the Anti-Extradition Bill Movement may have brought it very close to its breaking point, perhaps sliding towards an authoritarian era. It seems obvious that the challenges to Hong Kong's ROL are becoming even more numerous than before.

To provide a background to understanding the significance of these latest challenges to Hong Kong's ROL, Part I of this chapter examines the understanding of authoritarianism in relation with different conceptions of democracy and the ROL to illustrate the status of law in authoritarian systems. Part II provides an account of the backsliding to Hong Kong's system and how the opening of the era of authoritarian ROL happened. Part III discusses the challenges to Hong Kong's ROL arising from the encroachment of authoritarian ROL. Part IV concludes by suggesting ways that Hong Kong people may adopt to counteract these challenges.

DEMOCRACY, AUTHORITARIANISM AND THE ROL

Authoritarian regimes come in various forms: hereditary monarchy, military rule, personal dictatorship and the one-party state.[4] The most crucial factor in distinguishing a democratic from an authoritarian regime is *not* whether competitive elections with universal suffrage occur. Many authoritarian systems have such elections.[5] In truly democratic regimes, there must be a real chance for the legislative and Chief Executive offices to be filled by candidates from the opposition.[6] The ultimate goal of law in the governing process and how far citizens' civil and political rights are actually protected by law can reflect the varying degrees of democracy or authoritarianism in the system.[7]

Authoritarianism and the ROL

There is a general misconception that an authoritarian state does not incorporate laws and operates under a system of rule by persons. However, as revealed from numerous studies on the relationship between authoritarianism and law, not

[4] P Brooker, *Non-Democratic Regimes* (2014).
[5] L Diamond, 'Thinking about Hybrid Regimes' (2002) 13(2) *Journal of Democracy* 21–35.
[6] M Ottaway, *Democracy Challenged: The Rise of Semi-Authoritarianism* (2003).
[7] L Diamond, *Developing Democracy: Toward Consolidation* (1999).

only are there many locally made or imported legal rules, but laws are widely used to serve the needs of the authoritarian regimes. Because of law's concern with rules, rule-following, hierarchies of authority and coercion, the law can be a ready, efficient and effective tool of governing, social control and oppression.[8] Emphasising the central role of law in governing may also enhance the external legitimacy of an authoritarian regime.

Authoritarian regimes are always in search of legitimacy, ie the voluntary acceptance of the rightfulness of the authority by people under its rule, so that it can remain in power. If the supply from other sources of legitimacy comes up short, some elements of the ROL like judicial independence[9] and protection of legal rights in civil and commercial areas[10] might compensate the legitimacy deficit of the regime in question. Allowing the judiciary to enjoy some degree of independent authority may provide an image of constraining arbitrary powers. For example, establishing a neutral institution to protect property rights means that investor can be confident that there will be no interference with economic activity and development. If citizens' economic wellbeing leads to substantive improvement, the regime may also gain additional legitimacy.

However, providing political space for the ROL to thrive can be a double-edged sword. ROL, however thin, may still be used by the opposition to challenge the authority of authoritarian rulers. Citizens may also exercise their limited civil and political rights, posing a severe threat to the stability and continuation of authoritarian rule. Therefore, an authoritarian regime may have a political incentive to introduce some degree of the ROL but will never allow people to use the law to challenge its rule. The introduction of competitive elections in an authoritarian state serves similar purposes. Opening the highest offices of state power to competitive elections allows the authoritarian rulers to hold onto power by establishing an impression of popular consent, thus generating democratic legitimation.[11] However, authoritarian rulers also face the risk that the people might turn them out of power through elections. Therefore, they will use tools from a menu of manipulation[12] to tilt the playing field, making it very difficult for elections to generate a 'liberalising electoral outcome'.[13]

Democracy and the ROL

For a thicker understanding of democracy, in addition to the minimal requirement of competitive elections, the ROL must satisfy other substantial requirements.

[8] L Henderson, 'Authoritarianism and the Rule of Law' (1991) 66(2) *Indiana Law Journal* 356–379.

[9] T Moustafa, 'Law and Courts in Authoritarian Regimes' (2014) 10 *Annual Review of Law and Social Science* 281.

[10] J Rajah, *Authoritarian Rule of Law: Legislation, Discourse and Legitimacy in Singapore* (2012).

[11] A Schedler (ed), *Electoral Authoritarianism: The Dynamics of Unfree Competition* (2006).

[12] A Schedler, 'Menu of Manipulation' (2002) 13(2) *Journal of Democracy* 36.

[13] MM Howard and P Roessler, 'Liberalizing Electoral Outcomes in Competitive Authoritarian Regimes' (2006) 50(2) *American Journal of Political Science* 365.

First, legal rules are applied fairly, consistently and predictably across similar cases, irrespective of the class, status, or power of those subject to the rules. Second, the state and its agents are themselves subject to the law. The executive authorities are constrained, both constitutionally and by other government institutions. Executive powers are subject to review by an independent judiciary on their constitutionality and legality; there is policy and financial oversight by the legislature; and other mechanisms of horizontal accountability are established by law. Third, all citizens enjoy political and legal equality. Fundamental civil rights, including the right to freedom of expression, freedom of association and freedom of assembly must be constitutionally and legally protected.[14] Without the ROL, any competitive election may only be a kind of democratic façade.[15] On the contrary, the stronger the ROL is, the more stable and endurable the democracy will be.[16]

Similar to democracy and authoritarianism, the ROL can also contain different degrees. Dieter Grimm suggested a level approach to understanding the ROL: it is not a matter of all or nothing, but of more or less. Its realisation can take the form of a process, level by level. It is not possible to achieve all levels at the outset. Each new step means a step forward compared to the previous level and the realisation of the ROL becomes more demanding when advancing to higher levels.[17]

The minimal understanding of the ROL requires government officials and citizens to be bound and abide by the law.[18] There is no requirement that the laws must be enacted by a democratically elected legislature and implemented by executive authorities headed by a democratically elected Chief Executive. Also, there is no guarantee that the law will protect the fundamental rights of citizens.

However, ROL has a natural tendency to grow thick. To ensure government officials are bound and abide by the law, there must be effective mechanisms to limit their powers. Otherwise, the laws will be mere words on paper with no real use in guiding the action of government officials. Self-restraint by government officials cannot be an effective limitation measure. There must be external limitation mechanisms established by law. An independent judiciary is essential to ensure that government officials are held accountable. Judges are recognised to be the special guardians of the law. They are expected to be neutral, free of passion, prejudice and arbitrariness and loyal to the law alone when they

[14] Human Rights Committee, *General Comment No 25 of the International Covenant on Civil and Political Rights (1996)*. Adopted by the Human Rights Committee at its 1510th meeting, UN Doc CCPR/C/21/Rev.1/Add.7.

[15] Ottaway, n 6 above.

[16] R Dahl, *Polyarchy: Participation and Opposition* (1971).

[17] D Grimm, 'Levels of the Rule of Law on the Possibility of Exporting a Western Achievement' (2011) 1 *European-Asian Journal of Law and Governance* 5–11.

[18] B Tamanaha 'The History and Elements of the Rule of Law' (2012) *Singapore Journal of Legal Studies* 232.

interpret and apply the legal rules to actual dispute.[19] Institutional arrangements that protect the judiciary from outside interference are essential to the ROL.

However, the law cannot effectively constrain governmental powers by relying solely on judicial limitation. There must be other limitation mechanisms working together with an independent judiciary to impose proper and sufficient constraints on government.[20] One additional limitation mechanism is competitive elections for the offices of the Chief Executive and the legislature. Through voting in elections, citizens can exert influence on how the executive and legislative powers are to be defined and how the elected officials should use these powers.[21] Justice Bokhary, a retired permanent judge of the Court of Final Appeal of Hong Kong (HKCFA), once remarked that without democracy, there could only be something that is an 'approximation of the rule of law'.[22] Competitive elections may not need to take any particular form, but they must give effect to the free expression of the will of the electors. An electoral system must protect the political rights of voters. First, all electors have an equal number of votes. Second, the weight of the vote of each elector should be equal. Third, electors should have a free choice of candidates. Fourth, there cannot be any unreasonable restrictions on the right to stand for election; any restrictions must be justified on objective and reasonable criteria.

For the electors to exercise their right to vote effectively, adequate protection of citizens' civil rights is required. To make informed choices, electors must have the freedoms to debate public affairs, to hold peaceful demonstrations and meetings, to criticize and oppose, to publish political material, to campaign for election and to advertise political ideas. Citizens must be able to engage in political activity individually or through political parties and other organisations. They should have the right to form and join organisations concerned with political and public affairs. Other rights associated with these must also be protected. Electors must be free to visit the polling station so their right to freedom of movement must be protected. There must be free communication of information and ideas about public and political issues between citizens, candidates and elected representatives. The right to press freedom is implied. The list of associated rights can be further extended as fundamental rights become interconnected.

Democracy, therefore, has a complementary relationship with the ROL. It is a means as well as an end. Competitive elections are one of the limitation mechanisms to ensure that rights can be adequately protected. Democratic rights are the rights that should be protected by the ROL.[23] A full range of civil

[19] Ibid.

[20] JE Lane, *Constitutions and Political Theory* (2011).

[21] Human Rights Committee, n 14 above.

[22] The remark was made by Justice Bokhary in an interview with the *Hong Kong Economic Journal* on 1 October 2015.

[23] A Buchanan, *Justice, Legitimacy, and Self-determination: Moral Foundation for International Law* (2004).

rights must be protected by law for the effective exercise of democratic rights. Protecting the civil and political rights of citizens becomes the ultimate goal of the ROL.[24] Thus, the ROL and democracy overlap and are also interdependent. A democratic system needs the thin and the thick understandings of the ROL to avoid a decent into authoritarianism. The more ROL it can acquire, the stronger the democratic system will be. Similarly, without competitive elections, the ROL that can be realised may only be limited and more insecure. And in the end, no matter if one is looking from the perspective of democracy or the ROL, the law must adequately protect the civil and political rights of citizens.[25]

Semi-Authoritarianism or Semi-Democracy?

By integrating our understanding of authoritarianism, democracy and the ROL, we can understand more about the nature of an authoritarian system. There may still be elections, but there is no real chance for the opposition to win. There are many laws, but they only facilitate rather than constrain the power holders. The judiciary may be independent, but judges are politically shrewd and dare not question the legality and constitutionality of executive actions. Legal rights in the civil and commercial areas are protected, but citizens cannot exercise their civil and political rights to challenge the authority of those in power.

This kind of authoritarian system, different from the absolute form, can be called 'semi-authoritarian'. However, it may not be wrong to call it 'semi-democracy'[26] depending on whether the authoritarian or the democratic parts are being emphasised.[27] The direction of development also determines whether the system is semi-democratic or semi-authoritarian. If it is in the process of developing towards genuine democracy, calling the system a semi-democracy can highlight the dynamics of change.

If there is no way the system can evolve into a one that is fully democratic, then it is a semi-authoritarian regime. However, there are still dynamics and possibilities of change within a semi-authoritarian system. Semi-authoritarian regimes can have three different statuses. First, under a stable semi-authoritarian regime, a balance has been established among competing forces. There is no need to increase or reduce the degree of authoritarianism. Next, unstable semi-authoritarian regimes may experience dynamic change which undermines the government's ability to maintain the status quo. The power holders must open up new political spaces. The degree of authoritarianism will be reduced, providing the possibility of incremental progress toward democracy. Finally, in a decaying

[24] T Bingham, *The Rule of Law* (2010).

[25] J Habermas, 'On the Internal Relationship between the Rule of Law and Democracy' (1995) 3(1) *European Journal of Philosophy* 12.

[26] L Diamond, J Linz and SM Lipset (eds) *Democracy in Developing Countries* (1988).

[27] Brooker, n 4 above.

semi-authoritarian regime, there is a possibility that government will move to full authoritarianism. Weak counterbalancing factors may produce increasingly strong authoritarian tendencies.[28]

AN AUTHORITARIANISING HONG KONG

Hong Kong is neither genuinely democratic nor fully authoritarian. It belongs to a kind of hybrid system which contains both democratic and authoritarian elements.[29] Calling it semi-authoritarian may be correct, but many people in Hong Kong may prefer to call it semi-democratic because many democratic elements are still entrenched in the territory. One such element is the ROL which can provide adequate protection to the human rights of Hong Kong's citizens, including those who have been persistently fighting for genuine democracy. Another reason is that there is a timetable to the Basic Law (BL), Hong Kong's constitution, which clearly states that the ultimate aim of the development of the political system is to be democratic. Article 45 states that the ultimate aim is to select the CE by universal suffrage upon nomination by a broadly representative nominating committee in accordance with democratic procedures. There is a real possibility that Hong Kong may develop into a genuine democracy if the natural meaning of the BL provisions were to be implemented.

End of the Semi-Democracy Era

The Standing Committee of the National People's Congress (NPCSC), a legislative arm of the PRC, issued a decision on the election method of the CE on 31 August 2014 ('the 831 Decision'). It laid down rigorous requirements for the election method of the CE starting from 2017. The number of members, composition and formation of the nominating committee (NC) have to be made in accordance with the election committee for the previous CE. The NC can only nominate two to three candidates and each candidate must have the endorsement of more than half of all the members of the NC.

These specific arrangements for the nomination process allow the CCP to easily screen out undesirable candidates. They do not satisfy the international requirements on universal suffrage, as the Hong Kong electorate would not have a free choice of candidates and unreasonable restrictions would be imposed on the right of any person from the opposition to stand for future CE elections. The 831 Decision triggered the 79-day occupation during the Umbrella Movement in the autumn of 2014. It also formally ended Hong Kong's era of

[28] Ottaway, n 6 above.

[29] B Fong, 'State-Society Conflicts under Hong Kong's Hybrid Regime: Governing Coalition Building and Civil Society Challenges' (2013) 53(5) *Asian Survey* 854.

semi-democracy as it dashed any hope in the near future for genuine and equal universal suffrage in Hong Kong. The original plan of the CCP was to introduce a controlled form of competitive election to select future CEs to compensate the legitimacy deficit which had long been suffered by the Government of the HKSAR (HKSARG). The aim was to supply some measure of democratic legitimacy to the HKSARG, but also to ensure that the elected CE would still be under the CCP's control. However, the proposal to implement the 831 Decision was vetoed by the opposition as it failed to achieve the necessary support from two-thirds of the Legislative Council (LegCo).

The Umbrella Movement was the most direct confrontation between the CCP and the opposition. After the CCP decided that no genuine democracy could be given to Hong Kong, she adjusted her strategy to deal with the opposition voices in Hong Kong demanding democracy. If the system was not going to be liberalised, the remaining option was to find alternative ways to tighten political control in the territory to preserve a non-democratic regime.

Immediately after the Umbrella Movement, the CCP might not have decided to fully authoritarianise Hong Kong, as a semi-authoritarian Hong Kong could window-dress CCP's full authoritarian rule by demonstrating to the world that the Hong Kong people are still governing themselves and enjoy a high degree of autonomy. The processes to authoritarianise Hong Kong aim to achieve several strategic goals. One of which is to help the CE, who will never be democratically elected and is under CCP direction, find more political legitimacy. If successful, there will be no need to introduce genuine democracy in Hong Kong. The CCP's overriding concern is that that once democratic elections are fully implemented, it will lose control over the territory and Hong Kong could become a subversive base threatening its wider rule.

From the CCP's perspective, the past failures of CEs were caused by the constraints imposed by various checks and balances in the territory. If the CE could have a free hand to gain legitimacy by designing and implementing policies to improve the livelihood of Hong Kong citizens, this might weaken the voices demanding democracy. Therefore, the targets of authoritarianisation ROL are the sources of constraining power in Hong Kong, which focus on: the democratic camp, the Hong Kong courts and the civil society. Given the outbreak of the Anti-Extradition Movement, the CCP is prepared to further authoritarianise Hong Kong into becoming fully authoritarian.

Authoritarian ROL

Ironically, the CCP's most critical tool for advancing authoritarianism in Hong Kong is through the ROL, which has also been an essential component of Hong Kong's semi-democratic system since the colonial era. The ROL in the hands of the CCP is quite different from the ROL that has been embraced by Hong Kong. When the law is being captured and used to legitimise decisions made for authoritarian purposes, then the ROL can be referred to as an authoritarian ROL.[30] The law under authoritarian ROL does not need to constrain powerholders and protect the fundamental rights of citizens. The over-riding function of law is to maintain social order. This kind of law can still provide a varying degree of legitimation, depending on the legal culture of the community. This is why authoritarian rulers choose the law as one of their governing tools.

The CCP has used many different methods to implement authoritarian ROL. Various incidents before and after Carrie Lam's replacement of CY Leung as the CE indicate that Hong Kong is now clearly travelling in the direction of authoritarianism. What is unclear is just how far past the semi-authoritarian line it has gone.

Aggrandising the Constitution of the People's Republic of China

Many provisions of the Constitution of the People's Republic of China (PRC) contradict the Basic Law, which was the main reason why the CCP created the principle of 'One Country Two Systems' allowing Hong Kong to operate political, legal, social and economic systems that are very different from those on the mainland. Except for Article 31 of the PRC Constitution, which authorises the National People's Congress (NPC) to establish special administrative regions when necessary, the Basic Law avoids mentioning other provisions of the PRC Constitution. Article 11 provides that the systems and policies practised in the HKSAR should be based on the provisions of the BL. These include social and economic systems; the system for safeguarding the fundamental rights and freedoms of its residents; the executive; and the legislative and the judicial systems and their relevant policies.

Since 2014, the CCP has begun to emphasise the importance of the PRC Constitution in the governance of Hong Kong. It has not focused on the socialist provisions within the document but has instead emphasized the overriding interests of the nation, including national sovereignty, national security and development interests.[31] Although the provisions of the PRC Constitution may not be directly enforceable in the Hong Kong Courts, by aggrandising the Constitution, the CCP can reset Hong Kong's constitutional background, paving the way for advancing authoritarian ROL. This happens primarily through the power of interpretation of the Basic Law by the NPCSC.

[30] M Tushnet, 'Authoritarian Constitutionalism' (2015) 100 *Cornell Law Review* 391; Rajah, n 10 above.

[31] Xi JP, *Secure a Decisive Victory in Building a Moderately Prosperous Society in All Respects and Strive for the Great Success of Socialism with Chinese Characteristics for a New Era*. Delivered at the 19th National Congress of the Communist Party of China on October 18, 2017. Available at: www.xinhuanet.com/english/download/Xi_Jinping's_report_at_19th_CPC_National_Congress.pdf.

Normalising the Interpretation of the BL by the NPCSC

The Basic Law is Hong Kong's constitutional foundation. Through the power to interpret the Basic Law enjoyed by the NPCSC, the CCP can give any meaning to the BL whatever and whenever it desires. The meaning given may even distort the BL's original language and such additional meanings can also be applied retrospectively.

The CCP used to think that the power to interpret the Basic Law should only be used in exceptional circumstances as any such use would weaken Hong Kong's judicial authority. However, it is now more prepared to use this conveniently powerful constitutional tool. Once a legal basis can be established for a controversial political decision to be made through specific formal and authoritative decision-making procedures, many in Hong Kong may accept its legitimacy. Not many citizens seem to know or care too much about the specific source of the legal intervention, the integrity of the legal procedures in generating the legal justification, or whether the legal justification is itself liberal or equitable. Given this, the CCP will normalise the use of the interpretation process to provide constitutional and legal support for controversial political decisions.

Even if constitutional and legal disputes could have been resolved in Hong Kong's judicial proceedings, the CCP can issue an interpretation of the BL before the Hong Kong judges give a ruling. Thus, Hong Kong's judicial independence has been seriously eroded. The CCP does not trust Hong Kong judges and there is little respect for its judicial autonomy. The Hong Kong courts have unquestionably accepted the authority of the NPCSC interpretations. It appears that Hong Kong judges do not dare confront the sovereign power of the CCP and seem quite powerless to defend their understanding of the ROL in front of their sovereign master, who has a very different understanding of the ROL. An excellent example illustrating this is the interpretation by the NPCSC on Article 104 of the Basic Law (the Interpretation).[32]

The Interpretation in effect amended Article 104 and did not merely clarify the meaning of the constitutional provision. According to the Interpretation, an oath-taker must take the oath prescribed by laws accurately, completely, solemnly and sincerely. Failure to do so is considered as declining to take the oath. If an oath-taker is taken to have declined, they will be disqualified from assuming public office. Additionally, if the first oath taken is declared invalid, the oath-taker will not be given another opportunity to retake it. Thus, the NPCSC added details that can hardly be found in the legal text.

All levels of Hong Kong courts, including the HKCFA, accepted the Interpretation's constitutional authority. Six legislators of the opposition camp

[32] For further details of this incident, see Chapter 3 by Zhu Han in this volume.

were disqualified on the basis that they had failed to take their oaths accurately, completely, solemnly and sincerely, in accordance with the Interpretation.

Issuing Decisions on Compatibility with the Basic Law

Even though it is not explicitly mentioned in the Basic Law, the NPCSC has developed a new constitutional tool which can be considered as an extension of its power of interpretation. Foreseeing that there may be a constitutional challenge on a measure to implement authoritarian ROL, the NPCSC has acted pre-emptively, issuing decisions to confirm measures compatible with the Constitution and the Basic Law. In case these measures could still be legally challenged in the future, the NPCSC can give an Interpretation to grant constitutional status for the measures in question, with the hopes that people who want to challenge the measure would be dissuaded from doing so. A good example of this is the decision by the NPCSC confirming the constitutionality of the co-location arrangement of the high-speed rail between Hong Kong and Guangzhou (the Co-Location Decision).

In 2010, the HKSARG pushed through the LegCo a controversial project granting funding for the construction of a high-speed rail link from Hong Kong to Guangzhou via Shenzhen, to connect with the rail network on the mainland. The cost of the project increased from around HK$60 billion to close to 90 billion because of over-spending. One major attraction of the link is that there will be a co-location arrangement for passengers to complete clearance procedures for both Hong Kong and the mainland at a single location in one go. In 2017, the HKSARG proposed that the co-location arrangement would be conducted at the West Kowloon terminal. A Mainland Port Area (MPA) will be set up at the West Kowloon terminal, situated in the heart of the territory, in which the whole body of mainland laws will be applicable and mainland authorities will exercise jurisdiction over all matters except those reserved for the HKSAR.

Many people questioned whether the co-location arrangement was compatible with the provisions of the Basic Law. Article 18 provides that national law shall not be applied in the HKSAR except for those relating to defence, foreign affairs and other matters outside the limits of the autonomy of the HKSAR, listed in Annex III. Article 19 provides that HKSAR courts shall have jurisdiction over all cases in the territory, but that the restrictions on their jurisdiction imposed by the legal system and principles previously in force in Hong Kong shall be maintained. A December 2017 NPCSC decision confirmed that the co-location arrangement is compatible with the Basic Law. It states that the co-location arrangement will not change the HKSAR's territorial boundaries, nor affect its high degree of autonomy, or decrease the rights and freedoms enjoyed by Hong Kong residents. Also, it is beneficial to the economic development of Hong Kong. The Hong Kong Bar Association severely criticised the decision. All the provisions of the Basic Law referred to by the decision in their plain reading cannot provide a firm legal basis for the co-location arrangement and explain why it would not be contravening Article 18.[33]

With confirmation from the NPCSC, LegCo then enacted local legislation on the co-location arrangement, the law was challenged in the courts of Hong Kong on its compatibility with the Basic Law. The Court of First Instance ruled that the co-location arrangement is compatible with the Basic Law. The judge did not give direct constitutional status to the NPCSC Decision. However, he recognised that it ought to be admitted as relevant post-enactment extrinsic material, in aid of the construction of the Basic Law and has a high persuasive value in the particular circumstances of the case.

Like the oath-taking incident, this co-location incident severely undermines the ROL in Hong Kong. The CCP is now increasingly prepared to use the law to justify any decision it wants to make, as it controls the constitutional process to interpret the Basic Law. Even if the reading given by the NPCSC is beyond the natural and plain meaning of the legal text and is not in accordance with prescribed procedures of the Basic Law, no one can question its authority. As the Hong Kong Bar Association acknowledged, any act will be compatible with the Basic Law 'just because the NPCSC says so'. Law will be used in a manipulative fashion when the CCP believes that such 'good things' can be done.[34]

Acting through the HKSARG by Enforcing Existing Laws

The CCP now has the full cooperation of CE Carrie Lam's Administration. The spirit of authoritarian ROL utilises every possible space provided by the legal text to establish legal authorisation for authoritarianism. In so doing, the meaning of the legal text may be arbitrarily extended or twisted. Legal procedures may ignore the requirements of procedural fairness. Officials exercising the legal powers to fulfil an authoritarian task may face future judicial challenges. However, the CCP can easily pick an article from the Basic Law and issue an interpretation, thus providing a constitutional basis for that authoritarian measure. One example is the disqualification of candidates by returning officers, on the ground that they were not genuinely upholding the Basic Law.

After the successful disqualification of elected Legislative Councillors (noted above), the wave of disqualification was extended to cover undesirable

[33] Hong Kong Bar Association, Statement of the Hong Kong Bar Association on the Decision of the NPCSC of 27 December 2017 on the Co-operation Agreement between the Mainland and the HKSAR on the Establishment of the Port at the West Kowloon Station of the Guangzhou-Shenzhen-Hong Kong Express Rail Link for Implementing Co-location Arrangement. Available at: www.hkba.org/sites/default/files/20171228%20-%20Bar%20Co-Location%20Arrangement%20Statement%20%28English%29%20FINAL_0.pdf.

[34] Ibid.

candidates. Section 40 of the Legislative Council Ordinance provides that, for a person to be validly nominated as a candidate in the election of a constituency of the LegCo, they must sign a declaration to uphold the Basic Law and pledge allegiance to the HKSAR (the Declaration). Section 42A of the Legislative Council Ordinance authorises the Returning Office to decide whether a candidate is validly nominated. However, in the past, the relevant provisions of the Legislative Council Ordinance had only been used by returning officers to verify whether Declarations had been properly signed. Even though no express provision exists, since 2016 returning officers in LegCo elections have exercised the power to determine whether a nominee has a genuine and truthful intention to uphold the Basic Law. Nominations of several candidates have been declared invalid on the basis that they had expressed opinions supporting Hong Kong independence. In at least one case, a nominee had made a public statement that he no longer supported independence, but his nomination was still declared invalid. The returning officer's reason for disqualification was that she was not satisfied that the nominee had genuinely changed his stance.

The red line continues to be redrawn. In the March 2018 LegCo by-election, the nomination of a candidate supporting the right of the people to democratically decide Hong Kong's future was also declared invalid. The candidate was considered not to be upholding the Basic Law. Of course, 'To uphold of the Basic Law' is not defined in the Basic Law, nor in the Interpretation on oath-taking. However, since the 2016 LegCo election, all potential candidates must sign a confirmation form indicating their willingness to uphold the Basic Law, including Articles 1, 12 and 159(4).

Article 1 provides that the HKSAR is an inalienable part of the PRC. According to Article 12, the HKSAR shall be a local administrative region of the PRC, which shall enjoy a high degree of autonomy and come directly under the Central People's Government (CPG). Article 159(4) states that no amendment to the Basic Law shall contravene the established basic policies of the PRC regarding Hong Kong. Thus, returning officers could treat all opinions that deny, challenge, question or even suggest an alternative view to HKSAR's status as an inalienable part of China to not be upholding the Basic Law. However, nobody knows exactly what would be disallowed until the returning officer makes a decision. In other words, the returning officer now exercises arbitrary powers with no clear standard, which limits the rights of Hong Kong citizens to stand in elections. Even the Hong Kong courts confirmed that the returning officer does have such power and can satisfy specific requirements on procedural fairness in exercising it.

The CCP can now act through public servants in the HKSARG and achieve the objectives of the 831 Decision that triggered the outbreak of the Umbrella Movement, via another path. 'Undesirable' persons can now be easily screened out of standing for election. One can foresee that the returning officer will use the same power in the CE and the District Council elections going forward.

Clearing the Obstruction in the LegCo and Amending LegCo's Rules of Procedure

Even though the pro-CCP camp has always enjoyed a majority in the LegCo, the opposition camp can still use various mechanisms allowed by the Rules of Procedure, like filibustering or delaying controversial decisions of the HKSARG. The pro-CCP camp currently holds the special majority needed to amend LegCo's rules of procedure and the rules were recently amended. Thus, all allowable mechanisms in the legislative chamber to withstand the encroachment of the authoritarian regime by the opposition camp have been removed.

However, yet more manipulation of the Rules of Procedure by the pro-CCP camp is underway. The President of the LegCo and almost all chairpersons of LegCo's committees are from the pro-CCP camp. The President and the chairmen have the power to make final decisions on 'points of order' under Rule 45 of the Rules of Procedure. This should be a limited power and should only cover matters related to the observance of the rules of order during the meetings of the LegCo and its committees. Following the spirit of authoritarian ROL, the pro-CCP camp wants to extend the scope of this power, asserting that the President enjoys the power to make final decisions on all LegCo business. No debate would be allowed on the President's final decisions.

Additionally, it would be complicated to challenge a Presidential decision through judicial review, as the HKCFA has already ruled that the court will not interfere with the internal processes of the LegCo. As a result, LegCo proceedings are now dominated by the pro-CCP camp. Opposition camps are thus unable use the processes in the legislative chamber to defend thicker understandings of the ROL and to prevent authoritarian ROL.

Introduction of the Extradition Bill and Police Brutality

Before the recent Bill on national security was tabled, another Bill generated as much controversy. It is not clear who was the real initiator of the bill to amend the Fugitive Offenders Ordinance, the CCP or Carrie Lam. However, neither could have anticipated that its introduction would trigger another large-scale protest in the territory, not long after the Umbrella Movement. Under this Bill, a person in Hong Kong alleged to have committed an offence in Mainland China may be extradited there. The Bill was one of the measures designed to integrate the legal systems of Mainland China and Hong Kong and is an excellent example of China's power over Hong Kong.

The proposal generated a deep fear among Hong Kong people that a backdoor would open up in the 'legal firewall' separating Hong Kong's legal system from the Mainland's. Many people are concerned that the protection of fundamental rights in HK's common law system will be lost. On 9 June 2019, over 1 million people marched to protest against the Extradition Bill. However, the

HKSARG still did not back down. On 12 June 2019, the legislative process continued as scheduled. This triggered further protests, with thousands of protesters surrounding the legislative building and closing main access roads. The police fired tear gas and rubber bullets. The protests were cleared, but at a cost. Around 2 million people – about one-quarter of Hong Kong's population – took to the streets the following Sunday, demanding that the HKSARG withdraw the Extradition Bill (even though Carrie Lam had announced she was 'suspending' the Bill the day before). In the months following, roadblocks, the firing of tear gas, rubber bullets and water cannons, conflicts between the protesters and the police, arrests, injuries and fights between people holding different political views happened almost every weekend, sometimes even on weekdays. The police escalated their use of force to suppress the protests. The protesters responded to this brutality with even more violent acts.

The protesters also made other demands: there should be an independent inquiry to investigate the abuse of police powers used on 9 June 2019; the label of 'riot' should be removed from the incidents that happened on that date and all arrested protesters should be released; and universal suffrage should be introduced. The Extradition Bill was finally withdrawn almost 80 days later, on 4 September 2019. However, to date the HKSARG has not given any response to the other demands.

Enacting Laws for Hong Kong Directly by Adding National Laws to Annex III of the Basic Law

According to Article 18 of the Basic Law, national laws shall not be applied in the HKSAR except for those listed in Annex III to the Basic Law. The NPCSC may add a national law to Annex III if it is related to defence and foreign affairs, as well as other matters outside the limits of HKSAR autonomy, as specified in the Basic Law. The laws listed in Annex III will be applied locally by way of promulgation or legislation.

All the laws originally listed in Annex III were not politically controversial. The NPCSC has the ultimate power to determine whether a matter is within the scope of defence and foreign affairs or outside the HKSAR's autonomy. The CCP can easily use the backdoor process under Article 18 and Annex III to directly legislate for Hong Kong. Even if the law's real objective is to implement authoritarian ROL in Hong Kong, it can still be enacted.

Take the National Anthem Law (NAL). The NPC passed the NAL in September 2017. It was added to Annex III of the Basic Law by the NPCSC in November 2017. The local legislative process to implement the NAL was completed in June 2020. Several NAL provisions attracted widespread concern that freedom of expression in Hong Kong might be infringed.

The local legislation, the National Anthem Ordinance (NAO) has been adopted from similar Chinese legislation. Section 6 of NAO provides that it is an offence if a person, with intent to insult the national anthem, publicly and intentionally alters the lyrics or score of the national anthem, plays and sings the national anthem in a distorted or disrespectful way, or publicly and intentionally insults the national anthem in any way. The NAO defines 'insult' as 'to undermine the dignity of the national anthem as a symbol and sign of the PRC'.

These legal provisions might not be able to satisfy the constitutional requirements on limiting the right, because their ambiguity may not amount to being 'prescribed by law'. In effect, the NAO silences people from expressing legitimate criticism against the CCP. Even if one may want to challenge the constitutionality of the local legislation implementing NAO, Hong Kong courts do not have the jurisdiction to review its constitutionality.

Direct Enactment of a National Security Law for Hong Kong

The most devastating blow for Hong Kong's ROL is the direct enactment of a national security law. Based on an NPC decision, the NPCSC passed the 'The Law of the PRC on Safeguarding National Security in the HKSAR' (NSLHK) on 30 June 2020. The NSLHK's goal is to establish and improve the legal system and enforcement mechanisms for the HKSAR to safeguard national security, to effectively prevent, suppress and punish offences of secession, subversion, the organisation and perpetration of terrorist activities, including collusion with foreign countries or with external elements that may endanger the national security of HKSAR.

The NSLHK is included in Annex III of the Basic Law and has been promulgated and implemented in the HKSAR directly without going through a local legislative process for the law, drafted in Chinese terms to adopt to the common law environment in Hong Kong. It states that the principle of the rule of law shall be adhered to (Article 5). Yet, from its drafting, status, offences, jurisdiction and implementation, it is obvious that Hong Kong's ROL has suffered a near-fatal blow and the process of authoritarianising Hong Kong is nearly – if not entirely – complete.

The enactment of the NSLHK was a secretive process. People affected by the law had no chance to see a draft. No public consultation was conducted and the NPCSC showed no interest in understanding the views of Hong Kong citizens. The law prevails over any local law provisions that are inconsistent with the NSLHK (Article 62). The NPSCS is vested with ultimate authority to interpret the NSLHK (Article 65). The NSLHK in effect enjoys that same status of the Basic Law and has amended the Basic Law. However, the procedures of amending the Basic Law were not followed.

National security has been given a very wide understanding. Even many non-violent acts are now considered to be an offence if they are committed with the intention of undermining national unification or committing secession. Many offences are ill-defined, allowing significant discretion for law enforcement agencies to ban wide-ranging activities which have been permissible in the past. Punishments are disproportionately heavy for some prohibited acts.

The NSLHK claims an over-arching jurisdiction, which applies even to non-permanent residents of the HKSAR for acts committed outside HKSAR territory. People who may be remotely linked with Hong Kong could unknowingly commit an offence under the NSLHK by providing some kind of support to protesters in Hong Kong. Hong Kong Police can intercept communications and conduct covert surveillance on a person who is suspected of having been involved in the commission of an offence endangering national security. Only the approval of the CE, is needed, judicial approval is not required. Trials for offences under the NSLHK may be closed to the media and the public if it involves state secrets or public order. The Secretary for Justice may issue a certificate directing that the case to be tried without a jury on the grounds of protection of state secrets or involvement of foreign factors. The CE has the power to designate specific judges to handle cases concerning offences endangering national security.

The Commission for Safeguarding National Security, chaired by the CE, possesses primary responsibility for safeguarding national security in the HKSAR. The National Security Adviser, designated by the CPG, has the authority to give advice to the Commission. The decisions of the Commission are not reviewable by the court.

The Office for Safeguarding National Security (OSNS) is to be established by the CPG. It has the authority to oversee how the HKSAR is performing its duties under the law. In certain circumstances, the OSNS can exercise direct jurisdiction over a case concerning offences endangering national security with the approval of the CPG. For such cases, the person alleged to have committed an offence under the NSLHK will lose all protection under Hong Kong law. The OSNS and its staff are not subject to the jurisdiction of the HKSAR; they can be said to be above the laws of Hong Kong.

With the implementation of the NSLHK, the authoritarian regime has all it needs to enforce the authoritarian ROL in Hong Kong.

CHALLENGES TO HONG KONG'S ROL

For authoritarian ROL to be successful, people under its rule must voluntarily accept the authority of the regime. If most people under an authoritarian rule uncritically accept and obey the authority of law, then it can conveniently be used to oppress, punish, repress and dominate.

A Battle Over the ROL Discourse

In Hong Kong, as well as in other parts of the world, the ROL has a powerful legitimising effect. Once something is done, or said to be done, in accordance with the ROL, it will be considered by many as rightful and proper. However, ROL is also a contested concept. Even in the western world, the ROL has different thin and thick versions.[35] Different versions of the ROL will produce different assessments on whether a specific act is rightful or proper. Thin versions are more about specifying the features of a legal system for it to function effectively as a system of law. Thick versions build upon the thin versions, maintaining that human rights must be protected by law and attempting to ensure such protection is adequate.

The thinnest conception may only require power holders to conform to some general procedural requirements and implement decisions through independent courts in accordance with vaguely drafted legal rules. All laws, including the Constitution, can be given any meaning or even changed at their whim. Neither substantive legal rules nor government institutions, including the courts, can impose an actual constrain on powerholders. All government institutions are subject to the highest authority of the powerholder. Conversely, the thicker conception demands that the substantive contents of the law must protect the social and economic rights of citizens in addition to their civil and political rights.

Martin Krygier's teleological approach to the ROL may provide further insight in understanding the significance of the different versions. He emphasises the importance of understanding the ultimate and overriding goal of law under the ROL, before trying to say precisely what the elements of the ROL are and how it might be achieved.[36] The particular goal of the law taken as ultimate will determine its substantive meaning. It may also provide benchmarks to evaluate if an act done under the ROL has been carried out correctly. Using this approach, several options may be accepted to be the ultimate goal of law. For some, the overriding function of law is to maintain social order. Through constraining the behaviour of all government officials and citizens by law and emphasising the importance of obedience to the law, social order can be secured. If people uncritically accept the authority of law, the authority of those in power may be legitimised.

This rather thin version is the version of the ROL that the CCP, together with the CE and HKSARG, wishes to promote. To authoritarianise Hong Kong, people must uncritically accept the authority of law. To convince them that people's primary duty is to obey the law, maintaining social order is presented as the overarching goal. Therefore, any individual who breaks the law is disturbing the social order and damaging the ROL. This version of the ROL can be called 'Regulation by Law' or 'Rule by Law'.

However, many people in Hong Kong may take maintaining the social order as the foundation of more sophisticated and advanced goals. To some, the law

[35] B Tamanaha, *On Rule of Law: History, Politics, Theory* (2004).

[36] M Krygier, 'The Rule of Law: Pasts, Presents, and Two Possible Futures' (2016) 12 *Annual Review of Law and Social Science* 199.

must constrain governmental powers to prevent arbitrary abuse. An independent judiciary is one of the most important mechanisms to help constrain governmental powers. This version of the ROL can be called 'Limitation from Law'.

But having an independent judiciary does not mean that the powers of the government are adequately constrained. Also, even if the powers of the government are being constrained, there is no guarantee that the law can provide sufficient protection of citizens' rights. Therefore, some may expect the law to do more. The ultimate goal of the law is to provide substantive protection to a range of citizens' rights. This version of the ROL can be called 'Justice through Law'. If the law fails, citizens are justified under the ROL to resort to civil disobedience to change the law.[37] Thus, different versions of ROL will make different judgements on unlawful acts motivated by the spirit of civil obedience.

The ROL that Hong Kong has achieved throughout the years is not merely 'Regulation by Law'. It is at least 'Limitation from Law' or even 'Justice through Law'. But the CCP advocates redefining Hong Kong's ROL as only about maintaining social order, emphasising compliance and obedience. In other words, the battlefield of the ROL in Hong Kong is also about public discourse. What do Hong Kong people see as the ultimate goal of law in Hong Kong? Is it maintenance of social order ('Regulation by Law'), prevention of arbitrary powers ('Limitation from Law') or the protection of citizens' fundamental rights ('Justice through Law')? The answer can be found in the Hong Kong's legal culture.

In Search of a ROL Culture: Two Quantitative Studies

Legal culture is understood as the values, attitudes, beliefs and orientations prevalent among people in society towards legal institutions. It is an essential factor that explains how legal institutions operate and how people behave under a legal system. Within the concept of legal culture, there are two interactive elements: internal and external. The internal legal culture represents the cultural values held by the general public that provide the demand and expectations for the law. The external legal culture contains the values of the legal professionals that guide how the law is being framed, designed and operated.[38]

For the ROL to exist, there must be legal rules and legal institutions to enact, implement, interpret and adjudicate the legal rules. ROL values must also be socialised into the shared cultural beliefs of professionals who administer it and into the general public who are subject to legal rules and legal institutions.[39]

[37] BYT Tai, 'Rule of Law and Civil Disobedience' in M Ng and J Wong (eds) *Civil Unrest and Governance in Hong Kong: Law and Order from Historical and Cultural Perspectives* (2017), 141–162.

[38] L Friedman, 'The Concept of Legal Culture: A Reply' in D Nelken (ed) *Comparing Legal Cultures* (1996).

[39] Tamanaha, n 18 above.

Scholars generally accept the importance of having a ROL culture to support its foundations, but there is no consensus as to what those cultural values for the ROL should be.

Under different versions of ROL, different values are embraced in the legal culture. The culture needed may also depend on the ultimate goal of the law. Do the internal and the external legal cultures in Hong Kong support a minimal understanding of the ROL as being only about maintaining social order and obeying the law ('Regulation by Law')? Do they support a more sophisticated understanding of the ROL as constraining governmental powers and preventing arbitrary power ('Limitation from Law')? Or do they expect that the law should protect the civil and political rights of Hong Kong citizens ('Justice through Law')? I conducted an empirical study from April to August 2015 (2015 Study) to ascertain which versions of the ROL are present in Hong Kong's internal and external legal cultures. The findings reflect the internal and external legal culture of Hong Kong in the period immediately after the Umbrella Movement.

Using telephone polling, 3,500 randomly selected Hong Kong citizens were asked to comment on a list of statements to explore their orientation towards the nature, purpose and operation of legal rules, legal institutions and legal processes in Hong Kong. Their responses provided valuable information concerning the external legal culture of Hong Kong. The same set of questions was also sent to representatives randomly selected from different groups of legal professionals who were directly responsible for the operation of different legal institutions in Hong Kong. These groups include not only judges and lawyers who had received legal training, but also senior government administrators, senior law enforcement officials and legislators. Their responses provided valuable information concerning the internal legal culture of Hong Kong. Table 7.1 below lists the results of the study.

Respondents were asked whether they agreed with the following statements. The first three statements reflect whether the legal culture supports 'Regulation by Law': (1) All measures of the government must be based on law; (2) I always try to follow the law even if I disagree with it; and (3) Rulers should also follow the laws they make. The results overwhelmingly showed that both the internal and external legal cultures for 'Regulation by Law' are well entrenched in Hong Kong.

The internal and external cultures diverged in the next five statements: (4) In adjudicating major cases, judges should defer to the views of the executive authorities; (5) Maintaining social order is more important than protecting individual freedoms; (6) The rights possessed by an individual are not inborn but granted to him/her by society in reward for his/her good performance; (7) It is proper for civil society organisations to be under the supervision by government agencies; (8) Media has a duty to promote government policy.

Table 7.1

	External Legal Culture				Internal Legal Culture			
	A/SA	U	D/SD	DK	A/SA	U	D/SD	DK
(1) All measures of the government must be based on law.	90.0 %	4.6 %	3.8 %	1.5 %	92.3 %	3.6 %	4.2 %	0.0 %
(2) I always try to follow the law even if I disagree with it.	81.4 %	8.0 %	8.9 %	1.7 %	93.5 %	6.5 %	0.0 %	0.0 %
(3) Rulers should also follow the laws they make.	94.0 %	1.4 %	2.8 %	1.7 %	100.0 %	0.0 %	0.0 %	0.0 %
(4) In adjudicating major cases, judges should defer to the views of the executive authorities.	34.2 %	9.0 %	47.7 %	9.0 %	0 %	10.1 %	88.7 %	1.2 %
(5) Maintaining social order is more important than protecting individual freedoms.	57.6 %	16.9 %	23.0 %	2.5 %	10.7 %	17.5 %	71.8 %	3.6 %
(6) The rights possessed by an individual are not inborn but granted to him/her by society in reward for his/her good performance.	41.6 %	11.0 %	41.6 %	5.8 %	0.0 %	7.7 %	86.1 %	6.2 %
(7) It is proper for civil society organisations to be under the supervision of government agencies.	59.0 %	13.3 %	21.5 %	6.1 %	15.5 %	9.5 %	75.0 %	0.0 %
(8) Media has a duty to promote government policy.	60.4 %	13.8 %	23.1 %	2.8 %	4.2 %	26.4 %	68.2 %	0.0 %

* Agree (A); Strongly Agree (SA); Undecided (U); Disagree (D); Strongly Disagree (SD); Don't know (DK)

The results show that the external legal culture in Hong Kong failed to provide firm support for 'Limitation from Law' and 'Justice through Law'. Fewer than 50 per cent of the respondents from the general public who participated in the study gave favourable answers to these statements. In the period immediately after the Umbrella Movement, the general public tended to support only 'Regulation by Law'. The values supporting 'Limitation from Law' and 'Justice through Law' are well entrenched in Hong Kong's internal legal culture.

It seems that immediately after the Umbrella Movement, Hong Kong had only a rather thin external legal culture that could only sustain 'Regulation by Law' but not 'Justice through Law' or even 'Limitation from Law'. The results are cause for serious alarm regarding the ROL in Hong Kong. Unless there are changes in the external legal culture, then the strongholds of the more advanced understandings of the ROL, 'Limitation from Law' and 'Justice through Law', will only be defended mainly by the legal professionals in Hong Kong through the internal legal culture. In case they give up or give way to the CCP, Hong Kong's ROL may slide back to merely 'Regulation by Law'.

Fortunately, changes in the external legal culture do seem to have arisen. The Anti-Extradition Bill Movement might have generated a significant shift in external legal culture, bringing new hope and strength to the development of Hong Kong's ROL. Question 5 in the 2015 Study asked respondents to indicate their preference between 'protecting the fundamental rights and freedoms' and 'maintaining social order': 57.6 per cent preferred 'maintaining social order' over 'protecting the fundamental rights and freedoms'.

In a related study conducted at the height of the Anti-Extradition Movement, from mid-October to early November 2019 ('2019 Study'), around 1,000 randomly selected residents aged 15 or above were asked to choose several options that they considered to be the most important objectives for the ROL.[40] Amongst those who chose 'protecting the fundamental rights and freedoms' and 'maintaining social order', 57 per cent chose the former and 43 per cent the latter as the most important ROL objective. These findings present preliminary data that citizens may now see protecting fundamental rights and freedoms as being more important than maintaining social order. Evidence shows that age, level of education and place of birth are significant factors in determining people's attitudes. Those born in Hong Kong, aged under 55, with a tertiary or above level of education have a much higher tendency to accept 'protecting the fundamental rights and freedoms' as the ROL's most important objective.

Another question in the 2019 Study asks respondents whether they agreed with the statement that 'breaking the law for reasons of social justice is acceptable': 39.8 per cent of the respondents agreed with the statement, while

[40] Hong Kong Institute of Asia-Pacific Studies of The Chinese University of Hong Kong *Survey on public perceptions towards the rule of law in Hong Kong 2019*. Available at: www.bauhinia.org/assets/document/20191218/Executive_Summary_ENG_20191218.pdf.

31 per cent disagreed. This indicates the attitude of Hong Kong people towards civil disobedience. Most previous studies had consistently indicated that only around one-quarter of the population in Hong Kong supported civil disobedience. This is the first time that those favouring civil disobedience have outnumbered those who do not. Similarly, those born in Hong Kong, under 55, with a tertiary or above level of education are substantially more likely to favour civil disobedience.

Even though we should be very cautious about interpreting the 2019 results, given that the survey was conducted during a time of severely heightened tensions, the results do point to more Hong Kong citizens embracing thicker ROL values. Even outside the survey results, the 2019 Movement showed that more people either seem prepared to, or are at least sympathetic to, resorting to civil disobedience in advancing the ROL and appear more willing to defend Hong Kong's ROL in more energetic and creative ways. Thus, the Movement provides evidence that 'Justice through Law' may have been increasing in Hong Kong.

Legal Professionals in an Authoritarianising Hong Kong

Hong Kong citizens generally trust that judges can steadfastly guard the boundaries of the law, withstand interference from other branches of the government or outside powers and virtuously adhere to the spirit of the law, resisting the temptation to misuse powers for personal gain. 'Limitation from Law' heavily relies on judges' internalisation of the commitment to the ROL. Through training in legal knowledge and the craft of judging, taking a solemn oath to decide cases according to law and belonging to a community of legal practitioners devoted to upholding the ROL, its values can be integrated and sustained within the judiciary. It is assumed that legal professionals would similarly embrace ROL values. However, the position of legal professionals in authoritarian regimes remains precarious.

Authoritarian rulers have many methods to contain judges and other legal professionals without resorting to direct interference or attack. The anticipated threat of reprisal and the possibility that court rulings may simply be ignored or overruled by extra-legal measures may be sufficient to generate judicial self-restraint. Also, the internal structure of appointments and promotions may encourage voluntary compliance. Similarly, lawyers who uphold the more advanced ROL understandings may be silenced by the following authoritarian measures: (1) the professional autonomy of lawyers is to be dismantled; (2) politics is designated as a subject outside the valid concern of lawyers; and (3) the public domain is demarcated as a space for state dominance and any critique of state formulation of law is considered improper. Other legal professionals who are less independent than the judges will be even more vulnerable within authoritarian regimes.

Without democracy, the powers of the executive branch cannot be adequately checked. Their wigs and gowns have no magical power to protect them. It is doubtful how long they could withstand interference from an authoritarian regime.

Like other judges working under authoritarian systems, Hong Kong judges understand their political constraints. The overriding power of the interpretations of the Basic Law by the NPCSC cannot be questioned. But if they are not, Hong Kong's judicial autonomy will face an even greater danger.[41] Some judges have chosen to avoid controversial constitutional issues when adjudicating cases.[42] Others, along with some senior members of the legal profession, actively offer help to the CCP and the HKSARG by providing legal arguments to justify controversial constitutional decisions. Though all judgments of the court will be packaged by the judges as decisions made only in accordance with the law, politics can hardly be separated from the law, especially in controversial constitutional matters.

As controversial issues are less likely to be challenged in Hong Kong courts, the CCP is ready to make controversial constitutional decisions to consolidate authoritarian rule over Hong Kong. Legitimatised by Hong Kong courts, it will be increasingly difficult for the opposition camp to mobilise large-scale street action to challenge these controversial decisions. There is a genuine worry that Hong Kong's legal professionals will play it safe by avoiding any involvement in politically controversial issues. Some legal professionals may even openly embrace the authoritarian conception of the ROL and become useful ruling tools of the authoritarian regime. However, common law lawyers also have a long tradition of using various means, from electoral politics to civil disobedience, to defend the ROL and advance democracy in Hong Kong.[43] Prominent judges, lawyers and legal academics have played a vital role in shaping the understanding of the ROL in Hong Kong. In this battle over the ROL discourse, legal professionals must continue to stand firm. However, in light of the aggressive power of the authoritarian rulers, they also need to do it smartly.

Learning from the experiences of reform-orientated legal professionals in other authoritarian regimes, those in Hong Kong may try to apply subtle pressure for democratic reform at the margins, without directly impinging on the core interests of the authoritarian regime.[44] One method used by authoritarian regimes to isolate and contain legal professionals is to incapacitate their community support networks. The main actors are rights advocates in civil society who organise deliberate, strategic and repeated actions against

[41] BYT Tai, 'Judicial Autonomy in Hong Kong' (2010) 24(3) *China Information* 295.

[42] Yap PJ, 'Constitutional Review Under the BL: The Rise, Retreat and Resurgence of Judicial Power in Hong Kong' (2007) 37 *Hong Kong Law Journal* 449.

[43] K Lee, 'Lawyers and Hong Kong's Democracy Movement: From Electoral Politics to Civil Disobedience' (2017) 25(1) *Asian Journal of Political Science* 89.

[44] T Ginsburg and T Moustafa (eds), *Rule by Law: The Politics of Courts in Authoritarian Regimes* (2008).

authoritarian rule. In using their discretionary power under the law, the legal professionals in Hong Kong can strategically protect and create more political space for rights advocates to develop their organisational capacities. This may shield them from further direct and indirect interference from authoritarian rulers, thus defending and maintaining Hong Kong's ROL or even creating opportunities for Hong Kong to revert to a more democratic path.

Mutual support between the legal profession and the civil society is important in defending the ROL. This was recognised in a remark by Justice Tang, a retired permanent judge of the HKCFA, upon his retirement. He said:

> [A]lthough judges are prepared to uphold the rule of law as it has always been understood and applied in Hong Kong, the community must be willing to support them. In what form should the support take? I think the support should be all-embracing. If the judiciary is unfairly attacked, you should hold firm and stand up for them. But, support should not only be events driven. That is not enough. It may be too late. You should endeavour to nurture an atmosphere friendly to the rule of law. We have a free press and free elections in Hong Kong. Make your voice heard and your vote count. Believe me, the price of freedom is indeed eternal vigilance. Above all else, do not give up or underestimate your strength. If we as a community insist on the rule of law, it cannot be taken from us easily. Do not make it easy.[45]

The Rise of Uncivil Disobedience

In most social movements, there is disagreement among protesters over the strategic function of violence. When the non-violent means cannot deliver immediate results and protesters face imminent suppression, it is natural that some protesters in peaceful movements may shift to support the use of violence. Any attempt by power holders to supress the movement is usually what drives peaceful protesters to become violent.

Even to some non-violent protesters, it may be beneficial to the movement if there is a radical wing advocating the use of violence in advancing the same goal. If there is a radical flank effect,[46] powerholders may be more willing to listen to their claims and reach a compromise, because dealing with violent protesters is more challenging. However, the radical flank effect does not always produce positive results. These groups can also generate adverse outcomes because they may turn away many moderate supporters. Whether the radical flank effect will be positive or negative is often determined by the community's political culture.

The Umbrella Movement was a movement of civil disobedience. After it ended, there were clear signs of radicalisation in the democratic movement. Some groups are now asking not merely for democratic reform under the existing

[45] Farewell Sitting for the Honourable Mr Justice Tang PJ (2018) 21 *HKCFAR* 530, paras 17–19.
[46] K Schock, *Unarmed Insurrections: People Power Movements in Non-democracies* (2005).

constitutional framework, but demanding self-determination or even independence for Hong Kong. Some protesters also turned violent. On the eve of the Chinese New Year in February 2016, a conflict between protesters supporting unlicensed hawkers selling street-food during the festive occasion and the police, backing up the public hygiene officers, turned into a riot. These clashes have led some people to question whether violent protest can be justified in the context of Hong Kong's struggle for democracy.

The definition of civil disobedience adopted by the HKCFA was initially put forward by John Rawls.[47] Shaped by the specific political, historical, social and cultural backgrounds of United States' society, Rawls believed that civil disobedience is only applicable in a nearly just society, which sets a very high threshold. The act must be non-violent. Persons engaging in civil disobedience also must accept the legal consequences of their conduct, to express fidelity to the law. In a nearly just society, it is not easy to justify an illegal act and convince people that it is a sincere and conscientious expression of a public sense of justice.

However, in a society that is far from just, it is unreasonable to demand protestors satisfy such stringent requirements. 'Uncivil disobedience' may be needed to resist authoritarian rule. Covertness, evasiveness, violence and offensiveness are the features of uncivil disobedience. These acts can still be justified in an unjust society.[48] Although disobedience must be principled, vigilantism can be justified if there has been grave official misconduct and entrenched institutional inefficacy, such as when the state deploys force against its people or leaves some citizens vulnerable to grave harm. However, the harm inflicted by the vigilante must be a proportional response to an immediate threat.

Before the outbreak of the Umbrella Movement, Hong Kong was in a semi-democratic era and could be said to be a nearly just society. Abiding by the law was the dominant element in Hong Kong culture. In the years following the Umbrella Movement, with the encroachment of authoritarian ROL, this has wholly changed. Injustice in the territory has been amplified and the democratic movement is now facing a very different societal context. The rise of uncivil disobedience seems inevitable.

There is no question that some protesters have used violence in the Anti-Extradition Movement. Protesters often damaged traffic lights, targeting pro-CCP shops and symbolic subway stations. Arson and petrol bombs have not been uncommon. Police officers and pro-CCP citizens are being attacked. Interestingly, Hong Kong people seem to be much more tolerant of the use of violence.

In a survey conducted by the Lingnan University Public Governance Programme immediately after the 2016 riot,[49] around 1,000 adults aged 18

[47] J Rawls, *A Theory of Justice* (1999).

[48] C Delmas, *A Duty to Resist: When Disobedience Should Be Uncivil* (2018).

[49] Lingnan University Public Governance Programme, *Mongkok Incident Opinion Survey (2016)*. Available at: www.ln.edu.hk/pgp/pdf/mkincident.pdf.

and older were asked whether they thought the force that the participants used against the police in the clashes of recent years was excessive, appropriate or inadequate: 60.3 per cent considered the force excessive; 20.2 per cent, appropriate; and 6.7 per cent, inadequate. However, evidence shows that views have changed. In a survey conducted during the high time of the Anti-Extradition Movement in early October 2019, only 41.1 per cent of the 751 randomly selected respondents believed the force used by *protesters* was excessive.[50] Also, 59 per cent agreed that 'when large-scale protests cannot force the government to respond, it is understandable that protesters would take radical action'. One explanation may be that the public viewed the police as far more violent and abusive. In their eyes, the HKSARG and the police shoulder much of the blame.[51]

However, such incivility is only a sign of the challenge. The root cause of violence is the encroachment of authoritarian rule. Many people have already lost confidence in the law. The law in the hands of an authoritarian ruler is more a tool of suppression than a mechanism to protect people's fundamental rights and citizens have recognised this.

If injustices are not rectified, more protesters will be become uncivil. If Hong Kong is unwilling to follow the path of democracy, then its ROL is doomed to decay. In other words, uncivil disobedience, though unfortunate, may be a necessary evil in the struggle for democracy under authoritarian rule. And if authoritarianism persists, people may lose hope in the ROL entirely.

CONCLUSION: CIVIL RESISTANCE AND THE ROL

In the coming years, the CCP will further intensify its authoritarian measures in Hong Kong. If the Hong Kong people fail to effectively counteract the advancement of authoritarian ROL, Hong Kong's ROL will fade away, perhaps for a long while.

From Civil Disobedience to Civic Education

The above analysis demonstrates that the battle is not just legal or political, but a cultural one. We need to cultivate a stronger external legal culture. Various methods can be used to cultivate a more advanced ROL culture in Hong Kong, such as: strengthening civil society; investing in legal education at all levels of

[50] F Lee, 'Our research in Hong Kong reveals what people really think of the protesters – and the police' *Independent* (16 October 2019). Available at: www.independent.co.uk/voices/hong-kong-protests-police-violence-public-opinion-polling-support-a9158061.html.

[51] Hong Kong Public Opinion Research Institute, *We Hongkongers 'Special Module' Round Two Survey Results* (2019). Available at: https://static1.squarespace.com/static/5cfd1ba6a7117c000170d7aa/t/5de0bc2836172f0b2f7f44f5/1575009323786/6th_round_pt2.pdf.

education, from primary school to law school; and enlisting the help of the media to build a creative and multifaceted culture.[52] These methods may affect a change in the culture through a habit-building process and must continue.

However, long-lasting cultural change can also be brought about by 'cultural shock'. Civil disobedience can dramatise the injustice of a particular system in such a way that people can no longer ignore it.[53] People's established beliefs, values and attitudes may be challenged and questioned through civil disobedience and citizens are forced to reflect on the meaning and significance of truth and justice. Many may reconsider their existing attitudes towards current institutions thus forming new attitudes or consciousness. At times of political crisis or constitutional moment, civil disobedience can be a means for people to transform the system. Even if civil disobedience fails to bring about immediate institutional change, it can often lay the groundwork for future cultural and institutional change.

During an authoritarianising era, civil disobedience – with its ability to cause cultural transformation – is, therefore, still the most sustainable method of defending the ROL and striving for democracy. However, the cost for breaking the law may be much higher. The civil resistance movement in Hong Kong must be smarter and prepare itself better and more vigilantly for the next moment. It may be optimistic to say that there is still a slight chance that Hong Kong will revert to a democratic path. However, there can still be hope if the community is willing to band together to defend the ROL and prevent the further encroachment of authoritarianism.

From Street Protest to Protest by Votes

The latest challenges largely arose from the change of the CCP's policy towards Hong Kong after the Umbrella Movement. The movement's main aim was the introduction of truly democratic elections in Hong Kong, to realise the citizens' full political rights. Without this, however, a breakthrough may be arrived at by striving for liberalising electoral outcomes in the competitive elections that can still be conducted.

A necessary condition to successfully bring this about is that the opposition must be able to put aside differences and form coalitions. However, more is needed. It requires a further level of mobilisation, unity, skill and heroism far beyond what would normally be required for a normal democratic victory. There must be an ambitious political campaign organised by an election bloc, which includes most of the political parties and civil society groups, among the

[52] J Stromseth, D Wippman and R Brooks, *Can Might Make Rights?: Building the Rule of Law after Military Interventions* (2006).

[53] ML King, 'Letter from Birmingham City Jail' in H Bedau (ed) *Civil Disobedience in Focus* (1991).

opposition. The campaign should be able to: (1) orchestrate elaborate voter registration and voter turnout drives; (2) concentrate voters' choices; (3) send signals to voters for a strong commitment to win; (4) put in place electoral monitoring procedures that make opposition parties more politically attractive to voters; (5) demonstrate to voters that the opposition has the capacity to govern effectively; and (6) create a widespread sense that victory is possible.

Pro-democracy political parties and civil society groups in Hong Kong must establish a comprehensive election campaign to promote strategic voting in the coming elections to win more seats. If these can be achieved, the current trajectory will become more unstable. It will then be very difficult for the CCP to continue to manipulate the current system, so it must consider changing the systems.

The district council elections in 2019 resulted in a major success. Pro-democracy candidates won 388 out of the 452 seats and formed the majority in 17 out of 18 district councils. Though the main functions of the district councils are to advise the government on the provision and use of public facilities and services within the districts and they do not have actual power to govern, the landslide victory allows the pro-democracy camp to penetrate deep into the districts, consolidating the support of democracy in the community.

A more important election will be the next for LegCo. This was originally scheduled to be held in September 2020 but was delayed by one year. If the pro-democracy camp can control LegCo, this would provide it much more bargaining power, potentially being able to force concessions from the HKSARG and the CCP.

However, even if the opposition wins the election, there remains a chance that it will generate a 'deliberalising' outcome. Those in power may not want to step down and they will falsify the results, clamp down on the opposition, or even cancel all elections and impose full authoritarian rule. Given the current circumstances, this remains a distinct possibility in Hong Kong.

As the past few years have shown, Hong Kong is much more than a financial capital; it is also a highly political city.[54] Aspirations for democracy and self-government have been awakened. Although demands have been repeatedly suppressed, Hong Kong citizens have become more resilient, pluralistic and creative. They stand up to defend the universal values of freedom, the rule of law, human rights, democracy, fairness and justice. With a population of only 7 million people, Hong Kong has now become the frontline battle between the world of authoritarianism and the world of freedom and democracy. What happens here over the coming years may have implications far beyond Hong Kong; indeed, there may be significant implications for democracy and the rule of law around the world.

[54] Fu H, 'Political Protest in High-income Societies: The Case of the Occupy Central Movement in Hong Kong' in BC Jones, *Law and Politics of the Taiwan Sunflower and Hong Kong Umbrella Movements* (2017), 98.

8

Undemocratic Constitutional Law in Taiwan

LIN CHIEN-CHIH*

RECENT DECADES HAVE witnessed the emergence of populism around the globe,[1] which mirrors the distrust and dissatisfaction with the political branches. To many people, democracy has gradually deteriorated into plutocracy, in which the rich rather than the demos rule. Notwithstanding the surge of populism in both old and young democracies, democracy in Taiwan has remained stable since the late 1980s. While some democracies – even some long-established ones – have opted for quasi-authoritarian leadership, several signs suggest that Taiwan seems to be resilient to democratic regression.[2] For example, Taiwan had gone through its third party turnover peacefully in 2016 and, perhaps more importantly, nearly 80 per cent of Taiwanese had recently agreed that democracy is the best game in town, despite all its shortcomings.[3] Nevertheless, democracy in Taiwan is built on shaky constitutional grounds: the Constitution of the Republic of China (ROC Constitution). Enacted for the Chinese people, the ROC Constitution contains and entrenches several undemocratic elements which prolong the ideology of the self-deceiving one-China policy. This 'hegemonic preservation'[4] of the one-China policy has created several problems that may undermine constitutional democracy in Taiwan, such as the confusion of national identity, social division and political polarisation.

To address this issue, some scholars have argued that both formal and informal constitutional change, including constitutional amendments, social movements and judicial review, may be indigenising the ROC Constitution and healing

* Associate Research Professor, Institutum Iurisprudentiae, Academia Sinica.

[1] T Ginsburg and A Huq, *How to Save a Constitutional Democracy* (2018) 73–83.

[2] D Law and CC Lin, 'Constitutional Inertia in Asia' in MA Graber, S Levinson and M Tushnet (eds), *Constitutional Democracy in Crisis?* (2018) 423, 435–37.

[3] Taiwan Foundation for Democracy, 'A Political Profile of Taiwan's Youth: Democratic Support, Natural independence, and Commitment to Defense'. Available at: www.tfd.org.tw/opencms/english/events/data/Event0680.html.

[4] R Hirschl, 'The Strategic Foundations of Constitutions' in DJ Galligan and M Versteeg (eds), *Social and Political Foundations of Constitutions* (2013) 157, 166.

its democratic pathology.[5] Although this strategy has achieved some success, this chapter suggests that the written constitution in Taiwan, including both the Constitution and its amendments is, to a certain extent, both procedurally and substantively undemocratic. And informal constitutional change cannot fundamentally alter the undemocratic constitutional scheme. Consequently, the so-called 'Taiwanisation' or 'indigenisation' of the ROC Constitution has its limitations. The rest of this chapter proceeds as follows. In the first section, I will analyse how undemocratic the constitutional law in Taiwan is through the lenses of constitutional design, the rigidity of constitutional revision and the mandates of the Constitution. Tethered by the written constitutional text, Taiwanese people have relied on informal channels, such as social movements and judicial review, to ameliorate its democratic deficiencies. This approach has been praised as civic constitutionalism in Taiwan.[6] However, the second section argues that informal constitutional change fails to compensate for the undemocratic deficit. Finally, this chapter concludes that direct and decentralised forms of democracy[7] should be encouraged to enhance the quality of democracy in Taiwan.

THE UNDEMOCRATIC CONSTITUTIONAL LAW IN TAIWAN

A constitution, even if formally enacted by the people, is not necessarily democratic in substance. For example, the Constitution of the United States has been criticised as being undemocratic from time to time,[8] and some even argue that 'a substantial responsibility for the defects of [the United States] lies in the Constitution itself'.[9] It follows that a constitution can certainly deviate from public will and eventually become undemocratic once the sociopolitical conditions have changed as time goes by. This is particularly evident in the context of the ROC Constitution because of the Nationalist Party (KMT)'s retreat to Taiwan from China in 1949.

The Undemocratic ROC Constitution

In Taiwan, the supreme law is the ROC Constitution, which was promulgated in Nanjing, China on 1 January 1947. It was initially enacted for mainland China,

[5] See, eg, JR Yeh, *The Constitution of Taiwan: A Contextual Analysis* (2016) 4.
[6] Ibid 244–246.
[7] P Blokker, *New Democracies in Crisis?* (2015), 32.
[8] R Dahl, *How Democratic is the American Constitution?* (2002) 15–20; M Herz, 'Robert Dahl's How Democratic Is the American Constitution: An Introduction, with Notes on the Electoral College' (2005) 26 *Cardozo Law Review* 2515, 2516; T Marshall, 'Reflections on the Bicentennial of the United States Constitution' (1987) 101 *Harvard Law Review* 1; S Levinson, *Our Undemocratic Constitution: Where the Constitution Goes Wrong (And How We the People Can Correct It)* (2006).
[9] Levinson (n 8 above), 9.

but its jurisdiction has shrunk dramatically after the fiasco of the KMT in the Chinese civil war and its retreat to Taiwan in 1949. Although it was later amended in seven rounds after political liberation in 1987,[10] the ROC Constitution is still insufficiently democratic both procedurally and substantively.

Procedurally, the constitution-making project did not consider the interests and opinions of the Taiwanese people. To be sure, 18 representatives from the then Taiwan Province, along with representatives from other provinces, participated in the constituent convention in 1946.[11] Although these Taiwanese representatives were part of the constitution-building project, theirs was mainly a token appearance in Nanjing. One piece of evidence for this is that these 18 Taiwanese representatives only advanced three proposals among the 427 proposals in the constituent assembly;[12] all were rejected. Nor had they participated in the previous drafting process because, before 1945, Taiwan had been a colony of Japan.[13]

As a corollary, it should not be surprising that some of the constitutional designs in the ROC Constitution look bizarre. The Control Yuan and the system of provincial government are two cases in point. For starters, the existence of the Control Yuan after democratisation has created more problems than it solves and has long been criticised by constitutional scholars as unnecessary. It was originally established according to Sun Yat-sen's political thought, which was, in turn, modelled on the Censorate during the imperial period in China.[14] According to the framers' intent, its duty is to exercise the powers of consent, impeachment, censure and auditing[15] and its major goal is to hold high-ranking officials accountable. In theory, it might be suitable to have an independent supervisory institution that is exclusively responsible for holding other coordinate branches accountable.[16] However, remember that the ROC Constitution was enacted in 1947 when the KMT still ruled mainland China. In other words, the Control Yuan was designed for a geographically immense country, in which principal–agency problems were rampant. When the KMT brought the

[10] It has been amended respectively in 1991, 1992, 1994, 1997, 1999, 2000, 2005.

[11] JR Yeh and WC Chang, 'The Emergence of East Asian Constitutionalism: Features in Comparison' (2011) 59 *American Journal of Comparative Law* 805, 819.

[12] Compilation Commission of the Record of the National Assembly, *Record of the National Assembly* (Secretariat of National Assembly 1946) 685 (in Chinese).

[13] CJ Chen, 'A Feminist Critique of History and Traditions in Judicial Review' (2007) 7 *Academia Sinica Law Journal* 81, 94–95.

[14] E Caldwell, 'The Control Yuan and Human Rights in Taiwan: Towards the Development of a National Human Rights Institution?' in J Cohen, W Alford and CF Lo (eds), *Taiwan and International Human Rights. Economics, Law, and Institutions in Asia Pacific* (2019).

[15] Article 90 of the Constitution of the Republic of China (Taiwan) reads: 'The Control Yuan shall be the highest control organ of the State and shall exercise the powers of consent, impeachment, censure, and auditing.'

[16] B Ackerman, 'The New Separation of Powers' (2000) 113 *Harvard Law Review* 633; Ginsburg and Huq (n 1 above) 194; F Mahomed, 'The Fourth Branch: Challenges and Opportunities for a Robust and Meaningful Role for South Africa's State Institutions Supporting Democracy' in D Bilchitz and D Landau (eds), *The Evolution of the Separation of Powers* (2018) 177, 181–83.

constitution to Taiwan, a small island in the southeast of mainland China, the existence of the Control Yuan gradually became awkward. In many ways it has become a redundant government branch because its functions largely overlap with others, such as the national legislature and the prosecution service. It has been mocked and compared to a fly swatter, in that it can only investigate minor misdemeanors of low-ranking officials, but not serious crimes committed by those of higher rank.[17]

The impotence of the Control Yuan can be seen from the following political battle. In 2005, the KMT-controlled Legislative Yuan refused to confirm the nominees of the Control Yuan nominated by the Democratic Progressive Party (DPP) President. Consequently, the Control Yuan was paralysed for more than three years because no candidate could be appointed. This political impasse continued even after the Taiwan Constitutional Court stepped in and asked legislators to fulfill their constitutional obligations.[18] Ironically, this vacuum in the Control Yuan did not seem to affect the day-to-day governance of Taiwan at all. Today, the position of Control Yuan members is widely perceived as a 'pork barrel', used mainly by the ruling party to reward its loyalists. In 2014, the President of the Control Yuan, appointed by the KMT, opined that the Control Yuan should be downsized if not abolished completely.[19] In 2015, Current Vice President Lai also claimed that it should be abolished,[20] and this idea received support from some members of the Control Yuan itself.[21] This issue has been one of the few which has achieved bipartisan consensus in Taiwan in an age of political polarisation.

The other bizarre example involves the horizontal separation of powers between central and local governments. The ROC Constitution stipulates that local government includes two levels: provincial and county governments. The provincial governments, such as the Taiwan Province, enjoy local autonomy and have the power to enact provincial laws. This made sense when the Republic of China still reigned on mainland China, which was composed of thirty-five provinces before 1949. After the Chinese civil war, the KMT controlled only Taiwan and a few neighbouring islets. In practice, it was not necessary to maintain the Taiwan Province, given that the territory of the Republic of

[17] International Committee for Human Rights in Taiwan 'Military Authorities Burn Lei Chen Memoirs' (1988) 36 *Taiwan Communiqué* 4.

[18] JY Interpretation No 632 (2007). All Taiwan Constitutional Court judgments can be found here: https://cons.judicial.gov.tw/jcc/en-us/jep03. In this decision, the Constitution Court ruled that 'The Constitution does not allow for the event in which either the President or the Legislative Yuan fails to nominate or consent to the nomination of candidates so that the Control Yuan cannot exercise its power or function, thereby jeopardizing the integrity of the constitutional system.'

[19] HS Lee, 'Abolishing Control Yuan will be good for nation: Wang' *Taipei Times* (26 July 2014). Available at: www.taipeitimes.com/News/taiwan/archives/2014/07/26/2003595972.

[20] IS Loa, 'Lai issues threat to end Control Yuan' *Taipei Times* (20 August 2015). Available at: www.taipeitimes.com/News/front/archives/2015/08/20/2003625765.

[21] S Lin, 'Control Yuan nominees for its abolition' *Taipei Times* (13 January 2018). Available at: www.taipeitimes.com/News/taiwan/archives/2018/01/13/2003685687.

China largely overlaps with that of the Taiwan Province. The existence of the Taiwan Province became merely a symbol for the KMT government to justify its raving that it was still the only legitimate Chinese state in the world. After the myth had been dismantled by the rise of People's Republic of China (PRC), the KMT finally faced political reality and amended the Constitution in 1997, which declared that the Taiwan Province 'no longer has jurisdiction over matters regarding local self-government and has been deprived of the organic right of self-government'.[22] What is more absurd is that even the Fujian Province (a province in southeast China) was considered a 'local government' in Taiwan, because of the existence of Kinmen and Matsu. Similar to the Taiwan Province, the Fujian provinces had a provincial government, a provincial advisory council and some staff. That is, if adhering to formal constitutional orthodoxy, the Republic of China (Taiwan) still ostensibly controls two Chinese provinces, at least in part. It should be noted that the Taiwanese government finally decided to minimise the budgets of both provincial governments in 2018.[23] However, both provinces formally exist because they cannot be removed without amending the ROC Constitution.

To be sure, many constitutions are enacted in turbulent periods that are unfavourable to constitutional deliberation,[24] and this chapter does not intend to beat a dead horse. Nonetheless, unlike many other new democracies who have promulgated a brand-new constitution as a symbol to break with the past, Taiwan chose not to do so. Instead, the government decided to amend the old constitution. Most of these constitutional amendments were drafted and passed by representatives elected in Taiwan. They have greatly changed the contour of the original ROC Constitution, making it more tailored to Taiwan's political reality and social needs. Thus, some scholars take the view that these constitutional amendments have 'Taiwanised' the ROC Constitution. Jiunn-rong Yeh, for example, suggests that the constitutional amendments not only supported the legitimacy of the Constitution and prolonged its longevity, but they also simultaneously cultivated Taiwanese constitutional identity by reinforcing domestic representation.[25] He is certainly right insofar as Taiwanese citizens can now elect their political agents. Nevertheless, this contention merits further scrutiny because the democratic credibility of these constitutional amendments passed by the National Assembly was problematic both procedurally and substantively.

[22] Still, the Amendments of 1997 did not completely abolish the government of the Taiwan Province, which is still a local self-government in Taiwan, has certain legal rights and responsibilities under some conditions and may thus acquire the status of a public legal person. See JY Interpretation No 467 (1998).

[23] S Lin, 'Provincial government budget to be cut' *Taipei Times* (21 March 2018). Available at: www.taipeitimes.com/News/taiwan/archives/2018/03/21/2003689720.

[24] D Landau, 'Constitution-Making Gone Wrong' (2013) 64 *Alabama Law Review* 923.

[25] JR Yeh, *Democratic Transition and Constitution Development* (2003) 30–35 (in Chinese).

Undemocratic Constitutional Amendments

In terms of procedural issues, there are two layers of questions that must be addressed. The first involves the amount of civil participation during the process of constitutional revision, while the second refers to the procedural barriers these amendments erect to deter future constitutional revision. To begin with, whether and to what extent the current constitutional amendments are procedurally accountable is doubtful. In Taiwan, the National Assembly monopolised the power to amend the Constitution before it was completely abolished in 2005. The first-term representatives were elected in China in 1948 and continued to serve until December 1991 because national elections were suspended for four decades during the party-state era. Therefore, the first round of constitutional amendments were passed in May 1991. Given the Assembly's composition, the democratic responsiveness of the 1991 constitutional amendments is highly doubtful. Even after 1991, when members of the National Assembly were elected exclusively by Taiwanese citizens, electoral malpractice, such as vote-buying and cheating, were rampant,[26] probably because Taiwan was at an early stage of political liberation and democracy was not well entrenched at that time. As such, some members of the National Assembly were, indeed, hooligans. What is worse, it is sometimes unclear to what extent people sincerely care about the elections. For example, half of the people were unaware of the National Assembly elections in 2005[27] and less than a quarter (23.36 per cent) of the electorate eventually voted.[28] The reasons for this are complicated, but there is no denying that not many people paid attention to who would amend the Constitution. Because of this low turnout, the democratic legitimacy of the 2005 constitutional amendments has been questioned by three former constitutional court justices.[29]

Even if members of the National Assembly were properly elected, there is serious doubt as to whether the contents of the constitutional amendments reflect the popular will. In the first three rounds of constitutional revision, from 1990 to 1994, the constitutional amendments were initiated and passed chiefly by the KMT, which occupied a supermajority of seats in the National Assembly. Given the dominance of the KMT at that time, the criticism was made that members of the National Assembly listened to the will of the party boss, rather than that of the people. Under these circumstances and given the electoral malpractice mentioned above it is doubtful whether lay people had meaningfully participated in the constitutional revision, even if they had formally elected

[26] S Long, 'Taiwan's National Assembly Elections' (1992) 129 *China Quarterly* 216, 221–223.

[27] J Huang, 'Public clueless about assembly election, poll finds' *Taipei Times* (14 April 2005). Available at: www.taipeitimes.com/News/taiwan/archives/2005/04/14/2003250400.

[28] Central Election Commission, 'The Election of the National Assembly in 2005'. Available at: https://db.cec.gov.tw/histQuery.jsp?voteCode=20050501R1A9&qryType=prof.

[29] JY Interpretation No 721 (J Huang dissenting) (2014); J.Y. Interpretation No 721 (J Li concurring) (2014); JY Interpretation No 721 (J Chen concurring) (2014).

members of the National Assembly. In the last four rounds from 1997 to 2005, constitutional revision involved more cooperation and compromise between the KMT and the main opposition party, the DPP. From this perspective, constitutional amendment has been more like a contract between political elites than a social contract in the Lockean sense.[30] It is unclear to what extent these amendments reflected the people's will when partisan interests kicked in, particularly when the two were in conflict.

Some may argue that ex post public endorsement may heal the procedural imperfections. Taking the Fourteenth Amendment of the US Constitution as an example, Bruce Ackerman indicated that popular support justified the legitimacy of the post-Civil War Amendments despite their procedural controversies.[31] After all, if later generations are not satisfied with the amendments, they have the power to rewrite them. In the abstract, this argument is plausible, but, in practice, this is not persuasive in Taiwan because of the thresholds for constitutional amendments. Specifically, Article 12 of the Additional Articles[32] has erected procedural hurdles that are nearly impossible to overcome for future constitutional revision. Given the political stalemate and social division in recent years, this exceedingly high threshold has, in effect, rendered the Constitution untouchable. Admittedly, flexibility need not be the paramount virtue of a constitution, but excessive rigidity is arguably undemocratic[33] because it can eliminate people's capability to revise their fundamental law and reshape their constitutional identity.[34]

In addition to the procedural issues, the contents of some constitutional amendments reek of 'constitutional rent-seeking', which means the National Assembly would not have amended the Constitution unless it garnered something in exchange.[35] Monopolising the power to amend the constitution, in the constitutional amendments the National Assembly continually expanded its own power at the expense of other branches of government. For instance, it grasped the power to confirm the appointees of the other three branches in the 1991 constitutional amendments and conferred on itself the power to impeach the president and vice president in the 1997 constitutional

[30] T Ginsburg, 'Constitutions as Contract, Constitutions as Charters' in DJ Galligan and M Versteeg (eds), *Social and Political Foundations of Constitutions* (2013), 182.

[31] B Ackerman, *We the People: Transformation*, vol 2 (1998) 160–206.

[32] Article 12 of The Additional Articles of the Constitution of the Republic of China: 'Amendment of the Constitution shall be initiated upon the proposal of one-fourth of the total members of the Legislative Yuan, passed by at least three-fourths of the members present at a meeting attended by at least three-fourths of the total members of the Legislative Yuan, and sanctioned by electors … at a referendum … wherein the number of valid votes in favour exceeds one-half of the total number of electors.'

[33] Ginsburg and Huq (n 1 above) 139; Levinson, (n 8 above) 159–166.

[34] R Albert, 'Four Unconstitutional Constitutions and their Democratic Foundations' (2017) 50 *Cornell International Law Journal* 169.

[35] TS Wang, *The Process of Legal Modernization in Taiwan: From 'the Extension of Mainland' to 'Independent Reception'* (2015), 131 (in Chinese).

amendments. Both were examples of naked self-aggrandisement. Furthermore, its greed reached its zenith in the 1999 constitutional amendments, in which members of the National Assembly prolonged their own terms for two years in the name of institutional reform of the legislature. This constitutional revision had immediately enraged most Taiwanese people: according to an opinion poll, 75 per cent opposed the extension and 70 per cent believed the National Assembly should be abolished.[36] Pressured by the public, legislators of both parties thus petitioned the Constitutional Court, which invalidated the impugned 1999 constitutional amendments in Interpretation No 499. In this decision, the Court maintained that 'The amendment process … is in contravention of the principle of openness and transparency … to the extent of constituting manifest and gross flaws'.[37] In terms of the contents, the Court also pointed out that the 1999 constitutional amendments were 'in normative conflict with those provisions of the Constitution that are integral to its essential nature and underpin the constitutional normative order'.[38] Finally, the Constitutional Court declared the constitutional amendments unconstitutional and void on both procedural and substantive grounds. Eventually, the National Assembly was abolished in 2005.

Moreover, the constitutional amendments are undemocratic in a more fundamental sense: they still enshrine the one-China policy, a kind of political nostalgia if not an outright myth. During the authoritarian period, the KMT used the constitution to formally legitimise its claim of sovereignty over China's territory. Even after democratisation, this recurring nightmare continues to haunt Taiwan. Specifically, since 1991, the constitutional amendments have divided the Republic of China into two regions: Taiwan is the 'free area' of China and the People's Republic of China is the 'mainland area'. Therefore, the constitutional amendments prescribe in the preamble that the purpose of constitutional revision is to 'meet the requisites of the nation prior to national unification'.[39] Accordingly, Article 11 of the constitutional amendments demands that: 'Rights and obligations between the people of the Chinese mainland area and those of the free area, and the disposition of other related affairs may be specified by law.'[40] Given this constitutional mandate, the legislature has enacted the Act Governing Relations between the People of the Taiwan Area and the Mainland Area.[41]

[36] Chinese Television System, 'A Poll shows Opposition against the Extension of National Assembly terms'. Available at: https://news.cts.com.tw/cts/general/199909/199909050031749.html.

[37] JY Interpretation No 499 (2000).

[38] Ibid.

[39] Additional Articles of the Constitution of the Republic of China (ROC, Taiwan) (2005). Available at: https://english.president.gov.tw/Page/95.

[40] Article 11 of the Additional Articles of the Constitution of the Republic of China (Taiwan) (2005).

[41] The Article 1 of Act Governing Relations between the People of the Taiwan Area and the Mainland Area (2019) reads: 'This Act is specially enacted for the purposes of ensuring the security and public welfare in the Taiwan Area, regulating dealings between the peoples of the Taiwan Area and the Mainland Area, and handling legal matters arising therefrom before national unification.'

This constitutionalised one-China policy has aggravated political polarisation in Taiwanese society, partly because it has been invoked repeatedly both domestically and internationally. In 2016, Wang Yi, the Foreign Minister of China, took advantage of this constitutionalised one-China policy, arguing that even the ROC Constitution admits that there is only one China in the world.[42] For those who support democracy in Taiwan, this is embarrassing and actually hard to gainsay, constitutionally speaking. It has also become the most powerful legal discourse of the pro-unification camp. Former President Ma Ying-jeou, for example, has invoked this constitutional mandate from time to time to justify his claim that Taiwan should consider unification with China,[43] even though the majority of Taiwanese people oppose it, according to a public opinion poll carried out in 2017.[44]

This policy is repugnant to the majority of Taiwanese people: today almost 60 per cent of Taiwan's citizens identify as Taiwanese, as opposed to only 4 per cent who identify as Chinese.[45] Given these figures, it is not only unpopular but also highly undemocratic to force unification. Still, it has been etched into the constitutional amendments and Taiwan is unlikely to further amend the Constitution to remove this policy in the foreseeable future partly because of the excruciatingly high threshold mentioned above. It is also unlikely that the Taiwanese people can scrap the Constitution and enact a new one, because this may be perceived as attempting to secede from China.[46] Given China's formidable political, economic and military intimidation, it is explicable that Taiwanese people do not dare to rewrite the Constitution, even if it aligns with their current will. In May 2020, a group of DPP legislators proposed to remove the 'before national unification' from the Act Governing Relations between the People of the Taiwan Area and the Mainland Area.[47] Unsurprisingly, China responded by warning that: 'It is extremely dangerous that a handful of separatists have misread the situation and become unbridled in pushing Taiwanese independence.'[48] It is unclear whether the proposal will garner enough votes in the legislature even though the DPP controls an absolute majority.

[42] W Lowther, 'China touts Taiwan Constitution' *Taipei Times* (Taipei, 27 February 2016). Available at: www.taipeitimes.com/News/front/archives/2016/02/27/2003640311.

[43] S Hsu, 'Ma defends 'no opposition to unification'' *Taipei Times* (6 December 2018). Available at: www.taipeitimes.com/News/taiwan/archives/2018/12/06/2003705598.

[44] LH Chung, 'Poll: More than Half Taiwanese Oppose Unification' *Liberty Times Net* (28 March 2017). Available at: http://news.ltn.com.tw/news/politics/breakingnews/2018824.

[45] The Election Study Center of National Cheng Chi University (NCCU), 'Changes in the Taiwanese/Chinese Identity of Taiwanese as Tracked in Surveys (1992~2017.06)'. Available at: https://esc.nccu.edu.tw/app/news.php?Sn=166.

[46] Z Elkins, T Ginsburg and J Melton, *The Endurance of National Constitutions* (2009), 174; D Law, 'Imposed and Romantic Constitutions' in R Albert, X Contiades and A Fotiadou (eds), *The Law and Legitimacy of Imposed Constitutions* (2019), 41.

[47] S Lin, 'Proposal to remove 'unification' from law advances to committee review' *Taipei Times* (10 May 2020). Available at: www.taipeitimes.com/News/front/archives/2020/05/10/2003736129.

[48] Ibid.

Finally, the undemocratic nature of the Constitution can be observed from the fact that some constitutional provisions have essentially, but not formally, been repudiated in the sense that they are, in effect, not binding at all. Namely, '[w]here a textually entrenched provision loses its binding quality as a result of its non-use and sustained public repudiation by political actors, this provision may be understood as having been informally removed from the text'.[49] Yen-tu Su and I have pointed out elsewhere that the large-C constitution, including constitutional amendments, is supreme only insofar as it is consistent with what we call 'über-constitutional norms'.[50] That is, unwritten constitutional norms, such as judicial interpretation and sociopolitical movements, have become an important source in forging Taiwan's constitutional order.

Unfortunately, some undemocratic elements of the written Constitution, particularly the one-China policy, are particularly resilient to informal constitutional change and still function as a straitjacket which shackles the Taiwanese people. The main function of this constitutionalised policy is to clothe the unification (with China) with a veneer of constitutional legitimacy. Worse still, pro-China politicians can always claim that they are following constitutional requirements and advocates for Taiwanese independence are committing civil disturbance, if not treason. This may be even more relevant after the passage of the Hong Kong national security law. The following section analyses three social movements that have been motivated mainly by the desire to strengthen the constitutional democracy in Taiwan. Not surprisingly, the judiciary was embroiled with all three movements.

INFORMAL CONSTITUTIONAL CHANGE

If enacting a Constitution of Taiwan is too provocative and risky to be a viable option, can Taiwanese people indigenise the ROC Constitution through informal constitutional change? In Taiwan, social movements and judicial review have played a critical role in the process of constitutional development. The Wild Lily Movement in 1990 and JY Interpretation No 261 (1990) are two paradigmatic examples that have paved the way for political liberation. Moreover, they have also implicitly transformed constitutional identity to some degree, because both demanded *national* elections be held in Taiwan, rather than in China. This suggests that Taiwan is a country rather than a province (of China). Nevertheless, other social movements and judicial interpretations have been less fruitful. After the second party changeover in 2008, two social movements came into being because of the threat from China. Both failed to stimulate

[49] R Albert, 'How Unwritten Constitutional Norms Change Written Constitutions' (2015) 38 *Dublin University Law Review* 387, 400.

[50] YT Su and CC Lin, 'The Constitutional Law and Politics in Taiwan' in D Law et al, (eds), *Oxford Handbook of Constitutional Law in Asia* (forthcoming).

further constitutional revision. This section briefly compares the three social movements – Wild Lily, Wild Strawberry and Sunflower – and the role the judiciary played after these mobilisations.

The Limitations of Social Movements

The Wild Lily Movement took place in 1990 when the Temporary Provisions Effective During the Period of National Mobilization for Suppression of the Communist Rebellion remained in force. At that time, the Taiwanese people could not directly vote for their president, who was elected by members of the National Assembly, a body whose members had served continuously for four decades due to the suspension of national elections. Meanwhile, Taiwan was in the early stages of the third wave of democratisation.[51] On the one hand, the KMT regime faced overwhelming pressure for democratisation from both international and domestic forces; on the other hand, it also encountered internal resistance from its more conservative factions. In the face of pressure from the Wild Lily Movement, then-President Lee agreed with students' requests and held the first conference on national affairs, discussing the political agenda of democratic transition. Although some suggested that the reform-minded President Lee took advantage of this Movement to gain the upper hand in KMT's internal power struggle, the Wild Lily Movement still precipitated democratisation. This was a watershed moment in the history of Taiwan's political and constitutional developments. However, while electoral democracy has been stable, the Taiwanese people have gradually realised that regular elections alone cannot guarantee a constitutional democracy. Also, electoral democracy, however well it functions, cannot defuse the threat from China. The concerns revolving around these two problems–political dysfunction and external pressure – gave rise to two social movements that endeavoured to ensure democracy in Taiwan.

In contrast with the Wild Lily Movement, subsequent social movements were not as successful from the perspective of deepening Taiwan's constitutional democracy, partly because they addressed the most undemocratic part of the ROC Constitution: the one-China policy. Specifically, the Wild Strawberry Movement in 2008 aimed to protest human rights violations during the visit of Chen Yunlin, who was the President of the Association for Relations Across the Taiwan Straits, China. At that time, President Ma had just won a landslide victory over the DPP candidate Frank Hsieh, but his pro-China political agenda was controversial given China's explicit desire to isolate, attack and annex Taiwan. Many people claimed that Ma leant too heavily towards China at the cost of human rights and democracy in Taiwan. Chen's visit galvanised the fear that the KMT would collaborate with China in promoting unification and

[51] SP Huntington, *The Third Wave: Democratization in the Late 20th Century* (1993).

eliminating Taiwan's gains towards independence. The use of police violence during Chen's visit at the expense of freedom of expression further deepened this suspicion. Advocates for the independence of Taiwan and Tibet and members of Falun Gong were prohibited from waving their flags and slogan boards wherever Chen appeared due to 'security reasons'. Thus, thousands of students and citizens gathered in front of the Executive Yuan and the Chiang Kai-shek Memorial Hall, sat in and staged a protest march against the infringement of fundamental rights. The protest lasted a few days, but the protestors were purged and the movement did not lead to any formal constitutional changes or any significant political change.

The Wild Strawberry Movement was not alone. Beginning in March 2014, the Sunflower Movement aimed to protest the reckless passage of the Cross-Strait Service Trade Agreement, which was passed in an under-handed manner in a matter of 30 seconds. This farce clearly evinced the limitations of electoral democracy and the lack of deliberative democracy in Taiwan. All the legislators were popularly elected and should, in theory, have reflected the will of the people. Unfortunately, they not only passed an Agreement that was opposed by many if not most of the Taiwanese people,[52] but it was also passed in a potentially unconstitutional way. As a result, about 400 students occupied the Legislative Yuan on 18 March and were joined by tens of thousands of students and citizens in days that followed. In addition to returning the Agreement to the executive, the Sunflower Movement also demanded citizen conferences that would discuss, inter alia, the overhaul of the constitutional structure and the legal foundations of the cross-strait relationship. Like the Wild Strawberry Movement, Ma's cozying up to China created the Sunflower Movement. The occupation lasted about a month; eventually, the Agreement was suspended. It is widely believed that this event changed the political landscape in Taiwan and rendered Ma a lame-duck president.

In short, all three social movements, at least indirectly, resulted from the one-China policy enshrined in the Constitution and subsequent constitutional amendments: in the Wild Lily Movement, the National Assembly was monopolised by members who had been elected in China rather than in Taiwan; in the Wild Strawberry Movement, the protection of human rights yielded to the presence of an envoy from China; in the Sunflower Movement, many Taiwanese took the view that increased economic ties with China was simply a sugar-coated poison that would compromise democracy over the long haul.[53] Unfortunately,

[52] C Hsu, 'TRADE PACT SIEGE: Majority opposes trade agreement: poll' *Taipei Times* (27 March 2014). Available at: www.taipeitimes.com/News/taiwan/archives/2014/03/27/2003586647.

[53] CH Wu, 'Dancing with the Dragon: Closer Economic Integration with and Deteriorating Democracy and Rule of Law in Taiwan and Hong Kong', in BC Jones (ed), *Law and Politics of the Taiwan Sunflower and Hong Kong Umbrella Movements* (2017) 144, 158 (arguing that 'closer economic integration may result in worse governance in Taiwan and Hong Kong').

none of these social movements has successfully changed the one-China policy deeply rooted in the Constitution. Due to this confusing and, indeed, pernicious constitutional mandate, pro-China politicians can always claim that they are following constitutional requirements. This contention not only resonates with China's unrelenting propaganda, but also ignores mainstream opinion in Taiwan.

The Limitations of Constitutional Court Decisions

In addition to social movements, another common approach to bringing about informal constitutional change is through judicial review. Given the institutional constraints they face, judges are not supposed to be the best candidates in spearheading constitutional change. In practice, however. they are often embroiled in political frays of constitutional salience. In the three social movements identified above, the judiciary, including the Constitutional Court and ordinary courts, were asked to step in at various points. Their decisions demonstrate the limited role the judiciary usually plays in the process of democratisation: consolidators of electoral democracy.[54] Specifically, after the Wild Lily Movement, the Constitutional Court issued landmark Interpretation No 261 (1990). It demanded national elections and essentially abolished the Temporary Provisions, both of which were in harmony with the appeals of the Movement. After the Wild Strawberry Movement, the Constitutional Court delivered Interpretation No 718 (2014), in a case that involved the freedom of assembly and parade. In this case, one professor was prosecuted and convicted for inciting chaos when he protested the visit of Chen Yunlin in front of the Executive Yuan in 2008. Notwithstanding the failure of the Wild Strawberry Movement, the Constitutional Court expanded the scope of freedom of assembly six years later, holding that the impugned law unnecessarily constrained the freedom of assembly. And after the Sunflower Movement, several leaders of the occupation were prosecuted but this time, both the Taipei District Court and the Taiwan High Court ruled in their favour by invoking the concepts of civil disobedience and freedom of assembly.[55] In a nutshell, as a result of judicial decisions, national elections were restored in the 1990s and the scope of freedom of assembly was expanded at the dawn of the twenty-first century. It is fair to say that the judiciary responded positively to each of the three student movements.

[54] T Ginsburg, 'The Politics of Courts in Democratization: Four Junctures in Asia' in D Kapiszewski, G Silverstein and RA Kagan (eds), *Consequential Courts* (2013) 45, 50–51, 55–58.

[55] No 104 矚訴1, Taipei Dist Ct (2017); No 106 矚上訴1, Taiwan High Ct (2018) (in Chinese).

Table 8.1 Student Movements in Taiwan after Democratisation

	Origin	*Major Appeals*	*Response of Political Branches*	*Response of Judicial Branch*
Wild Lily (1990)	Suspension of Elections	Abolish the National Assembly; Repeal the Temporary Provisions; Hold Conference on National Affairs	National Assembly abolished; Temporary Provisions repealed; Conference on National Affairs held	Interpretation No 261
Wild Strawberry (2008)	Violation of the Freedom of Assembly	Revise the Assembly and Demonstration Act	No response; prosecute protestors	Interpretation No 718
Sunflower (2014)	Cross-Strait Service Trade Agreement	Return the Agreement; Establish Supervisory Mechanisms; constitutional reform	No response; prosecute protestors	No 106 矚上訴1, Taiwan High Court

Although the discussion seems to confirm that social movements and judicial review may have effectively changed the political landscape in Taiwan, their impact on the indigenisation of the constitution differ. The Wild Lily Movement undoubtedly has had a huge impact in both regards. The abolition of the Temporary Provisions not only precipitated political liberation but also gave birth to the 1991 constitutional amendments, which indigenised the ROC Constitution by requesting national elections be held in Taiwan. Compared with the Wild Lily movement, the Wild Strawberries and the Sunflower movements were not so fruitful. Both took place after Taiwan had passed the second party-turnover test, an indicator of stable democracy. Although they might have sown the seeds for the third-party turnover in 2016, they were relatively conservative in terms of requesting constitutional change. The Wild Strawberry Movement did not seek any constitutional reform, while Sunflower's cry for constitutional reform was simply ignored. Indeed, from the political development after the Sunflower Movement, it seems that the level of civil engagement in constitutional transformation did not change perceptibly. It is true that the DPP government is more alert to the economic and political threat from China but, in reality, it has done little to address the undemocratic constitution. If the Wild Lily Movement successfully spurred constitutional revision by holding national elections in Taiwan, neither the

Wild Strawberry nor the Sunflower brought about further constitutional change. Admittedly, there is no denying that activists in the Strawberry and the Sunflower Movements faced a higher threshold for the 2005 constitutional amendments. This chapter does not mean to devalue both movements; instead, it intends to point out the limitation of informal constitutional indigenisation through social movements.

Nor is judicial review able to further acclimatise undemocratic constitutional law. In Taiwan, the Constitutional Court has long been lauded as the guardian of the Constitution, which is true given its sterling record in striking down a constellation of laws that have infringed upon fundamental rights. Despite this reputation, the Constitutional Court is extremely careful not to step directly into the political thicket of controversies concerning national identity, operating at the margins rather than in the centre. On the one hand, the judiciary endeavoured to secure all basic rights necessary to bring about political change, such as the right to vote in Interpretation No 261 (the major appeal of the Wild Lily Movement) and the freedom of assembly in Interpretation No 718 (issues involved in the Wild Strawberry and Sunflower Movements).

On the other hand, it has refused to respond to the challenges of the one-China ideology. In Interpretation No 328 (1993), for instance, the controversy was how to demarcate the territory of the Republic of China: whether it still included mainland China and Mongolia or was limited to Taiwan and other neighbouring islets. The implication of this petition involved national identity and sovereignty: whether the Republic of China had essentially been replaced by Taiwan. By invoking the political question doctrine,[56] the Constitutional Court strategically evaded this issue. Although it was a legally and politically shrewd move, the evasion itself demonstrated that democratic deficiency in this regard cannot be ameliorated through judicial review. What is worse, the Constitutional Court has reinforced the one-China paradigm in some decisions, because it is also bound by the constitutional texts. In Interpretation No 329 (1993), for example, the majority opinion maintained that agreements between China and Taiwan are not international treaties, implicitly recognising the one-China policy. Moreover, in a series of cases concerning the Act Governing Relations between the People of the Taiwan Area and the Mainland Area, the Constitutional Court repeatedly upheld the principle that the relationship between Taiwan and China is one of area-to-area, rather than state-to-state.[57] These decisions demonstrate the international constraints imposed upon domestic constitutional courts. In the European context, courts may use these external pressures to facilitate and consolidate democracy

[56] JY Interpretation No 328 (1993). The Constitutional Court argued that 'The delimitation of national territory according to its history is a significant political question and thus it is beyond the reach of judicial review.'

[57] JY Interpretation No 497 (1999), JY Interpretation No 710 (2013) and JY Interpretation No 712 (2013).

when domestic human rights protection lags behind regional or international standards.[58] In the context of East Asia, however, the dynamic is reversed: China's ubiquitous clout means that the Taiwan Constitutional Court is unwilling to tackle some of the core issues of democracy. Unlike its heroic role in giving birth to electoral democracy, the judiciary has been more modest in indigenising constitutional identity.

Constitutional Desuetude

Admittedly, constitutional change can take place in a variety of forms; it need not be limited to judicial interpretation or formal amendment.[59] For instance, constitutional desuetude, occurs when a constitutional provision encounters 'conscious nonuse and public repudiation'[60] even if it is textually entrenched in the written constitution, eg when a constitutional provision has not only been ignored but also replaced by political elites consciously, continuously and publicly without invoking any formal process to amend the Constitution.[61] This usually happens when that clause is so inconsistent with mainstream public opinion that it is regarded as being effectively nullified. Under these circumstances, that written constitutional provision would cease to be binding.

In Taiwan, some constitutional provisions are close to constitutional desuetude. To name just one example: Articles 53 and 54 of the Constitution provide that the prime minister (the President of the Executive Yuan) should be the head of the executive branch.[62] These two articles have never been amended and remain in place. However, in reality, the popularly elected President is the head of the executive branch and the prime minister is only in charge of faithfully executing the President's policies. No prime minister has ever challenged the status of the President, notwithstanding the constitutional mandate and this political reality is crystal clear to all Taiwanese people. Nevertheless, the theory of constitutional desuetude cannot solve the undemocratic constitutional problem, because, as mentioned above, some pro-unification politicians continuously invoke the one-China policy etched in the Constitution.

[58] N Maveety and A Grosskopf, '"Constrained" Constitutional Courts as Conduits for Democratic Consolidation' (2004) 38 *Law and Society Review* 463, 467.

[59] C Bernal, 'Foreword-Informal Constitutional Change: A Critical Introduction and Appraisal' (2014) 62 *American Journal of Comparative Law* 493.

[60] R Albert, 'Constitutional Amendment by Constitutional Desuetude' (2014) 62 *American Journal of Comparative Law* 641, 653.

[61] Ibid 674–675.

[62] Article 53 of the ROC Constitution reads: 'The Executive Yuan shall be the highest administrative organ of the State.' Article 54 reads: 'The Executive Yuan shall have a President, a Vice President, a certain number of Ministers and Chairmen of Commissions, and a certain number of Ministers without Portfolio.'

CONCLUSION: DEEPENING DEMOCRACY IN TAIWAN THROUGH REFERENDUM

The fact that neither formal constitutional amendment nor informal constitutional change can deal with the undemocratic constitution does not mean there is nothing we can do to deepen democracy in Taiwan. Given China's bullying, it is unrealistic to indigenise the ROC Constitution through formal constitutional revision, even if the threshold for constitutional amendments is lowered. One viable approach is to empower civil society and deepen civil constitutionalism, which may increase popular participation in normal politics beyond elections.[63]

Referendums may be worth considering in undergirding Taiwan's democracy. Article 17 of the ROC Constitution protects the people's right of election, recall, initiative and referendum.[64] The legislature enacted the Referendum Act in 2004. Nevertheless, for a variety of reasons, the original Referendum Act did not really encourage more civil participation. First, the threshold of proposal and approval were too high to get a referendum on the ballot. Specifically, it required at least 5 per cent of the total electors in the most recent election of President and Vice President to propose a national referendum. The proposal would not be adopted unless half of the eligible voters vote and half of the voters assent. Meanwhile, citizens must have reached the age of 20 to be eligible to vote. More importantly, the scope of issues eligible for both national and local referenda was limited. Given these constraints, the Referendum Act was widely labelled as a 'birdcage' Referendum Act, because all six of the proposals[65] that went forward were vetoed, as each one failed to pass the statutory thresholds.

Since 2017, these constraints have been considerably loosened: the voting age has been reduced to 18, the issues eligible for referendums have been enlarged and the thresholds have been lowered.[66] Of course, these revisions should partly be attributed to the change of political climate after the Sunflower Movement, which resulted in Taiwan's third political turnover. Notably, under the amended Act, a proposal will now be adopted as long as valid ballots of assent are more than ballots of dissent and reach a quarter of eligible voters. Moreover, people may advance initiatives or referendums on important policies at both national and local level. This change has greatly increased the public's ability to participate in direct policymaking. In 2018, for example, 10 proposals were on the ballot including issues such as: same-sex marriage, thermal power plants, nuclear power plants and whether Taiwan should participate in the 2020

[63] J Colón-Ríos, *Weak Constitutionalism: Democratic Legitimacy and the Question of Constituent Power* (2013) 35.

[64] Article 17 of the Constitution of the Republic of China (Taiwan) (1947): 'The people shall have the right of election, recall, initiative and referendum.'

[65] Central Election Commission, 'Referendums Profile' (24 October 2019). Available at: www.cec.gov.tw/english/cms/rProfile.

[66] S Lin, 'Referendum Act amendments approved' *Taipei Times* (13 December 2017). Available at: www.taipeitimes.com/News/front/archives/2017/12/13/2003683881.

Summer Olympics under the name of 'Taiwan' rather than 'Chinese Taipei'. Of course, a referendum is not a silver bullet that ensures democratic accountability. During the referendum process of 2018 some misconduct was detected, such as a huge number of forged signatures.[67] The sheer number of questions (10) also spawned several unexpected controversies and eventually the chairman of the Central Election Commission was forced to step down.[68]

In conclusion, this chapter suggests that the domestication and indigenisation of the ROC Constitution through formal constitutional amendment has been unsuccessful. Worse still, these constitutional amendments not only obstruct future constitutional revision but also etch the one-China policy into the supreme law. Aware of the limitations of formal constitutional change, some have turned to informal constitutional change, such as social movements and judicial review. This strategy, however, does not change the undemocratic nature of the ROC constitutional framework. To enhance the quality of civil constitutionalism in Taiwan, this chapter suggests that we may consider a direct and decentralised form of political participation, such as plebiscite. It is certainly not a panacea for democratic backsliding and may be misused, if not intentionally abused. The anti-marriage equality proposals in the 2018 referendum were good examples. Still, it may be a viable mechanism to deepen Taiwan's constitutional democracy in the face of unrelenting pressure from China.

[67] R Drillsma, '10 referendums to be held alongside Taiwan's local elections on Nov. 24' *Taiwan News* (24 October 2018). Available at: www.taiwannews.com.tw/en/news/3559435.

[68] D Deaeth, 'Chairman of Taiwan's Central Election Commission resigns' *Taiwan News* (25 November 2018). Available at: www.taiwannews.com.tw/en/news/3583110.

9

Law in the Shadow of the Political

XIAOBO ZHAI*

THE PARTY'S RULE-OF-LAW IDEAL

A HOTLY DEBATED issue nowadays is determining what conceptual framework of the rule of law should be used to evaluate China's 40-year rule-of-law history. This chapter is not a project of so-called legal orientalism; that is, taking the 'Ideal Western Legal Order' (IWLO) as superior and shaming and blaming China for falling short of it.[1] One of my tasks is to examine whether the Party has achieved the rule of law that it claims to be pursuing. I will predominantly adopt an internal perspective, taking as my conceptual framework the Chinese Communist Party (CCP or Party)'s self-understanding of the rule of law. Albert Chen and Randall Peerenboom suggested that the Party's notion of the rule of law was a thin version of the rule of law.[2] I disagree. The rule of law that the Party originally set out to achieve is fairly thick. I will demonstrate this by a brief historical account of the Party's discourse on the rule of law.[3]

The Party made the decision for the rule of law immediately after the conclusion of the Cultural Revolution (CR). For the post-CR leadership, the cause of the CR was the lack of a robust rule of law and the way to prevent repeating the CR was to transform China into a rule of law country. The Party's discourse on

* Associate Professor, University of Macau. The research for this chapter was supported by the University of Macau (MYRG2016-00094-FLL). I thank Brian Christopher Jones for his valuable comments and suggestions.

[1] For the Ideal Western Legal Order (IWLO) approach, see D Clarke, 'Puzzling Observations in Chinese Law', in CS Hsu (ed), *Understanding China's Legal System* (2003), 93. This model is also branded as 'Legal Orientalism', see T Ruskola, *Legal Orientalism: China, the United States, and Modern Law* (2013).

[2] A Chen, 'China's Long March towards Rule of Law or China's Turn against Law' (2016) 4 *The Chinese Journal of Comparative Law* 1, 11–12. R Peerenboom, *China's Long March Towards Rule of Law* (2002), 212.

[3] As EP Thompson once said, discourse is 'something a great deal more than sham' and cannot be dismissed as a mere hypocrisy. EP Thompson, *Whigs and Hunters: The Origin of the Black Act* (1975), 267.

the rule of law has been largely consistent throughout the four generations of the Party's leadership in the post-Mao era.

Many of the first-generation leaders suffered severely from the lack of the rule of law during the CR. They were eager to advocate the importance of law, especially the legal protection of citizens' rights. The Party's 11th Central Committee pointed out that one major cause of the CR was that the Party 'had failed to institutionalize by law the intra-Party democracy and the democracy in the political and social life of the country' and that 'the relevant laws we had made lacked due authority'.[4] The paramount leader Deng Xiaoping (1904–1997) believed that the rule of law was the only way to prevent repeating a tragedy like the CR.[5] Ye Jianying (1897–1986) stressed that the CR 'taught us a painful lesson, and made us realize that a country cannot flourish without law and institutions'.[6] Peng Zhen (1902–1997) said, 'Nobody would like to see again the tragedy like the CR, but hope alone will not help, and we need a guarantor, which can only be a robust Socialist Rule of Law (SROL): the whole population must all behave according to the Constitution and laws'.[7]

These leaders believed that the rule of law was the negation of the CR. The CR was 'catastrophic turmoil',[8] in which the following were rampant: framed or false verdicts, torture, arbitrary arrests and detentions, private courts, smashing and looting and personality insults; people lived in a chaos of terror where the Constitution and laws were entirely ignored.[9] Ye characterised the CR as follows: The Gang of Four 'arrested anyone they wanted to arrest' and 'imposed fascist dictatorship upon our cadres and people'.[10] They 'brutally persecuted the revolutionary masses and cadres, seriously undermined the SROL, thereby leaving unprotected people's legitimate democratic rights and personal safety'.[11]

[4] *Resolution on Certain Questions in the History of our Party since the Founding of the People's Republic of China* (关于建国以来党的若干历史问题的决议), adopted by the Sixth Plenary Session of the Eleventh Central Committee of the Communist Party of China on 27 June 1981). Available at: http://news.sina.com.cn/c/nd/2016-05-16/doc-ifxsenvn7202369.shtml.

[5] X Deng, 'Answers to the Italian Journalist Oriana Fallaci' ('答意大利记者奥琳埃娜-法拉奇问') (21 and 23/08/1980), in *Selected Works of Deng Xiaoping* (邓小平文选) (1994) vol 2, 348.

[6] J Ye, 'A Speech at the Concluding Session of the Central Work Conference' (在中央工作会议闭幕会上的讲话) (13/12/1978. Available at: www.aisixiang.com/data/23237.html.

[7] Z Peng, cited in Zheng Liu (刘政), 'The Features and History of the System of People's Congresses' (我国人民代表大会制度的特点及其历史发展). Available at: www.npc.gov.cn/npc/c541/199809/ef185e57149c49999cab7ee04ae1835a.shtml.

[8] *Resolution on Certain Questions*, n 4 above.

[9] The Research Office of the Central Committee of the CCP (中共中央党史研究室), *The History of the CCP* (中国共产党历史) (2002) vol 2 (1949–1978), 966–982.

[10] J Ye, 'A Talk on the Rule of Law with Journalists of Xinhua News Agency' (接见新华社记者谈法制建设)(14 February 1979) in Wang Yuming (ed), *The Legal Thought of Mao* (毛泽东法律思想库) (1993), 50.

[11] J Ye, 'Report on the Revision of the Constitution' (关于修改宪法的报告)(1 March 1978) Available at: www.reformdata.org/1978/0301/8945.shtml.

Drawing on lessons from the CR, the Party made the decision for the rule of law. In his speech at the Central Party Work Conference (中央工作会议) on 13 December 1978, Deng declared:

> The rights of citizens, party members, and the members of the Party Committees stipulated in the Constitution and the Party's Charter must be firmly guaranteed, and be infringed by no one. … In order to protect democracy, we must strengthen the rule of law. We must institutionalize democracy by law so that these institutions and laws will not be changed by the change of leaders, or the changes of leaders' opinions and attention. … There must be laws to follow, laws must be enforced, the enforcement of law must be strict, and the violations of law must be investigated and punished.[12]

On 22 December 1978, *the Communiqué of the Third Plenum of the 11th Party Congress* repeated Deng's words verbatim, adding that 'law and institutions must have stability, continuity, and the supreme authority', that 'the procuracy and the judiciary should have its proper independence, and be faithful to law and institutions' and that 'all are equal before law and no one is allowed to enjoy privileges above law'.[13] Deng, in fact, suggested that the rule of law he had in mind was the rule of law in western liberal democracies. He said, 'Mao once said that Stalin had severely broken and damaged the SROL, and this kind of things could never happen in western countries like the UK, the US and France'.[14] One obstacle to the rule of law in China, Deng claimed, was 'the feudalistic despotism China inherited from its old past'.[15] Similarly, Peng Zhen stressed the necessary relationship between democracy and the rule of law.[16] 'How could it be possible to have the rule of law without democracy, unless what you want is a reactionary and undemocratic legal system?'[17] These views were reiterated and expanded upon by Deng and other paramount leaders of the second generation. Meanwhile, Deng laid down as unchallengeable the leadership of the Communist Party.[18]

A landmark in the Party's rule of law discourse is the amendments of the Charter of the Party and the Constitution in 1982. The Party's 12th Congress

[12] X Deng, 'Liberate Our Thought, Seek Truths from Facts, and Unite and Look to the Future'(解放思想，实事求是，团结一致向前看)(13 December 1978. Available at: http://cpc.people.com.cn/n1/2018/0531/c69113-30025177.html.

[13] '*The Communiqué of the Third Plenum of the 11th Party Congress*' (中国共产党第十一届中央委员会第三次全体会议公报) (22 December 1978). Available at: http://cpc.people.com.cn/GB/64162/64168/64563/65371/4441902.html.

[14] X Deng, 'The Reforms of the System of the Leadership of the Party and the State'(党和国家领导制度的改革), *Selected Works of Deng Xiaoping*, vol 2 (1975–1982), 333.

[15] Ibid, 332, 334–336.

[16] Z Peng, 'Some Questions regarding the SROL' (关于社会主义法制的几个问题), (1979) (11) *Red Flag* (红旗).

[17] Z Peng, 'A Speech to Cadres of Legislative Work' (对立法工作干部培训班学员的讲话) (1 July 1985), in *The Legal Thoughts of Mao*, 50–51.

[18] X Deng, 'Uphold the Four Cardinal Principles'(坚持四项基本原则)(30 March 1979), *Selected Works of Deng Xiaoping*, vol 2, 169–171.

this year provided that 'the Party (including the Party organs and members) must act within the limits of the Constitution and laws'. Besides, the revised Charter of the Party specifies that 'the Party's leadership means mainly political, ideological and organizational leadership'. According to Hu Qiaomu, this provision 'clarifies the relationship between the Party, the state and the non-Party organizations, prevents the confusion between the Party and the state, between the Party and the enterprises, … and guarantees that the legislature and the judiciary work independently and responsibly'.[19] Hu Yaobang, then general secretary of the CCP, emphasised that 'the party, including the Party organs and members, must act within the limits of the Constitution and laws is a principle of extreme importance. … The Party leads the people to make the Constitution and laws; once the Constitution and laws are made, the whole party must strictly abide by them'.[20] Peng Zhen explained that it was thanks to the CR that this principle was enshrined in the Charter of the Party.[21] Using this principle, the Party's 12th Congress theoretically solved the problem of the relationship between the Party's leadership and the rule of law.[22] In the same year, the 1982 Constitution stipulated in its Preamble that:

> This Constitution … is the fundamental law of the state and has the supreme legal validity. The people of all nationalities, all state organs, the armed forces, all political parties and public organizations, and all enterprises and institutions must take the Constitution as the fundamental norm of conduct, and they have the duty to uphold the dignity of the Constitution and ensure its implementation.

It removed the 1978 Constitution's provision that 'the CCP is the leadership core of all Chinese people'. Article 5 of 1982 Constitution provides that:

> the state upholds the uniformity and dignity of the socialist legal system. No law or administrative or local ordinance and regulation shall contravene the Constitution. All state organs, the armed forces, all political parties and public organizations, and all enterprises and institutions must abide by the Constitution and laws. All acts in violation of the Constitution and laws must be investigated and punished. No organization or individual may enjoy the privilege of being above the Constitution and laws.

The consensus among constitutional scholars is that 'all political parties' here includes the CCP itself.

[19] Q Hu (胡乔木), 'Answers to the Journalists of Xinhua News Agency on the Revisions of the Charter of the Party' (关于《党章》修改问题答新华社记者问), *Works of Hu Qiaomu* (胡乔木文集)(人民出版社, 2012), vol 2, 195–208.

[20] Y Hu (胡耀邦), 'Comprehensively Open Up a New Prospect for Socialist Modernization'(全面开创社会主义现代化建设的新局面) (1 September 1982). Available at: www.gov.cn/test/2007-08/28/content_729792.htm.

[21] *Developing Socialist Democracy, and Improving SROL: A Collection of Important Excerpts* (发展社会主义民主，健全社会主义法制：有关重要论述摘编) (1988), 177.

[22] D Cai (蔡定剑), *History and Reform: The Journey of the Rule of Law Construction in New China* (历史与变革: 新中国法制建设的历程（1999), 129.

The CCP's 13th Congress in 1987 was regarded as the best conference in the Party's history.[23] The communiqué of the Congress pointed out, 'the aim of our political reform is to improve socialist democracy and rule of law, and eliminate bureaucratism and feudalism, which is the fundamental guarantor against repeating the CR', and 'the key priority of the political reform is the separation of the Party and the state'.[24]

China's march towards the rule of law suffered a temporary setback after the 1989 Tiananmen Square Incident. However, three months later, President Jiang Zemin declared that 'we will never allow the government or the law to be replaced by the Party, which is about the choice between the rule of men and the rule of law. We must follow the policy of the rule of law'.[25] China's discourse on the rule of law reached its climax in 1997 when the Party's 15th Congress officially endorsed 'ruling the country in accordance with law and establishing a socialist rule of law state' as a basic principle of the Party's leadership.[26] The 15th Congress also made the decision to 'push forward the judicial reform, and guarantee institutionally the judiciary to exercise its powers independently and justly'.[27] In 1999, the Constitution was amended and the following phrase was added: 'the PRC will rule the country in accordance with law, and build a socialist rule of law state'. In 2011, Wu Bangguo, China's top legislator, announced that a socialist legal system with Chinese characteristics had taken shape.[28]

Since President Xi took power, the rule of law has been flagged as one of the four priorities of the CCP.[29] In 2014, the 4th Plenum of the Party's 18th Central Committee made the rule of law as its main topic: this was the first time in the Party's history that such a high-profile meeting had focused on the rule of law. This plenum passed a 'Decision on Some Major Issues About Comprehensively Pushing Forward the Rule of Law', which states:

> all organizations or individuals must respect the authority of the Constitution and laws, and must act within the limits of the Constitution and laws, must all exercise

[23] W Wu (吴伟),' The Drafting Process of the Report of the Party's 13th Congress' (中共十三大报告起草过程述实). Available at: www.yhcqw.com/30/9464.html.

[24] Z Zhao (赵紫阳), 'Advance Along the Path of Socialism with Chinese Characteristics' (沿着有中国特色的社会主义道路前进) (25 October 1987). Available at: http://fuwu.12371.cn/2012/09/25/ARTI1348562562473415.shtml.

[25] Cited in B Li (李步云), 'Ruling the Country According to Law, and Constructing a SROL Country' (依法治国，建设社会主义法治国家). Available at: www.npc.gov.cn/npc/c541/199808/001dcc045c1e42ccb01e59ab395153a2.shtml.

[26] Z Jiang, 'Fly High the Great Flag of the Deng Xiaoping Theory, and Advance Comprehensively into the 21th Century the Project of the Socialism with Chinese Characteristics' (高举邓小平理论伟大旗帜, 把建设有中国特色社会主义事业全面推向二十一世纪) (12 September 1997). Available at: http://cpc.people.com.cn/GB/64162/64168/64568/65445/4526285.html.

[27] Ibid.

[28] B Wu (吴邦国), 'The Socialist Legal System with Chinese Characteristics has Taken Shape'(中国特色社会主义法律体系已经形成) (10 March 2011). Available at: http://news.sina.com.cn/c/2011-03-10/102222087632.shtml.

[29] They are called four comprehensives: comprehensively building a moderately prosperous society, deepening reform, advancing the rule of law and strictly governing the Party.

> their powers or rights, and perform their duties and responsibilities according to the Constitution and laws; none should have privileges outside of the Constitution and laws. … the main task of the rule of law is to regulate and restrain public powers.

It also emphasises that 'the Party's leadership is the most fundamental guarantor of the socialist rule of law'.[30]

The above brief account shows that, during the past four decades, the CCP has taken every opportunity to emphasise the importance of the rule of law and to declare its resolve to entrench the rule of law in China. Its commitment to the rule of law is serious and sincere. According to the Party's discourse, one major point of the SROL is to guard against repeating the CR, which was considered a kind of fascist dictatorship or totalitarianism. The CCP's leadership emphasised that the rule of law is the opposite of the rule of men: it aims to constrain the arbitrary exercise of public powers, to shut the power in the cage of institutions and laws.[31] The CCP reiterates that even the supreme power holder, ie the Party, must behave within the limits of the Constitution and laws.[32] Xi stressed in 2015 that 'every organization of the Party, and every cadre of the Party, must obey and comply with the Constitutional and laws'.[33] It is a mistake to think that 'Chinese law, including the Constitution, simply does not *attempt*' to constrain the Party's leadership.[34]

The Party's discourse also shows that the SROL is comprised of many requirements.[35] First, there are a set of formal and procedural requirements: the supremacy of the Constitution and laws; the implementation of the Constitution and laws; the clarity, accessibility, continuity, publicity and non-retrospectivity of laws; the equality before law; and independent adjudication according to law, etc. Second and, more importantly, the SROL also includes some substantive requirements: its aim is not only to develop the economy, but also to protect human dignity and human rights, which are enshrined in the Constitution.[36] The SROL allegedly is not just the rule of any kind of law, but it is the rule of good law. According to the Party, 'good laws are a prerequisite

[30] 'The CCP's Central Committee (CCPCC)'s Decision on some Major Questions regarding Comprehensively Moving Forward the Project of Ruling the Country According to Law' (中共中央关于全面推进依法治国若干重大问题的决定). Available at: http://cpc.people.com.cn/n/2014/1029/c64387-25927606.html.

[31] J Xi, *The Governance of China* (习近平谈治国理政) (2014), 388.

[32] This is exactly the core of the rule of law, see G Postema, 'Law's Rule: Reflexivity, Mutual Accountability, and the Rule of Law', in X Zhai and M Quinn (eds), *Bentham's Theory of Law and Public Opinion* (2014), 10–11.

[33] 'Xi Jinping's Speech to Provincial Leaders on Ruling the Country According to Law' (习近平在全面推进依法治国专题研讨班上的讲话) (2 Feburary 2015). Available at: www.csoa.cn/doc/16149.jsp.

[34] T Zhang and T Ginsburg, 'China's Turn toward Law' (2019) 59 *Virginia Journal of International Law* 306, 316.

[35] 'The CCPCC's Decision on Major Questions', n 30 above.

[36] Arts 33 (3) and 38. On human dignity under China's Constitution, see X Zhai, 'Personal Dignity under Chinese Constitutional Law', in JC Hsu (ed), *Human Dignity in Asia: Dialogue Between Law and Culture* (2021).

for good governance. … Justice, fairness, and publicity must guide all aspects of legislation'.[37] Additionally, the SROL must institutionalise and promote socialist democracy.

In short, the original conception of the rule of law, as the Party itself has professed, is not a thin version of the rule of law, as Peerenboom and Chen have suggested;[38] nor is it the rule by law, which means that law is only used as a tool to rule and govern the society, and imposes no meaningful limits upon high powers. It is quite a thick version of the rule of law.

However, I would like to add three provisos to the above claim. First, the relationship between the Party and the law is 'the core issue of the rule of law construction in China':[39] on the one hand, the Party emphasises that it 'must behave within the limits of the Constitution and laws'; on the other hand, it insists that 'the rule of law must be promoted *under* the leadership of the Party'.[40] Second, there were also changes in the Party's discourse on the rule of law, the most important of which concerns the relationship between the Party and the state. Since Xi came to power, the principle of the separation between the Party and the state has been abandoned. The best example of this was the statement that 'the leadership of CCP is the defining feature of the socialism with Chinese characteristics', which was added to Article 1 of the Constitution in 2018. Third, the Party has constantly insisted that China would not adopt the political system of western liberal democracies, including Western constitutionalism, the separation of powers, judicial independence, or party rotation.[41]

BETWEEN OPTIMISM AND SCEPTICISM

Since the Party made the decision for the rule of law, more than four decades have elapsed. Looking back, many experts agree that China made obvious progress towards the rule of law in the first three decades, ie roughly from the end of the CR to 2008 when Wang Shengjun was appointed as the President of the Supreme People's Court (SPC).[42] China's rule of law reforms in the post-Mao era have

[37] 'The CCPCC's Decision on Major Questions'.

[38] R Peerenboom, 'The X-Files: Past and Present Portrayals of China's Alien "Legal System"' (2003) 2 *Washington University Global Studies Law Review*, 57–59; A Chen, 'China's Long March', n 2 above, 10–11.

[39] J Xi, 'Some Explanations about "The CCP's Central Committee's Decision on some Major Questions"'(关于《中共中央关于全面推进依法治国若干重大问题的决定》的说明'). Available at: www.qstheory.cn/dukan/2020-06/04/c_1126073326.htm.

[40] 'The CCPCC's Decision on Major Questions'.

[41] J Xi, 'Strengthening the Party's Leadership over Comprehensively Ruling the Country According to Law' (加强党对全面依法治国的领导) (24/08/2018). Available at: www.xinhuanet.com/politics/2019-02/15/c_1124120391.htm.

[42] B Liebman, 'Assessing China's Legal Reforms' (2009) 23(1) *Columbia Journal of Asian Law* 17, 18; Peerenboom n 38 above, 55; S Lubman, *Bird in a Cage: Legal Reform in China after Mao* (2002) xvi, 2.

been well documented.[43] It is more difficult to evaluate the state of the rule of law since Wang Shengjun's appointment. In an article published in 2011, Carl Minzner argued that China had turned against the rule of law in the first decade of the twenty-first century.[44] Jiang Ping, one of the most influential and outspoken legal scholars, pointed out in 2010: 'Looking at China's current situation, I think we are in a period where the rule of law is in retreat. Or perhaps, the rule of law, judicial reform, and political reform are all moving backwards.'[45] The scepticism recently has only deepened and widened.[46] It is not about the importance of the law in China: the Party continues to use the Constitution and laws to empower, legitimise and thereby strengthen itself.[47] It is about the rule of law in China: ie, whether law can really constrain the arbitrariness of high power-holders. The Party announced in 2014 that it had made 'historical achievements' in the rule of law. However, it meanwhile acknowledged that there remained many problems, including:

- law-breaches with impunity（有法不依、违法不究）and non-strict law enforcement（执法不严）are grave;
- duplicate law enforcement (多头执法) and selective and corrupt law enforcement remain;
- law enforcement and adjudication are non-standardised, opaque and uncivilised;
- many people do not have the proper consciousness of respecting the law, trusting the law, obeying the law, using the law and safeguarding their rights by means of the law;
- some officials' – especially the leading cadres'– awareness and ability to tackle issues according to the law are disappointing; laws are knowingly violated, the word of officials are taken as the law, so the law is trumped by power and is manipulated to benefit private interests.[48]

These problems, diagnosed by the Party, were common and deeply embedded. In addition, the Party's strong tendency to politicise non-political issues, the tightened ideological control, the frequent sentences of 'picking quarrels and

[43] For example, The State Council Information Office (国务院新闻办公室), 'China's Efforts and Achievements in Promoting the Rule of Law' (中国的法治建设白皮书) (28/02/2008; 'Judicial Reforms in China' (中国的司法改革白皮书) (9 October 2012).

[44] C Minzner, 'China's Turn against Law' (2011) 59 *American Journal of Comparative Law* 935.

[45] P Jiang (江平), 'China's Rule of Law Is in Full Retreat'. For an English translation of Jiang Ping's speech, see https://lawprofessors.typepad.com/china_law_prof_blog/2010/03/jiang-ping-chinas-rule of law-is-in-full-retreat.html. See also P Jiang, *I Remain Cautiously Optimistic* (依然谨慎的乐观) (2016), 51, 88.

[46] Zhang and Ginsburg have offered a comprehensive overview of the pessimistic literature, see n 34 above, 104, fn 1.

[47] Ibid.

[48] 'The CCPCC's Decision on Major Questions', n 30 above.

provoking troubles'(寻衅滋事),[49] the promotion of mediation, the shift from professionalism to populism, the pervasive role of guanxi (personal networks 关系), have all been cited to support this scepticism. In the following, I point to three deep structural factors which need to be addressed in China's march towards the rule of law. These demonstrate that, currently in China, the law only rules in the shadow of the political.

THE PARTY AND THE LAW

In China, a basic difficulty for the SROL is how to deal with the relationship between the Party on the one hand and the Constitution and laws on the other. Xi said that 'the relation between the Party and the SROL is the core issue of the construction of the SROL', that the Party's leadership was 'the fundamental guarantor' and 'fundamental requirement' of the SROL, and that the former is consistent with the latter.[50] Cai Dingjian, a late liberal constitutional scholar, wrote that 'the serious problem facing the SROL is that its destruction seriously comes from the Party, the government, and their leaders'.[51] Some have even suggested that the leadership role of the Party is 'at odds with rule of law'.[52] In the following, by focusing on the Party's unusual legal status, I will provide a more complex account of the possible challenges that the Party's leadership poses for the rule of law.

The Party's Legal Immunity

It has been reiterated by the Party itself that the Party must behave within the limits of the Constitution and laws. Although the Party's leadership is mentioned in the Preamble of the Constitution and other laws and was written into the Constitution in 2018, the Party does not possess legal powers. Under Chinese law, the Party does not exist as an institution of state power and has no power to issue legally binding decisions. But, in real politics, the Party is omnipotent and supreme. It is in charge of the military and monopolises all coercive force and

[49] D Roberts, '"Picking Quarrels and Provoking Troubles" – the Crime Sweeping China'. Available at: www.bloomberg.com/news/articles/2014-05-12/picking-quarrels-and-provoking-troubles-the-crime-sweeping-china.

[50] Xi, 'Some Explanations', n 39 above.

[51] Cai, *History and Reform*, n 22 above, 296.

[52] R Peerenboom, 'Fly High the Banner of Socialist Rule of Law with Chinese Characteristics! What Does the 4th Plenum Decision Mean for Legal Reforms in China?' (2015) 7 *Hague Journal on the Rule of Law* 49, 55. See also A Chen's Review of Tong Zhiwei's *The Reform of China's Constitutional System* (中国宪制之维新), (2018) 16 *International Journal of Constitutional Law* 728, 729–30; WP Alford, 'How Law Does – and Doesn't –Matter in the PRC', in National Taiwan University College Law (ed), *Fifth Herbert Han-Pao Ma Distinguished Lectureship* (2015), 123, 138.

can always implement its will if it decides to do so. Under Chinese law, except in purely civil or commercial cases, there is no effective legal way to hold the Party to account. The Party's decisions are not amenable to judicial review, so it has legal immunity. The following are some examples illustrating this immunity.

First, as a legal person under the civil law, the Party often enjoys privileges. In a defamation case, the High Court of Guangdong Province replied to the Intermediate Court of Meizhou City:

> the Party's committees are like state organs, and have legal standing in civil litigation … However, as civil law persons, they are very special. The cases involving the Party's organs should be concluded by mediation as much as possible. If it has to be concluded by formal adjudication, the trial judges must report the case to the Party's higher committee, and seek its understanding and support.[53]

Second, according to the Administrative Litigation Law, the Party's organs cannot be sued.[54] Because of this legal immunity, officials usually choose to make their decisions not as the agents of the state or government, but as the agents of the Party, in order to avoid being sued.

Third, it is not clear whether the Party's organs are, in fact, bound by law. In 2018, according to *Regulations on Open Government Information*, Guo Xiaobing submitted an application to the Government of Jiangsu Province, asking for information on a plan for county reform. The case reached the Supreme People's Court, which rejected Guo's application, stating that '*Regulations on Open Government Information* does not apply to the information possessed by the Party's organs or a joint decision made by the Party and the Government'.[55]

Fourth, at the central level, the Party's legal immunity is well captured by its ambivalent attitude towards the relationship between law and the Party. The Party has always stressed two underlying – but potentially competing – theses: one is that the Party must behave within the Constitution and laws; the other is that the rule of law must be constructed under the Party's leadership. In reality, the Party can change the Constitution and laws by a recommendation or proposal which the NPC never refuses. The Party insists that these two theses are compatible with each other.[56] Addressing the debate about whether the Party is above the law, Xi declared, 'the question is a political trap, a false question'.[57]

[53] 'The High Court of Guangdong Province's Reply to the Question Whether the Party's Local Committee can be a Subject of Civil Litigation' (广东省高级人民法院关于基层党委可否作为民事诉讼主体问题的批复) (16 August 2006) (粤高法民一复字[2006]3 号). Available at: www.cnlawyers.top/guangdong/news/bencandy.php?fid=33&id=5484.

[54] Administrative Litigation Law, arts 2, 6 and 12.

[55] 'SPCXingshenNo789(2018)AdministrativeDecisionoftheSPC' (中华人民共和国最高人民法院行 政 裁 定 书 （2018） 最高法行申 798 号). Available at: https://kuaibao.qq.com/s/20180716B1QEOA00?refer=spider.

[56] 'The CCPCC's Decision on Major Questions', n 30 above.

[57] 'Xi Jinping's Speech to Provincial Leaders', n 33 above.

The Party's leading legal theorist, Xu Xianming, once said that 'the Party is above, within and below the Constitution and laws'.[58]

The Party and the State: Separation or Integration?

The relationship between the Party and the state is a perennial problem vexing Chinese politics, which can be traced to the politics of Soviet communism and to that of Kuomintang's 'the Party ruling the country'.[59] How the Party's leadership could be reconciled with democracy and the rule of law was a question with which the early reformers had struggled. Since the end of the CR, the CCP has been determined to reform its political regime to prevent repeating the CR. The Party's 12th and 13th national congresses worked out a solution in theory, which included two principles: the first was that the Party behave within the limits of the Constitution and laws, and the second was the separation between the Party and the state. Deng Xiaoping considered the separation between the Party and the state (the principle of separation) the central guiding principle of political reform and the precondition for democracy and the rule of law in China.[60]

According to the principle of separation, first, the CCP's leadership is mainly three-fold: political, ideological and organisational. Political leadership is to formulate major policies and to translate these policies into state laws according to legal procedure; ideological leadership is to improve the political understanding of the people through disseminating Marxism; and organisational leadership is to recommend excellent political officials to the state, so that they be appointed to leading state posts. Second, the Party would not, or at least would less and less, directly exercise state power and issue legally binding decisions. Instead, it would only rule the country indirectly through state organs. The Party leads but does not rule. The leadership is realised not by coercive power, but by means of the Party's morality and wisdom. The CCP's organs ought not to interfere with, but to respect and support, the normal operations of state organs and NGOs.[61] Since the Party does not rule by means of coercive power and since the exercise of powers by the government will be held to account according to law, the Party's leadership and its legal immunity are compatible with the rule of law.

There will be tension between the Party's legal immunity and the rule of law when integrating the Party and the state (the principle of integration) becomes the guiding idea of the regime. The Party recently has abandoned

[58] X Xu (徐显明), 'The Party is above, within and below the Constitution and laws' (共产党既在法律之中，也在法律之下，还在法律之上), Available at: www.sohu.com/a/134191503_662101.

[59] See Wang Guixiu (王贵秀), *The Path of China's Political Reform* (中国政治体制改革之路) (2004) 157–68.

[60] *Selected Works of Deng Xiaoping* (邓小平文选), vol 3, 177–178.

[61] 'The CCPCC's Decision on Major Questions', n 30 above.

the principle of separation and managed to merge the Party and the state by expanding and strengthening the Party's control. The result is that the Party dictates to the state and has started to exercise state powers. In January 2019, the CCPCC passed the Political-Legal Work Regulation (政法工作条例),[62] which stipulates that the first requirement of political-legal work is to 'uphold the absolute leadership of the Party, and implement the Party's leadership in all aspects and the whole process of political-legal work'. So-called political-legal work includes legislation, judicial adjudication and law-enforcement. If all state powers (including those regulating the public media) are under the Party's absolute leadership and if the Party's decisions are not subject to judicial review and cannot be held to account according to law, then only the Party's self-restraint can be relied upon to ensure that it behaves within the limits of the Constitution and laws.

The Conflict of Officials' Recognition

Another issue caused by the relationship between the Party and the state is the conflict between officials' recognitions of norms. Hart takes officials' recognition of norms as the foundation of a legal system.[63] In China, there are two types of conflict regarding the recognition of norms. First, due to a lack of effective judicial review of the constitutionality and legality of the actions of the Party and the state, officials' recognition of lower norms prevails over their recognition of higher laws and the Constitution. Second, most civil servants in China are also Party members;[64] as such, their recognition of the Party's norms prevails over their recognition of the law. When the Party's norms are inconsistent with state laws, civil servants are required to obey the Party's norms: the Party requires civil servants (including legal professionals, such as judges and lawyers) 'to be absolutely loyal to the Party' and to 'always to be ready to sacrifice everything for the Party'.[65]

The Party's norms are sometimes inconsistent with the requirements of the rule of law. They are more Leninist. Guided by the idea of integrating the Party and the state, ongoing reforms focus on incorporating the state into the Party and legalising the Party's Leninist regulations and ideology into state laws. The

[62] The CCPCC, 'The CCP's Political-Legal Work Regulation' (中国共产党政法工作条例). Available at: www.gov.cn/zhengce/2019-01/18/content_5359135.htm.

[63] HLA Hart, *The Concept of Law* (1994), 100–110.

[64] According to Xi's speech in January 2016, more than 80 per cent of civil servants are Party members and more than 95 per cent of the leading cadres are Party members. 'Xi's Speech at the Sixth Meeting of the 18th *Central Commission* for *Discipline Inspection* (CCDI)'(在第十八届中央纪律检查委员会第六次全体会议上的讲话) (12 January 2016).

[65] See Civil Servants Law arts 4, 13(3), 14(1), 59(1); arts 3(4) and 6 of the Charter of the Party; 'The CCPCC's Decision on Major Questions: VI', n 30 above.

National Supervision Committee (NSC) is an archetypal example of such reforms, a close reading of which can reveal the prospects for the rule of law in China.

The NPC passed the National Supervision Law (NSL) in 2018 and created the NSC, legalising and expanding the Party's anti-corruption practice. There are two broad approaches to fighting corruption. One is the democratic and rule of law approach, emphasising official transparency and public access to official information. This had been the CCP's longstanding efforts. However, implementation of the NSL represents an authoritarian approach. As the Party repeatedly emphasises, the NSC is 'a *political* organ … Its nature and status are different from those of administrative and judicial organs. … It is essentially the Party's organ'.[66] The NSC has combined the investigation roles of the Party's Committee of Disciplinary Inspection (CDI), the supervision ministry and the procuratorate, and it ranks higher than the courts and the procuracies. The NSL extends the CDI's extra-judicial approach to all public servants and the managers at universities and state-owned enterprises (Article 15). Supervision Commissions have broad investigative powers, including the power to question (Articles 20 and 21), detain (Article 22), freeze assets (Article 23) and search premises (Article 24) without charge. The Party's frightening Shuanggui (双规)[67] was given a new name Liuzhi (留置 detention in custody), which can last six months (Article 43). A Supervision Commission does not need to notify the family about a suspect's detention if it thinks that this will affect its investigation (Article 44). Those under investigation are denied access to a lawyer. A Supervision Commission's decisions and measures are not subject to judicial review. Supervision commissioners are not required to pass a bar exam. The NSL says that procuratorates could decide to drop a case transferred from a Supervision Commission (Article 47), but this has never happenend.[68] In corruption-related crimes, the NSL has superseded the Criminal Litigation Law.[69]

THE PROBLEM OF THE LEGALITY AND CONSTITUTIONALITY OF GENERAL NORMS

When exercising their powers, officials in China are at first guided by lower norms, but in their absence they are allowed to ground their decisions in higher norms. The hierarchy of norms in China includes administrative decisions and orders of general binding force (行政机关制定、发布的具有普遍约束力的决定、命令,

[66] 'Supervision Committees are political organs' (监察委员会是政治机关). Available at: www.ccdi.gov.cn/yaowen/201803/t20180308_165743.html.

[67] *Shuanggui*, or 'double designated', refers to a notice informing a Party member to come to a designated place at a designated time for questioning.

[68] An earlier draft proposed that a procuratorate would need the SC's approval to abandon prosecution.

[69] 'Seven Experts on the Draft of the National Supervision Law' (七位法学家锐评《监察法(草案)》). Available at: www.jmkdwh.com/m/NewsDetail.aspx?Id=702.

'administrative orders'), administrative regulations (行政规章, made by ministries, other departments directly under the State Council and governments at the levels of provinces and cities with subordinate districts (设区的市)), local ordinances (地方性法规, made by people's congresses at the levels of provinces and cities with subordinate districts), administrative ordinances (行政法规, made by the State Council), laws by NPCSC, laws by NPC and at the top: the Constitution.

China does not have an effective system of judicial review regarding the legality of general norms. It is also well known that China's system of constitutional review is not particularly effective. Thus, the legality and constitutionality of general norms are not effectively guaranteed. Illegal or unconstitutional general norms will violate people's legal rights in a far wider and therefore more serious way than illegal concrete decisions or actions, ie the applications of the general norms of governments.

Regarding the legality of general administrative norms, China first allowed administrative litigation in 1982,[70] and it passed its first Administrative Litigation Law (ALL) in 1989. This was revised in 2014. Over the course of its development, the scope of acceptable cases has gradually expanded. The legality of administrative orders, administrative regulations and ordinances should have been guaranteed by the system of administrative litigation. However, these general norms cannot be challenged in the courts (Article 13(2), ALL).

According to China's system of legislation, administrative ordinances and local ordinances must be scrutinised for their legality and constitutionality, while the laws made by NPC and NPCSC must be scrutinised for their constitutionality. We will call the issue here 'review of the legality and constitutionality of legislation' (立法的合法性与合宪性审查).

As part of the Party's post-CR decision for the SROL, the implementation of the Constitution was in the minds of the early reformers. According to Wang Hanbin's recollection:

> During the public discussions of the draft of the Constitution, many people were not confident whether the Constitution could be implemented, and they had three worries. First, the lawless chaos of the CR would recur; second, the Constitution would be shelved and become empty words; third, the problem of power trumping law would not be solved. We had a Constitution in the past, but some leaders violated it at will and kicked it away whenever they lost sense. This was a bitter lesson taught by the CR, and we should not allow it to happen again.[71]

The drafters hotly debated what kind of institutional arrangements should be adopted to implement the Constitution. The majority supported the idea of establishing a Constitutional Committee directly under the NPC. However, the leaders did not endorse this idea. The Constitution of 1982 provides that the

[70] Art 3(2) of Civil Litigation Law (民事诉讼法试行) (1982).
[71] *Interviews with Wang Hanbin* (王汉斌访谈录) (2012), 123.

NPCSC has the power to interpret the Constitution and supervise its implementation (Article 67(1)); that the NPCSC has the power to annul any administrative ordinances made by the State council that contravene the Constitution and laws, local ordinances that contravene the Constitution, laws and administrative ordinances (Article 67(7) and (8)). To facilitate the NPCSC's supervision, the Constitution, the Law of Legislation (passed in 2000 and revised in 2015) and the Law of Supervision (监督法) (2006) require administrative and local ordinances (including the SPC's judicial interpretations) to be reported to the NPCSC. China's current constitutional regime presupposes that the laws of the NPC and the NPCSC have equal validity with the Constitution, so they cannot be challenged constitutionally.[72]

The Constitution of 1982 set up the framework for China's constitutional review, but did not establish a functional procedure for giving the initiative to those who really wish to challenge the constitutionality or legality of administrative and local ordinances. The result has been that the Constitution was not satisfactorily implemented: no ordinances have ever been declared unconstitutional or illegal. There have been increasing calls for reform, and many scholars have advocated the judicialisation of the Constitution, some of which have made an important impact on legal practice. On 13 August 2001, the SPC issued 'A Reply to Whether a Person Should be Held Liable for Violating a Citizen's Constitutional Right of Education by Infringing his Right of Name'. On the same day, the SPC's organ *The Daily of People's Courts* (人民法院报) published an article 'The Judicialisation of the Constitution and Its Meaning: A Comment on an SPC's Reply of Today' by Judge Huang Songyou, the Head of the SPC's Civil Law Chamber. Huang stressed, 'An important solution to the problem of the implementation of the Constitution in our country is the judicialization of the Constitution', which he defined as follows: 'the Constitution can be used directly as a legal ground for adjudicating cases, in the same way as other laws and ordinances are used'.[73] But this type of judicialisation of the Constitution will ultimately lead to American-style judicial review, which is a departure from the Chinese Constitution. In 2008, the SPC quietly cancelled this reply. This sent the message that the current official position was that the Constitution should not be applied as a legal ground for adjudication.

Around the same time, many scholars suggested that the implementation of the Constitution should be improved within the current constitutional structure. The Law of Legislation is an nod in this direction. Central state organs and provincial legislatures can now submit a *request* (要求) to the NPCSC asking for a review of an ordinance. This will start a review procedure. However, other state organs, citizens and NGOs can only submit a *suggestion* (建议) for review,

[72] For a detailed analysis, see X Zhai (翟小波), *The People's Constitution* (人民的宪法) (2009), 53–57.

[73] S Huang (黄松有), 'The Judicialization of the Constitution and its Meaning' (宪法司法化及其意义) (*The Daily of People's Courts* (人民法院报) (13/08/2001). Available at: www.gongfa.com/huangsyxianfasifahua.htm.

which may or may not start the review procedure, depending on the discretion of the NPCSC.

On 14 May 2003, Chinese citizens Yu Jiang (俞江), Teng Biao (滕彪) and Xu Zhiyong (许志永), invoking Article 99(2), submitted to the NPCSC a suggestion for a review of the constitutionality and legality of '*the Measures for Internment and Deportation of Urban Vagrants and Beggars*' enacted in 1982 by the State Council. One month later, the State Council abolished the ordinance on its own initiative. So far, the NPCSC has never pronounced an ordinance unconstitutional or illegal and thereby annulled it. In 2017, Shen Chunyao (沈春耀), the director of the NPCSC's Legislative Affairs Commission (LAC), made the first report to the NPCSC on the work of constitutional and legal review; so far, the LAC has reported its review work to the NPCSC three times. From these reports, it is clear that the aims of the review work are (in the order of importance): (1) to guarantee that the Party's orders are obeyed, (2) to guarantee the Constitution and laws are implemented, (3) to improve the quality of legislation and (4) to protect citizens' lawful rights. Since the 12th NPC, the NPCSC has received 2,894 suggestions for review from citizens and NGOs and no requests or suggestions from state organs.[74]

China's current constitutional review regime has many problems. First, the policies and norms subject to constitutional and legal review are strictly limited. Second, the Law of Legislation gives the power to request constitutional and legal review to high state organs, who are too busy to be concerned with whether ordinances contravene the Constitution and laws, and have no motivation to request the NPCSC to review the constitutionality and legality of ordinances; whereas those who are so concerned and do have the motivation can only make a *suggestion* for review. Whether the review will be initiated is at the discretion of the NPCSC. The citizens and NGOs who have made suggestions lack the legal means to push a review forward and cannot participate in the process. Third, the review process and the result are not transparent: the review is essentially an internal negotiation among state organs.

EXTRA-LAW, SENSITIVE CASES AND POLITICAL MOVEMENTS

China's legal practice has long been troubled by extra-legal factors. Benjamin Liebman's research shows that even in routine cases of civil and commercial law, courts are not just law-appliers; they serve as 'problem solvers for society, and for the party-state'.[75] Courts do not necessarily focus on determining the truth of what happened or the laws that should be followed. The different parties

[74] For the NPCSC's LAC's Reports on the Reporting and Review Work in 2017, 2018 and 2019, see *China's People's Congress* (中国人大), No 1 of 2018, No 3 of 2019, No 5 of 2020.

[75] B Liebman, 'Ordinary Tort Litigation in China: Law versus Practical Justice?' (on file with author).

involved in a lawsuit (litigants, insurance companies, governments, etc) all have different motivations, very few of which are purely legal. Courts 'must respond to these varied uses and litigant goals; doing so requires doing more than resolving legal or factual issues'.[76] Various factors influence the resolution of routine civil cases in China: political interference or corruption is only one; others include: the principle of fairness and justice (天理); conventional morality (人情); public opinion (民意or 輿情); guanxi (关系, personal relationships and connections); a high degree of deference to state actors; judges' desire to avoid responsibility; the possibility of solving the dispute; the enforceability of the judicial decision; its possible social effect (社会效果); and concerns about social stability. In his article on China's medical malpractice, Liebman concluded that 'courts seek to mollify parties', and 'the formal legal system operates in the shadow of protest and violence'.[77]

In contrast to ordinary routine cases, the law's influence is even more marginal in so-called 'politically sensitive' cases (敏感案件). Fu Hualing claimed that China was ruled by three types of regime: law, extra-law and extra-extra-law. The extra-law regime exists where power is neither explicitly derived from law nor subject to judicial oversight, eg anti-corruption practice and media governance. The extra-extra-law regime refers to the measures that lack legality and essentially operate using intimidation or terror, eg 'black jails', forced disappearance, etc.[78]

The most worrying feature of these politically sensitive cases is their wide range and indeterminate nature. In 2006, the All-China Lawyers Association (中华全国律协, ACLA) passed its *Guiding Opinions on Lawyers Handling Mass Cases*. according to which mass cases (群体性案件) are 'cases involving 10 or more plaintiffs or defendants who filed a common lawsuit or a series of non-litigation legal proceedings on a common or similar issue of fact or law'.[79] The ACLA pointed out that 'mass cases' have been mainly caused by:

(a) the taking of land,
(b) urban housing demolition,
(c) relocation from reservoir areas,
(d) enterprise restructuring,
(e) environmental pollution, and
(f) violation of the rights of migrant workers.

[76] Ibid.

[77] B Liebman, 'Malpractice Mobs: Medical Dispute Resolution in China' (2013) 113 *Columbia Law Review* 181, 210.

[78] H Fu, 'The Varieties of Law'. Available at: https://lawprofessors.typepad.com/china_law_prof_blog/2011/06/fu-hualing-on-the-varieties-of-law.html.

[79] 'Guiding Opinions on Lawyers Handling Mass Cases' (中华全国律师协会关于律师办理群体性案件[的]指导意见) (adopted on a trial basis on 20 March 2006, by the Standing Committee of the ACLA). Available at: www.acla.org.cn/article/page/detailById/21911.

They 'often involve complex social, economic, and political factors, and have varied important impact on the state and society'.[80] The ACLA's *Guiding Opinions* also applies to those cases that have 'attracted nationwide or international attention, or are of huge social influence', or 'influential sensitive cases'.[81]

Following the adoption of the ACLA's *Guiding Opinions*, many local governments passed regulations, which were far more restrictive. The scope of mass or sensitive cases has been hugely widened. According to the regulations of Shenzhen (深圳) and Xiangtan (湘潭), sensitive cases or incidents are defined as 'criminal, administrative, and even civil cases that likely lead to social contradictions and influence social stability'. They include:

(a) major criminal cases relating to national security;
(b) criminal and civil cases which are of great influence and in which the masses are interested;
(c) incidents of profound influence relating to reforms of the political or economic systems;
(d) incidents that are likely influence the relation between the masses and the cadres;
(e) civil disputes relating to the purchase or management of real estate;
(f) administrative disputes caused by the government's infringement of the interest of the masses;
(g) disputes caused by unfair law enforcement;
(h) major cases in which the leadership has intervened; and
(i) other major criminal, administrative and civil cases that likely cause social contradictions and influence social stability.[82]

According to the regulation of Henan (河南) Province, sensitive cases can also include cases affecting the government's image or involving high-level cadres.[83] Very often, a case suddenly becomes a sensitive case simply because it involves a sensitive person.

Zhang and Ginsburg claim that 'in the vast majority of cases, and specifically in nearly all civil and commercial cases, courts tend to operate in a highly professional, law-oriented manner', and that only in a 'small minority of social and politically charged cases' are the courts 'under significant outside pressure

[80] Ibid.

[81] Ibid.

[82] Xiangtan City's Judicial Bureau (湘潭市司法局), 'Provisional Regulation on Lawyers Handling Sensitive and Mass Cases' (关于律师代理群体性敏感案（事）件管理暂行规定) (1 September 2010). Available at: www.ts12348.com/news/109.html, art 2. Shenzhen City's Judicial Bureau（深圳市司法局）, 'Provisional Regulation on Lawyers Handling Sensitive and Mass Cases' (关于律师代理群体性敏感案（事）件管理的暂行规定) (29/06/2006), art 2. This regulation has disappeared from the internet, but it has the same content.

[83] Henan Provincial Judicial Bureau(河南省司法厅), 'Opinion on Strengthening the Guidance and Supervision for Lawyers' Handling Important, Sensitive, and Mass Cases' (关于进一步加强律师办理重大、敏感、群体性案件指导监督工作的意见) (18/3/2006), which has disappeared from the internet.

to reach specific outcomes'.[84] However, many cases which are considered politically sensitive are actually ordinary civil and commercial cases. The key problem is not the number of the cases, but that the wide scope and the vague, empty and expansive formulations of the so-called 'sensitive' cases means that any case can arbitrarily be deemed 'politically sensitive', no matter how far removed it appears from politics.[85]

When dealing with sensitive cases, the ACLA requires lawyers 'to manage carefully and properly their relations with the litigants, judicial bureaus, the governments, the media, and the public'. For example, they should share information with the government and must safeguard the country's stability.[86] Lawyers handling sensitive cases, according to these regulations, are subject to the Party's political and propaganda discipline and the supervision and punishment of the government.[87] They are discouraged from publicising the cases, and they must not conduct any interview with foreign media without the approval of the relevant government department.[88] Once a case is deemed politically sensitive, it becomes a political problem to be eliminated: an ordinary dispute turns into a struggle between friends and enemies, and a *de facto* state of emergency occurs. As Stanly Lubman, Benjamin Liebman and Fu Hualing have argued, in this situation, the law can be entirely ignored and political mobilisation (or extra-extra-law) will prevail.[89]

If the task is a national problem to be addressed, the party-state will use its habitual way of ruling inherited from its revolutionary past: war-like or tempestuous mass political movements. As the CR and other political movements have illustrated, the party-state will mobilise its vast power, concentrating all its energy on a single task: using the most effective measures to eliminate the problem. During these periods, all legal, institutional and professional boundaries or spaces disappear into one force, other values are surrendered, the rights of citizens are negligible and laws (delimitations of powers and legal procedures) are only obstacles which must be overcome.

Dong Biwu (1886–1975), the main founder of China's legal system, was well aware of the negative effect of mass movements on the rule of law. As early as the 1950s, he pointed out that, 'mass movements do not rely on laws … they break pre-existing laws' and 'foster among people a psychology of despising law', noting that 'we therefore should not always launch movements'.[90] Professor Chen Shouyi (1906–1995), one of the founders of China's legal education and

[84] Zhang and Ginsburg, n 34 above, 316.

[85] See also Liebman, 'Ordinary Tort Litigation in China', n 75 above; 'Authoritarian Justice in China', in W Chen (ed), *The Beijing Consensus? How China Has Changed Western Ideas of Law and Economic Development* (2017), 246.

[86] ACLA's 'Guiding Opinions', n 79 above.

[87] Henan Provincial Judicial Bureau's 'Opinion', n 83 above.

[88] Xiangtan City's Judicial Bureau's 'Provisional Regulation', art 7, n 82 above.

[89] Lubman, *Bird in a Cage*, n 42 above, 86, 88; Liebman, 'Authoritarian Justice in China', n 85 above, 246; Fu, 'The Varieties of Law' n 78 above.

[90] *Dong Biwu's Writings on Law* (董必武法学文集) (2001), 311, 350, 380.

jurisprudence, wrote in the 1990s: 'in the past, we put laws aside, and launched political movements one after another. … From now on, we should never launch any political movement'.[91] However, during the last 40 years, mass movements have been launched one after another. This has become a deeply ingrained habit for the party-state, who often believe that mass movements are a more effective way to rule the country than the rule of law.

CONCLUSION

As a response to the CR, the CCP made a decision to embrace the rule of law. In the past four decades, China's legal system has been hugely improved, and law has become more important than before. The early reformers' vision was an order where 'the institutions and laws will not be changed by the change of leaders, or the change of leaders' opinions and attention',[92] where 'the Constitution must be completely implemented: from the principle and spirit to the concrete words', and where people's human dignity and legal rights must be protected.[93] Forty years later, the vision remains unfulfilled. The Party's legal immunity when exercising power, in addition to the ongoing reforms to integrate the Party and the state, has created a system within which there is no effective legal way to hold the high decision-makers to account. The absence of an effective judicialised review of legislation or general norms means that the legality and constitutionality of the authorities' decisions cannot be guaranteed. Even the most ordinary case can suddenly be deemed as 'politically sensitive', and politics then replaces the law. To achieve its objectives, the party-state still frequently turns to mass political movements. 'Chinese courts', as Liebman stated, 'are both weak political actors and are extremely political. … [They] remain an instrument of party-state governance'.[94]

Despite the achievements in legal development, the law remains weak: the partial rule of law in private and commercial fields is fragile; and the law has difficulty guarding the powerful guardians.[95] The problem today is the same as 40 years ago: as the CCP pointed out in 1981, 'We made laws, but they lacked due authority'.[96] Xi recognised this problem when he emphasised: 'The life force of law lies in its implementation, so does the authority of law. … When comprehensively advancing the law-based governance, the focus should be to guarantee the law to be strictly implemented'.[97] The problem is essentially this: How can law be empowered in China?

[91] S Chen (陈守一), *On Legal Studies and Legal Education* (法学研究与法学教育论) (1996), 38.
[92] Deng, 'Liberate Our Thought, Seek Truths from Facts, and Unite and Look to the Future', n 12 above.
[93] Ye, 'Report on the Revision of the Constitution', n 11 above.
[94] Liebman, 'Authoritarian Justice in China', n 85 above, 243–244.
[95] Peerenboom, n 2 above, 217.
[96] 'Resolution on Certain Questions', n 4 above.
[97] Xi, 'Some Explanations' n 39 above.

'Laws do not, indeed laws cannot, rule, only *people* rule'.[98] The rule of law is, in fact, a sophisticated mode of the rule of men and is ultimately a matter of interest, power and force. Commenting on the Rule of Law in China, Alford said: 'I am not naive about the possibility that self-interested senior political figures may have personal pecuniary, as well as ideological, reasons to resist according real autonomy to the courts'.[99] The law must be empowered, so that it is capable of guarding the powerful guardians. If law is to control or tame the prince, its force must be the people's force. People must (a) be willing and able to hold each other to account and (b) be willing and able to hold those in power to account according to law.[100] A rule of law polity is not only incompatible with, but diametrically opposite to, a 'deplorably sheep-like' society.[101] For the law to work, there must be ways in which it can be valued, trusted and empowered. The rule of law is significantly bolstered when democracy, checks of powers, and public opinion align with it. There are some deep connections between the rule of law, democracy and a robust public opinion tribunal: they are vital for holding those in power to account, a fact that was well recognised by the CCP's leadership. Peng Zhen once said: 'How could it be possible to have the rule of law without democracy?'[102] According to Xi, to 'shut the power in the cage of institutions', 'the key is to construct a system of checks and supervisions on powers: the exercise of powers should be watched by the people, and be exposed to the sunshine'; 'publicity must be improved, and the process of the exercise of powers must be publicized … Institutions should not be paper tigers or scarecrows'.[103] Xi further stressed, 'a major measure of shutting the power in the cage of institutions is the tribunal of public opinion, including the internet'. 'A good tribunal of online public opinion should not be comprised of only one voice or one melody'.[104] Looking at the current reality, Xi's words seem to have been ignored.

[98] G Postema, 'Law's Sovereignty: How Can Law Rule?' (unpublished manuscript, on file with author)

[99] Alford, n 52 above, 143.

[100] G Postema, 'Law's Rule: Reflexivity, Mutual Accountability, and the Rule of Law', in X Zhai and M Quinn (eds), *Bentham's Theory of Law and Public Opinion* (2014), 7–39.

[101] Hart, *The Concept of Law* n 63 above, 117.

[102] Peng, 'A Speech to Cadres of Legislative Work', n 17 above.

[103] Xi, n 31 above, 391–392, 395.

[104] Ibid., 337.

10

Developing a Human Right to Democracy in International Law: Protection by the Rule of Law?

GLENN PATMORE*

INTRODUCTION

A DECLARATION ADOPTED by the United Nations (UN) General Assembly at a High-level Meeting on the Rule of Law at the National and International Levels in 2012 reaffirmed 'that human rights, the rule of law and democracy are interlinked and mutually reinforcing and that they belong to the universal and indivisible core values and principles of the United Nations' (the Core Values Principle).[1]

This Declaration makes a familiar claim about the relationship between democracy, human rights and the rule of law.[2] The chapter critiques that claim, especially in regard to the meaning of 'democracy' and its connection to human rights and the rule of law. It focuses on the definitions adopted by the UN, noting the influence of Asian countries on the development of these ideas and highlighting the shortcomings of the definitions of 'democracy' and 'democratisation'. My contention is that the UN has not yet developed a human right to democracy for the rule of law to protect and that this necessitates reform.

The argument consists of three parts. The first demonstrates that there has been no express human right to democracy developed by the UN; the second describes the principle of 'the rule of law', dispelling the view that the UN cannot provide definitions of such contested concepts. The third

* I wish to thank, for their assistance, Brian Christopher Jones, Sarah Biddulph, Hilary Charlesworth, Cassie O'Regan, Sarah Shrubb, Sophie Ward and the Melbourne Law School Academic Research Service.

[1] Declaration of the High-Level Meeting of the General Assembly on the Rule of Law at the National and International Levels, GA Res 67/1, UN Doc A/RES/67/1 (30 November 2012) para 5 ('Declaration of the High-Level Meeting').

[2] The Core Values principle features in United Nations General Assembly resolutions and resolutions of the Human Rights Council as well as in reports by the Secretary-General of the United Nations.

evaluates the rule of law at the international level, noting UN limitations in establishing a human right to democracy. The chapter considers the potential development of such a right by democratic states, drawing upon the treaty provisions of regional organisations like the European Union, which commit their members to introduce and maintain a democratic system of government. It argues that a human right to democratic government would have benefits at the national and international levels and could address critical problems in democratic law and practice.

The need for reform is even more pressing given the recent assertiveness of China and the decline in friendly relations amongst states. In addition, China has a longstanding opposition to Western ideas of democracy and constitutionalism,[3] and has refrained from supporting liberal democracy and democratisation of states within the UN.

DEMOCRACY

The legal definition of 'democracy' has been most extensively developed in the arena of human rights law.[4] The origins of the definition can be traced to the Universal Declaration of Human Rights (UDHR), which provides an 'election-focused' conception of democracy in Article 21:[5]

> 1. Everyone has the right to take part in the government of his country, directly or through freely chosen representatives.
>
> 2. Everyone has the right of equal access to public service in his country.
>
> 3. The will of the people shall be the basis of the authority of government; this will shall be expressed in periodic and genuine elections which shall be by universal and equal suffrage and shall be held by secret vote or by equivalent free voting procedures.

Similarly, Article 25 of the International Covenant on Civil and Political Rights (ICCPR) includes the following:[6]

> Every citizen shall have the right and the opportunity, without discrimination and without unreasonable restrictions:
>
> (a) To take part in the conduct of public affairs, directly or through freely chosen representatives;

[3] BG He, *In Search of a People-Centric Order in Asia* (World Scientific, 2017) xxv.

[4] H Charlesworth, 'Democracy and International Law' (2015) 371 *Collected Courses of the Hague Academy of International Law* 43, 81. In this part, I draw from and adopt the argument of Brett Bowden and Hilary Charlesworth that the UN definitions of democracy are inadequate in most democratisation circumstances: B Bowden and H Charlesworth, 'Defining Democracy in International Institutions' in Brett Bowden, H Charlesworth and JM Farrall (eds), *The Role of International Law in Rebuilding Societies After Conflict: Great Expectations* (2009) 90, 93.

[5] Universal Declaration of Human Rights, GA Res 217A (III), UN GAOR, UN Doc A/810 (10 December 1948) art 21. See Bowden and Charlesworth, n 4 above.

[6] International Covenant on Civil and Political Rights, opened for signature 16 December 1966, 999 UNTS 171 (entered into force 23 March 1976) art 25.

(b) To vote and to be elected at genuine periodic elections which shall be by universal and equal suffrage and shall be held by secret ballot, guaranteeing the free expression of the will of the electors;
(c) To have access, on general terms of equality, to public service in his country.

Notably, neither treaty right refers to the term 'democracy'.[7] Article 25 is thus not a right to democracy but rather a right to political participation, accountability through elections and equal access to the public service.[8] Henry Steiner explains that the limited rights in Article 25 permitted each side in the Cold War to claim that their political system complied with the treaty obligations.[9] While both treaties protect freedoms of speech, association and assembly,[10] Gregory Fox notes that these treaties guarantee 'rights that many viewed as constituent elements of democracy but not a right to democracy itself'.[11] This is significant, as it allows the treaty rights to be interpreted as compatible with different normative outlooks and political systems.[12]

The UN Human Rights Council (HRC) and its predecessor, the Commission on Human Rights, have both developed definitions of 'democracy'.[13] Hilary Charlesworth points out that since 1997 there has been a series of non-binding resolutions that highlight a disagreement over the definition of 'democracy' between the North and the South.[14] This disagreement is illustrated by two opposing resolutions passed by the Council in 2012. Resolution 19/36, 'Human Rights, Democracy and the Rule of Law', stressed that democracy includes free and fair elections and freedoms of speech, association and assembly. It advocated

[7] There is a reference in each treaty to 'a democratic society', but this is as 'a possible limitation on the exercise of rights': Charlesworth, n 4 above, 82. See, eg, Universal Declaration of Human Rights, GA Res 217A (III), UN GAOR, UN Doc A/810 (10 December 1948) art 29(2). International Covenant on Civil and Political Rights, opened for signature 19 December 1966, 999 UNTS 171 (entered into force 23 March 1976) arts 14, 21–22.

[8] Charlesworth, n 4 above, 83; GH Fox, 'Democracy, Right to International Protection' in R Wolfrum (ed), *Max Planck Encyclopedia of Public International Law* (2008); Human Rights Committee, General Comment No 25: The Right to Participate in Public Affairs, Voting Rights and the Right of Equal Access to Public Service (Art 25), 57th sess, UN Doc CCPR/C/21/Rev1/Add.7 (12 July 1996).

[9] HJ Steiner, 'Political Participation as a Human Right' (1988) 1 *Harvard Human Rights Journal* 77; Charlesworth, n 4 above, 82.

[10] Universal Declaration of Human Rights, GA Res 217A (III), UN GAOR, UN Doc A/810 (10 December 1948) arts 19–20; International Covenant on Civil and Political Rights, opened for signature 19 December 1966, 999 UNTS 171 (entered into force 23 March 1976) arts 19, 21–22.

[11] Fox, n 8 above, para 1.

[12] Cf R Janse, 'The UNGA Resolutions on the Rule of Law at the National and International Levels, 2006–Post 2015' (2014) 18(1) *Max Planck Yearbook of United Nations Law* 258, 285.

[13] The Human Rights Council is a subsidiary body of the UN General Assembly and its purpose is to promote human rights globally. Human Rights Council, GA Res 60/251, UN Doc A/RES/60/251 (15 March 2006); GD Triggs, *International Law: Contemporary Principles and Practices* (2nd edn, 2011) 1020.

[14] Charlesworth, n 4 above, 100; On related resolutions in the General Assembly, see JE Alvarez, *The Impact of International Organizations on International Law* (2016), 167–168.

a process of democratisation and the principle of the rule of law.[15] This resolution was supported by Western countries like the United States, Italy and Spain and some Asian countries, such as Malaysia, the Philippines, Indonesia and India. China and Cuba abstained.[16]

Resolution 21/9, 'Promotion of a Democratic and Equitable International Order', stressed that democracy has political, social and economic dimensions.[17] While it referred to the procedural right to participate in elections and government, it did not refer to the process of democratisation nor to freedoms of expression, association or assembly. Rather it emphasised concepts often propounded by the Global South: permanent sovereignty over natural wealth and resources, equitable access to benefits from the international distribution of wealth, self-determination and international solidarity; values of equity and justice; and rights to development and a healthy environment.[18] Resolution 21/9 was supported by China, Cuba, some Asian countries, such as Malaysia, the Philippines, Indonesia and India and was opposed by the Western countries on the Council.[19]

The two resolutions reflect two different conceptions of democracy, procedural and substantive. The former invokes a substantive definition 'by reference to a series of rights and social goods said to be interrelated and mutually reinforcing'.[20] In this conception, free and fair periodic elections are reinforced by other individual rights and freedoms necessary for a democracy to function and also protected by the rule of law.[21] It is a liberal definition because it provides legal protection for the rights of individuals and groups, such as civil, political and minority rights.[22] The latter adheres to a procedural definition of 'democracy' focusing on participation in elections and government, with an 'emphasis on development and social and economic rights',[23] but does 'not involve other human rights that protect citizens against forms of governmental overreaching'.[24] Overall, it has relatively little to say about democratic governance and the rule of law.

Asian countries have responded in diverse ways to Western liberal conceptions of democracy within and outside the UN. China rejects Western definitions of democracy and constitutionalism,[25] and voted for the resolution containing the procedural definition of democracy. Interestingly, other Asian members

[15] Human Rights, Democracy and the Rule of Law, HRC Res 19/36, UN Doc A/HRC/RES/19/36 (19 April 2012). See also Charlesworth, n 4 above, 100.

[16] Ibid.

[17] Promotion of a Democratic and Equitable International Order, HRC Res 29/1, UN Doc A/HRC/RES/21/9 (11 October 2012).

[18] Ibid. See also Charlesworth, n 4 above, 100.

[19] Ibid.

[20] Fox, n 8 above, para 10.

[21] Ibid; KA Alfadhel, *The Right to Democracy in International Law: Between Procedure, Substance and the Philosophy of John Rawls* (2017), 5.

[22] T Landman, *Human Rights and Democracy: The Precarious Triumph of Ideals* (2013), 27–29.

[23] Charlesworth, n 4 above, 106.

[24] Fox, n 8 above, para 8.

[25] He, n 3 above, xxv.

on the HRC supported both resolutions – declining to endorse one over the other. Evidently, both forms of democracy resonate with the values of these countries. Even so, disagreements have emerged over the compatibility – and the application – of democracy in Asia. Democracy has been criticised as a tool of the West and as inappropriate in non-Western contexts.[26] This critique emerged during the process of decolonisation and subsequent debates about the compatibility of democracy in Asian countries with a Confucian heritage.[27] For example, the former Prime Minister of Singapore, Lee Kuan Yew, distinguished between Confucian and Western values, arguing in 1994 that democracy was a Western concept. He did not accept the democratic maxim 'that all men are equal' nor was he 'intellectually convinced that one-man, one-vote is the best'.[28] The critique that democracy is inconsistent with Confucian values was vigorously challenged by Anwar Ibrahim, a former Foreign Minister of Malaysia. Ibrahim maintained in 2006 that 'the experiences of South Korea and Taiwan, two states with a clearly Confucian ethical heritage, further lay waste to the notion that Western concepts of democracy are incompatible with Asian civilization'. He noted that Asian peoples have promoted democratic principles and have sustained democratic institutions and freedoms.[29]

Overall, disagreements over the definition of 'democracy' between the North and South, as well as contention over the meaning of 'democracy' in Asia, have hampered the development of a clear and widely shared understanding of the concept.[30] Moreover, '[t]he critique of democracy as a Western concept has influenced the willingness of the United Nations to develop a substantive notion of democracy'.[31] For instance, at the 2005 World Summit, heads of state and government gathered to mark the sixtieth anniversary of the UN. The General Assembly Summit Outcome, a non-binding resolution,[32] noted that 'democracy does not belong to a single country or region' and rejected the idea that it has a 'single model'. It referred to democracy's 'common features', but 'did not identify any'.[33] Thus, the General Assembly endorsed democracy, but remained unclear about its meaning.[34]

While the UN has not committed to a definition of democracy, scholars have debated whether a human right to democratic governance is recognised

[26] Bowden and Charlesworth, n 4 above, 94.

[27] Ibid, 94. See, eg, F Zakaria, 'Culture Is Destiny: A Conversation with Lee Kuan Yew' (1994) 73(2) *Foreign Affairs* 109; A Ibrahim, 'Universal Values and Muslim Democracy (2006) 17(3) *Journal of Democracy* 5.

[28] Zakaria, ibid. Bowden and Charlesworth, n 4 above, 94.

[29] Ibrahim, n 27 above.

[30] Fox, n 8 above.

[31] Bowden and Charlesworth, n 4 above, 95.

[32] 'UNGA resolutions cannot, except for certain internal matters, bind its members and are purely recommendatory. They merely constitute evidence of State practice and State understanding as to the law': Janse, n 12 above, 261; see also Charter of the United Nations arts 10, 14.

[33] 2005 World Summit Outcome, GA Res 60/1, UN GAOR, 60th sess, 8th plen mtg, Agenda Items 46 and 120, UN Doc A/RES/60/1 (24 October 2005) [135]; Charlesworth, n 4 above, 101.

[34] Bowden and Charlesworth, n 4 above, 90, 95.

in international law. The end of the Cold War, a revival of electoral democracy and the rise of election monitoring by international organisations saw Thomas Franck argue that democracy was emerging as a global right promoted and protected by collective international processes.[35] Others argued that there was an existing human right to democratic government.[36] Sceptics responded that recognition of a human right to democracy in international law is doubtful either because of an absence of 'international institutional support',[37] or a lack of empirical evidence that democratic governance is 'treated as an essential prerequisite to membership in the community of nations'.[38]

As we have seen, there is no express UN treaty right to democracy. Rather, there is a limited procedural right to participate in elections and government. Different conceptions of democracy have been expressed through non-binding resolutions of the HRC, but these are competing and contested. The 2005 General Assembly Summit Outcome endorsed democracy as a principle, without developing a procedural or substantive conception of the term. Ultimately, at present there is no express human right to democracy for the rule of law to protect.

The Core Values principle from the 2012 UN General Assembly Declaration refers to 'human rights, the rule of law and democracy' as being 'interlinked and mutually reinforcing'. This is a substantive conception of democracy. However, the claim that this represents the 'universal and indivisible core values and principles of the United Nations'[39] remains doubtful, since democracy is conceived of differently in international treaties, the HRC and General Assembly resolutions.

THE RULE OF LAW

While the core value of democracy remains contested among UN Member States, the principle of the rule of law is more widely accepted. The UN has provided a substantive definition of 'the rule of law' and guidance for its practical implementation in Member States. In 2008, Secretary-General Ban Ki-Moon published the 'Guidance Note on the UN Approach to Rule of Law Assistance',

[35] TM Franck, 'The Emerging Right to Democratic Governance' (1992) 86(1) *American Journal of International Law* 46; Charlesworth, n 4 above, 85–86.

[36] CM Cerna, 'Universal Democracy: An International Legal Right or the Pipe Dream of the West?' (1995) 27(2) *New York University Journal of International Law & Politics* 289; GH Fox and G Nolte, 'Intolerant Democracies' (1995) 36(1) *Harvard International Law Journal* 1. JH Fahner, 'Revisiting the Human Right to Democracy: A Positivist Analysis' (2017) 21(3) *International Journal of Human Rights* 321.

[37] Charlesworth, n 4 above, 87.

[38] S Marks and A Clapham, *International Human Rights Lexicon* (2005), 68. For a recent discussion of these issues, see, T Ginsburg, 'Introduction to the Symposium on Thomas Franck, "Emerging Right to Democratic Governance" at 25' (2018) 112 *AJIL Unbound* 64; A Rubinstein and Y Roznai, 'The Right to a Genuine Electoral Democracy' (2018) 27(1) *Minnesota Journal of International Law* 143, 168 ff. Note also that 'Membership in the United Nations is open to all other peace-loving states which accept the obligations contained in the present Charter': Charter of the United Nations art 4(1).

[39] Declaration of the High-Level Meeting, n 1 above, para 6.

which applied to all national circumstances, including pre- and post-conflict and development contexts.[40] It adopted former Secretary-General Kofi Annan's definition of 'the rule of law':

> For the United Nations system, the rule of law is a principle of governance in which all persons, institutions and entities, public and private, including the State itself, are accountable to laws that are publicly promulgated, equally enforced and independently adjudicated, and which are consistent with international human rights norms and standards. It requires as well measures to ensure adherence to the principles of supremacy of the law, equality before the law, accountability to the law, fairness in the application of the law, separation of powers, participation in decision-making, legal certainty, avoidance of arbitrariness, and procedural and legal transparency.[41]

This definition invokes some essential features of the rule of law,[42] both procedural and substantive. The procedural or rule-based standards include accountability, public promulgation, legal certainty and procedural and legal transparency.[43] The substantive or rights-based standard, under which rules encapsulate 'moral' and 'political rights,' is that rules be 'consistent with international human rights norms and standards'.[44] Most importantly, the definition sets up a relationship of reciprocity between the law-giver and the law-follower, whereby the state not only promulgates the rules but is also held accountable to them.[45] While the term 'democracy' does not appear in the definition of the rule of law, it is explicitly referred to in a restatement of the Core Values principle in the report.[46] In addition, the report provides a Framework for Strengthening the Rule of Law, outlining the fundamental constituent elements of rule of law efforts, which reflect the essential features of a constitutional democracy:

- 'a constitution' as 'the highest law of the land';
- a 'legal framework … consistent with international norms' which protects human rights including 'free association and assembly' and 'free expression, opinion and information'; and
- an 'electoral system' which assures, through periodic and genuine elections, that the basis of the authority of government shall be 'the will of the people'; guarantees universal and equal suffrage; secures an electoral atmosphere free of intimidation; and provides for the peaceful transfer of power.[47]

[40] Secretary-General of the United Nations, 'Guidance Note of the Secretary-General – UN Approach to Rule of Law Assistance' (Report, April 2008) (2008 Guidance Note).
[41] Ibid, 1; 'The Rule of Law and Transitional Justice in Conflict and Post-Conflict Societies – Report of the Secretary-General', UN Doc S/2004/616 (23 August 2004).
[42] C Stewart, 'The Rule of Law and the Tinkerbell Effect: Theoretical Considerations, Criticisms and Justifications for the Rule of Law' (2004) 4 *Macquarie Law Journal* 135, 138.
[43] L Fuller, *The Morality of Law* (1969) ch 2.
[44] R Dworkin, *A Matter of Principle* (1985) 11–12; Stewart, n 42 above, 138.
[45] Stewart, n 42 above, 139–40.
[46] Secretary-General of the United Nations, 2008 Guidance Note, n 40 above, 2.
[47] Ibid, 4–7.

In the way the constituent elements of the rule of law are described, they certainly seem to be expressed as reinforcing the core principles and values of a constitutional democracy. The Guidance Note also envisages a constitutional democracy as integral to the protection of the rule of law, by referring to the democratic and constitutional features of the rule of law. The report therefore incorporates a substantive definition of democracy into the Framework for Strengthening the Rule of Law.

Ban Ki-Moon's 2008 Note also provides guiding principles for UN rule of law activities at the national level.[48] The guiding principles explain how the rule of law can be implemented as an international norm in national contexts. The Secretary-General insists that the UN will only offer rule of law assistance where it is requested by the state or mandated by the Security Council and eschews 'one-size-fits-all formulas' and the 'importation of foreign models'.[49] Instead it adopts a flexible approach based on a process of 'national assessments, local needs and aspirations, and broad participation', basing its assistance on 'international norms and standards'.[50]

While the 2008 Note references the essential features of constitutional democracy, it refrains from explicitly defining the term. Previous Secretary-Generals have been active in providing reports and guidance notes on democracy and democratisation, but these too have refrained from defining the term.

For instance, Boutros Boutros-Ghali's 'An Agenda for Democratization', published in 1996,[51] does not provide a definition of 'democracy' referring instead to the 'undeniable fact [that] there is no one model of democratization or democracy suitable to all societies'. The report maintains that it is not the role of the UN to promote a particular model of democracy or democratization; it can only assist each country to 'choose the form, pace and character of its democratization process'.[52]

In 2009, 13 years after Boutros-Ghali's report, Ban Ki-Moon's 'Guidance Note of the Secretary-General on Democracy'[53] once again maintains: 'while democracies share common features, there is no single model of democracy'.[54] The Guidance Note does, however, provide an explanation of 'democratisation':

> Democratization, furthermore, is neither linear nor irreversible and thus both state institutions and citizens must monitor and maintain oversight of this process. Accordingly, all countries, as well as the international community itself, could benefit from continued strengthening of, and support to, their democratic processes.[55]

[48] Ibid, 2–4.
[49] Ibid, 2.
[50] Ibid.
[51] B Boutros-Ghali, 'An Agenda for Democratization' (Report, 1996).
[52] Ibid, 1, 4.
[53] Secretary-General of the United Nations, 'Guidance Note of the Secretary-General on Democracy' (Report, 2009).
[54] Ibid, 2.
[55] Ibid, 1.

The Note alludes to the ordinary meaning of 'democratisation' as a non-linear movement towards democracy but does not fully explain this process.[56]

Nevertheless, the criticism that there is no one model of democracy and thus it is impossible for the UN to substantively define it, is dispelled by the 2008 Guidance Note. As we have seen, the Note's Framework outlines the essential features of a constitutional democracy, albeit in furtherance of the rule of law. It also provides guiding principles for implementation of its Framework in Member States in conformity with international norms. Yet the substantive definition of 'democracy' in the Guidance Note has not been taken up in later declarations and resolutions.

In 2012, the UN General Assembly issued the 'Declaration of the High-level Meeting of the General Assembly on the Rule of Law at the National and International Levels'.[57] The high-level meeting involved heads of government and state. The Declaration defined the rule of law in Article [2]:

> We recognize that the rule of law applies to all States equally, and to international organizations, including the United Nations and its principal organs, and that respect for and promotion of the rule of law and justice should guide all of their activities and accord predictability and legitimacy to their actions. We also recognize that all persons, institutions and entities, public and private, including the State itself, are accountable to just, fair and equitable laws and are entitled without any discrimination to equal protection of the law.[58]

Again, this definition consists of both 'procedural' and 'substantive' criteria of the rule of law. The definition distinctively highlights the substantive requirements of equal protection of law and non-discrimination. In the definition, the rule of law also makes law givers 'accountable' to law followers.[59]

The Declaration both defines the rule of law and sets out additional 'minimum standards which States should respect in their domestic legal systems'.[60] These include the independence, impartiality and integrity of the judicial system, provision of informal justice mechanisms and provision of legal aid.[61] Ronald Janse argues that these standards at least confirm a core element of the international rule of law – the guarantee of legal protection.[62] Helmut Philipp Aust and Georg Nolte maintain that the normative standard of international law protection described here 'can be conceived as a contemporary expression of the traditional international 'minimum standard of justice'.[63] Consequently,

[56] However, the Note does briefly refer to the transition to and consolidation of a democracy: ibid, 4–5.

[57] Declaration of the High-Level Meeting, n 1 above.

[58] Ibid, para 2. See Janse, n 12 above, 277.

[59] Stewart, n 42 above, 139–40.

[60] Janse, n 12 above, 285.

[61] Declaration of the High-Level Meeting, n 1 above, paras 12–15.

[62] Janse, n 12 above, 285.

[63] HP Aust and G Nolte, 'International Law and the Rule of Law at the National Level' in M Zurn, A Nolkaemper and R Peerenboom (eds), *Rule of Law Dynamics: In an Era of International and Transnational Governance* (2012) 48, 48.

the 2012 UN General Assembly Declaration recognises the current conception of the rule of law at the international level.[64] But what of its conception of democracy?

The UN General Assembly Declaration refers to the Core Values principle.[65] However, nowhere does the Declaration provide a definition of 'democracy'. Its references to democratic rights and freedoms remain sparse and therefore cannot be conceived as, in the words of Aust and Nolte, a contemporary expression of traditional minimum standards of a democratic state. The Declaration upholds the right to self-determination of peoples which remain under colonial domination and foreign occupation.[66] Though it expresses respect for fundamental rights and freedoms,[67] it does not mention freedom of speech, association and assembly nor a right to participate in free and fair elections. Rather than acknowledging a right to democracy, it stresses a procedural right of participation in governance and legal process, especially on the basis of non-discrimination against women.[68] Moreover, the Declaration contains 'very few action-oriented proposals' and no follow-up mechanism to determine whether or not states are implementing their commitments.[69]

While the Declaration provides a sparse explanation of the Core Values principle, in 2015 the HRC passed a resolution to establish a forum on Human Rights, Democracy and the Rule of Law.[70] The forum meets every two years at the United Nations in Geneva. It aims to provide 'a platform for promoting dialogue and cooperation on issues pertaining to the relationship between' the three principles and to identify and analyse best practices and opportunities for states.[71]

But the forum is inherently limited because in its preamble it provides no substantive conception of democracy and it emphasises that it must defer to state sovereignty. The resolution reaffirms the now-familiar UN mantra that 'while democracies share common features, there is no single model of democracy and … democracy does not belong to any country or region' and further reaffirms 'respect for sovereignty and self-determination'.[72] Countries who voted for the establishment of the first forum included the United States, the United Kingdom, Canada, Indonesia, Japan and the Philippines. China, Cuba, Pakistan and Vietnam abstained.[73]

[64] Janse, n 12 above, 285.
[65] Declaration of the High-Level Meeting, n 1 above, para 5.
[66] Ibid, para 3.
[67] Ibid, paras 3, 6, 7.
[68] Ibid, para 16.
[69] Janse, n 12 above, 283.
[70] Human Rights, Democracy and the Rule of Law, HRC Res 28/14, UN Doc A/HRC/RES/28/14 (9 April 2015).
[71] Ibid, para 1.
[72] Ibid, Preamble.
[73] Ibid.

The subsequent resolutions of 2017[74] and 2019[75] to establish the second and third forums were accepted without a vote. It is telling that reference to the three principles as forming the core values of the UN is no longer found in these resolutions.[76] While this might simply acknowledge the reality of Member State commitments, it can be seen as weakening the UN's commitment to these fundamental principles.

We may now assess the Core Values principle and its reference to the rule of law. The UN has provided a substantive definition of 'the rule of law' in the Secretary-Generals' reports and the High-level Declaration. If it is possible to define the meaning of a broad concept such as 'the rule of law', why not 'democracy?' In fact, the 2008 'Guidance Note on the UN Approach to Rule of Law Assistance' does provide a substantive conception of constitutional democracy, but this definition has not been widely endorsed or adopted. The UN also continues to exhibit a reluctance to adopt a definition of 'democracy' at all.

THE RULE OF LAW AT THE INTERNATIONAL LEVEL

The principles for strengthening the rule of law at the international level, in addition to the current state of international relations, make it difficult for the UN to develop a human right to democracy. The UN's promotion of the rule of law in the international realm is explained in Secretary-General Ban Ki-Moon's 2011 'Guidance Note on the UN Approach to Assistance for Strengthening the Rule of Law at the International Level'. It established a framework which guides UN departments, offices, funds, agencies and programmes in their promotion of the rule of law 'in the relations between States, between States and international organizations' and within the UN.[77]

The ideal of the rule of law at the international level is founded on the UN Charter, which expresses a determination to 'establish conditions under which justice and respect for the obligations arising from treaties and other sources of international law can be maintained'.[78] The framework provides specific UN principles that guide assistance for strengthening the rule of law at the international level, including the promotion of the uniform and consistent application of international law, technical assistance on international law matters and '[a]ssistance in the progressive development of international law

[74] Human Rights, Democracy and the Rule of Law, HRC Res 34/41, UN Doc A/HRC/RES/34/41 (6 April 2017).

[75] Human Rights, Democracy and the Rule of Law, HRC Res 40/9, UN Doc A/HRC/RES/40/9 (5 April 2019).

[76] HRC Res 28/14, n 70 above, Preamble.

[77] Secretary-General of the United Nations, 'Guidance Note of the Secretary-General – UN Approach to Assistance for Strengthening the Rule of Law at the International Level' (Report, May 2011) 3 ('2011 Guidance Note').

[78] Charter of the United Nations Preamble; ibid, 3.

and its codification'.[79] However, UN principles are subject to their own limits which constrain their implementation in Member States.

While the UN provides rule of law and democracy assistance at the domestic level,[80] the ICCPR and the UN Charter only provide a right to participate in government, not a human right to democracy. Consequently, there is an absence of guidance for the UN in the uniform and consistent application of these treaties in the context of promoting democracy and democratisation. Disagreements about the term 'democracy' within the UN may permit contested understandings regarding the implementation of technical assistance to nation states on such international law matters.

The mandate of the General Assembly under Article 13(1)(a) of the Charter to provide assistance in the 'progressive development of international law and its codification'[81] offers the tantalising prospect that the UN could adopt a substantive definition of 'democracy' or establish a human right to democracy by resolution of the General Assembly. However, the current prospects for this remain doubtful.

The UN's objective is to develop international law by drafting conventions and instruments on subjects that are not regulated, or in regard to which state practice is not yet sufficiently developed and by systematising existing rules.[82] In doing so, the General Assembly must take into account the interests of states and the international community and their different social and legal systems.[83]

Despite considerable support within the UN for promoting democracy and democratisation, the UN General Assembly mandate to draft new conventions and instruments in this field is likely to be frustrated; state practice may be relied upon to demonstrate that no human right to democracy exists,[84] rather than as a reason to establish one. Many UN Member States are not democratic, so it is not in their interest to develop a human right to democracy.[85] The state of international relations also makes it difficult to systematise existing rules. Overall, the UN General Assembly's capacity to draft conventions or instruments establishing a human right to democracy is constrained by the requirement that it must take into account the interests of non-democratic states and their different legal systems.

Also, the possibility of the UN developing a norm of democratic governance has been hindered by the deterioration in relations between the Chinese

[79] Secretary-General of the United Nations, 2011 Guidance Note, n 77 above, 5–9.

[80] See, eg, 'United Nations Democracy Fund', United Nations. Available at: www.un.org/democracyfund/; 'Political and Peacebuilding Affairs: Elections', United Nations. Available at: https://dppa.un.org/en/elections.

[81] Charter of the United Nations art 13(1)(a); Secretary-General of the United Nations, 2011 Guidance Note, n 77 above, 6.

[82] Secretary-General of the United Nations, 2011 Guidance Note, n 77 above, 6–7. Charter of the United Nations art 13(1)(a).

[83] Secretary-General of the United Nations, 2011 Guidance Note, n 77 above, 6.

[84] For a discussion of state practice, see Alfadhel, n 21 above.

[85] See Economist Intelligence Unit, 'Democracy Index 2019: A Year of Democratic Setbacks and Popular Protest' (Report, 2020) 3.

Communist Party (CCP) and democratic states. Just as Cold War tensions restrained the UN's development of the concept of democracy,[86] so too current international tensions are not likely to favour the development of an international norm of democratic governance. The assertiveness of states in the South China Sea and cyber-attacks against the democratic states underscore the challenges to the maintenance of friendly relations among states. We have also entered a time of international relations marked by belligerence and bellicosity, especially between China and the United States and other democratic Asian and Australasian countries.

The territorial claims over the South China Sea are evidence of ongoing tensions in the region. The CCP has claimed historical title and sovereignty over the South China Sea since 1948, through its self-drawn 'nine-dash' or 'dotted' line on its official maps.[87] Other countries, including Brunei, Malaysia, the Philippines, Vietnam and Taiwan, have each expressed similar territorial claims.[88] In 2013 the Philippines brought a case against China to the Permanent Court of Arbitration under the UN Convention on the Law of the Sea (UNCLOS).[89] The Tribunal rejected China's claims to historic rights or other sovereign rights or jurisdiction over the South China Sea to the extent that they exceed their UNCLOS entitlements.[90] The Tribunal found in favour of the Philippines on almost every issue.[91] China has refused to accept the Tribunal's 2016 ruling[92] and has resisted pressure from Australia, the US and the EU to honour it.[93] In 2020, Australia and the US wrote to the UN Secretary-General, formally rejecting China's claims as being inconsistent with UNCLOS.[94] China's building of

[86] H Charlesworth, 'International Legal Encounters with Democracy' (2017) 8(6) *Global Policy* 34, 35; GH Fox, 'Internationalizing National Politics: Lessons for International Organizations' (2007) 13(2) *Widener Law Review* 265.

[87] *South China Sea Arbitration (Philippines v China) (Award)* (Permanent Court of Arbitration, Case No 2013-19, 12 July 2016) [181].

[88] 'Troubled Waters in South China Sea', *The Straits Times* (29 February 2016). Available at: http://graphics.straitstimes.com/STI/STIMEDIA/Interactives/2016/02/turf-wars-on-the-south-china-sea/index.html; 'Why Is the South China Sea Contentious?', *BBC* (12 July 2016). Available at: www.bbc.com/news/world-asia-pacific-13748349.

[89] *South China Sea Arbitration*, n 87 above.

[90] Ibid, [1203][B][2].

[91] Ibid, [1203].

[92] Ministry of Foreign Affairs of the People's Republic of China, 'MFA Spokesperson Hong Lei's Remarks on the Arbitral Tribunal's Claim that It Would Soon Issue the So-called Final Award of the South China Sea Arbitration Unilaterally Initiated by the Philippines' (29 June 2016). Available at: www.fmprc.gov.cn/mfa_eng/xwfw_665399/s2510_665401/2535_665405/t1376307.shtml.

[93] BG He, 'Regionalism as an Instrument for Global Power Contestation: The Case of China' (2020) 44(1) *Asian Studies Review* 79, 79, 87.

[94] Letter from Permanent Mission of the Commonwealth of Australia to the United Nations to the Secretary-General of the United Nations, 23 July 2020. Available at: www.un.org/depts/los/clcs_new/submissions_files/mys_12_12_2019/2020_07_23_AUS_NV_UN_001_OLA-2020-00373.pdf; Letter from Ambassador Kelly Craft, United States Representative to the United Nations to the Secretary-General of the United Nations, 1 June 2020. Available at: https://usun.usmission.gov/wp-content/uploads/sites/296/200602_KDC_ChinasUnlawful.pdf.

military bases on disputed islands,[95] the sinking of a Vietnamese fishing boat by the Chinese coastguard in April 2020[96] and continued military exercises in the region have only heightened tensions. Since 2002, China and the Association of Southeast Asian Nations (ASEAN) have been in ongoing negotiations to prevent conflict and contestation within the region. Since 2017, they have been consulting over a Draft South China Sea Code of Conduct. The Code of Conduct is principally concerned with the management, settlement and prevention of incidents and disputes in the South China Sea, but its purpose is not to resolve the underlying territorial and sovereignty disputes.[97] As Baogang He has remarked, 'if the SCS issue cannot be mentioned and discussed in regional and global forums, there is no way that China and ASEAN can develop a successful resolution to territorial disputes'.[98] China's claims and actions represent a disengagement with UN processes of international governance and dispute settlement. These developments starkly illustrate the very significant deterioration in regional and global relations.

China's assertiveness now extends well beyond the South China Sea and is leading to a further deterioration in friendly relations among states. Its cyber activities currently target democratic governance in Australasia and Asia. In August 2020, it was reported that Chinese-linked hacking groups launched cyber-attacks against at least 10 Taiwanese government agencies and some 6,000 government e-mail accounts.[99] The Chinese Foreign Ministry denied Taiwan's 'accusation' as 'nothing but a vicious slander to instigate cross-strait confrontation and to seek political gains out of selfish motives'.[100] In 2020, cyber-attacks by a 'sophisticated state actor', thought to be China,[101] targeted 'Australian

[95] 'China Has Built Seven New Military Bases in South China Sea, US Navy Commander Says', *South China Morning Post* (15 February 2018). Available at: www.scmp.com/news/china/diplomacy-defence/article/2133483/china-has-built-seven-new-military-bases-south-china.

[96] 'Vietnam Protests Beijing's Sinking of South China Sea Boat' *Reuters* (4 April 2020). Available at: www.reuters.com/article/us-vietnam-china-southchinasea/vietnam-protests-beijings-sinking-of-south-china-sea-boat-idUSKBN21M072; Ministry of Foreign Affairs of the People's Republic of China, 'Foreign Ministry Spokesperson Hua Chunying's Regular Press Conference on April 3, 2020' (3 April 2020). Available at: www.fmprc.gov.cn/mfa_eng/xwfw_665399/s2510_665401/2511_665403/t1765751.shtml.

[97] C Thayer, 'A Closer Look at the ASEAN-China Single Draft South China Sea Code of Conduct' *The Diplomat* (3 August 2018). Available at: https://thediplomat.com/2018/08/a-closer-look-at-the-asean-china-single-draft-south-china-sea-code-of-conduct/; He, 'Regionalism', n 93 above, 86–88.

[98] He, 'Regionalism', n 93 above, 93.

[99] Y Lee, 'Taiwan Says China Behind Cyberattacks on Government Agencies, Emails' *Reuters* (19 August 2020). Available at: https://uk.reuters.com/article/us-taiwan-cyber-china/taiwan-says-china-behind-cyberattacks-on-government-agencies-emails-idUKKCN25F0JK?il=0.

[100] Ministry of Foreign Affairs of the People's Republic of China, 'Foreign Ministry Spokesperson Zhao Lijian's Regular Press Conference on August 20, 2020' (20 August 2020). Available at: www.fmprc.gov.cn/mfa_eng/xwfw_665399/s2510_665401/2511_665403/t1807885.shtml.

[101] 'Exclusive: Australia Concluded China Was Behind Hack On Parliament, Political Parties – Sources' *Reuters* (16 September 2019). Available at: www.reuters.com/article/us-australia-china-cyber-exclusive/exclusive-australia-concluded-china-was-behind-hack-on-parliament-political-parties-sources-idUSKBN1W00VF.

organisations across a range of sectors, including all levels of government, industry, [and] political organisations'.[102] In response to media reports that China was responsible, China said that Australia, a member of the Five Eyes, 'has been a fervent intelligence gatherer in relevant countries', intruding on state sovereignty and was playing 'the part of the victim, peddling rumors and stoking confrontation by staging a farce of the thief crying "stop thief"'.[103] Both countries agree that cyber espionage is contrary to sovereignty and international law.[104] While international espionage is not an unusual practice in international relations, as the Australian Defence Minister remarked in September 2020, cyber-attacks blur the distinction between 'peace and war'.[105]

The recent assertiveness of the CCP not only challenges the democratic policies but is a threat to the governing institutions and political organisations of democratic states. This climate reduces the likelihood of the UN developing a human right to democracy. As we have seen, the UN can muster only limited commitment to popular governance. However, the preservation of liberal democratic institutions is critical to the very existence of democratic states.[106] Could the democratic states establish a human right to democracy? What would a potential human right to democracy require? According to Charlesworth, it would necessitate 'local adoption, clarity about the elements of the right and some measures of accountability for its breach'.[107] We can see that these requirements, even if in a minimal form, are attributes of liberal democratic regimes. As Noberto Bobbio explains,[108] liberal democracies confer rights to directly or indirectly participate in collective decisions and procedures for making decisions, such as majority rule. They guarantee fundamental freedoms of expression, of assembly, of association and so on. These freedoms permit those making decisions or elected to do so to be offered real alternatives and be in a position to choose between them. Insofar as constitutional law establishes these basic rules and confers these rights, powers and freedoms on almost all adult citizens, they become legal rights. Constitutional law protects democratic rights through rules which are either written or customary and subjects their violation to political accountability or administrative and judicial review.

[102] Prime Minister Scott Morrison, Minister for Home Affairs and Minister for Defence, 'Statement on Malicious Cyber Activity Against Australian Networks' (19 June 2020). Available at: www.pm.gov.au/media/statement-malicious-cyber-activity-against-australian-networks.

[103] Ministry of Foreign Affairs of the People's Republic of China, 'Foreign Ministry Spokesperson Zhao Lijian's Regular Press Conference on June 29, 2020' (29 June 2020). Available at: www.fmprc.gov.cn/mfa_eng/xwfw_665399/s2510_665401/2511_665403/t1793120.shtml.

[104] Morrison, n 102 above; PRC Ministry of Foreign Affairs, n 100 above.

[105] A Galloway, 'Cyber Attacks from State-based Actor Increasing', *Sydney Morning Herald* (4 September 2020). Available at: www.smh.com.au/politics/federal/cyber-attacks-from-state-based-actor-increasing-20200903-p55s0g.html.

[106] N Bobbio, *The Future of Democracy* (1987).

[107] Charlesworth n 4 above, 87.

[108] Bobbio, n 106 above, 24.

The Asian and Australasian region consists of numerous democratic states, including Australia, India, Indonesia, Japan, Malaysia, New Zealand, Papua New Guinea, South Korea and Taiwan.[109] Democratic governance is already established in these countries, providing fertile ground for establishing an international human right to democracy. After all, the norm of democratic governance rests on common assumptions, commitments and practices amongst the leaders and peoples of the democratic states. Nevertheless, more is required to establish a human right. Peggy Levitt and Sally Merry argue that the drafters of human rights documents must 'wrestle with the dilemma' of ensuring that international standards have resonance with local communities.[110] Many states within this region are well placed to address this dilemma, because their democracies have evolved within diverse and localised histories and religions and legal, political and economic systems.

The establishment of a human right to democracy would be attractive for several reasons.[111] First, democracies are associated with peaceful international relations, which international relations scholars have backed up by evidence.[112] This does not mean that democracies do not engage in war;[113] rather, it means that democratic states 'are not likely to fight interstate wars against each other'.[114] More generally, 'democracy has an important pacifying impact on international politics'.[115] Various arguments have been advanced for the existence of the democratic peace. Both within and among democratic states, there is an assumption shared by political leaders that conflicts are to be resolved through a peaceful rule-based order. Democratic leaders also run the risk of losing the confidence of their party, interest groups and electorates if they engage in a war. They are likely to be suspicious of autocratic leaders who do not share their commitment to peaceful rule-based relations and need only convince a relatively small number of loyal supporters to undertake hostilities.[116] These considerations make democracies cautious about entering militarised conflicts, particularly against other democracies.[117]

Secondly, democracy is a form of governance protective of human rights. Andrew Clapham and Susan Marks describe the relationship as one

[109] Economist Intelligence Unit, Democracy Index 2019, n 85 above at 26.

[110] P Levitt and S Merry, 'Vernacularization on the Ground: Local Uses of Global Women's Rights in Peru, China, India and the United States' (2009) 9(4) *Global Networks* 441, 447.

[111] Marks and Clapham, n 38 above, 68.

[112] JL Ray, 'Democratic Peace' in B Badie, D Berg-Schlosser and L Morlino (eds), *International Encyclopedia of Political Science* (2011).

[113] Bobbio, n 106 above, 41.

[114] Ray, n 112 above.

[115] Ibid; see also JL Ray and A Dafoe, 'Democratic Peace Versus Contractualism' (2018) 35(2) *Conflict Management and Peace Science* 193. Ray reviews the literature and empirical data on the correlation between democracy and peace.

[116] Ray, n 112 above. Of course, some non-democratic states may well adhere to the rule-based settlement of disputes and democratic leaders may start wars to maintain or enhance their popularity.

[117] Ibid.

of 'mutual dependence'.[118] Charlesworth explains it as symbiotic: 'human rights form central components of democracy and in turn democracy is critical to the protection of human rights'.[119] Scholars have provided evidence that democracy has demonstrably positive effects on civil and political rights.[120] Of course, autocratic governments can protect and enhance economic and social rights; China, for example, has been very successful over the past three decades in lifting people out of poverty and meeting its Millennium Development Goals.[121] But liberal democratic states such as Australia, Japan and South Korea are similarly successful in protecting economic, cultural and social rights,[122] and authoritarian states such as China offer little protection for the freedoms of speech, association, religion and the right to participate in free and fair elections.[123]

The establishment of a human right to democracy would not only have benefits at the national and international levels but could also address important problems in democratic law and practice. Despite earnest efforts by the UN to promote democratisation, with several reports on the subject by the Secretary-General, it has not established a human right to democratic governance. By contrast, a number of regional organisations have committed their member states to introduce and maintain a democratic system of government,[124] including the African Union,[125] the European Union, the Organization of American States[126]

[118] Marks and Clapham, n 38 above, 71.

[119] Charlesworth, n 4 above, 87.

[120] Empirical studies have demonstrated the relationship, but the absence of a standard legal definition of 'democracy' in domestic and international agreements (compared to the clearly enunciated human rights) has hampered a more nuanced analysis: T Landman, 'Democracy and Human Rights: Concepts, Measures, and Relationships' (2018) 6(1) *Politics and Governance* 48, 56.

[121] Landman, *Human Rights and Democracy*, n 22 above, 38. On China's progress on the Millennium Development Goals, see United Nations, 'The Millennium Development Goals Report' (2015) 15, 21; Ministry of Foreign Affairs, People's Republic of China, 'Report on China's Implementation of the Millennium Development Goals (2000–2015)' (July 2015).

[122] For each country's recent ICESCR reports, see Australia: Periodic Report, UN Doc E/C12/AUS/5 (16 February 2016); Republic of Korea: Periodic Report, UN Doc E/C12/KOR/4 (21 July 2016); Japan: Periodic Report, UN Doc E/C12/JPN/3 (16 May 2011).

[123] 'China', *Freedom House* (2020). Available at: https://freedomhouse.org/country/china/freedom-world/2020.

[124] S Wheatley, *Democracy, Minorities and International Law* (2005), 132; A Duxbury, *The Participation of States in International Organisations: The Role of Human Rights and Democracy* (2011).

[125] The Constitutive Act of the African Union provides as an objective the promotion of 'democratic principles and institutions, popular participation and good governance' and 'Governments which shall come to power through unconstitutional means shall not be allowed to participate in the activities of the Union': Constitutive Act of the African Union, opened for signature 11 July 2000 (entered into force 26 May 2001) arts 3(g), 29, 30. See also African Charter on Democracy, Elections and Governance, opened for signature 30 January 2007 (entered into force 15 February 2012) arts 23–26.

[126] In the OAS Inter-American Democratic Charter, '[t]he peoples of the Americas have a right to democracy and their governments have an obligation to promote and defend it' and Member States may be suspended for 'an unconstitutional interruption of the democratic order or an unconstitutional alteration of the constitutional regime that seriously impairs the democratic order': Organization of Inter-American States, Inter-American Democratic Charter (11 September 2001) arts 1, 19–21. See also the Charter of the Organization of American States, opened for signature 30 April 1948, 119 UNTS 39 arts 2(b), 3(d), 4–9.

and the Pacific Island Forum.[127] For example, the Treaty on European Union provides that the 'Union is founded on the values of respect for ... democracy ... [and] the rule of law' and that sanctions may be imposed for 'serious and persistent breaches' of these values, such as suspension of voting rights in the European Council.[128] These regional instruments foreground the possibilities of developing a human right to democratic government at the international level. Nevertheless, none of these reports or instruments adequately address the current challenges that democracies face.

Recently there has been a decline in political rights and civil liberties in democracies around the world.[129] Democracy is not fully developed in most of the world's democratic states;[130] most democratisation projects occur in the non-Western world and are criticised by scholars for being overly technical and lacking nuance regarding the local context.[131] Regional treaties and instruments promoting democracy have their own limitations. Even the European Union, which has strong legal commitments,[132] has seen a decline in democracy in countries such as Poland and Hungary.[133] In addition, the ASEAN Charter highlights once again some familiar problems of treaties protecting democracy. While the Charter states that members 'shall act in accordance with' the principle of 'adherence to the rule of law ... the principles of democracy and constitutional government', these obligations are vague and imprecise

[127] The Pacific Islands Forum, an international organisation of 18 Pacific countries, adopted the *Biketawa Declaration* in 2000, which commits its members to guiding principles, including 'Upholding democratic processes and institutions which reflect national and local circumstances, including the peaceful transfer of power, the rule of law and the independence of the judiciary, just and honest government': Pacific Islands Forum, Biketawa Declaration (28 October 2000). Available at: www.ramsi.org/wp-content/uploads/2014/07/Biketawa-Declaration.pdf. '[T]he Biketawa Declaration was invoked in 2009 to prevent Fiji's participation in the Pacific Islands Forum': Charlesworth, n 4 above, 104.

[128] Treaty on European Union, opened for signature 7 February 1992, [2009] OJ C 115/13 (entered into force 1 November 1993) arts 2, 7 and 49.

[129] According to Freedom House, the decline in democracy began in 2005, representing a decline in freedom around the world: Freedom House, 'Freedom in the World 2020: A Leaderless Struggle for Democracy' (Report, 2020) 1, 33.

[130] 'According to The Economist Intelligence Unit's measure of democracy, almost one-half (48.4%) of the world's population live in a democracy of some sort, although only 5.7% reside in a "full democracy", down from 8.9% in 2015': 'Global Democracy in Retreat' *The Economist Intelligence Unit* (21 January 2020). Available at: www.eiu.com/n/global-democracy-in-retreat/.

[131] Charlesworth, n 4 above, 115–16; T Berger and M Lake, 'Human Rights, the Rule of Law, and Democracy' in A Draude, TA Börzel and T Risse, *The Oxford Handbook of Governance and Limited Statehood* (2018), 416.

[132] Charlesworth, n 4 above, 101.

[133] Significantly, the European Union has been slow to impose sanctions on states under art 7 that derogate from their respect for democracy, such as Hungary and Poland: see L Gall, 'EU Leaders Drag Their Feet on Hungary Sanctions' *Human Rights Watch* (31 January 2019). Available at: www.hrw.org/news/2019/01/31/eu-leaders-drag-their-feet-hungary-sanctions; European Parliament, 'Hungary's Emergency Measures: MEPs Ask EU to Impose Sanctions and Stop Payments' (Press Release, 14 May 2020). Available at: www.europarl.europa.eu/news/en/press-room/20200512IPR78917/hungary-s-emergency-measures-meps-ask-eu-to-impose-sanctions-and-stop-payments.

and there is no express provision for sanctioning or suspending members for a breach.[134]

In response to these challenges, there is a burgeoning field of scholarship on democratic decay and renewal that could be drawn on in defining and promoting 'democracy' and 'democratisation'.[135] The protection of democracy and democratisation raises a number of research questions. One is how the terms 'democracy' and 'democratisation' are to be defined in the contemporary context. Another is how a human right to democratic government might apply in the overlapping sphere of domestic constitutional law and international law. A final question is how a human right to democracy could be developed and promoted by Australasian and Asian democracies.

The establishment of a human right to democracy must, of course, comply with the principles of the sovereign equality of all nations and the international prohibition on the use of force.[136] Like the development of the Anti-Personnel Landmines Convention, a treaty for democracy negotiated by democratic states in conjunction with a campaign by NGOs outside the UN could subsequently be endorsed and promoted by it.[137] If the number of democracies around the world increases, this may fortify support for the endorsement of such a treaty.

CONCLUSION

To return to the UN 2012 Declaration, the Core Values principle proclaims 'that human rights, the rule of law and democracy are interlinked and mutually reinforcing and that they belong to the universal and indivisible core values and principles of the United Nations'. The UN has not adequately explained the relationship between the three terms – 'human rights', 'democracy' and 'the rule of law' – nor has it established a human right to democracy for the rule of law to protect. While such a right could be established by the democratic

[134] Charter of the Association of Southeast Asian Nations, opened for signature 20 November 2007, 2624 UNTS 223 (entered into force 15 December 2008) arts 2(h), 6(2)(d). Serious breaches of the Charter can be referred to the ASEAN Summit for a 'decision': art 5(3). See M Davies, 'Regional Organisations and Enduring Defective Democratic Members' (2017) 44(1) *Review of International Studies* 174, 179–181; Duxbury, n 124 above, 198–9.

[135] See, eg, KL Scheppele, 'Autocratic Legalism' (2018) 85 *The University of Chicago Law Review* 545, especially 564–565; A Huq and T Ginsburg, 'How to Lose a Constitutional Democracy' (2018) 65(1) *University of California Law Review* 78, especially 86–92, nn 28–30.

[136] Charter of the United Nations art 2.

[137] See, eg, Implementation of the Convention on the Prohibition of the Use, Stockpiling, Production and Transfer of Anti-Personnel Mines and on Their Destruction, GA Res 64/56, UN Doc A/RES/64/56 (12 January 2010). While there are 164 parties to this Convention China, Russia and the US have not joined it, but are 'de facto respecting many of its provisions': S Casey-Maslen, 'Convention on the Prohibition of the Use, Stockpiling, Production and Transfer of Anti-Personnel Mines and on their Destruction: Introductory Note', *United Nations Audiovisual Library of International Law*. Available at: https://legal.un.org/avl/ha/cpusptam/cpusptam.html.

states themselves, significant challenges remain. Democracy is in decline around the world and the current state of international relations, especially with the assertiveness of China, militates against the UN developing a human right to democracy. As bellicosity, belligerence and war remain a scourge on human society, there is a pressing need to revisit the advancement, articulation and protection of democratic principles at the international level.

11

Democracy, Rule of Law and Resisting the Creep of Authoritarianism

AMY BARROW*

THE PEOPLE'S REPUBLIC of China (PRC), a one-party state, which practises what it refers to as the 'Socialist Rule of Law', has long impacted relations with Taiwan, which China claims as its territory. However, China's authoritarian governance practices increasingly risk undermining the rule of law and democracy in other political contexts. As with writing any book that seeks to advance theoretical enquiry through empirical case studies, it is difficult to predict how the actions of lawmakers, politicians and civil society actors will unfold and what their implications will be for the rule of law, democracy and social change. All of the book's authors are acutely aware of China's increasing assertiveness in the Asia-Pacific region and globally. Perhaps it could have been predicted that the Hong Kong Special Administrative Region (SAR) would experience further civil and political unrest as the territory inches towards 2047, the end of the fifty-year transitional period for the operation of One Country, Two Systems (OCTS) and potentially also the end of Hong Kong's Basic Law. However, this edited volume was conceived of prior to the advent of the anti-extradition law amendment bill (anti-ELAB) movement in Hong Kong and the imposition of national security laws in the territory, both of which have fundamental consequences for the rule of law and any aspirations for democracy that Hong Kong citizens may hold. Additionally, the authors could not have foreshadowed that a global pandemic would ensue, infecting millions worldwide and causing more than 2.4 million deaths and counting.[1]

In 2019, Hong Kong experienced protracted protests and civil unrest, triggered by the government's attempt to legislate the Fugitive Offenders and Mutual Legal Assistance in Criminal Matters Legislation (Amendment) Bill 2019. As the year drew to a close, the protests showed no signs of abating. The anti-ELAB movement continued as rumours circulated of a SARS-like coronavirus causing

* Senior Lecturer at the Macquarie Law School, Macquarie University.

[1] World Health Organisation, 'Covid-19 Dashboard'. Available at: https://covid19.who.int/.

pneumonia in Wuhan, China at the end of 2019. With human-to-human transmission confirmed, mass travel in the lead up to the Lunar New Year spring festival had already begun by the time the government imposed a lockdown of Wuhan and Hubei province.[2] International news footage of people being welded into their own homes,[3] and being forcibly separated from their families and quarantined,[4] appeared highly symbolic of China's authoritarian regime and the type of measures it imposes on its own citizens to control freedom of expression, information and movement. Yet, as the seeds of the novel coronavirus scattered around the world, liberal democratic states also initiated emergency measures and powers, impinging on democratic decision-making processes and restricting civil liberties in an attempt to curb the spread of the COVID-19 pandemic.

As the pandemic took hold globally and the protests in Hong Kong waned, the National People's Congress took the unprecedented step of promulgating the Law of the People's Republic of China on Safeguarding National Security in the Hong Kong Special Administrative Region[5] (National Security Law). The law came into force on 30 June 2020, just hours before the 1 July anniversary of Hong Kong's transfer to Chinese sovereignty, usurping the Basic Law's requirement that only the Hong Kong SAR Government should enact national security legislation for the territory.[6] The National Security Law ushers in a new era for Hong Kong's relationship with China and arguably demonstrates the failure of One Country, Two Systems.

In this concluding chapter, I tease out several key themes examined by the authors in this volume including how the rule of law has been shaped across jurisdictions; how civil and political rights are recognised; and how the political trajectory of Taiwan and Hong Kong have increasingly diverged. While protest has increasingly been utilised as a highly visible form of resistance by successive social movements in China, Hong Kong and Taiwan,[7] I specifically examine Hong Kong's anti-ELAB leaderless movement, which preceded the imposition of the National Security Law on the Hong Kong SAR. I then contextualise these dynamics in light of recent international developments

[2] MM Kavanagh, 'Authoritarianism, outbreaks, and information politics' (2020) 5 *The Lancet* E135.

[3] H Wu, 'Sealed in: Chinese trapped at home by coronavirus feel the strain' *Reuters* (22 February 2020). Available at: www.reuters.com/article/us-china-health-quarantine-idUSKCN20G0AY.

[4] J Page, 'China's Progress against Coronavirus used draconian tactics not deployed in the west' *Wall Street Journal* (24 March 2020). Available at: www.wsj.com/articles/the-west-is-misinterpreting-wuhans-coronavirus-progressand-drawing-the-wrong-lessons-11585074966.

[5] The Law of the People's Republic of China on Safeguarding National Security in the Hong Kong Special Administrative Region (2020).

[6] Article 23 of the Basic Law states: 'The Hong Kong Special Administrative Region shall enact laws on its own to prohibit any act of treason, secession, sedition, subversion against the Central People's Government, or theft of state secrets, to prohibit foreign political organizations or bodies from conducting political activities in the Region, and to prohibit political organizations or bodies of the Region from establishing ties with foreign political organizations or bodies.'

[7] See Fu Hualing and Michael Jackson's chapter in this collection.

including the impact of the COVID-19 pandemic. I conclude that the adoption of Hong Kong's National Security Law has wider implications for the rule of law and democracy, not only in Hong Kong but also in the Asia-Pacific and beyond.

RIGHTS, THE RULE OF LAW AND RESISTANCE

Within their analysis, the authors of this volume explore the development and functioning of the rule of law, democratic processes and the protection of civil and political rights in China, Hong Kong, Taiwan and other jurisdictions. Collectively, their analyses indicate the divergent political trajectories of Taiwan and Hong Kong in the face of China's increasing assertiveness within the region, under the leadership of Xi Jinping. As explored by Zhai, in his chapter examining the evolution of the rule of law in China, the separation between party and the state has been a perennial problem in Chinese politics and can be traced back to the Chinese Nationalist Party's (Kuomintang) rule of the country. Zhai rebuts the suggestion made by some scholars that China has a 'thin rule of law' arguing that the conception of the rule of law is both substantively and procedurally 'thick'. Zhai does, however, acknowledge that under Xi Jinping, pessimism that the rule of law is in retreat has deepened. Zhai points to the crackdown on activist lawyers; the 'tightening ideological control and repression' including criminal sentencing for actions deemed to be subversive, or provoking trouble; and the use of televised confessions.

Whereas once Hong Kong and Taiwan were perceived to share similarities – both are post-colonial societies and have enjoyed economic success –Taiwan's transformation towards a robust and pluralistic democracy has increasingly diverged from Hong Kong's gradual slide towards authoritarianism and shrinking civic space. Hong Kong's Legislative Council (LegoCo) is situated only 600 metres away from the Central Barracks, which houses the People's Liberation Army (PLA). LegCo's position in the shadow of the PLA is symbolic of Hong Kong's transition to an authoritarian future. Taiwan, once an authoritarian regime scarred by martial law and the suppression of political dissidents during the White Terror period, is now recognised as a progressive and pluralistic liberal democracy. This does not suggest that Taiwan's democracy is built on strong legal foundations and as Lin explains in his chapter, the Republic of China's (ROC) Constitution, initially enacted for China by the Kuomintang, 'prolong[s] the ideology' of the One China Policy. Lin explores the role of informal constitutional change through 'constitutional amendments, judicial review and social movements', which have gone some way to indigenise the ROC Constitution. However, informal constitutional change cannot fundamentally alter or indigenise what he refers to as the 'undemocratic constitution', due to 'China's bullying'.

Similar to Taiwan, Hong Kong's population has not always enjoyed robust civil liberties. The 1967 riots, triggered by an industrial labour dispute, resulted in widespread civil unrest across the territory. To quell the riots, the British Colonial Government invoked the Emergency (Principal) Regulations Cap 241 (1967), which were used to adopt a series of draconian measures including the detention of individuals for up to one year without trial.[8] While a series of labour and policy reforms were initiated following the 1967 riots, the British Colonial Government only extended a number of international human rights treaties[9] to the territory after the signing of the Sino-British Joint Declaration in 1984, when the United Kingdom agreed to rescind its sovereignty and cede Hong Kong to China. The British Colonial Government adopted the Bill of Rights Ordinance Cap 383 (1991) (BORO) to formally implement the International Covenant on Civil and Political Rights (ICCPR) in domestic law as a means of shoring up public and investor confidence in the handover following the 1989 Tiananmen Massacre in Beijing.[10]

Hong Kong's rights-based legal framework has allowed for some 'constituent elements of democracy'. The Basic Law 1990 (which entered into force in 1997) and the BORO create a rights-based architecture which supports civil and political liberties including freedom of speech, freedom of the press and freedom of association, assembly, procession and demonstration.[11] While the exercise of civil and political rights is not absolute,[12] given Hong Kong's democratic deficit, public protest has increasingly been used as a strategy in claims-making. As Fu and Jackson explain, despite limited public space, Hong Kong's citizens have regularly participated in public meetings and processions to 'air grievances and express popular demands'. The Civil Human Rights Front's annual rally held on 1 July, the anniversary of the 1997 handover, has become highly symbolic of the contentious relationship between Hong Kong and China. On 1 July 2003, more than 1 million protestors took to the streets to demand the withdrawal of the Hong Kong SAR Government's proposed Bill to implement Article 23 of the Basic Law on National Security. On 1 July 2012, protestors again took to the streets to oppose the appointment of then Chief Executive Leung Chun-ying, who was perceived to be too pro-Beijing. Indeed, protest has been a valuable way for Hong Kong citizens to express public sentiment throughout the years. In 2011, members of the Hong Kong Journalists Association protested the

[8] 'EMERGENCY (PRINCIPAL) REGULATIONS' *Historical Laws of Hong Kong Online*. Available at: https://oelawhk.lib.hku.hk/items/show/2955.

[9] For example, the Convention on the Elimination of All Forms of Discrimination against Women (CEDAW) 1979 was only extended to the territory in 1996.

[10] P Yu, 'Succession by Estoppel: Hong Kong's Succession to the ICCPR' (1999) 27 *Pepperdine Law Review* 53 at 64.

[11] Basic Law, art 27; Bill of Rights Ordinance Cap 383, arts 16, 17 and 18 (1991).

[12] Restrictions may be placed on the exercise of these civil and political rights provided that they conform with law and are 'necessary in the democratic society for the interests of national security or public safety, public order (ordre public), the protection of public health or morals or the protection of the rights and freedoms of others' (International Covenant on Civil and Political Rights, art 21).

'heavy-handed security' used during the visit of then Vice-Premier Li Keqiang to the territory[13] and, in 2012, the Hong Kong SAR Government's 'national education' proposal to promote Chinese civic education in Hong Kong's primary and secondary schools also triggered mass protests.[14] More broadly, as several authors in the volume explore, a wave of social movements challenging the 'core of each political system' occurred across the region in 2013–2014, from the New Citizens Movement in China, to the Sunflower Movement in Taiwan and the Occupy Central Movement in Hong Kong. But the way these movements were treated in each jurisdiction was starkly different. As explored by Fu and Jackson, in China, protest and collective action are perceived as a 'symbol of disorder and instability,' which challenges the legitimacy of the Party-state.

Fu and Jackson explain that 'entrenched beliefs in the rule of law and judicial independence' have played an integral role in shaping Hong Kong's identity. And yet, its aspirations for genuine democracy have not been realised and its relationship with China has become increasingly contentious. Since 1997, Hong Kong's high degree of autonomy in governance has been tested by a series of interventions in its internal legal and political affairs by the Chinese Government,[15] and this interventionism has triggered protests by a variety of interest groups including journalists, lawyers and, exceptionally in 2019, Hong Kong's civil servants.[16] Tai suggests that in the aftermath of the Occupy Central Movement, Hong Kong's era of semi-democracy has ended and it is now moving towards semi-authoritarianism.

Fu and Jackson point to a sharp increase in the number of assemblies in Hong Kong post-handover. Significantly, a marked increase[17] in public meetings and processions appears to have coincided with the 2016 oath-taking scandal, when the oaths of two pro-independence activists elected to the LegCo, Leung Chung-hang and Yau Wai-Ching, were declared invalid. As Zhu explains in her chapter for this volume, in China – and now in Hong Kong – law has been used as a tool to stifle 'those who challenge the existing constitutional configuration'. In contrast, during Taiwan's democratic transition, the political process – as opposed to legal means – has predominantly been used to mediate disputes and such oath-taking disputes have petered out as Taiwan's democracy has strengthened.

[13] 'Hong Kong Journalists Warn of Self-Censorship' *Wall St Journal* (28 June 2012). Available at: www.wsj.com/articles/BL-CJB-16015.

[14] A Lai, '"National education" raises furor in Hong Kong' *CNN* (30 July 2012). Available at: https://edition.cnn.com/2012/07/30/world/asia/hong-kong-national-education-controversy/index.html.

[15] See Zhu Han's and Benny Tai's respective chapters in this collection.

[16] T May, 'Hong Kong's Civil Servants Protest Their Own Government' *New York Times* (2 August 2019). Available at: www.nytimes.com/2019/08/02/world/asia/hong-kong-civil-servants-protest.html.

[17] 'Public Order Event Statistics' (2020) Hong Kong Police Force. Available at: www.police.gov.hk/ppp_en/09_statistics/poes.html.

Zhu suggests that an increased focus on 'One Country' rather than OCTS in Hong Kong has produced a lower threshold for undesirable speech than in democratic jurisdictions. On 3 November 2016, in a judicial review application hearing brought by the Chief Executive and Secretary for Justice to disqualify Leung Chung-hang and Yau Wai-Ching, the Court of First Instance in Hong Kong reserved judgment.[18] Within days of the judgment, on 7 November 2016, the Standing Committee of the National People's Congress (NPCSC) delivered its interpretation of what constitutes a 'valid oath' under Article 104 of the Basic Law. In a rare public display of opposition,[19] Hong Kong's legal community, dressed all in black, silently marched from the High Court to the Court of Final Appeal to condemn the NPCSC's intervention in Hong Kong's independent legal system. Since the oath-taking scandal, Leung Chun-hang and Yau Wai-Ching have faced punitive measures, been forced to pay back their salaries and have effectively been bankrupted.[20] The targeting of Hong Kong legislators is reminiscent of the actions of the ruling People Action Party in Singapore (PAP), which 'seeks to undermine the opposition, portraying it as irresponsible and a threat to Singapore's future'.[21] As Lee and Neo explore in their chapter, the PAP has long dominated Singaporean politics, but as the country's democracy matures, concepts such as 'representation' and the 'rule of law' are also changing. Singaporean citizens appear less willing to be subjected to authoritarian rule of law, but communitarian values continue to infuse governance approaches rather than individual rights. Scholars have suggested that China strives to achieve Singapore's model of 'resilient authoritarianism', whereby political stability and governance endure despite advanced economic development.[22]

In Hong Kong, the courts have increasingly become embroiled in mediating contentious disputes between the government and pro-democracy activists, opening up scrutiny of judicial independence and the rule of law. As Jones explores in his chapter examining court criticism and the rule of law, judiciaries often find themselves in the complicated position of having to adjudicate issues involving major societal clashes. Jones explores the labelling of 'dinosaur' judges in Taiwan and 'foreign' judges in Hong Kong, explaining that there is a marked distinction between helpful speech, which may help to hold the judiciary

[18] When the CFI delivered its judgment on 15 November 2016, its findings echoed those of the NPCSC. See *The Chief Executive of the HKSAR and Another v Yau Wai Ching and Others* HCMP 2819/2016.

[19] E Cheung and T Phillips, "Hong Kong: Lawyers and activists march against Beijing 'meddling'" *The Guardian* (8 November 2016). Available at: www.theguardian.com/world/2016/nov/08/hundreds-silently-march-in-hong-kong-in-protest-at-beijing-meddling.

[20] T Cheung and K Cheung, 'Bankruptcy ruling sought as disqualified Hong Kong lawmaker Baggio Leung fails to repay HK$930,000 owed to legislature' *South China Morning Post* (7 July 2020). Available at: www.scmp.com/news/hong-kong/politics/article/3092202/bankruptcy-ruling-sought-disqualified-hong-kong-lawmaker.

[21] MR Thompson and S Ortmann, 'Mis-modelling Singapore: China's Challenges in Learning from the City-state' (2018) *The China Quarterly* 1014, 1021.

[22] Ibid, 1015.

accountable and harmful speech, which potentially threatens the rule of law. While the author suggests that court criticism forms an important part of democratic debate, he has developed a three-part test to distinguish harsh criticism from criticism which violates the rule of law. Criticism that is (1) targeted; (2) abusive or belligerent; and (3) focused on the validity or legitimacy of the decision maker, may be perceived to have transgressed the rule of law. He finds that, in certain situations, judicial criticism in Hong Kong has transgressed these boundaries, while in Taiwan judicial criticism has not gone as far.

As Jones notes, Hong Kong's Basic Law 'explicitly allows' foreign judges from other common law jurisdictions,[23] yet criticism towards foreign judges has increased even in circumstances that fall outside of democratic reform-related challenges. On their appointment to the Court of Final Appeal in 2018, non-permanent 'foreign' judges' Brenda Hale's and Beverley McLachlin's perceived support of LGBT rights was called into question by some pro-Beijing lawmakers.[24] More broadly, Chinese officials' sharp rhetoric that 'foreign forces are at play' has punctuated the political landscape in Hong Kong, particularly since the Occupy Central Movement of 2014.[25] Cheng's research on contentious politics and protest in Hong Kong has examined how the Chinese Government's rhetoric on 'the need "to stop violence and end chaos" (止暴制亂) and to combat foreign interference' has been utilised as a means to classify the anti-ELAB movement as a national security threat.[26]

HONG KONG'S ANTI-EXTRADITION PROTESTS AND THEIR AFTERMATH

Hong Kong's Chief Executive, Carrie Lam, first tabled the Fugitive Offenders and Mutual Legal Assistance in Criminal Matters Legislation (Amendment) Bill 2019 on 3 April 2019. If enacted, the Bill would have allowed for the extradition of fugitives to countries with which Hong Kong has no extradition agreement, including China and Taiwan.[27] The Civil Human Rights Front organised two mass public protests against the Bill on 31 March and 28 April 2019.[28] Prior to

[23] Article 19, Hong Kong Basic Law ('Judges and other members of the judiciary of the Hong Kong Special Administrative Region shall be chosen on the basis of their judicial and professional qualities and may be recruited from other common law jurisdictions').

[24] A Lum, 'Pro-Beijing lawmakers voice concerns over foreign judges' support for gay rights' *South China Morning Post* (28 April 2018). Available at: www.scmp.com/news/hong-kong/politics/article/2143767/pro-beijing-lawmakers-speak-out-against-two-female-foreign.

[25] A Barrow, 'Sexual Orientation, Gender Identity, and Equality in Hong Kong: Rights, Resistance, and Possibilities for Reform' (2020) 15 *Asian Journal of Comparative Law* 126.

[26] EW Cheng, 'United Front Work and Mechanisms of Countermobilization in Hong Kong' (2020) 83 *The China Journal* 1 at 30.

[27] Fugitive Offenders and Mutual Legal Assistance in Criminal Matters Legislation (Amendment) Bill 2019, Part 3, cl 10.

[28] FLF Lee, S Yuen, G Tang and EW Cheng, 'Hong Kong's Summer of Uprising' (2019) 19(4) *China Review* 1, 2.

the Bill's second reading, 3,000 lawyers, again dressed in black, marched silently from the Court of Final Appeal to the LegCo to call for the Bill's withdrawal. Despite widespread opposition, Carrie Lam attempted to push the Bill through the LegCo. As the protests and violence escalated, Hong Kong's Police Force came under intense scrutiny for deploying tear gas and rubber bullets to disperse the protesters and the Hong Kong Government was criticised for referring to the protestors as rioters.

The movement evolved from one focused on opposing the Extradition Bill to a more holistic movement framed around five key demands. In addition to their call for the full withdrawal of the Extradition Bill, protestors sought a commission into alleged police brutality; the re-classification of rioters as protestors; amnesty for those protestors arrested – and echoing earlier social movements – universal suffrage of the Chief Executive and LegCo.[29] In contrast to the 2014 Occupy Central Movement, the movement, marked by five key demands has been described by scholars as 'leaderless and decentralised'.[30] Protestors engaged in the Anti-ELAB movement used encrypted messaging services such as Telegram to mobilise.[31] An editorial in the *China Daily* condemned the 'foreign forces [that] are trying to hurt China by creating chaos'.[32] In October 2019, the Hong Kong Government invoked colonial-era emergency powers under section 2 of the Emergency (Principal) Regulations Cap 241, 1967, to impose a blanket ban on face masks, which many protestors had used to protect their identity – a move which triggered further civil unrest. In November 2019, following sustained violent clashes between protestors and the police at Hong Kong Polytechnic University and the Chinese University of Hong Kong, universities across the territory took the unprecedented decision to end the semester early and transition to online teaching. Although the anti-ELAB movement continued into 2020, the COVID-19 pandemic created a period of what Chung refers to as 'enforced abeyance'.[33] In April 2020, the Court of Appeal found that the government's blanket ban on face masks was unconstitutional given the public health risks posed by the pandemic.[34] Indeed, the emergence and spread of COVID-19 has exposed China's public health response and behaviour to heightened international scrutiny.

[29] Ibid. Currently, only geographical constituency seats are directly elected, with functional constituency seats, representing industry and other sectors, elected only by members of the functional constituency.

[30] Lee et al., n 28 above, 14.

[31] Ibid.

[32] B Blanchard, 'Chinese paper says "foreign forces" using Hong Kong havoc to hurt China' *Reuters* (10 June 2019. Available at: www.reuters.com/article/us-hongkong-extradition-march-china-idUSKCN1TA0U4.

[33] HF Chung, 'Changing Repertoires of Contention in Hong Kong: A Case Study on the Anti-Extradition Bill Movement' (2020) 3 *China Perspectives* 57.

[34] *Leung Kwok Hung v Secretary for Justice and Another* [2020] HKCA 192, para 355.

FREEDOM OF SPEECH, WHISTLE BLOWING AND THE EMERGENCE OF COVID

In December 2019, when Dr Li Wenliang, an ophthalmologist at Wuhan Central Hospital, alerted colleagues to the emergence of what appeared to be a SARS-like virus causing pneumonia, he, along with seven other clinicians, was reprimanded by the authorities for spreading rumours.[35] Sharing the information privately in a closed group on WeChat, Li Wenliang did not intend to be a whistle-blower and only alerted the press after being forced to sign a letter of reprimand.[36] Following Li's death from the disease to which he helped to alert the world, widespread anger ensued both within China and internationally regarding his silencing and humiliation.[37]

The COVID-19 pandemic has undoubtedly heightened worldwide tensions. Both the US and China have blamed one another for the spread of the virus.[38] China favourably compared its efforts to stem the virus to Washington's bungled COVID-19 response.[39] Within the Asia-Pacific region, China and Australia have long been considered economically interdependent, but bilateral relations have deteriorated since 2017 when then Prime Minister, Malcolm Turnbull questioned the extent of 'foreign interference' in Australian politics.[40] China's influence on university campuses has also been called into question following a number of incidents, which have tested the parameters of academic freedom.[41] Tensions between the two countries have accelerated during the political fallout from COVID-19. Since Australia's call for an independent enquiry into the origins of COVID-19, China has targeted several Australian industries, including the export of beef, wine, coal and cotton and placed an 80 per cent tariff on Australian barley.[42] According to a poll conducted by a Sydney-based independent think tank, the Lowy Institute, only 23 per cent of Australians trust China to 'act responsibly in the world'.[43] Yet, the COVID-pandemic has also raised the spectre of what Thomson and Ip refer to as 'the impending authoritarian pandemic'.[44]

[35] Kavanagh, n 2 above.

[36] JB Nie and C Elliott, 'Humiliating Whistleblowers: Li Wenliang, the Response to COVID-19, and the Call for a Decent Society' (2020) *Journal of Bioethical Inquiry* (Advance publication: 25 August 2020).

[37] Ibid.

[38] B Gill, 'China's Global Influence: Post-COVID Prospects for Soft Power' (2020) 43(2) *The Washington Quarterly* 97.

[39] Ibid, 102.

[40] N Kassam, 'Great Expectations: The unravelling of the Australia-China Relationship' *Brookings* (20 July 2020). Available at: www.brookings.edu/articles/great-expectations-the-unraveling-of-the-australia-china-relationship/.

[41] L Bochner, 'China's influence on our campuses', Australian Strategic Policy Institute (31 August 2020), Available at: https://www.aspi.org.au/opinion/chinas-influence-our-campuses.

[42] Kassam, n 40 above; 'Australia's cotton the latest target for China' *Asia Times* (16 October 2020), https://asiatimes.com/2020/10/australian-cotton-the-latest-target-for-china/.

[43] Kassam, n 40 above.

[44] S Thomson and EC Ip, 'COVID-19 emergency measures and the impending authoritarian pandemic' (2020) *Journal of Law and the* Biosciences (Advance publication: 29 September 2020). [doi:10.1093/jlb/lsaa064.

AUTHORITARIAN GOVERNANCE PRACTICES UNDER THE COVER OF COVID

Patmore, in his chapter on developing a right to democracy in international law, explains that 'authoritarian governance offers a fragile protection of fundamental freedoms' and proposes that the 'promotion of a norm of democratic governance' may support peaceful international relations. While this may be the case, the sharp divide between democratic and authoritarian governance appears to be increasingly less pronounced. As Lin points out in his chapter on Taiwanese constitutional law, although Taiwan's democracy has remained relatively stable, there has been a global emergence of 'quasi-authoritarian leadership' even in long-established democracies. Indeed, as others have explored, authoritarianism is a phenomenon not 'merely observable in unitary state form but one that exists across a wide range of contexts, in societies ruled by authoritarian states as well as enclaves with ostensibly liberal democratic ones'.[45] These words ring especially true when looking to authoritarian governance practices during the COVID-19 pandemic, which have called into question the proper balance between the power of the state and individual freedom.

While in times of public emergency rights may legitimately be subject to limitation or derogation, some rights are non-derogable.[46] Thomson and Ip point to authoritarian governance practices during the pandemic, which are marked by 'diverse combinations of governmental and administrative overreach, the adoption of excessive and disproportionate emergency measures, [the] override of civil liberties and fundamental freedoms, failure to engage in properly deliberative and transparent decision-making, and even the suspension of effective democratic control'.[47] Globally, the imposition of strict lockdown laws, quarantine, curfews and social distancing measures have restricted freedom of assembly and movement in both authoritarian governance regimes and established liberal democracies. To illustrate, Australia first closed its borders to China in February 2020,[48] then to other states including Iran,[49] and then enforced an international travel ban preventing its citizens and permanent residents from leaving the country.[50] The development of the COVIDsafe App as a tool to identify those

[45] LJ Chua, 'Legal Mobilization and Authoritarianism' (2019) 15 *Annual Review of Law and Social Science* 355, 356.

[46] Article 4 of the ICCPR outlines non-derogable rights, which include arts 6, 7, 8 (paras 1 and 2), 11, 15, 16 and 18.

[47] Thomson and Ip, n 44 above, 4.

[48] 'Australia to shut border to foreign nationals arriving from China to fight spread of coronavirus' *South China Morning Post* (1 Feb 2020). Available at: www.scmp.com/news/asia/australasia/article/3048525/qantas-air-nz-suspend-china-flights-japan-declares.

[49] D Conifer, 'Australia announces Iran travel ban amid COVID-19 coronavirus outbreak' *ABC News* (29 February 2020). Available at: www.abc.net.au/news/2020-02-29/australia-announces-iran-travel-ban/12013884.

[50] S Meixner, 'Australia's outbound travel ban is one of the strictest coronavirus public health responses in the world' *ABC News* (31 August 2020). Available at: www.abc.net.au/news/2020-08-31/coronavirus-covid-outbound-international-travel-ban-morrison/12605404.

exposed to COVID-19 raised privacy concerns about how the data could be used both during and beyond the pandemic.[51] Concerns have also been raised that emergency powers may be utilised by some states as a way to consolidate executive power and suppress dissent,[52] potentially threatening the rule of law.

In Hong Kong, the government's public health measures adopted in response to COVID-19 have impacted on organising and activism, with riot police enforcing powers under the public health emergency regulations to arrest protesters.[53] In July 2020, the Hong Kong Journalists' Association condemned riot police for allegedly abusing their powers during a protest to mark the anniversary of the 21 July mob attack at Yuen Long Mass Transit Railway (MTR) station.[54] Similarly, police forces in New South Wales and Victoria, Australia, have been criticised for using public health emergency laws and orders as a means of policing and punishing protestors.[55]

Despite the widespread adoption of draconian measures during the COVID-19 pandemic, as Tsung Ling-Lee explains, 'in liberal democracies, law is central to [a] pandemic response'.[56] In Taiwan, one major factor contributing to the government's success in responding to the COVID-19 pandemic has been its legal preparedness, which draws on pre-existing public health legislation, developed after lessons learnt following the 2003 severe acute respiratory (SARS) epidemic.[57] Three principal factors have played a role in Taiwan's legal and policy response to the pandemic – its mask policy to prevent the spread of the virus, 'the use of big data and technology to enhance effective implementation of disease prevention and detection measures, and strong state-society relations favouring transparency, communication and collaboration'.[58] Taiwan did not declare a public health emergency during the first 100 days of the pandemic and, similar to its ordinary administrative law procedures, public health measures remain amenable to judicial review.[59] However, in May 2020,

[51] JJ Kang and P Haskell-Dowland, 'How safe is covidsafe? What you should know about the apps issues and Bluetooth related risks' *The Conversation* (7 May 2020). Available at: https://theconversation.com/how-safe-is-covidsafe-what-you-should-know-about-the-apps-issues-and-bluetooth-related-risks-137894.

[52] A Zouev, COVID and the Rule of Law: A Dangerous Balancing Act' *United Nations*. Available at: www.un.org/en/coronavirus/covid-and-rule-law-dangerous-balancing-act.

[53] Thomson and Ip, n 44 above, 24.

[54] Ibid.

[55] N Chrysanthos, 'Head of Sydney Law School condemns 'hard' policing of student protests' *Sydney Morning Herald* (15 October 2020). Available at: www.smh.com.au/national/nsw/head-of-sydney-law-school-condemns-hard-policing-of-student-protests-20201015-p565je.html; 'Harsh Police Response During Covid-19' Human Rights Watch (24 September 2020). Available at: www.hrw.org/news/2020/09/24/australia-harsh-police-response-during-covid-19.

[56] Tsung LL, 'Legal preparedness as part of COVID-19 response: the first 100 days in Taiwan' (2020) 5(5) *BMJ Global Health* 1 at 1.

[57] Ibid.

[58] WT Yen, 'Taiwan's COVID-19 Management: Developmental State, Digital Governance, and State-Society Synergy' (2020) 12(3) *Asian Politics and Policy* 455 at 455.

[59] Tsung, n 56 above, 1.

when Taiwan sought to participate in the World Health Assembly as an observer, China attempted to discredit Tsai-Ing Wen's government's intentions, with state media reporting that 'seeking independence under the pretext of [a] pandemic response is doomed to fail'.[60] This type of rhetoric has regularly been deployed by China in its relations with Taiwan, but has increasingly been applied in Hong Kong to quash any anti-government or anti-Beijing sentiment. In another move perceived to demonstrate Beijing's increasing assertiveness, in 2020 the annual 4 June Tiananmen vigil was cancelled for the first time in 30 years, ostensibly due to the COVID-19 pandemic. However, the move failed to deter thousands of protestors from defying the ban to hold city-wide vigils.[61]

HONG KONG'S NATIONAL SECURITY LAW

In a highly political and symbolic move by the Chinese Government, the National Security Law entered into force at 23:00 on 30 June 2020, just hours before the 1 July 'handover' anniversary, a date which has become synonymous with pro-democracy protests in the territory. The law seeks to prevent, suppress and impose punishment for four broadly defined offences: secession (Article 20); subversion (Article 22); organisation and perpetration of terrorist offences (Article 24); and 'collusion with a foreign country or with external elements to endanger national security in Hong Kong' (Article 29). Reference is made to existing human rights protections contained in the Basic Law and the ICCPR (Article 4). However, the reported arrest of eight protestors holding up blank placards within days of the National Security Law coming into force[62] is illustrative of the 'swiftly escalating repression' in Hong Kong,[63] and will have done little to reassure Hong Kong citizens that their rights and civil liberties under the Basic Law will be respected and protected.

Some China analysts have questioned whether the National Security Law can be effectively framed as a 'law', given its vague and broad-reaching terms and the way in which it was imposed on the territory – by circumventing procedural justice.[64] The interpretation of the malleable language that runs through

[60] 'Taiwan seeking independence under pretext of COVID-19 doomed to fail: Chinese FM' *China Daily* (15 May 2020). Available at: www.chinadaily.com.cn/a/202005/15/WS5ebe9c1ca310a8b24115618b.html.

[61] 'Tiananmen vigil as it happened: Thousands of Hongkongers defy ban to mark anniversary of June 4 crackdown' *South China Morning Post* (4 June 2020). Available at: www.scmp.com/news/hong-kong/society/article/3087496/tiananmen-vigil-hong-kong-defies-covid-19-social-distancing.

[62] T Grundy, 'Security Law: Hong Kong Police arrest 8 at 'blank placard' silent protest' *Hong Kong Free Press* (6 July 2020). Available at: https://hongkongfp.com/2020/07/06/security-law-hong-kong-police-arrest-8-at-blank-placard-silent-protest/.

[63] E Pils, 'From the "rule of law" to "rule by fear": Hong Kong's National Security Law' *Right Now* (3 August 2020). Available at: http://rightnow.org.au/analysis/hong-kong-national-security-law/.

[64] P Poon, 'Is the "National Security Law" for Hong Kong really a "law"?' (15 July 2020). Available at: https://patrickpoon.medium.com/is-the-national-security-law-for-hong-kong-really-a-law-6ac5025c7277.

the National Security Law risks being subjected to abuse. The law calls for the establishment of the Committee Safeguarding National Security, the duties and functions of which include 'advancing the development of the legal system' (Article 14(2)), which suggests that the Committee will be a driver for the implementation of Article 23 of the Basic Law on National Security. However, the scope of what is meant by 'development' is not defined and could have wider ramifications for Hong Kong's legal system. Significantly, the law precludes the Committee's decisions from being amenable to judicial review, in direct contravention of Article 35 of the Basic Law, which states that 'Hong Kong residents shall have the right to institute legal proceedings in the courts against the acts of the executive authorities and their personnel'. Not only does the National Security Law pose a significant risk for the operation of Hong Kong's rule of law, but it also substantially weakens the SAR's general autonomy.

Given the significant opposition to the proposed extradition law, many activists will be deeply concerned by the inclusion of Articles 55–57 of the National Security Law which, in the absence of explicit language of extradition, nevertheless raise 'the feared sceptre of extradition to the mainland a distinct possibility'.[65] Article 68 clearly states that the National Security Law will prevail where local laws are inconsistent. The law's reach is significant and applicable to any persons in the Hong Kong SAR (Article 36) including non-permanent residents (Article 38). Some international universities have subsequently adapted their teaching and assessment processes such as allowing anonymous submission of work related to China so as to protect students from the reach of the law while upholding freedom of expression.[66] Several states including Australia, Canada, Germany, New Zealand, the US and the UK have subsequently suspended their extradition treaties with Hong Kong. Further, a number of UN human rights experts drafted a letter citing their concern regarding the repression of fundamental freedoms and emerging legal developments in Hong Kong, the Xinjiang and the Tibet Autonomous Regions.[67] As Pils explains, 'Hong Kong's new National Security Law must be understood as a transnational, as well as a local mechanism for repression'.[68] Propper argues that China intends the law serve as a signal not only to its own citizens, but also to Taiwan and the United States, that the 'Communist party will take all measures it views as appropriate to maintain stability, unity, and sovereignty'.[69]

[65] Pils, n 63 above.

[66] MJ Richardson, 'Oxford is protecting students from China's national security law – other universities must follow suit' *The Conversation* (7 October 2020). Available at: https://theconversation.com/oxford-is-protecting-students-from-chinas-national-security-law-other-universities-must-follow-suit-147399.

[67] 'UN experts call for decisive measures to protect fundamental freedoms in China' United Nations (26 June 2020). Available at: www.ohchr.org/EN/NewsEvents/Pages/DisplayNews.aspx?NewsID=26006&LangID=E.

[68] Pils, n 63 above.

[69] E Propper, 'The National People's Congress 2020: The Hong Kong National Security Law and China's Enhanced Presence' INSS Insight No 1329 (3 June 2020), 4.

Since the law entered into force, several high-profile arrests have been made in the territory.[70] Following Carrie Lam's suggestion that no official separation of powers exists, Judge James Spigelman, an Australian, non-permanent Judge of the Court of Final Appeal resigned citing concerns regarding the content of the National Security Law.[71] Although many western liberal democracies have enacted national security laws, Lai and Chan suggest Hong Kong's National Security Law is problematic because it operates to suppress civil and political liberties rather than protect national security.[72] And, as Poon explains, Hong Kong citizens will now be subjected to the type of offences that Chinese citizens have been subjected to for decades.[73]

CONCLUSION

As the authors within this volume have explored, in the shadow of China's authoritarianism, the space within which democracy and the rule of law operate is fraught with tensions. With the imposition of the National Security Law, Hong Kong currently sits at a crossroads in its legal and political development. The National Security Law's malleable language and overreach has transnational implications for both the rule of law and democratic governance practices in the region and more broadly. In the immediate future, we can expect to see the strengthening of 'One Country' and potentially the end of Hong Kong's autonomy. The model of 'One Country, Two Systems' is incompatible with the Chinese Government's aspirations to rule by resilient authoritarianism. This development is deeply concerning not only for Hong Kong, but for Taiwan and the Asia-Pacific more broadly. Expansive in scope, yet vaguely drafted, the National Security Law attempts to export a highly repressive model of authoritarian governance. Given that many well-established liberal democracies have also adopted draconian responses to the COVID-19 pandemic, these developments pose important questions regarding how these practices will shape the

[70] J Lau, 'Hong Kong national security law: 26 arrests so far, resignation of a foreign judge, and suspension of a middle school pupil mark third month' *South China Morning Post* (30 September 2020), Available at: www.scmp.com/news/hong-kong/politics/article/3103600/hong-kong-national-security-law-26-arrests-so-far.

[71] 'Australian judge steps down from Hong Kong court over new national security law' *The Guardian* (18 September 2020). Available at: www.theguardian.com/world/2020/sep/18/australian-judge-steps-down-from-hong-kong-court-over-new-national-security-law.

[72] LCB Lai and DSW Chan, 'National Security Laws in General are not a problem. Hong Kong's is' *The Diplomat* (5 June 2020). Available at: https://thediplomat.com/2020/06/national-security-laws-in-general-are-not-a-problem-hong-kongs-is/.

[73] P Poon, 'Hong Kong Free Press National security law: Hongkongers will soon face what Chinese people have suffered for decades' *Hong Kong Free Press* (4 June 2020). Available at: https://hongkongfp.com/2020/06/04/national-security-law-hongkongers-will-soon-face-what-chinese-people-have-suffered-for-decades/.

future of civil liberties and the rule of law. One can only hope that these temporary measures do not erode the rule of law and the rights and liberties citizens possess in democratic countries. After all, as this edited volume has demonstrated, if law is used to suppress rather than enhance the democratic spirit, then the creep of authoritarianism may become even more prevalent.

Index

www.ingramcontent.com/pod-product-compliance
Ingram Content Group UK Ltd.
Pitfield, Milton Keynes, MK11 3LW, UK
UKHW020251290926
15470UKWH00002B/858

9 781509 933969